MW01005926

CLEOPATRA'S KIDNAPPERS

Also by Stephen Dando-Collins

*Caesar's Legion: The Epic Saga of Julius Caesar's
Elite Tenth Legion and the Armies of Rome*

*Nero's Killing Machine: The True Story of Rome's
Remarkable Fourteenth Legion*

CLEOPATRA'S KIDNAPPERS

HOW CAESAR'S SIXTH LEGION GAVE EGYPT TO ROME AND ROME TO CAESAR

STEPHEN DANDO-COLLINS

WILEY

John Wiley & Sons, Inc.

Published by John Wiley & Sons, Inc., Hoboken, New Jersey
Published simultaneously in Canada

For general information about our other products and services, please contact our Customer Care Department within the United States at (800) 762-2974, outside the United States at (317) 572-3993 or fax (317) 572-4002.

Wiley also publishes its books in a variety of electronic formats. Some content that appears in print may not be available in electronic books. For more information about Wiley products, visit our web site at www.wiley.com.

Library of Congress Cataloging-in-Publication Data:

Dando-Collins, Stephen, date.
    Cleopatra's kidnappers : how Caesar's sixth legion gave Egypt to Rome
and Rome to Caesar / Stephen Dando-Collins.
      p. cm.
    Includes bibliographical references and index.
    ISBN-13 978-0-471-71933-5 (cloth)
    ISBN-10 0-471-71933-1 (cloth)
    1. Caesar, Julius—Military leadership. 2. Rome. Legion VI Ferrata—History.
3. Rome—History, Military—265-30 B.C. 4. Rome—History—Civil War, 49-45 B.C.
5. Alexandrine War, 48-47 B.C. 6. Cleopatra, Queen of Egypt, d. 30 B.C. I. Title.
    DG266.D36 2006
    932'.021—dc22

                                          2005003082

Printed in the United States of America

10 9 8 7 6 5 4 3 2 1

CONTENTS

ATLAS

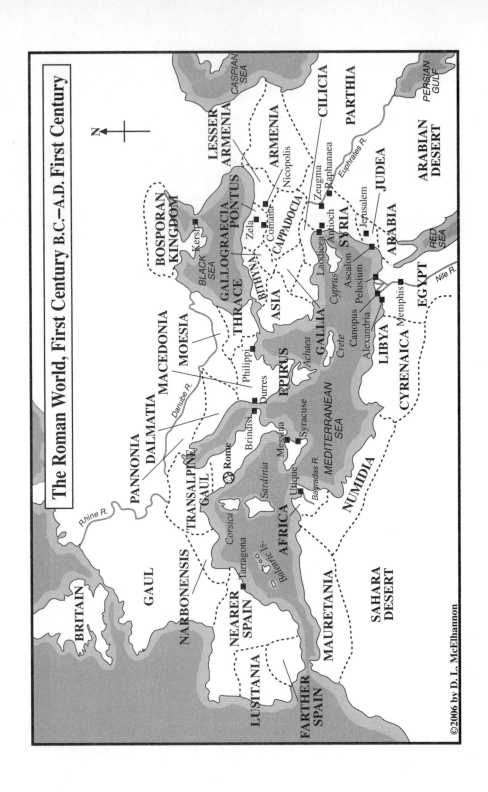

The Roman World, First Century B.C.–A.D. First Century

©2006 by D. L. McElhannon

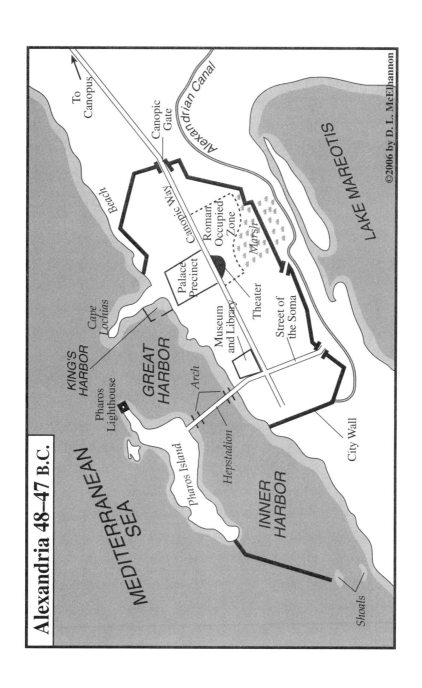

Alexandria 48–47 B.C.

MEDITERRANEAN SEA

To Canopus

Canopic Gate

Alexandrian Canal

Beach

Canopic Way

Palace Precinct

Roman Occupied Zone

Marsh

Theater

Street of the Soma

Museum and Library

Cape Lochias

KING'S HARBOR

Pharos Lighthouse

GREAT HARBOR

Arch

Hepstadion

Pharos Island

City Wall

LAKE MAREOTIS

INNER HARBOR

Shoals

©2006 by D. L. McElhannon

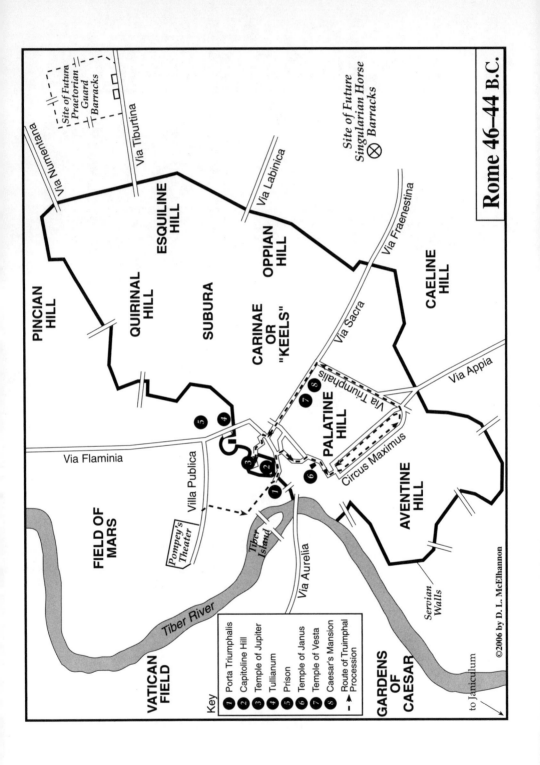

Rome 46–44 B.C.

Site of Future Praetorian Guard Barracks

Site of Future Singularian Horse Barracks

Via Numentana

Via Tiburtina

Via Labinica

Via Fraenestina

Via Sacra

Via Appia

Via Triumphalis

Via Flaminia

Via Aurelia

PINCIAN HILL

QUIRINAL HILL

ESQUILINE HILL

SUBURA

CARINAE OR "KEELS"

OPPIAN HILL

CAELINE HILL

PALATINE HILL

AVENTINE HILL

Circus Maximus

FIELD OF MARS

Villa Publica

Pompey's Theater

Tiber Island

Tiber River

VATICAN FIELD

GARDENS OF CAESAR

Servian Walls

to Janiculum

©2006 by D. L. McElhannon

Key

1. Porta Triumphalis
2. Capitoline Hill
3. Temple of Jupiter
4. Tullianum
5. Prison
6. Temple of Janus
7. Temple of Vesta
8. Caesar's Mansion

- - - Route of Truimphal Procession

ACKNOWLEDGMENTS

This book would not have been possible without the immense help provided over many years by countless staff at libraries, museums, and historic sites throughout the world. To them all, my heartfelt thanks. Neither they nor I knew at the time what my labor of love would develop into. My thanks, too, to those who have read my research material as it blossomed into manuscript form and made invaluable suggestions.

I wish to record my gratitude to several people in particular. To Stephen S. Power, senior editor with John Wiley & Sons, for his continued enthusiasm, support, and guidance. And to Wiley's patient production editor, John Simko, who has had to chase me halfway around the world at times, and copy editor Bill Drennan. To Richard Curtis, my unrelenting and all-conquering New York literary agent, who was determined from the start that the stories of the legions should and would be a series of books, and has been the general of the campaign to make it so.

And my wife, Louise. Quite simply, without her, I would not be who I am, be where I am, or do what I do. As Pliny the Younger was to say of his wife, Calpurnia: "All this gives me the highest reason to hope that our mutual happiness will last forever and go on increasing day by day."

AUTHOR'S NOTE

Read most modern histories of Rome or biographies of the lives of Julius Caesar and Cleopatra and you will be told that Caesar "dallied" in Egypt with Cleopatra for several months in 48–47 B.C., following his defeat of Pompey the Great at the Battle of Pharsalus. What those books don't tell you is that "dalliance" was a bitter, life-or-death struggle for Caesar that lasted for seven long months against a well-equipped, well-led, and determined Egyptian army that had just murdered Pompey and was bent on also eliminating Caesar.

This book tells the story of those desperate, bloody months, when Caesar was cut off from reinforcements and supplies and apparently ignored by his deputy Mark Antony at Rome, when Caesar's life and career were on the line day after day after day.

Most importantly, this is also the story of the little more than nine hundred men of the 6th Legion, the key troops in Caesar's little force with him in Egypt, hardened Spanish soldiers with seventeen years of military service under their belts. For, without these men, Cleopatra's kidnappers, Caesar would not have survived the war in Egypt or gone on to Pontus to achieve one of his most famous victories, after which he would boast, "I came, I saw, I conquered."

This is the third book in this series of histories of individual legions of ancient Rome, following my previous books on the subject, *Caesar's Legion*, the story of the 10th Legion, Julius Caesar's favorite unit, and *Nero's Killing Machine*, the history of the remarkable 14th, a legion that in the course of its career went from the shame of being wiped out to fame as the victors over Queen Boudicca and her rebel British army.

Prior to the 2002 publication of *Caesar's Legion*, never before had a comprehensive history of an individual Roman legion been published. Because ancient history is often seen as a subject too dry to be interesting, a subject to be left behind in the schoolroom, in writing these books I made the conscious decision to make the histories of the legions as interesting and as exciting as I could without losing sight of the facts.

In my American histories, books such as *Standing Bear Is a Person*, I have gone to great lengths to include copious endnotes and detailed citations, because the sources are many and varied, and because the story affects the lives of people today, descendants of the people I've written about, and I owe it to them to support the details I've put on paper with relevant attributions.

These legion histories are different. I chose not to load them down with footnotes, often a barrier to readership by newcomers to history. In the place of footnotes, on the pages of these legion books I tell you which classical author was the source of a conversation, speech, or claim I document. And in the appendices you'll find, in addition to a detailed list of my secondary sources, extensive summaries of the lives and works of my primary classical sources, with comments on their accuracy and usefulness.

In writing these books I have relied heavily on classical sources. Even then, Caesar and other classical authors colored and propagandized their personal accounts of the events they describe. Recorded Roman history is full of holes, and modern authors usually can only fill those holes with informed speculation. Just the same, some obvious clues abound in ancient texts if the reader is prepared to look for them, and to look for them in more than one source.

I have also brought to light several aspects overlooked by other authors. One is the reenlistment factor. In the imperial era each legion generally discharged its men en masse when their twenty-year enlistments were up and filled their places with mass enlistments of new recruits. These discharge and reenlistment dates vary by legion. Read Tacitus in particular and you will be able to calculate the discharge and reenlistment years for virtually every legion and the Praetorian Guard for several hundred years. Pinpoint one date, and then work forward and back for the others—twenty years in the imperial era, sixteen years prior to it. By going back to the year an Augustan legion was founded, you can even establish in which year its enlistment period was upped from sixteen to twenty years by Augustus between 6 B.C. and A.D. 11. (Not surprisingly, the Praetorian Guard was the last unit to make the change.) The foundation dates of some legions are easier to establish than others—for the survivors of the large number of units founded by Caesar in his massive 49 B.C. conscription program, for instance.

Then there are the gaps in Caesar's memoirs, gaps apparently created by his editor Hirtius and publisher Balbus. Some of their erasures are obvious, with the text saying "as stated before," but with no such previous statement remaining. Other erasures are less obvious, with events suddenly jumping to a new episode. The strike by Caesar's legions following the Battle of Pharsalus is a typical example. The strike is simply deleted, and the next thing we know, Caesar is riding off with his still-loyal cavalry to give chase to Pompey, with the 6th Legion (up to that point a Pompeian legion) marching on his heels to support him. Yet, *not one* of the legions that had fought for Caesar at the Battle of Pharsalus follows him. Every one is taken back to Italy by Mark Antony, and no explanation is given why. But we are told that the four legions made to camp at Rome continued to be in a state of mutiny for the next eighteen months. Either Caesar himself or his contemporary editor and publisher could not bring themselves to admit the strike took place and simply glossed over the event.

At other places in Caesar's memoirs, and the accounts appended to them, one legion or another mysteriously turns up on a different side, or on the other side of the Roman world, the explanation having been eliminated from the original text. Or, as in the case of the 4th and 6th Legions at the Battle of Pharsalus, Caesar can only bring himself to describe them as "the Spanish cohorts." And Caesar's editors provide no explanation for the 6th Legion serving both Pompey and Caesar.

By knowing that the 6th Legion was one of those Pompeian units that surrendered to Caesar in Spain in 49 B.C.; by knowing that Afranius escaped from Spain by sea with a number of men and joined Pompey in Greece; by knowing, from Caesar, that Pompey had seven "Spanish cohorts" in his army at Pharsalus, units that had not escaped from Italy with him; by knowing, again from Caesar, that less than a thousand men of the 6th Legion followed Caesar from the Pharsalus battlefield while all Caesar's own infantry remained behind, the truth can be deduced.

The accounts of other authors often fill in the gaps in Caesar's own story. Appian, for example, while not always the most accurate of historians, provides otherwise missing details such as the events of the night Caesar was lured into an ambush at the port town of Durrës (Dyrrhachium) in 48 B.C., events not described in Caesar's commentaries.

On the other hand, some other classical authors can confuse the picture—the ever unreliable Suetonius, for example, in his life of Caesar, has the 6th Legion on Caesar's side at the Battle of Dyrrhachium, and suffering heavily during one of Pompey's attacks. Yet all the other evidence tells us that at that time the 6th was on Pompey's side, while, from Caesar, we know that the Caesarian legion that took the heavy casualties at Dyrrhachium was actually the 9th, not the 6th.

Spend time reading a variety of classical authors covering the same events with the eye of a detective, applying a modicum of logic, and the picture becomes clearer.

The works of numerous classical writers who documented the wars, campaigns, battles, skirmishes, and most importantly the men of the legions of Rome have come down to us. Apart from Caesar, Appian, Plutarch, and Tacitus, those authors include Suetonius, Polybius, Cassius Dio, Josephus, Cicero, Pliny the Younger, Seneca, Livy, and Arrian. Without the labors of these writers the books in this series would not have been possible.

All speeches and conversations in this book are taken from dialogue and narrative in classical texts, and are faithful to those original sources. For the sake of continuity, the Roman calendar—which in republican times, until Caesar changed it in 47 B.C., varied by some two months from our own (it was a difference of sixty-seven days by 46 B.C., when Caesar corrected the calendar), is used throughout this work.

Place names are generally first referred to in their original form and thereafter by their modern name, where known, to permit readers to readily identify locations involved. Personal names created by English writers of more recent times and familiar to modern readers have been used instead of those technically correct—Mark Antony instead of Marcus Antonius, Julius Caesar for Gaius Julius Caesar, Octavian for Caesar Octavianus, Pompey for Pompeius, Caligula for Gaius, Vespasian for Vespasianus, Trajan for Traianus, Hadrian for Hadrianus, and so on.

In the nineteenth and twentieth centuries it was fashionable for some authors to refer to legions as regiments, cohorts as battalions, maniples as companies, centurions as captains, tribunes as colonels, and legates as generals. In this work, Roman military terms such as legion, cohort, maniple, and centurion have been retained, as it's felt they will be familiar to most readers and convey more of a flavor of the time. Because of a lack of popular familiarity with the term legate, "general" and/or "brigadier general" is used here. "Colonel" and tribune are both used, to give a sense of relative status.

Likewise, so that readers can relate in comparison to today's military, when referred to in the military sense praetors are given as "major generals," and consuls and proconsuls as "lieutenant generals." In this way, reference to a lieutenant general, for example, will immediately tell the reader that the figure concerned is or has been a consul. I am aware this is akin to having a foot in two camps and may not please purists, but my aim is to make these books broadly accessible.

In this book I have quite deliberately skipped over the early battles of the civil war, in Italy and Spain, the Battle of Dyrrhachium in Albania, and the later key Battles of Thapsus in Africa and Munda in Spain, because these are covered in considerable detail in other books in this series—

Caesar's Legion and *Nero's Killing Machine*. In the former I also give a detailed account of the Battle of Pharsalus, but from the point of view of the 10th Legion, on Caesar's side. In this book I again describe Pharsalus, but this time from the point of view of the 6th Legion, on Pompey's side, to depict the path to the 6th Legion's change of sides in 48 B.C.

For this book is essentially about the 6th Legion. If it had not been for the tough veterans of the 6th, who fought and won desperate battles for Caesar against enormous odds, Caesar's career, and his life, would have ended in Egypt, or at the subsequent Battle of Zela in Turkey. These are the men who made Rome great—one or two extraordinary men, and many more ordinary men who often did extraordinary things. I hope that via these pages I can help you come to know them.

INTRODUCTION:
CAESAR IN CONTEXT

In 1961, Norman Schwarzkopf, then a young U.S. Army officer, attended an advanced training course at Fort Benning, Georgia. While in that course, he wrote an essay that won him an award from the army. Titled "The Battered Helmet," it told of a weary, mud-splattered general entering his tent after a battle and tossing his battered helmet onto the cot in the corner. As the essay unfolded, the reader came to realize that the author was not talking about a modern-day general or a contemporary battle, but was referring instead to Julius Caesar following his defeat of Pompey the Great at the Battle of Pharsalus in 48 B.C. It was a highly original treatise on the fact that while times have changed, the basic human element in war has not.

Schwarzkopf, later a famous general himself as commander of coalition forces in the 1991 Gulf War (Operation Desert Storm), made one or two small errors in his 1961 essay. For instance, the day of the Battle of Pharsalus was hot and dry, so Caesar could not have been wearing mud-splattered boots. But Norman Schwarzkopf made a much more fundamental error, an error frequently made down through the ages since the time of Caesar—he described Pompey as the "rebel" general in the affair. In reality, Julius Caesar was the rebel—a rebel who went to war against his own country and was declared an enemy of the state.

To put the civil war initiated by Julius Caesar in a modern context, what he did in 49 B.C. when he crossed the Rubicon River and invaded Italy was the equivalent of General Schwarzkopf in 1991 returning from commanding coalition forces in the Persian Gulf and invading the United States with part of his army, intent on deposing President George H. W. Bush and overthrowing Congress. The modern counterpart of Caesar's chief military opponent, Pompey the Great, would have been General Colin Powell, chairman of the U.S. Joint Chiefs of Staff.

1

Caesar's defeat of Pompey at Pharsalus in Greece in 48 B.C. was like General Schwarzkopf defeating General Powell at a battle in Florida, after which Powell would have fled to Mexico, just as Pompey fled to Egypt. And just as Caesar arrived in Egypt in search of Pompey, and became entangled in a prolonged conflict in Alexandria, General Schwarzkopf would have reached Mexico with a small force and occupied part of Mexico City. And there he would have taken the four leading members of the ruling Mexican dynasty hostage. In Caesar's case, in Egypt, the kidnap victims were the siblings Cleopatra, Ptolemy, Arsinoe, and the younger Ptolemy.

It is on Egypt in 48–47 B.C. that this book focuses, as the rebel Caesar arrived in pursuit of Pompey, to eliminate his rival and become ruler of the Roman world. This is the story of Caesar's life-and-death struggles in Egypt; of months of vicious street fighting that culminated in an all-out battle beside the Nile River; and of the short, bloody Battle of Zela immediately after, in Turkey. It's also the story of Caesar's romance with Cleopatra, a girl young enough to be his daughter who made a career of attaching herself to Roman strongmen.

Most importantly, this is the story of the nine hundred Spanish legionaries of the 6th Legion who kidnapped Cleopatra and led the way for Caesar in three successive battles, nine hundred men who made it possible for Caesar to come, to see, and to conquer. Shortly before, these soldiers had been members of a defeated army, and stood on the brink of annihilation as the troops of Mark Antony surrounded them. Yet, within months, these few men of the 6th Legion were to prove so invincible it was as if they were clad in iron, as they helped Julius Caesar go from rebel general and from a declared enemy of the state to ruler of the Roman world.

I

LAST STAND
IN ALEXANDRIA

Death in Egypt. It was not an end the men of the 6th Legion or those of the 28th Legion would have imagined for themselves or their general, Julius Caesar, when they set foot here in Alexandria at the beginning of October 48 B.C. This was only meant to be a brief stopover, after all. Now, months later, as the legionaries filed through the darkness of night into the half-moon theater of the royal palace of the Ptolemies close to Alexandria's docks, and crowded toward the front to hear Caesar speak, many of them were afraid. Some were on the verge of panic.

Back in August, Caesar had been the victor in a battle that had given him control of much of the Roman world. An army of tens of thousands of men served him. But here, now, Caesar commanded little more than three thousand legionaries and several hundred cavalry, and he was surrounded and cut off in the Egyptian capital by as many as seventy thousand well-equipped Egyptian troops.

To many members of his little force, Caesar's cause looked lost, and their future bleak. He had ignored their requests to lead them out of Alexandria. Why, they didn't know. He had lingered here until the Egyptians had sealed them all inside the city. They were surrounded by determined Egyptian regulars and militia who consistently tried to dislodge them from their fortified positions in fierce assaults and brutal street fighting. Caesar's orders to commanders he'd left behind in Greece and Syria to urgently send him reinforcements seemed to have gone unheeded, his requests for help from the minor potentates of the Middle East had apparently been ignored.

Arguments had begun to break out among Caesar's rank and file. Some men said that he had lied to them when he had recently said he would soon give the order to break out of this fatal place. Others took Caesar's part, saying that it would be impossible to break out without the enemy getting wind of their intentions and setting an ambush for them, because townspeople trapped in the Romans' sector of Alexandria would see what they were up to and covertly alert the besiegers. But those who had lost their courage and their faith in Caesar outnumbered those who defended him.

It seemed to many of Caesar's troops that they were doomed to perish here, forgotten and forsaken by their countrymen. No reinforcements had reached them. Their food was almost exhausted. But worse, they had that morning discovered that their water supply, precarious at the best of times, had been poisoned by the Egyptians. Certainly it was winter here now, and the locals had told them they could soon expect thunderstorms that would bring rain, and even hail. But a man without water can last only a matter of days. The Romans could all be dead from thirst before the first winter storms brought rainwater sluicing down from the stone-clad rooftops of the city.

The warships that had brought them here were still at anchor in the harbor. Why couldn't they make a sudden dash from the sector of the city they held, force their way to the docks, and board the waiting ships and make good their escape? It seemed a simple enough solution to simple soldiers.

When the panicky clamor from his troops, led by his younger, inexperienced Italian legionaries of the 28th—mostly mere boys in their teens and twenties—had that morning begun to sound threateningly like the first stages of mutiny, Caesar had quickly called this assembly. Caesar had seen more than enough mutinies of late. The previous year he had punished the 9th Legion at Piacenza in northern Italy by decimation for refusing to obey the orders of his deputy Mark Antony. And he wouldn't be here with so pitifully few troops if it hadn't been for a massive strike by all his best legions in Greece this past August. It was time to put his famed oratorical powers to use, to dampen fears, to embolden faint hearts.

Yet not all the legionaries assembling in the low light of spluttering torches and spreading on the stone tiers of the theater were anxious or fearful. While the youngsters of the 28th talked incessantly among themselves, repeating the sentiment now prevalent in their ranks that they must escape Alexandria to survive, most of the older soldiers of the 6th Legion, less than a thousand men in their thirties and forties, quietly, calmly took their places.

These men of the 6th were tough, vastly experienced veteran soldiers. Recruited in eastern Spain seventeen years before by Pompey the Great, they had subdued the Celtic natives of Portugal and western Spain, they had been commanded by Caesar for two years during his conquest of Gaul, they had fought in the major conflicts of the civil war. These men of the 6th had stared death in the face for almost two decades. Over the years they had seen a third of their comrades die, as they stormed villages and towns and fought set piece battles across western Europe. They had starved and gone without water before now, too.

Folding their arms, swarthy, battle-scarred Spanish veterans of the 6th such as Publius Sertorius, his brother Marcus, and their good friends the brothers Quintus and Gaius Tetarfenus would have studied the overtalkative, edgy youths of the 28th Legion with distaste. Made arrogant by their experience of war and by the special trust that Caesar had placed in them of late, the legionaries of the 6th stood aloof from these foolish, frightened Italian boys. "Make way for your betters," they would have said as they came to the assembly at the theater.

Some of Caesar's cavalry troopers also would have been looking and sounding alarmed—men who had been among the seven hundred Gallic cavalry that Caesar had taken into battle in Greece against Pompey. Two hundred of their number had died in the Battle of Pharsalus. The five hundred survivors, here, now, were conscious that they were a long way from their homeland in France. None had ever been so far from home before. This hot, dry place was alien to them, and worse, they had been forced to dismount and fight as foot soldiers in the streets of Alexandria; this wasn't what their elders had told them to expect when they signed up with Julius Caesar.

These troopers, all wearing breeches—unlike the Romans, who wore tunics to their knees but no trousers—were cavalrymen, the best horsemen in Europe, not infantry. They were neither equipped nor trained for close-quarters fighting on foot. Since boyhood they had practiced launching lances and darts at the gallop at enemy infantry, to wield their large cavalry sword, the *spatha*, from horseback, slicing off heads as if they were cutting chaff. Their round shields were small, their leather vests only light, unlike the Roman legionaries they fought alongside, whose shields were almost as big as they were, their chain mail armor thick, and their training designed around close combat with their short swords.

Other troopers would have appeared more stoic and less troubled—the three hundred long-haired, bearded Germans of Caesar's bodyguard—tall, broad-shouldered, and fiercely brave Batavians from modern-day Holland and Treverans from the Moselle River. These Germans, most of them fair of hair, some redheaded, none of them Roman citizens, had served as Caesar's personal bodyguards for a decade. Rating them the best cavalry he had ever seen, Caesar paid them well, and in return their loyalty was to him, and to him alone. Never once had they questioned his orders or let him down. That attitude would not change here at Alexandria; the Germans had blind faith in Caesar. If only that faith was shared by his own countrymen of the 28th Legion.

Not all the troops were here. Some were on guard duty, at the walls and guard towers of the fortifications they had built around their sector of the city, a sector centered on the theater, which Caesar had turned into a citadel. Other troops were guarding four special prisoners, surviving members of the Egyptian royal family, who had been kidnapped by the men of the 6th and their colleagues and held here with the Romans. Chief among them was fourteen-year-old Ptolemy XIII, king of Egypt. With him were his youngest sister, the fifteen-year-old Arsinoe; his little brother, another Ptolemy; and the elder sister who had until recently shared the throne with him as queen of Egypt until he had deposed her—the enigmatic twenty-one-year-old Cleopatra VII.

There was movement in the wings of the tall back stone wall of the theater; a curtain covering a doorway parted, and Julius Caesar was walking out onto the stage in front of his troops, bareheaded, in his armor, with his rich scarlet general's cloak, the *paludamentum*, flowing behind him. He was not tall, nor was he handsome, possessing a long nose and balding pate. Yet there was something magnetic about Gaius Julius Caesar.

"Hail, Commander!" came the characteristic greeting of three thousand chorused voices, led by their officers. Expectantly, and in some cases nervously, Caesar's men stood on the tiers of the theater before him in full equipment, with their helmets under their arms. And then they lapsed into silence as they watched their general reach the front of the stage. He stood there for a moment, his long, serious face lit by torches burning in a row along the front of the stage.

"Comrades," Caesar began. Unlike other Roman generals, who addressed their men simply as "Soldiers," Caesar would often refer to his rank and file as his fellow soldiers or comrades in arms when he spoke to them. Caesar's contemporary, the great Roman orator Marcus Cicero, wrote to a friend, "Do you know any man who, even if he has concentrated on the art or oratory to the exclusion of all else, can speak better than Caesar?" The speaking style Caesar used was grand and noble. Sometimes he was wonderfully witty, and he displayed a varied yet exact vocabulary. He'd even written a book on the subject of public speaking and the appropriate use of words. Yet, when he spoke to his troops, he spared his men the rhetorical flourishes that impressed the likes of Cicero.

With a staff officer noting down his words, Caesar spoke to the hushed theater, characteristically pitching his voice high so that all could hear

him. Impatient by nature, he was never one to beat about the bush. Coming straight to the point, he immediately addressed the problem at hand,
the lack of freshwater, by reasoning with his men.

"Comrades, if you dig wells, freshwater will be found. Every coastal district naturally has veins of freshwater." It sounded like such an easy solution. Besides, Caesar went on, even if the Egyptian coast turned out to be
different from every other coastline in the world and devoid of freshwater,
the Romans could still send their small fleet to fetch water farther to the
east or west. The way Caesar spoke, water was only a minor problem.

"As for flight," he went on, sounding more like a friendly adviser than
a commander, "that is out of the question. Not merely for those for whom
their reputation comes first, but even for those who think of nothing but
their lives. It's only with great effort that we've beaten back the onslaughts
of the enemy on our fortifications. If we abandon those fortifications, we
will be no match for the enemy either in numbers or in position. Besides,
embarkation, especially from small boats, involves difficulty and delay,
while the Alexandrians have on their side extreme speed and familiarity
with the areas and the buildings." Made insolent by their successes so far,
Caesar said, the Egyptians would react quickly and lethally to any attempt
at a mass breakout to the sea by the Romans. "They would dash ahead
seizing the higher ground and the buildings, and so prevent you from
withdrawing and reaching the ships."

Murmurs of agreement ran through the assembled soldiers. Heads
among the ranks of the 6th Legion were nodding. Many legionaries could
now picture themselves being cut to pieces in the open by the vastly more
numerical enemy troops as they made a headlong dash for the harbor, or
on the harbor itself as the Egyptians flooded onto it in small boats, as they
had previously. What Caesar said made sense.

Caesar could sense a mood change. "So you should put that idea out of
your heads." His voice became less friendly, more steely. "Concentrate on
conquering. At all costs!"

Caesar now prepared to give an order to his centurions, an order that
went against the mood prevailing in this theater when he had strode onto
the stage. If that order was not obeyed by the rank and file, his power of
command would be at an end; many of his troops would disregard their
officers and try to escape from Alexandria any way they could, or surrender. With the inevitable result that the Egyptians would overrun Caesar's
positions and he would be a dead man. "Centurions . . ." He paused, looking around the assembly and catching the eye of his centurions, all men
he knew by name. "You are to cease all current operations."

Julius Caesar had a new operation for them all.

II

TRAPPED

T he sounds of battle came from behind them, and away to their left. Cries of pain, shrieks of terror, bellows of command, the clash of iron on wood, iron, and bronze. The surviving men of two cohorts of the proud 6th Legion, less than a thousand of them, stood silently in their circular *orbis* formation, ten men deep. Their large, curved, rectangular shields bearing the 6th's charging bull emblem were raised on their rippling left arms and locked together to create a series of almost impenetrable walls of wood, leather, and iron. In their right hands each man held his short sword, the twenty-inch *gladius*, known as the "Spanish sword" among the rank and file.

Few men of the 6th had bloodied their blades this hot summer day, for the tide of battle had quickly turned against their army after their cavalry had been sent fleeing from the field. And here they were on the plain of Farsala, Pharsalus as the Romans called it, in the Thessaly region of eastern Greece, surrounded, trapped, without the opportunity to show their worth. It was August 9, 48 B.C., and this was the Battle of Pharsalus, the battle in the now eighteen-month-old civil war that would decide who controlled Rome and her empire.

These legionaries were Spaniards, among the six thousand men recruited into the Roman army's new 6th Legion by Gnaeus Pompeius Magnus—Pompey the Great—seventeen years before in the Roman province of Tarraconensis, better known as Nearer Spain, the eastern part of Spain. Back then, in 65 B.C., most of these men had been raw recruits, a few of them penniless, homeless volunteers, but draftees in the main, as young as seventeen, averaging twenty years of age. Clean-shaven and wet behind the ears, they had been town laborers, farm boys, fishermen; poorly educated, and most of them poorly off. They were all Roman citizens, but they spoke their Latin in accents tainted by local Spanish dialects.

Sorted into ten cohorts, the equivalent of modern battalions, each of six hundred men, they were then subdivided into maniples, or companies, of two hundred men marching behind a standard bearing the emblem of an open hand, a symbol of power. These had been subdivided again into centuries of a hundred men, with every century commanded by a centurion. Centuries were in turn divided into ten *contuberniums* or squads, each of ten men. Once their units had been sorted out, with NCOs appointed—a centurion, an optio or sergeant major, and a tesserarius, an orderly sergeant, to every century—their officers had told the recruits to team up with a comrade in their squad, a buddy who would watch the other's back in combat, who would hold his last will and testament, and, if necessary, bury him and act as executor of his estate.

The equipping of a Roman legionary was by this time a methodical and well-organized affair. Each recruit had been provided with a standard dark-red Roman army tunic that reached almost to the knee, plus a red woolen cloak, an armored vest made of chain mail sewn to an armless leather waistcoat, and a bronze helmet with a jutting neck protector, a plume of yellow horsehair, and cheek flaps that tied under the chin. They wore heavy-duty, hobnailed military sandals on their feet.

Each recruit was armed with a gladius, the short, pointy-tipped sword, worn in a scabbard on the right side, plus a *puglio* army knife worn on the left hip, and several javelins that had weighted ends and were designed to bend behind the head once they hit a target—so that no opponent could throw them back.

Finally, they were given their shields. Made from strips of wood glued together, not unlike modern plywood, the shield had a leather surface covering. Four feet long and two and one-half feet across, the shield was curved, to provide better body protection, rimmed with metal, and equipped with a metal boss at the center. The handle was attached to the reverse side of the boss, to be gripped in the left hand. A leather strap slipped over the elbow to help support the shield's weight. Most of the legions raised in Spain during this period took as their emblem the bull, a symbol of religious sacrifice. The 6th Legion's symbol of a charging bull was painted on every man's shield and appeared on every standard. When not on parade or in battle order, each soldier protected his shield with a slip-on leather weather cover.

Legionaries also were provided with an entrenching tool, a scythe for foraging, a water bucket, bedroll, and eating and cooking implements. Some were given a pickax, a turf-cutter, and a wicker basket. All were equipped with a pair of picket stakes; combined, the twelve thousand pickets carried by the men of a legion would form the top of the legion's camp wall when they were in the field. All this equipment had to be carried in a backpack slung from a pole over the soldier's right shoulder when on the march.

As legionaries, they were no longer subject to civil law. After they had sworn to obey their officers and serve the Senate and people of Rome, their centurions read aloud the strict military regulations that would govern their lives for the next sixteen years of their enlistment, if they lived that long. They could not marry. Homosexual acts were punishable by death, as was desertion and even falling asleep on guard duty. Minor infractions would bring various punishments, starting with a beating from the vine stick carried by every centurion. Three minor infractions also added up to the death penalty—the original three-strikes-and-you're-out policy.

Now that they were professional soldiers, their rations would be supplied by the state and they would be paid a salary, at that time a meager 450 sesterces a year, doubling to 900 sesterces a year on the initiative of Caesar during the 50s B.C. As the recruits got to know each other in camp, scratching their names inside their new shields and helmets (one helmet found in modern times had four names scratched inside, indicating four different owners at various times), sharpening their blades, and sorting out their equipment, they would have talked about the likelihood of making money in the years ahead.

The army's rules of plunder meant that if they stormed an enemy town the troops kept all the booty they looted from it. But if the town surrendered, the loot went to their commanders. Likewise, proceeds from the sale of prisoners who were fighting men went to the legionaries, while their officers received the money generated by the sale of civilians. The new recruits of the 6th Legion would have all heard how during the past decade the men of Pompey the Great's legions had come back rich men after conquering the East. From Asia Minor to Palestine, Pompey's legionaries had stormed cities and towns and enriched themselves—and their general, who was now considered Rome's wealthiest man. There were still considerable parts of the known world to conquer and troublesome allied states to keep in order, so a profitable future would have seemed an excellent prospect to the recruits of the 6th.

Enlisted men also could improve their financial positions via promotion. A senior centurion could earn a handsome 20,000 sesterces a year, and received the lion's share of booty and bonuses. Promoted from the ranks, and in eleven grades, a legion's sixty centurions had money, prestige, and power. Prior to the major Roman army reforms instituted by the consul Gaius Marius during his seven consulships between 107 and 86 B.C., centurions had been elected by the rank and file. Now a centurion was chosen, promoted, and demoted or dismissed on the say-so of his superiors, based on his courage, performance, and leadership qualities.

Technically, a legion was commanded by its six tribunes. Six young men from leading Roman families, all members of the Equestrian Order of knighthood, in their late teens and twenties, they had no previous military experience and served for just a year before going home to Rome to commence their civil service careers. Over the twelve months the tribunes spent with a legion they would take turns commanding it—every two months the command would rotate. For his remaining ten months, each tribune commanded two of the ten cohorts of the legion. Some of these young tribunes would prove exceptionally able, and would go on to one day become famous generals, but many were far from equipped to lead men in battle, and in practice the leadership of a legion in republican times fell to its centurions.

Those centurions were responsible for the training of their men. With their own lives depending on how well their men performed in combat, centurions were tough, even brutal with their recruits. They taught them how to march, how to run twenty-five miles in full equipment, and how to build a fortified camp in hours at the end of every day's march. But most of all they taught their men how to fight—not as individuals but as members of a close-knit team.

A century later, in another civil war, two thousand gladiators would be drafted into a Roman army to fight on the battlefield for the emperor Otho. The gladiators would ultimately prove a failure as soldiers. Trained to fight as individuals, they did not have the skills to work as a unit. Those skills, once ingrained into legionaries through grinding, painful training and later in battle, meant that a legionary would obey his centurion's commands in combat without thinking, would instinctively cooperate with his comrades around him. He knew exactly what to do and where to go when his centurion called for various offensive and defensive formations. There was the wedge, a standard defense against cavalry attack. And the crescent, designed to suck the enemy into the center before the wings wrapped around behind them. Then there was the *testudo*, or tortoise, a formation used for attacking enemy fortifications where legionaries locked their shields over their heads as protection from missiles flung from above. And the *orbis*, or ring, often a formation of last resort.

Publius Sertorius and his brother Marcus were among these soldiers of the 6th. Their father, Marcus, had apparently been granted Roman citizenship by Quintus Sertorius, rebel Roman governor of Spain, taking Sertorius's last name as his own. Perhaps these soldiers' father had marched for Sertorius against the Roman general sent to regain Spain from him, Pompey the Great, returning to civilian life after Sertorius's assassination in 72 B.C. The Sertorius boys had been caught up in Pompey's mass intake of thirty-six thousand Spanish legion recruits authorized by the Senate in 65 B.C. From that intake, in addition to the 6th, Pompey also created the new 4th and 5th Legions, units that would march with the 6th for decades to come, and the 7th, 8th, and 9th, legions that would form the backbone of Julius Caesar's army in Spain and later in Gaul during his 58–50 B.C. conquests there.

Legionaries Publius and Marcus Sertorius were here now in the ranks at Farsala, along with comrades including Lucius Caienus, Quintus Tetarfenus, Gaius Tetarfenus, Lucius Labicius, Gaius Figilius, Lucius Acilius, Gaius Numisius, and Quintus Nonius. And a question was exercising the minds of them all. Had they survived seventeen years of battles, sieges, and assaults, only for their careers and their lives to come to an end here in a Greek wheat field?

During their early years in the legion, the men of the 6th had garrisoned eastern Spain; before, from 55 to 52 B.C., they marched on bloody campaigns in Lusitania, today's Portugal, against the wild Celtic tribes of the region. Led by a dashing, ambitious, short-tempered general, Marcus Petreius, they had subdued the locals, who made excellent cavalry but poor infantry, after many a battle in which the men of the 6th had adopted unorthodox but ultimately successful tactics.

In 52 B.C., Pompey, who maintained overall control of Spain from Rome, had loaned the 6th Legion to Julius Caesar, to help him out in Gaul after the recently conquered Gallic tribes had risen in revolt. That revolt, led by a young Gallic chief from the Auvergne Mountains named Vercingetorix, was extinguished before the 6th Legion had a chance to get a major piece of the fighting or the booty. But with minor manifestations of the revolt erupting around Gaul like brush fires even after Caesar had forced Vercingetorix to surrender at Alesia that same year, Caesar had retained the 6th as part of his army in Gaul.

At first, because it had been one of Pompey's legions, Caesar hadn't entrusted the 6th with important tasks, relegating it to guarding baggage and harvesting wheat in southern France with the 14th Legion, a Caesarian unit in which he had lost faith after it had been wiped out once and savaged again by Belgian and German tribesmen. But in the winter of 52–51 B.C. the proximity to the action of their camp had meant the 6th and 14th had been called in to put down unrest in central France, marching north to occupy the city that was to become modern Orléans. In the new year, the 6th and the 14th had worked together to terminate unrest in western France before conducting the successful siege of the rebel hill town of Uxellodunum in the Department of Lot, where Vercingetorix's deputy had holed up. This turned out to be the last engagement of the Gallic War.

By 50 B.C., with resistance quashed and Gaul, Belgica, and western Germania—France, Belgium, Luxembourg, Holland, and Germany west of the Rhine—under the Roman yoke, Caesar had turned to matters political. During the turbulent year that he had served as consul of Rome, in 59 B.C., Caesar had done much good for the republic. Among numerous initiatives, he had created the world's first daily newspaper, the *Acta Diurnia* (Daily News), written by hand at Rome every day and circulated throughout the Roman world. Caesar also had brought in the capital's first traffic laws, banning most wheeled traffic from the city's narrow, congested streets by day, so that all night, every night, wagons and carts rolled in and out of the city, those coming in loaded with farm produce and foreign imports, those departing taking out the manufactured goods of the capital.

But in his impatience to make his mark on Rome and her administration, Caesar had cut many corners and made many enemies in 59 B.C. Deferring to no man, he'd defied anybody who stood up to him, even forcing his antagonistic fellow consul Marcus Calpurnius Bibulus to retire behind closed doors for the latter part of his consulship. Throughout his career, Caesar was never afraid to offer a bribe to win his way, and once his consulship ended, many accusations were circulating that he'd played fast and loose with treasury funds.

Moves to bring Caesar to court to face charges of illegal acts during his consulship were circumvented when he left Rome in 58 B.C. to take up his governorship of Cisalpine Gaul, Transalpine Gaul, and Illyricum—a current consul or proconsul could not be taken to court. But when in 50 B.C. those governorships were coming to an end, Caesar's enemies in the Senate began to agitate to bring him to trial on the old charges when he was once again a private person. If found guilty, he could face the death penalty, or, at least financial ruin and banishment. To prevent this, Caesar proposed that he be given a new appointment to govern just one of his provinces, supported by two legions. When this idea failed to win support, he set his sights on again being elected consul, with his talented deputy during the Gallic War, General Titus Atius Labienus, as his coconsul.

Yet, while Caesar managed, via elections and bribery, to cement the loyalty of three key supporters, including his relative Marcus Antonius (Mark Antony), who all had power of veto over Senate votes as Tribunes of the Plebeians, it became increasingly obvious to him that his many opponents in the Senate would never let him again become consul. Even his old ally Pompey the Great, who had been married to Caesar's daughter Julia until her death in 54 B.C., began to back away from him.

In the summer of 50 B.C., Pompey had sent a trusted senior officer to southern France to collect the 6th Legion and lead it out of Caesar's area of control and back to his, in Nearer Spain, where the legion was due to undergo discharge and reenlistment in the new year, at the end of their sixteen years' contracted military service. This officer was identified by Plutarch as General Appius. Lieutenant General Appius Claudius Pulcher, a consul in 54 B.C., governor of Cilicia in 52 B.C., was close to the Pompey family—his daughter had married Pompey's eldest son, Gnaeus.

When Caesar learned that he was being deprived of the 6th Legion, in the hope of securing their loyalty he sent a gift to the men of the 6th as they prepared to leave the camp they'd been sharing with the 14th Legion in France—1,000 sesterces per man, more than their annual salary of 900 sesterces, for by then Caesar had decided on his future course. Denied what he saw as his due, prevented from retaining gubernatorial power or again becoming consul, he had decided to grab total power for himself, using his loyal legions while he still had control of them.

"I see quarrels ahead in which strength and steel will be the arbiters," former Tribune of the Plebs Marcus Caelius Rufus wrote to his patron Marcus Cicero at the end of that summer of 50 B.C. "Fate is preparing a mighty and fascinating show." He was one of the few to fully realize what Caesar had in mind. Pompey and the Senate had been lulled into a false sense of security, never expecting Caesar to go to war with his own country.

That sense of security had several origins. First, one of the consuls for 50 B.C., Gaius Claudius Marcellus, had ordered Caesar and Pompey to each provide a legion for a force that would invade Parthia from Syria. Primarily this was intended to punish the Parthians for defeating General Crassus at Carrhae, in today's Iran, three years before. But the plan also was sponsored by reports of movement by Parthian forces on the northeastern rim of Rome's provinces in the East. Caesar had not been happy to give up a legion, but when Pompey sent his elite 1st Legion marching up from Rome into Caesar's province of Cisalpine Gaul as his contribution, Caesar had been forced to hand over the 15th Legion.

After taking the 6th Legion back to Spain, General Appius had led the 1st and the 15th to Rome as a prelude to their embarkation for the East. At that point, the Parthians had ceased to threaten Roman territory in the East, and the Senate had canceled the Parthian operation and given both the 1st and the 15th over to Pompey's control. He had subsequently sent the two units into winter camp at Luceria in the Puglia region of southeastern Italy.

Privately, Caesar had been furious at losing both the 6th and 15th Legions from his army, but said nothing publicly—although he would rail about it in his memoirs. This silence led his opponents in the Senate to believe they had the better of him. But, never one to be outwitted, Caesar promptly replaced the 15th Legion by recruiting six thousand men from Celtic tribes in Transalpine Gaul to form a new legion. He did this without the permission or prior knowledge of the Senate—all provincial governors were required to seek Senate approval before they enrolled new units. None of his new recruits was a Roman citizen, but Caesar soon fixed that by unilaterally granting them citizenship. For the time being, Caesar called his new legion the Alaudae, which was a Celtic word meaning "crested larks," apparently deriving from these soldiers' long Celtic-style helmet plumes.

There was another factor that had made Caesar's opponents believe he would not embark on what they felt was the insane course of armed conflict with his own countrymen. After General Appius returned to Rome with the 1st and the 15th, the handsome, vain Appius, who was both fickle and prone to poor judgment, had assured Pompey and his colleagues that Caesar's legions had no stomach for civil war. Plutarch says that Appius even told Pompey that if Caesar were to overstep the mark, such was the loyalty of Rome's legions to Pompey that they would all flock to Pompey's banner. As it was to prove, Appius was way off the mark. Even if Appius had genuinely felt Caesar's troops were loyal to Pompey—rather than telling Pompey what he felt he wanted to hear—Appius had mixed primarily with the men of the 6th and the 1st, both of them Pompey's legions, and had no real feel for the attitude of Caesar's troops then stationed in Gaul other than those of the 15th.

Pompey took Appius's view as his own. "Should Caesar take leave of his senses," Marcus Cicero wrote to his friend Titus Atticus after a meeting with Pompey during which he had raised the possibility of Caesar resorting to military action, "Pompey is quite contemptuous of anything he can do and confident in his own and the republic's forces."

When the men of the 6th Legion had tramped back over the Pyrenees Mountains to their old base in eastern Spain, toting their by then bulging purses, there would have been much talk among the ranks of the likelihood of Caesar going to war against the Senate, of what stand Pompey might take, and where the men of the 6th stood in the eventuality that it came to civil war.

By the time the year was ending and the confrontation between Senate and Caesar was coming to a head, Pompey had decided on his position, prompted by a December 21 speech in the Senate in which Caesar's former quaestor, or chief of staff, Mark Antony, had condemned Pompey out of hand. Four days later, in another meeting with Marcus Cicero, Pompey had declared: "How do you expect Caesar to behave if he gets control of the state, when his feckless nobody of a quaestor dares to say this sort of thing?"

In Cicero's opinion, far from seeking a peaceful settlement, Pompey had come to dread such an option. Unless Caesar backed down, as most people thought he would, war was inevitable.

When, in January 49 B.C., just weeks before his 7th, 8th, and 9th Legions were—like the 6th—due to receive their sixteen-year discharge, Caesar crossed the Rubicon River, invading Italy and launching into a civil war against his own countrymen, the 6th had stayed firm in its loyalty to Pompey. This was despite the bribe Caesar had paid them the previous summer, and even though it meant that hard fighting lay ahead. Discharge was on hold for all legions on both sides of the conflict, both those serving Caesar and those, like the 6th, serving the Senate of the republic and its appointed military commander, Pompey. They could go home only once this civil war initiated by the rebel Caesar had been decided.

Even though there were seven republican legions in Spain—six of them made up of long-serving, highly experienced soldiers—their generals, although loyal to Pompey, were not in either Pompey's or Caesar's league as strategists or leaders. As Caesar set off from Rome to take command of his forces in Spain, he was confident of quickly dealing with Pompey's best soldiers and poorest generals. Suetonius says that Caesar, who was fond of witticisms and wordplay, told his staff at the time: "I'm off to meet an army without a leader. When I come back I'll meet a leader without an army."

The 6th Legion was one of five experienced legions, along with the 3rd, 4th, 5th, and Valeria, that went up against six of Caesar's legions in eastern Spain that summer. After some initial success in battles and skirmishes outside the city of Lérida, the Roman Ilerda, the republican legions, low on supplies, had been led north by their generals, Lucius Afranius and Marcus Petreius, toward the mountains, in search of food. Outmaneuvered and cut off on the plain by Caesar, Afranius and Petreius had surrendered their starving legions.

Surrender had been an ignoble end to an illustrious career for the men of the 6th, but at least Caesar discharged them, even paid them their back pay—having to borrow from his own officers to do it—and sent them home. So, disarmed, but carrying full purses, on August 4, 49 B.C. the men of the 6th legion had set off to tramp back to their homes in eastern Spain with their fellow discharged veterans of the 4th Legion, to surprise families they had not seen in sixteen years, to find and marry old sweethearts or new ladyloves, to buy a farm or set up in business, to look forward to a retirement, with a "home and a pleasing wife," as the Romans said. Within days, Caesar also discharged the Spanish legionaries of Pompey's surrendered 5th Legion and sent them on their way toward their homes farther west, while he sent the 3rd and the Valeria marching under escort of two of his legions to Transalpine Gaul, where they, too, would be discharged, at the Var River, which formed the border with Cisalpine Gaul. Caesar then quickly set off for western Spain, to deal with the two republican legions still under arms and to secure the province of Baetica, Farther Spain.

The Pompeian commanders, Generals Afranius and Petreius, also were set free, after giving Caesar their parole that they would take no further part in the civil war. Ignoring his parole, Afranius, in his fifties, an old friend of Pompey's and fellow native of the Picenum region of eastern Italy, had immediately hurried with the younger Petreius to Tarragona, the Roman Tarraco, principal city of the province of Nearer Spain. On the Mediterranean coast, Tarragona was not yet in Caesar's hands. The initial intent of the two generals was to find a ship that would take them to Greece to join Pompey.

Other surrendered Pompeian officers joined Afranius and Petreius in Tarragona, several of whom had been captured and released on parole once before by Caesar, during his drive down through eastern Italy in the spring. Back in March, after hearing that these officers had broken their parole, Caesar had commented in a letter to Cicero: "I'm not worried by the fact that those whom I have released are said to have left the country in order to make war against me again. Nothing pleases me more than that I should be true to my nature and they to theirs." But a second violation of their parole would try Caesar's patience.

There in Tarragona, to their delight, Generals Afranius and Petreius found that a fleet of eighteen heavy warships under the Senate's Admiral Lucius Nasidius had just pulled into port. Admiral Nasidius had been sent west from Greece by Pompey with sixteen battleships and cruisers with orders to help the people of Marseilles, Roman Massilia, in southern France, who were holding out against three of Caesar's attacking legions. Capturing and manning an additional cruiser when he raided Messina on Sicily along the way, Admiral Nasidius had linked up with eleven Marseilles warships and gone into battle off the city against a Roman fleet led by Caesar's Admiral Decimus Brutus. Nasidius's allies had fared badly in the battle, losing nine ships. One of the survivors had joined Nasidius as he withdrew his battered vessels and headed for the nearest friendly port, Tarragona.

Now, Generals Afranius and Petreius had an idea. Sending messengers around Nearer Spain, they hastily recalled thirty-five hundred of their best soldiers of the 4th and 6th Legions, enough men to make three cohorts of the former and four of the latter. The number of men summoned was dictated by the number of Nasidius's warships—about two hundred men could be crowded onto the deck of each ship together with all the supplies and war matériel they could carry. Then, with their paid oarsmen straining at their banks of oars, the big ships departed Tarragona and set a course for Greece. The exact route taken by the little fleet of crowded ships is unknown, but they succeeded in reaching Greece late in the summer without encountering any opposition, for Caesar's naval forces were limited.

Generals Afranius and Petreius then led the cohorts of the 4th and 6th overland to link up with Pompey at Veroia in northeastern Macedonia, where Pompey was building up his forces for an inevitable battle against Caesar. Afranius seemed to think that Pompey would be pleased that he had brought him thirty-five hundred of his best men. But Pompey was staggered that Afranius also brought him the news that he had lost him eastern Spain, and five legions, with western Spain and the remaining two republican legions sure to soon follow.

For his dismal performance in Spain, Afranius suffered continual criticism from the hundreds of senators and senior officers accompanying Pompey. There were even accusations that Afranius was a traitor who had deliberately given up his legions to Caesar. As a result, he would never be completely trusted by those in Pompey's camp. But the men of the 4th and the 6th were indeed welcome additions to Pompey's army. Apart from his crack 1st Legion, which had served Pompey for decades, and the 15th, which had been raised by Caesar and had seen service in the conquest of Gaul, Pompey's legions were composed of a combination of new recruits and men who had not seen action in years. While marching behind their own eagle standards still, the 4th and the 6th were ordered by Pompey to act as a single unit.

There in Macedonia, through the fall and early winter of 49 B.C., the seven Spanish cohorts of the 4th and the 6th had trained together, watching the other units of the senatorial army go through their paces. Fifty-seven-year-old Pompey himself trained with his troops, on foot and horseback. He had gained weight in the decade since he'd last marched at the head of an army, and was no longer the lithe, trim twenty-three-year-old who had led his first legions to victory after victory back in the civil war between Sulla and Marius. Yet, despite the passing of the years, the added pounds, and the fact that he had been gravely ill the previous year when Caesar crossed the Rubicon, Pompey looked fit and well, and he had galvanized his troops by displaying the energy and skill of a youngster.

Inspired by their famous general, who had never been beaten in battle—Pompey was still "a match for all comers," according to first-century writer Seneca—they vied for his approval. As it went through its formation drills, the 1st Legion would have shown a machinelike discipline that impressed all who saw it. The men of the 6th would have been amused when they heard from their comrades of the 1st Legion that after Pompey had sent the 1st to Caesar in Cisalpine Gaul as his contribution to the soon-to-be-aborted Parthian operation, when Caesar sent the 1st on its way back to Rome with General Appius and the 15th, he had paid the men of the 1st a bonus of 250 sesterces each. Caesar had obviously been trying to buy the loyalty of the 1st ahead of his planned invasion of Italy.

What would have amused the men of the 6th most was not that Caesar had attempted to bribe the men of Pompey's most elite and most loyal unit, but that he had given the men of the 1st Legion only 250 sesterces. He'd paid the legionaries of the 6th four times as much the previous year! And how that information would have swelled their heads. As it turned out, Caesar didn't value the 6th above the 1st; he was just running out of money.

The six-year veterans of the 15th Legion also would have been in good form as they trained in Macedonia. Caesar would have been hoping that their long association with him in Gaul would see them desert Pompey, but he had been disappointed; the 15th had stayed firmly behind the Senate's commander. The Italians of the five cohorts of the new 28th Legion would have trained enthusiastically, but they were worryingly inexperienced. After being caught on the Adriatic in an abortive amphibious landing in Illyricum led by Mark Antony's brother Gaius, they had deserted their commander and come over to Pompey and the republic. But they were raw draftees, enrolled eighteen months before in central Italy, and while they had performed creditably in the Durrës breakout, they were yet to prove themselves in a full-on battle.

There were also two four-year-old legions made up of Italians, which had been stationed in Syria. But they were survivors of the mayhem of the Battle of Carrhae against the Parthians, in modern-day Iran, four years before, when Roman general Marcus Licinius Crassus and thirty thousand Roman legionaries had been wiped out by ten thousand mounted Parthians in one of Rome's greatest defeats. The men of this pair of surviving legions had not seen action since, and a question mark hung over their dependability once memories of Carrhae were revived in a combat situation.

Pompey's newly created Gemina Legion had been put together using men from two legions stationed in Cilicia since being recruited in eastern Italy two springs before. Immediately after they'd arrived in Cilicia in 51 B.C. they had seen some action under their then governor Marcus Cicero, first skirmishing with the advance guard of a Parthian expeditionary force that had pushed up into Cilicia but then withdrew after its general died, and then successfully conducting an eight-week siege of a town held by "Free Cilician" rebels in the Amanus Mountains. But to veteran soldiers such as the men of the 6th Legion this was mere child's play and did nothing to equip the men of the Gemina for a set-piece battle against Caesar's best troops.

The men of the last of Pompey's twelve legions, three units hurriedly raised the previous spring in southern Italy, were as green as grass. Although they had been given experienced centurions, and several cohorts of discharged veterans recalled from retirement in Macedonia and on the island of Crete had been salted through their formations, their lack of battle experience could be expected to show when the signal for battle was given and they came up against Caesar's legions.

Six of Caesar's nine legions had seen extensive experience in his bloody conquest of Gaul, with the longest-serving of Caesar's legionaries having accumulated, like the men of the 4th and the 6th, seventeen years' combat experience. Pompey's new recruits would have boasted that their youth would give them the advantage against the "old-timers" in Caesar's ranks, but the men of the 6th were "old-timers," too, and they would have shaken their heads at the naïveté of the youngsters. "Deeds, not words," they would have mumbled disparagingly, repeating a proverb of the day and raising their eyes.

In fact, the tough veteran men of the 6th were, along with their comrades of the 4th, now by far Pompey's most experienced troops. Even the majority of the rank and file of the vaunted 1st had only joined Pompey's most elite legion at its latest reenlistment three years back and had no combat experience. But at least the proud senior centurions of the 1st had been enlisted by Pompey, many in his native region of Picenum in eastern Italy, and some had served him faithfully for thirty years or more. None would let the renowned legion's lofty reputation be forgotten by their troops, or by anyone else.

As for the "Allied" troops, auxiliary light infantry, archers, slingers, and cavalry supplied by kings and minor potentates from throughout the

East who owed their thrones to Pompey, only Pompey's cavalry, by its sheer size—seven thousand troopers in all—would have impressed Publius Sertorius and his comrades of the 6th. The eastern foot soldiers, the Greeks in particular, looked soft and easily spooked, but at least the cavalry, sixteen hundred of them Gauls who had previously ridden for Caesar, seemed formidable enough.

More than that, the legionaries of the 6th would have been impressed that Pompey's cavalry commander was General Titus Atius Labienus. For nine years Caesar's brave and brilliant deputy during his conquest of Gaul, Labienus, a republican at heart, had not believed in Caesar's self-serving cause and had changed sides to follow Pompey and the Senate at the outbreak of the civil war, bringing two-thirds of his cavalry with him.

Where and when Pompey would finally come to grips with Caesar had still been a mystery to the men of the 6th as they broke camp in the first week of January 48 B.C. and joined the line of march as Pompey's entire army of forty thousand men set off west along the paved Egnatian Way military highway, heading for the Adriatic port of Dyrrhachium. Located in Albania today and known as Durrës, this was Rome's principal port in the Epirus region, immediately opposite Brundisium, today's Brindisi. At Durrës, Pompey had stockpiled enough food to last him many months, and with rations fast running out he was taking the army to the supply dump to stock up for the spring—the time when he expected Caesar to cross to Greece from Italy to confront him.

On the march, word had reached Pompey that on the night of January 4–5 Caesar had made an amphibious landing on the Epirus coast some distance below Durrës with elements from seven legions. As the news rippled through Pompey's army, many an Allied infantryman had begun to look pale and fearful. Although stunned that Caesar had attempted a sea crossing in winter, when the Adriatic was storm-tossed, and pulled it off, Pompey reacted quickly. He set off at double time to reach Durrës, and his supplies, before Caesar did. Pompey had won the race, and then set up a camp on the coast south of the port to defend it. The town's senatorial garrison was commanded by famous senator, writer, and orator Marcus Cato—known to history as Cato the Younger. Formerly governor of Sicily, Cato had escaped to Greece when four Caesarian legions were about to land at Messina and take Sicily.

Once Caesar had landed in Greece, he had marched toward Durrës and, reinforced in February by Mark Antony and another ten thousand legionaries from Italy, had surrounded Pompey's camp with a fifteen-mile trench line dotted with twenty-four forts and had begun a siege. Caesar and his officers were confident of a swift victory. One of his young colonels, the twenty-one-year-old Publius Dolabella, who was related to Caesar, wrote a gloating letter to his father-in-law, Cicero, saying of Pompey's plight: "Driven out of Italy, Spain lost, his army of veterans taken prisoner, and to crown everything he is now blockaded in his camp, a humiliation that I believe has never before fallen a Roman general."

For all this, the expected swift victory had not come Caesar's way. For months there were skirmishes along the trench line south of Durrës, until, one night in June, with Caesar decoyed away to Durrës town in the belief that the locals were going to let him in behind Cato's back, Pompey had launched a carefully prepared assault, based on intelligence provided by defectors, against a fort in the encirclement held by Caesar's weakened 9th Legion. The defenders were overwhelmed and Pompey's breakout was successful. Although Caesar hastily returned and led a counterattack in daylight, his forces failed to seal the breach in the encirclement. Caesar suffered heavy casualties and was forced to withdraw from the untenable Durrës position.

In the wake of his first serious reverse of the civil war, Caesar had led his hungry troops east, toward the wheat-growing region of Thessaly in eastern Greece. The latest wheat crop would soon be ready to harvest, so when Caesar made camp on a wheat-covered plain at Farsala, his men looked forward to soon filling their grain sacks and their bellies. Pompey and his now confident army had shadowed them all the way to Thessaly, and set up camp on high ground several miles away from Caesar's position.

Pompey's officers had urged him to give battle, here on the plain of Farsala. The success at Durrës had convinced them that Caesar could be beaten. But Pompey had held back for weeks—like the men of the 6th, he had his doubts about the abilities of most of his infantry. Finally he relented, basing his battle plan on a decisive flanking maneuver by his cavalry, which outnumbered the men of Caesar's mounted force seven to one.

And now here the day was, August 9, 48 B.C. At dawn that morning, just as Caesar was breaking camp, planning to march away, Pompey had lined his army up on the plain in battle order. And the men of the 6th Legion would have contemplated a smashing victory over Julius Caesar's army, outnumbered as it was two to one. Once Caesar was dealt with, the men of the 6th could look forward to their discharge, now a year overdue, a victory bonus from the Senate, and a grant of farmland where they could at last settle down and raise a family.

The most honored place for a Roman legion in any battle line was the right wing. Only the best troops were placed on the right, because soldiers stationed there, carrying their shields on their left arms, were exposed on their right side. Many a battle was won and lost on an army's right wing. This day, the men of the 6th and the 4th Legions had been assigned Pompey's right wing. Their divisional commander, the general in charge of Pompey's right wing, mounted behind his frontline troops with his staff, was Lieutenant General Lucius Cornelius Lentulus. A consul the previous year, about forty-three years of age, Lentulus had no military reputation, but his rank as a recent consul and an intense personal dislike of Caesar had qualified him for this command.

Beside the seven cohorts from the two Spanish legions ran the Enipeus River. Filling the gap between the 4th and the 6th and the river, Pompey had stationed lightly armed Greek auxiliaries and six hundred slingers. Because the river's high banks prevented mounted troops from outflanking him on the right, Pompey hadn't given the 4th and the 6th any cavalry cover, instead massing all seven thousand of his mounted troops away on his left for his strike against Caesar's flank.

Pompey lined his foot soldiers up in three successive battle lines, the usual Roman military tactic. Each legion was spread between all three lines—full-strength legions had four cohorts in the front line and three in each of the second and third lines. The 4th and the 6th Legions, working together as a single legion, would have spread their cohorts three-two-two through the three lines.

The centuries within each cohort of each legion stood ten men deep, and, if a century was at full strength, eight men across. Their centurion stood at the left end of the front line, while their optio, or sergeant major, stood at the right end of the rear line, and their tesserarius, or sergeant, occupied the left rear position—the two NCOs being in the best places to prevent desertions. There was a gap of about three feet between each legionary and his immediate neighbor, room enough for him to launch his javelins. On the command "Close ranks," the legionary would step up to form a solid mass, shoulder to shoulder, with his comrades.

On that still, baking hot morning, looking across a field of ripening wheat to the troops immediately opposite them, and wiping sweat from their eyes as it rolled down from beneath their helmets, the men of the 6th would have recognized the bull emblems on the shields of the adjacent 7th, 8th, and 9th Legions, and realized that they would soon be coming to grips with fellow Spaniards, and killing them.

Not an ideal prospect, but better than facing their old marching companions of Caesar's 14th Legion, the unit the 6th had spent two years campaigning with in Gaul. The northern Italians of the 14th had never regained Caesar's favor because of their unit's bloody and disgraced past—any legion that lost its eagle standard carried the shame long after. Likewise, the 6th, because it was one of Pompey's units, had not been entrusted to major campaigns by Caesar. Their shared status as outcasts had brought the two legions together, like two gawky kids who become friends because they're never picked for schoolyard teams. True to form, Caesar had left the 14th in Spain after he'd accepted the final Pompeian surrender on the Iberian Peninsula; it had been the only one of Caesar's experienced "veteran" legions he'd left behind in Spain as he turned east to tackle Pompey himself in Greece.

Pompey's infantry had been carefully briefed on what they had to do here on the Farsala plain. Their commander in chief would launch a flanking attack with his cavalry, an attack designed to get behind the 10th Legion, Caesar's best, which occupied the extremity of his right wing, and, hopefully, wrap up the Caesarian line like a shovel driving snow. While the cavalry was doing its job, Pompey's legions were to stand their ground; they were not to charge. If, however, Caesar's infantry had the opportunity to launch a charge against Pompey's front line, Pompey's legionaries were under instructions to continue to stand where they were, immobile, instead of also charging. A countercharge was the usual response to a charge by the opposition, to meet the enemy on the run, but Pompey was hoping that Caesar's troops would be winded by the 450-yard dash from their position to his waiting front line, which was to act as a solid barrier from which Caesar's troops would rebound like surf from a seawall.

That, at least, had been the theory behind the tactic, a tactic that revealed Pompey's lack of confidence in his infantry's ability to match it in the open with Caesar's men. With luck, Pompey had hoped, it would never come to that—if General Labienus's cavalry did the task he had assigned to them, all his infantry would have to do was mop up after the cavalry charge. But it was a tactic that Caesar later roundly condemned as detrimental to both the morale and the attacking power of the troops involved. Certainly, the men of the 6th Legion wouldn't have been enamored of the idea of just standing there, waiting for their opponents to come charging into them, remembering the old Roman saying "He who does not advance goes backward."

Still, all had begun well enough for Pompey's side. In the middle of the morning General Labienus had set the battle in motion by leading his cavalry in a charge that killed two hundred of Caesar's troopers when they tried to stand in his way, and sent the remaining eight hundred Caesarian cavalry galloping from the field. Labienus had then led his excited horsemen into the side and rear of the 10th Legion. But Caesar had anticipated Pompey's maneuver and had stationed a reserve of heavy infantry as a fourth line—out of sight, on the ground—behind his standing third line. On Caesar's command, this reserve force had sprung up and charged into the tightly packed Pompeian cavalry, thrusting their javelins lancelike into their faces. Caesar's cavalry had returned, and between them, the 10th Legion and the reserve, they'd killed a thousand of Labienus's mounted men. The rest of the Pompeian cavalry had turned and fled, exposing Pompey's left wing.

When his reserve had spontaneously surged across the battlefield toward Pompey's 1st Legion, Caesar had ordered his entire first line to charge. His banner dropped, trumpets sounded "Charge," and with a roar the men of the first line had rushed forward. As ordered, the men of the 6th Legion and their comrades of the republican infantry had stood their ground. Halfway across the gap separating the two armies, Caesar's charging thousands had halted, regained their breath, then charged anew through the wheat stalks, launching their javelins as they came. They had crashed into the shield line of the republican army and come to a dead stop. Pompey's line held firm. There, toe to toe, shield to shield, the opposing front lines had fought it out.

Without cavalry covering their wing, the men of Pompey's elite 1st Legion had soon found themselves under sustained attack from front and flank. With Caesar's troops threatening to get behind it, the 1st closed up and began to slowly move back to cover its rear. It did so in tight, disciplined formation, fighting with each backward step, but this forced the 15th Legion beside it to also begin a slow fighting retreat. Seeing this withdrawal on their left, men in the less experienced legions in Pompey's center lost their nerve and their discipline. Many broke, pushing their way through the lines behind them to get to the rear, throwing away their equipment, and running for the hills. Men in the rear lines, experiencing wide-eyed deserters pushing back through their ranks from the battlefront, began to look uncertainly around them as their centurions called for them to hold their positions. Roman historian Tacitus was to write that the spread of fear and panic starts with the eyes. That infectious fear, transmitted from eye to eye, began to make the legs of men in the stationary rear lines at the republican center weak and wobbly.

At this point, Caesar ordered his second line to also charge into the fray. Once these troops came at the run and entered the battle, Pompey's center gave way completely, through all three lines, as whole units turned and ran. This allowed Caesar's men to advance through the center and split Pompey's army in two, then wrap around the still solid and defiant wings. Pompey had held back no reserves who might have bolstered his center. Seeing that the day was lost, and in a shocked daze, he left the battle and rode to his camp on the heights. On the Pompeian left, as the 1st backpedaled with determined discipline, the 15th disintegrated.

On the right, the 4th and the 6th stuck together like glue and stubbornly held their ground against the men of the 8th and the 9th Legions, fellow Spaniards, who were urged forward by their divisional commander, Mark Antony. But as the men of the 6th saw the Greek auxiliaries and the slingers to their right turn and flee blindly toward the rear, and saw the Gemina Legion to their immediate left quickly crumble and the well-led opposition Spaniards of their brother 7th Legion close in along their left flank and push toward their rear, threatening to swing behind them, they knew that, like the 1st, they must retreat. Behind them, General Lentulus, the 6th's divisional commander, had turned his horse around and, emulating Pompey, fled at a gallop to the camp on the hill. The men of the 6th were on their own.

With iron discipline, step by deliberate step, guided by the barked orders of their centurions, hounded all the way by their opponents, the 4th and the 6th began to pull back, with shields raised and locked, and with swords jabbing and flashing over the top. But unlike the 1st Legion over on the far left of the battlefield, their withdrawal was not speedy enough. Caesar's troops hurried down the left side of the Spanish formation and came around behind them. The two under-strength legions were compressed beside the tall bank of the Enipeus. With the 6th taking the pressure from their assailants, men of the 4th behind them began deliberately sliding down the steep riverbank. Soon all fifteen hundred men of the 4th had managed to cross the river and clamber up the far bank. Men of the 6th able to cast a quick glance over their shoulder would have seen Eagle-Bearer Marcus Caesius bearing away the silver eagle of the 4th and fleeing west across the plain with his comrades, toward the town of Farsala.

Half the men of the 6th were able to follow the troops of the 4th. But the last thousand men of the 6th Legion, acting as rear guard so their own eagle could also be carried safely from the field, weren't so lucky; they were completely surrounded by Mark Antony's troops. They could see Antony himself, on horseback, with his staff officers, directing operations quite close by. They would have recognized him, having seen him in Gaul during their two years' service there, when he was one of Caesar's generals—a tall, solidly built man of thirty-four with curly hair and a square jaw. They knew him by reputation as a man with a not entirely honorable past who liked wine, women, and song off the battlefield but who was a fiercely brave soldier on it, fighting like a demon, flinching at nothing.

These last defiant fighters of the 6th Legion prepared to die in the field of flattened wheat. Covered in perspiration under the hot August sun, bleeding from wounds, their muscles aching under the weight of the equipment that gave them the label of "heavy infantry," encircled and vastly outnumbered, they expected to be overwhelmed at any minute. But not one of them would ask for quarter; they would go down fighting, "claws and beak" as the Romans said. If they were to die here on Greek soil, across the world from their Spanish homeland, that would be all right. The legions had a saying, "Every soil is a brave man's country."

There was also a prayer prevalent among the rank and file of Rome's legions, and recorded on a roughly scrawled inscription: "Jupiter, Best and Greatest, protect this cohort, soldiers all." Many a soldier of the 6th would have uttered that prayer as the battle began that day, and many would have been saying it to themselves now with the fervor of men who could see death closing in around them and all possibility of escape apparently denied them.

But today was not to be the final day of life and breath of these men of the 6th. As Suetonius and Appian both record, at that moment mounted messengers were galloping urgently about the battlefield calling out an order from Caesar: "Spare your fellow Romans!"

Caesar only wanted troops from the Allied states killed, because they had actively sided with Pompey and the Senate. By his reckoning, Pompey's Roman legions were only following orders. Later in this protracted civil war Caesar would not be quite so magnanimous when it came to sparing his fellow countrymen, but right now he wanted to give legionaries, Roman citizens, the opportunity to surrender and be accorded all the rights of prisoners of war. He had written in a note to his staff officers Gaius Oppius and Lucius Balbus in March of the previous year: "Let this be the new style of conquest, to make mercy and generosity our shield."

Now Mark Antony himself was yelling to the men of the 6th that if they stood their ground and threw down their weapons they would not be harmed. Sympathetic fellow Spaniards in the ranks encircling them, men such as Marcus Aemilius and Lucius Mestrius of the 9th Legion and Gaius Canuleius of the 7th, began repeating the call, as their officers told them that they could each personally spare a fellow legionary from the other side.

The soldiers of the 6th looked at each other, with questions in their eyes. They had survived more than a decade and a half of battles, sieges, and skirmishes via a combination of fighting skill and good, old-fashioned luck. Was their luck holding, or was it about to run out? Could they trust the word of Julius Caesar and Mark Antony?

III

ACCORDING
TO BRUTUS

T o escape from the death and mayhem of the Battle of Pharsalus, Marcus Junius Brutus had waded through reed-filled swampland north of Mount Dogandzis that hid him from Caesar's foot soldiers and prevented cavalry from pursuing him, then walked all the way to the ancient citadel city of Larissa, today's Greek town of Larisa, on the plain near the eastern coast of Thessaly, traveling without stop through the night of August 9–10.

This was the Brutus who would be made famous by historians and playwright William Shakespeare as one of Caesar's chief assassins. The thirty-seven-year-old Brutus, whose family was descended from Junius Brutus, one of the revered founders of the Roman Republic, was a nephew of the famous philosopher Marcus Cato, the so-called Cato the Younger, one of the Senate's senior commanders in the civil war being waged against Caesar. Brutus's mother, Servilia, Cato's sister, was reputedly one of Rome's most beautiful women. His father—officially, at least—was Marcus Junius Brutus Sr., Servilia's husband at the time Marcus was born. But it was widely rumored that young Marcus's father was in fact Julius Caesar.

That Caesar and Servilia had a teenage affair was well known, but with Caesar aged fifteen at the time of the younger Marcus's birth, later historians would say that he was much too young to be the father. Yet, Romans began their sex lives young—while Servilia had been just thirteen when she gave birth to Marcus, under Roman law women could become engaged at ten and could marry at twelve, and Roman men officially came of age at fifteen. And Caesar was notoriously virile. He was to have three wives; the first died young; the next, Caesar divorced. His last marriage was, by 48 B.C., more than a decade old. And through all his marriages he'd had numerous amorous affairs, including, reputedly, an incautious fling with Mucia, a wife of his then friend and now opponent Pompey the Great.

While Caesar's paternity of Brutus was never officially acknowledged, Caesar treated Brutus like a son, and it had been assumed at the outbreak of the civil war that Brutus would side with Caesar, especially as Pompey had some years before executed Marcus Junius Brutus Sr., the man who raised Brutus as his son. But the younger Brutus was a passionate believer in the Roman Republic. So, rather than support the rebel autocrat Caesar, Brutus had thrown his loyalty behind Pompey and the Senate—in the words of Plutarch, "judging Pompey's to be the better cause."

In 49 B.C., while the civil war was spinning out its early, murderous months in Italy, then in Spain and the south of France, Brutus had accepted a posting from the Senate to join the staff of Major General Publius Sestius, governor of the province of Cilicia—Anatolia in modern-day Turkey. By the end of 49 B.C. Brutus had quit his job in Cilicia and brought himself to Macedonia to join Pompey's army.

Though Pompey greeted Marcus warmly—the highly intelligent and famously ethical Brutus was a popular and respected figure, and his involvement with the cause was good for the army's morale—the Senate's commander had no post for Marcus. There were upward of four hundred senators and hundreds more knights in Pompey's camp, all offering Pompey advice and clamoring for military appointments, and Brutus had no military experience to speak of.

So, unemployed, he'd spent the days leading up to the Pharsalus battle keeping out of the way, reading and studying in the vast senatorial camp on the hillside overlooking the plain and Caesar's distant camp. On August 8 Brutus had remained in his tent all day, writing a condensed Latin version of a work by Greek writer Polybius, keeping to himself as the army readied for combat the next day after the Senate's war council had decided to bring Caesar to battle.

As Pompey's army had marched down the slope from their camp on the morning of August 9 and lined up in battle order on the plain, like Pompey's eldest son, Gnaeus, Brutus had remained in camp on the hill, along with a camp guard of seven cohorts of legionaries and Greek auxiliaries under General Lucius Afranius, the 6th Legion's former commander in chief in Spain. Unbeknownst to Brutus, as Caesar gave orders for the disposition of his troops for battle that morning, he had also ordered that should his soldiers come across Brutus on the battlefield, they must allow him to surrender and then bring him to Caesar. But if Brutus refused to surrender, said Caesar, his troops were to allow the young man to escape, unharmed.

Brutus had watched the events of August 9 unfold from the ramparts of the senatorial camp's earthen walls, while thousands of servants laid out tables in the massive, almost deserted encampment and set up decorations—for the victory feast that was expected to soon follow.

When the battle turned against the republicans and General Afranius had hustled Pompey's heir Gnaeus Pompey from the camp, heading west, Brutus also had escaped, in his case heading north. He had seen enough at Pharsalus, in the senatorial camp with its bickering knights and senators, and then on the battlefield, to know that the republican cause was doomed. Despite his exhaustion, as soon as he arrived at Larisa he wrote a letter to Julius Caesar, then sent a mounted messenger to find Caesar and deliver the letter.

Pompey had escaped, too. Dragged in a daze from the camp by a loyal subordinate as Caesar's troops were breaking in, he had ridden north, also heading for Larisa, accompanied by just his secretary and three generals, including the 6th Legion's divisional commander, General Lentulus. Picking up an escort of a fleeing thirty-man republican cavalry troop along the way, Pompey had reached Larisa well before Brutus arrived.

By the morning of August 9, Caesar also was heading for Larisa, chief city of Thessaly, determined to track down Pompey and eliminate him from the picture—either through his capitulation or his death. At dawn, Caesar had accepted the surrender of many thousands of Pompeian troops sheltering on a hillside to the north of the Pharsalus battlefield, having surrounded the hill with his four Spanish legions, the 7th, 8th, 9th, and 10th, the previous evening. Learning from prisoners that Pompey had headed north, he then prepared to march his troops on his opponent's trail. But at that point, Caesar's Spanish legions refused to take another step for him.

This action began, most likely, with the 9th Legion, which had mutinied against Caesar once before in this civil war and suffered the punishment of decimation as a result. But the strike soon spread to the three other units. The 9th, 8th, and 7th were all now eighteen months past their due discharge date. They'd beaten Pompey, as Caesar had asked them to do, and now they wanted the financial rewards that Caesar had promised them, and their discharges, so they could finally hang up their swords.

Furious with his mutinous legions, Caesar had ordered them to escort the republican prisoners back to their camp six miles away on the Farsala plain, telling them he would address their grievances once he returned. At the same time he sent orders for another four legions at the camp to join him, with his now reassembled cavalry. The four replacement legions and cavalry had arrived in the middle of the morning. By that time Brutus's letter had reached Caesar, who was overjoyed to hear that Brutus was alive and well. Taking the cavalry with him, Caesar set off at a gallop for Larisa, for Brutus's letter also had told him that Pompey had come through the city.

In fact, Pompey had spent only a few hours in Larisa before continuing his flight. Commandeering an empty grain ship he found anchored off the town of Paralia, Pompey had sailed for the island of Lesbos, where his wife, Cornelia, and youngest son, Sextus, were waiting.

When Caesar reached Larisa, a community that had enthusiastically supported Pompey, he found that the city fathers had decided that resistance was futile and, probably at the instigation of Brutus, they opened the city gates as Caesar approached and sought his pardon. Caesar wasn't so much interested in the surrender of Larisa as in finding Brutus. Caesar and Brutus soon reunited, apparently there at the city gates, and Caesar embraced Brutus. Caesar immediately forgave him for siding with his enemies, and welcomed him into his fold. Together the pair then rode a short distance from Caesar's staff and bodyguards. Dismounting, they then walked through the countryside, deep in conversation.

The fifty-two-year-old Caesar, short, slight, long-faced, with his hair combed forward to hide his increasing baldness, listened as Brutus, an earnest man with handsome features, a small chin, and his thick, straight hair cut in a severe fringe across his forehead, pleaded for a pardon for his brother-in-law, Gaius Cassius Longinus, who was married to Brutus's half sister Junia. Cassius had been chief of staff in Marcus Crassus's doomed army at Carrhae in 53 B.C., and through his tough determination and calm leadership had been responsible for saving the two legions that ultimately had joined Pompey's army at the Battle of Pharsalus from Syria. Siding with the Senate in the civil war, Cassius was at this time commanding a powerful senatorial fleet somewhere in the Aegean Sea.

Agreeing to pardon Cassius, Caesar then plied Brutus with questions about Pompey's likely future course. What had Pompey said to Brutus? Where would Pompey go from Thessaly? To Asia? Or farther afield, to Syria? Would he perhaps try to win the support of the Parthians? As members of Pompey's party later revealed, the Parthian option actually did occur to Pompey as he fled Greece, until his companions talked him out of involving Rome's old enemy in her internal affairs.

No, said Brutus, in his estimation Pompey would head for Egypt. Pompey had strong connections with Egypt. He had been responsible for cementing King Ptolemy XII, father of the current rulers of Egypt, on his throne, and could rightfully expect those current corulers—a teenaged King Ptolemy XIII and his sister Cleopatra VII—to repay him with military and financial support as he set about building a new army for a second tilt at Caesar. After all, the Egyptian royal house was fabulously wealthy, and they had a well-equipped and well-trained army, which included Roman troops stationed in Egypt some years back by Pompey— Pompey's son Gnaeus had brought five hundred Roman cavalry from Alexandria, where he had been stationed with the Roman forces assigned to Egypt, to join his father's army at Pharsalus.

Caesar agreed that it would make sense for Pompey to head south for Egypt, although he could not afford to discount the possibility that he was making for the East, where many local potentates also owed him favors and had money and troops—both of which Pompey was in dire need of. Thanking Brutus, Caesar mounted and headed back to the Pharsalus battlefield with his large cavalry escort. Pharsalus beckoned because before he could set off in pursuit of Pompey, Caesar had to resolve the mutiny of his four best legions.

IV

THE DEAL

On the Pharsalus battlefield, the men of the 6th had agreed to surrender on August 9, and true to the word of Caesar and Mark Antony they had not been harmed once they threw down their weapons. Meanwhile, all around them, Allied troops and noncombatants had been slaughtered. Appian records the surrendered legionaries standing stock still while Caesar's troops had run by them and even through their ranks to attack the fleeing Allies.

Caesar, in his "commentaries," his memoirs, would give an inflated casualty list for Pompey's army at the Battle of Pharsalus. His staff officer Colonel Gaius Asinius Pollio, who was at Caesar's side throughout the battle and also later as the bodies were counted, and who was considered a particularly reliable witness by Roman authors, later wrote an account of the civil war in which he put Pompey's Pharsalus losses at 6,000. At most, Caesar had lost 1,200 men, 200 of these cavalry. A total of 24,000 Pompeian soldiers had surrendered and been made prisoners of war. Another 18,000, including survivors from the 4th and 6th Legions and the almost intact 1st Legion, had escaped west.

Because Caesar's legions did not pursue them, over the coming weeks these 18,000 escapees would be loaded aboard the ships of the senatorial fleets based on Greece's western coast. It was an efficient evacuation organized by Marcus Brutus's uncle Cato the Younger, who came down from Durrës to Buthrotum, today's Buthroton, and the waters around Corfu, where the bulk of the senatorial ships were based, and calmly took charge.

When Cato was joined by Pompey's leading generals after they'd escaped from the debacle of Pharsalus—Labienus, Afranius, Petreius, and Pompey's father-in-law, Scipio—they agreed that they would transfer the surviving troops to the province of Africa, modern Tunisia, still firmly in senatorial hands and which held a large number of friendly forces, there to regroup before going against Caesar again.

When Caesar returned to his camp on the Farsala plain on August 11, it was to find that not only were the 7th, 8th, 9th, and 10th Legions in revolt in their commander in chief's absence, but they had also infected all his other legions with the same mutinous spirit. Now all nine of his legions were on strike, demanding discharge for the legions who were entitled to it, and payment to every single surviving legionary of the bonus that Caesar had promised at an assembly of his army at Brindisi in December prior to their embarkation for Greece: 20,000 sesterces per man.

Caesar didn't have anywhere near the sort of money the legions were demanding. The costs of the civil war to date had left his purse bare. Besides, he was determined not to give in to blackmail. So on August 11, while his eight hundred loyal cavalrymen—three hundred Germans and five hundred Gauls who possessed neither Roman citizenship nor a grievance against their general—stood guard duty at his Farsala camp and watched over the Pompeian prisoners encamped with Caesar's legions, he sent his most trusted officers ranging through the POW camp. He had briefed them to talk to the prisoners and determine who among them would be prepared to march for him in several new Caesarian legions that would be formed entirely from POWs. Just as he had promised his own men big rewards at the outset of his invasion of Greece, Caesar now promised the POWs the same rewards—to be paid once this civil war was concluded.

Throughout his career, Caesar considered his Spanish legions by far his best and used them at the forefront of his operations. When he'd served as governor of Baetica, or Farther Spain, for a year in 61 B.C., he had inherited a garrison made up of two legions, the 8th and the 9th, both of which had been raised locally by Pompey four years earlier. Caesar had immediately raised a new legion, the 10th, in his province. He'd then led his three legions on a rampaging and profitable campaign against the towns and villages of the unconquered tribes of Lusitania, to the north of his provincial capital, Corduba, today's city of Córdoba.

Later, when he took up his commands in Gaul in 58 B.C., Caesar had received Senate approval to summon the 8th, 9th, and 10th, and their brother legion the 7th, then stationed in eastern Spain, for his advance north into what today is France and Belgium. These four Spanish legions had been at the forefront of his conquests ever since. Tough, determined, courageous, slow to panic, and quick to respond to orders, Caesar's Spaniards had never let him down in battle.

And it so happened that among the tens of thousands of Pompeian prisoners on the Farsala plain were the men of the 6th Legion—less than a thousand of them, but veteran Spanish legionaries just the same. What was more, Caesar well remembered that these men had marched for him in Gaul for two years, so he directed his officers to initially concentrate on the legionaries of the 6th. Not only were these men of the 6th Legion the best soldiers among all the surrendered Pompeians, but also if they signed up for Caesar they were so well respected by the other prisoners that many others could be expected to follow their lead.

It didn't trouble Caesar that these men of the 6th had previously made a moral choice against him and for Pompey and the republic, and had ignored the bounty he'd given them two years before when they were led back to Spain. Suetonius said of him, "He judged his men by their fighting record, not by their morals."

The precise details of the deal the soldiers of the 6th made that day with Caesar are unknown. To win them over, Caesar would no doubt have offered them considerably more than he had been prepared to pay his own men. They would have known that at Brindisi the previous fall he had promised his legions 20,000 sesterces per man to defeat Pompey. Later he would up this to 24,000 sesterces to convince reluctant legionaries to fight one more campaign for him. The men of the 6th, being hard-dealing Spaniards, would have hung out for even more, knowing how important their defection was to Caesar's fortunes.

There was another factor to be considered. When the men of the 6th had marched down the slope to the Farsala plain on the morning of August 9, they had left their personal possessions behind at the sprawling republican camp on the hill. Those personal possessions had included all their noncombat equipment, spare clothing, their utensils, as well as the souvenirs of the many victories they had won over the years while marching for Pompey the Great and also, briefly, for Caesar. Most important of all was the money they had left at the camp, their savings from seventeen years' military service, their horde of gold accumulated from their annual salary payments, bonuses, and the proceeds of the sale of booty.

There is no record of the amounts involved, but within twenty years or so Rome's legions would have banks, administered by the standard-bearer of each cohort, in which the savings of every man were preserved. Following a rebellion on the Rhine in A.D. 89, which was financed by their general robbing the troops' savings then in the banks of two legions, the emperor Domitian would limit the amount that a soldier could save in these banks thereafter to just 1,000 sesterces a man. Such savings would amount to tens of thousands of sesterces per man as they neared the end of their enlistment. And on August 9, 48 B.C., the men of the 6th Legion had lost every penny they had put away over almost two decades, as Caesar's troops fought their way into Pompey's camp, then progressively looted it of everything that was valuable and killing every noncombatant who stood in their way or tried to save packmules or their master's silver plate.

No one could deny that the men of the 6th Legion had lost everything they possessed other than what they had on them when their camp fell to the other side. But they had no way of proving any claims of losses they might have made, or of reclaiming those losses from Caesar's men. It was a classical case of finders keepers. No general in his right mind would ask his troops to hand back their loot, certainly not Caesar, faced now as he was with his legions on strike as they demanded even more. So not only would the men of the 6th now have demanded at least the same victory bonuses that Caesar's troops were being promised by their commander, they also would have wanted restitution for what they had lost at Pompey's camp. And realizing how badly Caesar needed them, they would have exaggerated their losses and pitched their demands high when Caesar's recruiting officers came to them in the POW camp.

Even if Caesar had to pay these men double what he had previously offered his own men, it would have been worth the cost to attract what he considered the best soldiers from among the prisoners to march for him. Whatever Caesar ultimately offered the men of the 6th, it was enough to convince the Spaniards to change sides. As the Spanish say, there is no lock that a golden key will not open, and there in the POW camp the men of the 6th were tempted by the promise of sufficient gold coin to enter into a contract with Caesar's officers and change sides and loyalties, at least until the civil war was settled.

But there was more to the deal than money. In addition to the promise of a considerable financial reward for each man who survived this next episode in their military careers, Caesar also agreed to give the men of the 6th their now well overdue discharge from military service once the contract expired, plus grants of farmland; retiring veterans during this period received around fifty acres each.

In agreeing to the deal, the men of the 6th stipulated that the land involved in this instance was not to be confiscated from other owners, who might later challenge the legality of their tenure. There had been examples of this in the recent past, and the troops didn't want their land grants to be contested later. The land they were given had to be state-owned land, with no strings attached.

The full package was to be delivered by Caesar once his troops had won this conflict for him. No money changed hands up front. The men of the 6th would rely on Caesar to keep his word, confident that they had the backup of the contracts they now put their names to, and their swords.

It is apparent that in addition to their agreed rewards, Publius Sertorius and his comrades of the 6th set down two key final conditions before
they would march for Caesar. First, they would not join a new unit containing other POWs. If Caesar wanted them on his side, they would not
be assimilated into other units—he had to take them as the 6th Legion,
marching behind their own eagle, even if their unit was well below
strength; nor would they permit their numbers to be bolstered by the addition of men from other units. And, most importantly, they would not
under any circumstances fight their comrades of the 6th who had escaped
from Greece to Africa after the Battle of Pharsalus.

Caesar quickly acceded to these requirements; the 6th Legion was
reinstated, and its men included on the pay lists of his army. He ordered
his quartermaster, General Quintus Cornificius, to rearm the men of the
6th and to provide them with the best equipment available. The 6th was
to be ready to march as soon as possible.

There was also the matter of the 6th's eagle standard. Nine silver eagles
and many more cohort standards had been captured from Pompey's twelve
legions during and after the Battle of Pharsalus. As with the eagles of the
1st and 4th Legions, the eagle of the 6th had been preserved and carried
away by the men of the legion who had escaped from Farsala. It seems
that the men of the 6th who would now march for Caesar were provided
with one of the captured eagle standards, which Roman priests would
have blessed in a hurried performance of the *lustratio exercitio,* or Lustration Exercise, the traditional religious ceremony in which a legion's standards were dressed with garlands and perfume in the spring, prior to each
campaigning season, before Caesar formally presented it to the 6th Legion.

In later centuries some confusion would arise about the 6th and its
role in Caesar's army at this time, prompted in part by the Roman writer
Suetonius, who, in his book *Lives of the Caesars,* written 150 years after
the event, would put the 6th Legion on Caesar's side in an engagement
against Pompey's army during the Battle of Dyrrhachium. Suetonius confused the 6th Legion with the 9th Legion in that engagement, as we know
from Caesar's own memoirs. The 6th was always in Pompey's army until
this deal following the Battle of Pharsalus.

On the morning of August 12, Caesar would have called an assembly
of his legions and informed them that he was continuing this war without
them, and with the help of Pompey's surrendered troops. His own legions
would be taken back to Italy by Mark Antony, he said, where they were to
await his pleasure. He then departed Farsala, accompanied by a small staff
and his cavalry, heading for Macedonia, with the intent of crossing the

Dardanelles into the province of Asia and then marching overland down to Syria as he attempted to track down Pompey. If necessary, he was prepared to march all the way to Egypt to find him.

As Caesar galloped away to the north with his eight hundred horsemen, the camp he left behind was full of activity. The men of the 6th Legion were hastily preparing to also march. Antony would lead the striking legions to Durrës, where they would obtain shipping for a return to Italy. With them would go those POWs who chose not to march for Caesar, about thirteen thousand of them.

In the end, another ten thousand agreed to change sides, and these ex-Pompeians were formed into two new Caesarian legions. Over the past sixteen months, Caesar had conscripted twenty-one new legions in Italy and Cisalpine Gaul, some of them from republican troops who had surrendered to him during his advance into Italy after crossing the Rubicon. Those legions had been numbered 17 to 35, so that the two new legions formed from POWs at Farsala were assigned the numbers 36 and 37.

Caesar had left orders for Lieutenant General Gnaeus Domitius Calvinus, who had commanded his center at the Battle of Pharsalus, to lead on his heels those men other than the legionaries of the 6th who changed sides, as soon as they were ready to march. On Caesar's instructions, General Domitius was to take charge of the province of Asia, and it was there that Caesar wanted Pompey's former troops to link up with him and the 6th Legion.

At the same time that Caesar and his cavalry rode north, messengers galloped south from Farsala, to the region of Achaea, south of Athens. Since his invasion of Greece, Achaea had been occupied for Caesar by General Quintus Fufius Calenus with the 27th Legion and the five cohorts of the 28th Legion that had not been involved in the aborted invasion of Illyricum by Gaius Antony. Caesar's messengers carried orders for General Fufius to immediately send the five cohorts of the 28th—containing a little over twenty-two hundred men, according to Caesar himself—marching to join him, the 6th, and the former republican troops in Asia, at once. As for the 27th Legion, Fufius was to send it to join General Domitius and the men who would make up the 36th and 37th Legions, as soon as practicable.

On the same day when Caesar set off, the 6th Legion departed the plain at Farsala at forced march pace, leaving behind Caesarian mutineers and Pompeian POWs. The 6th's orders were to follow Caesar with all speed, bringing a baggage train of war supplies with them. It must have been with mixed thoughts that the men of the 6th marched rapidly up the road toward Macedonia. Only days before, they had been preparing to die. Now, not only were they very much alive, they had been welcomed into Caesar's army, they had been provided with the best equipment, and they had been given the role of Caesar's most elite foot soldiers.

Their change in fortune came at the price of a change in allegiances, and with the knowledge that Caesar wanted them to link up with him in Asia and help him track down their former commander, Pompey. This may have bothered some of them. As later events were to show, Spaniards held Pompey and his family in high regard. But it didn't bother the men of the 6th enough to cause them to have second thoughts.

With luck, many of the legionaries of the 6th would have hoped, Pompey may well come to terms with Caesar before any more blood had to be shed. And then, with peace, they could start new lives, enriched by Caesar, before they had to kill anyone.

V

CLEOPATRA'S WAR

I n late August 48 B.C., in southern Palestine, messengers reached the encampment of a twenty-one-year-old Egyptian woman to say that Pompey the Great had been defeated in battle by Julius Caesar in Thessaly. Pompey was fleeing east, said the messenger, and Caesar was giving chase. This information would have greatly troubled the recipient of that message. Her name was Cleopatra.

By the time that the Battle of Pharsalus was decided in Greece, Cleopatra VII, Queen of Egypt, was a young woman on the run and in fear for her life. The daughter of King Ptolemy XII of Egypt—known as Ptolemy the flute player—Cleopatra had come to the throne of Egypt three years before jointly with her now fifteen-year-old brother Ptolemy XIII, on the death of their father, who had owed his throne to Rome—or more specifically to Pompey the Great.

The Ptolemaic dynasty had been founded in Egypt in 323 B.C. by Ptolemy I, senior Macedonian general of Alexander the Great, conqueror of much of the known world. Descendants of General Ptolemy had ruled Egypt ever since. Ptolemy XII was the illegitimate son of Ptolemy IX, and while he had been invited by the people of Alexandria to take the Egyptian throne on the death of his uncle Ptolemy XI, doubts were raised in the Roman Senate about his right to the throne—by senators with avaricious eyes on Egypt. Plutarch quotes Cato the Younger remarking to Ptolemy XII that some greedy Roman senators would not be satisfied even if all of Egypt were turned to silver.

In 59 B.C., Ptolemy had paid Julius Caesar, then a consul of Rome, a huge bribe to pass a law at Rome acknowledging his right to rule. According to Suetonius, this bribe was shared by both Caesar and Pompey and totaled 15 million sesterces. While this legislation was duly passed it didn't prevent Rome from the following year annexing the island of Cyprus, until then an Egyptian possession. After grassroots Egyptian dissent over this loss of Cyprus grew and spread to the Egyptian army, in 58 B.C. Ptolemy hurried to Rome seeking military support for his continued rule. In Ptolemy's absence the Alexandrians installed Ptolemy's eldest daughter, Berenice, on the throne as a puppet ruler.

For many months Ptolemy had stayed at Rome, as a guest of Pompey the Great in one of Pompey's mansions. All the while he was there, Ptolemy paid millions of sesterces in bribes to leading Roman senators to win their support, and employed assassins who killed the members of Egyptian delegations sent by the Alexandrians to Italy before they could testify against him to the Senate. Eventually he ran out of money, and was forced to borrow millions of sesterces from Caesar, who had unsuccessfully applied to the Senate for approval to personally oversee a settlement in Egypt.

In late 57 B.C. Pompey succeeded in pushing a vote through the Senate approving the restoration of Ptolemy to his throne with Roman military help. But opponents were soon able to unearth an influential ancient prophesy that forbade active aid to the king of Egypt, and Ptolemy was forced to leave Rome empty-handed, going into exile at Ephesus in the Roman province of Asia in present-day eastern Turkey. But Pompey had given his word to Ptolemy that he would be reinstated on his throne, and as one of Rome's most powerful men, if not the most powerful, he was never one to be thwarted for long.

In 55 B.C., on orders from Rome drafted by Pompey, Lieutenant General Aulus Gabinius, governor of Syria, who had recently put down a Jewish insurrection in Judea, accepted a bribe of 24 million sesterces from Ptolemy—to be paid from the rich Egyptian treasury once the mission was completed—and invaded Egypt with several legions from the Syria station. The Egyptian army did not resist, and Gabinius was able to swiftly reinstall Ptolemy as king of Egypt. Ptolemy's first act had been to execute his daughter Berenice for reigning in his stead. This made the then fourteen-year-old Cleopatra his eldest surviving daughter.

Among Gabinius's officers during this 55 B.C. invasion of Egypt had been a dashing cavalry colonel with a growing reputation for bravery—Marcus Antonius, or as we know him, Mark Antony. To maintain Ptolemy in power and prevent any further Egyptian insurrections, when General Gabinius returned to Syria he left a number of Roman officers, foot soldiers, and cavalry in Egypt with orders to equip, train, and then lead an Egyptian army in the Roman style. This continued Roman military presence was also designed by Pompey the Great to ensure future Roman control over Egypt.

That control was strengthened by a treaty of friendship and alliance between Rome and Egypt drafted by Pompey and signed by Ptolemy. In addition to guaranteeing Roman military aid for Egypt against outside aggressors, and in return Egyptian contributions to Roman military campaigns in the East, the treaty also gave the consuls of Rome power to arbitrate in any subsequent dispute over who would take the throne of Egypt following Ptolemy's death.

With Ptolemy XII's will stipulating that his eldest son and eldest daughter should jointly take his throne on his demise, when in 51 B.C. he died of natural causes Cleopatra became ruler of Egypt in partnership with her brother Ptolemy XIII. This arrangement emulated the old Ptolemaic custom where brother and sister ruled as husband and wife—although there is no evidence that Cleopatra and young Ptolemy actually had sexual relations.

Cleopatra's brother and fellow sovereign, only twelve when he took the throne, was surrounded and manipulated by advisers whom Cleopatra neither liked nor trusted. And the feeling was mutual. Convinced that these advisers wanted her out of the way so they could rule without restraint, Cleopatra was able to maintain her position and her power by fostering a close relationship with the most senior Roman officer then stationed in Egypt—Colonel Gnaeus Pompey, eldest son of Pompey the Great. Gnaeus, only a year or two older than Cleopatra, was married—to the daughter of the General Appius mentioned earlier. But this didn't stop strong rumors emerging that Gnaeus and Cleopatra were lovers while he was in Egypt—his wife being back at Rome throughout his eastern posting.

If Cleopatra's subsequent relationships with leading Romans is any guide, it is more than likely that she shared arrogant young Gnaeus's bed. And in return he acted as her champion and protector to counter the political maneuvering of the members of her brother's scheming circle. As Pompey's son, and in effect Roman royalty, Gnaeus was not a man the Egyptians dared antagonize. So while Cleopatra had the support of the powerful young Roman, her position was secure.

But all things change sooner or later. And change they did for Cleopatra once Gnaeus Pompey heeded his father's summons in the spring of 48 B.C. and sailed to join him and the senatorial forces in Greece for the war against Caesar, taking with him from Alexandria the Egyptian battle fleet and five hundred Roman cavalry who had been based in Egypt. Without her influential Roman lover to watch out for her and keep her safe, Cleopatra's position had become more and more precarious, with her brother increasingly determined to remove her.

In late July or early August of that year, in Julius Caesar's own words, "by means of his intimates and his favorites," Ptolemy had Cleopatra expelled from Alexandria. With a small band of staff and supporters she had fled east across the Nile Delta, setting up a camp in southern Palestine. From here the exiled Cleopatra had sent out messages seeking money and supporters from throughout the Middle East for a war against her brother. And there she waited for news of the outcome of the conflict between Pompey and Caesar in Greece, confident that Pompey would prevail and she would soon have Roman help to regain her Egyptian throne.

The news that Pompey had been defeated and was on the run would have been devastating for Cleopatra. She would have been counting on Pompey winning, counting on his son Gnaeus returning to resume his posting in Alexandria and coming back to her, counting on regaining her position in Egypt with his help. Gnaeus would not return—he was fleeing to Africa with the remainder of the surviving republican leaders. At the same time, the news of Pompey's defeat and flight had a galvanizing affect on her brother's entourage at Alexandria. They knew that Cleopatra would have been banking on the Pompey family for aid, and now that aid was unlikely they mobilized the Egyptian army to deal with the young queen and the ragtag band of refugees, mercenaries, and runaway slaves she had gathered around her.

The Egyptian army that had been created on Pompey's orders less than a decade earlier contained twenty thousand foot soldiers and two thousand cavalry. These troops had been organized in Roman military fashion and trained in Roman military tactics. Some of them—the middle-ranking officers—were themselves Romans, but the vast majority were Easterners. Their unit standards, uniforms, and equipment were similar to those of the Roman legions, with some units carrying the curved, rectangular Roman shield, the *scutum,* and others equipped with round shields. Frescoes in Italy dating from this period depict Egyptian military officers in bronze armor, wearing Roman-style cloaks and tunics, some white, others brown, others again orange, and wearing Roman-style helmets with long plumes like horses' tails.

By the last week of September, the majority of the men of that Egyptian army had departed from Alexandria with young King Ptolemy XII and his advisers, and marched up the coast to Pelusium, a town at the mouth of the easternmost branch of the Nile. A long-established Egyptian fort at Pelusium commanded the narrow strip of land between the Mediterranean and the Gulf of Suez, a strip that acted as a gateway to Egypt and that any army coming from the north must use. Here the Egyptian army camped while the king took up residence on Mount Casius, overlooking Pelusium.

On September 28, a small Roman fleet of four cruisers and a dozen frigates dropped anchor in Pelusium Bay alongside a much larger Egyptian fleet of fifty battleships and cruisers sitting at the anchorage. A ship's boat soon ground into the sand, bringing several senior Roman officers ashore with a message for the Egyptian authorities. Pompey the Great was aboard the flagship of their fleet and needed King Ptolemy's help, they said. Pompey respectfully requested an interview with the king in Alexandria.

Pompey's flight from Thessaly in a commandeered grain ship had taken him to the island of Lesbos, where, at the capital, Mytilene, modern Mitilini, he had collected his young wife, Cornelia. A beauty by all accounts, Cornelia was his fifth wife, having been made a widow when her previous husband, Publius Crassus, son of the triumvir Crassus, was killed by the Parthians along with his father at the Battle of Carrhae in 53 B.C. With Cornelia were Sextus, Pompey's teenage youngest son from an earlier marriage, and a number of servants and supporters. Pompey crammed the entire party aboard four cruisers he found at Mitilini; then, sending Generals Lentulus and Spinther in other vessels to attempt to wring support from cities and potentates of the East, Pompey himself had set off south. At Attalia in Pamphylia, on the southern coast of present-day Turkey, he had taken on board a contingent from the republican legion based in Cilicia, making the two most senior centurions his personal bodyguards.

When Pompey reached the island of Cyprus he had learned that Antioch, capital of Syria, had closed its gates to him and that he would be unwelcome if not unsafe in the rest of Syria, which no longer had a Roman garrison since its governor, Pompey's father-in-law, Scipio, had led the two legions stationed there to their doom at the Battle of Pharsalus. So Pompey raised money from the Cypriots, commandeered a dozen frigates, and armed two thousand slaves and put them aboard his little fleet. As Brutus had guessed, Pompey then decided to make for Egypt and call in the favor he considered he was owed for putting Ptolemy XII back on his throne and for maintaining Ptolemy's heirs on theirs.

Once they had delivered their message to the Egyptians, Pompey's officers began to talk freely with Romans in the Egyptian army, and they urged the "Gabinians," as these former soldiers of General Aulus Gabinius were known, to give Pompey their services and ignore his recent bad luck. All this information was relayed to the king on Mount Casius.

The Egyptians did not respond at once. They kept Pompey waiting many hours for a reply while they held a meeting of their royal council convened by Ptolemy's tutor and chief secretary, Pothinus, a eunuch who had been castrated as a boy. With young Ptolemy sitting at the head of this council, all its members were invited by Pothinus to express their views on what should be done about Pompey.

Plutarch says that the council members were primarily chamberlains and royal servants. Among them was the commander of the Egyptian army, the locally born Greek general Achillas. The general said little at this point, as his fellow council members fell into two camps. One group was for sending Pompey away, while the other favored inviting him ashore and receiving him.

Ptolemy's rhetoric master, Theodotus, originally from the Greek island of Chios, then spoke at length, suggesting that neither option was safe. If the Egyptians entertained Pompey, he argued, they would make Caesar their enemy and Pompey their master. But if they dismissed Pompey, they would offend him and engender Caesar's wrath for letting Pompey get away. The only course that Theodotus could see was to invite Pompey ashore here at Pelusium and then kill him. In that way they would ingratiate themselves with one Roman leader and have nothing to fear from the other. Plutarch says that Theodotus added, with a smile, "Dead men don't bite."

There was also the likelihood that if Pompey were to rebuild his power he would bow to the wishes of his son Gnaeus and restore Cleopatra to her place on the throne beside her brother. It was even possible that, angry at Ptolemy for chasing out his sister, once Pompey again had a large army behind him he might decide to punish Ptolemy, or remove him permanently. Now, defeated and for the moment next to powerless, accompanied by just a hundred or so legionaries and some armed slaves—as the Egyptians knew from Pompey's loose-lipped envoys—he was as vulnerable as he would ever be. So a fateful decision was made by the Egyptians.

General Achillas then called in the most senior Roman officer attached to the Egyptian army, a colonel, the tribune Lucius Septimius. Nineteen years before, Colonel Septimius had served under Pompey as a young centurion commanding a century in the Roman army that Pompey had used to eliminate powerful fleets of Cilician pirates then ranging the Mediterranean. Normally a centurion could not be promoted to tribune, a rank reserved for the knights of the Equestrian Order. Septimius would have been one of the small number of knights who, in these late days of the republic, was forced by dire financial circumstances to join in the army as an enlisted man, and had been promoted to centurion.

This anomaly involving Equestrian Order centurions would continue for another fifty years or so until, during the reign of the first Roman emperor, Augustus, the practice was phased out and Equestrians were not permitted to literally lower themselves to the ranks. By way of compensation, Augustus was to decree that Equestrians who had served as centurions were eligible for seats in the Senate despite their military service among the enlisted men.

Now, after several years based in Egypt, the middle-aged Colonel Septimius and his men had grown accustomed to royal privileges and the Egyptian way of life. Ignoring Roman military regulations that prevented Roman soldiers from marrying, they had taken Egyptian wives and now had children and comfortable homes. Respected, if not feared by the locals, they had begun to feel more Egyptian than Roman. Now General Achillas made the tribune an offer: if he were to kill Pompey, he would cement his future in Egypt and be well rewarded by the king.

Colonel Septimius would have briefly conferred with his fellow Roman officers, telling them that, as Pompey's envoys had let slip, Pompey intended to enlist the Roman troops stationed in Egypt in his bid to regain power. This would mean leaving the country they now called home and joining Pompey for a renewed war against Caesar. It turned out that none of them was prepared to give up what they had for a dubious if not ill-fated future with Pompey. Septimius soon informed Achillas that he and his fellow Romans agreed to go along with the general's proposition.

That afternoon, the Egyptian army came marching down to the Pelusium seashore. The Egyptian troops and their Roman officers silently formed in neat ranks behind their standards, facing the sea. At the same time, the crews of the Egyptian warships anchored in the bay and drawn up on the shore began to board their craft. King Ptolemy and his entourage arrived from the royal encampment on Mount Casius, and the king seated himself on a throne on the beach in front of his army, flanked by the spear-bearers of his bodyguard.

A fishing boat then rowed out to the cruiser that Pompey was using as his flagship—a craft from Seleucia in Turkey. Typical fishing boats of this period were open and possessed twelve oars. This particular fishing boat soon bumped alongside the warship. As the cruiser's crew and the members of Pompey's entourage watched, not a little warily, up the cruiser's side climbed General Achillas, followed by Colonel Septimius and a Roman centurion from the Egyptian army named Salvius.

"Hail, Imperator," said Colonel Septimius in greeting to Pompey, courteously extending to him the honorific title that had been conferred on Pompey by his victorious troops many years before, a title sported by only a few other living Roman generals, Julius Caesar among them. While General Achillas watched in silence, the colonel then extended an invitation for Pompey to come ashore with his party for a meeting with young King Ptolemy here, now, on the beach at Pelusium.

Pompey's young wife, Cornelia, could sense that there was danger here, and urged him not to go ashore in the mean fishing boat. But Pompey agreed to accompany the Egyptian party. His spirits had lifted after he'd been shrouded in gloom for weeks. At first gripped by shock at his defeat at Pharsalus, he had later berated himself for failing to have his navy in support off the eastern coast of Greece. Now he was feeling more like his old self. It was an auspicious day, he would have reminded Cornelia, the anniversary of the Triumph he had celebrated at Rome for his defeat of Mithradates the Great and the Cilician pirates. What was more, the next day would be his fifty-eighth birthday, and he seemed to think the Fates were with him. Besides, he was in no position to offend the Egyptians; he needed their king's help.

After saying farewell to his wife and his aides, Pompey climbed down into the waiting boat, accepting a helping hand from a crewman. In addition to the Egyptian party, he was accompanied by his secretary, a personal servant, and his pair of centurion bodyguards, the latter wearing helmet, armor, and sheathed swords. He took a seat with his back to the shore, with his bodyguards on either side of him on the same wooden seat.

Pompey had an excellent memory for faces, and as the boat was being rowed to shore he recognized Colonel Septimius, who was sitting opposite, as an officer who had once served under him. When Pompey put this to the colonel, Septimius nodded in affirmation of the fact that he had indeed formerly served under Pompey, but said nothing.

The fishing boat slid into shore. Pompey and his two bodyguards came to their feet and turned around to disembark. Ahead, an Egyptian reception party was walking down the beach toward the boat. Behind Pompey and his centurions, General Achillas, Colonel Septimius, and Centurion Salvius also came to their feet, and drew their swords.

VI

MARK ANTONY, RULER OF ROME

Mark Antony was in his element. The thirty-four-year-old Master of Horse was in effect ruler of Rome. By early October he had shipped all Caesar's mutinous legions from Durrës back across the Strait of Otranto to Brindisi in southeastern Italy. Almost as soon as he set foot back in Italy, the other consul for the year apart from Caesar, Publius Servilius Isauricus, appointed by Caesar before he left Rome to undertake the invasion of Greece, bowed to orders from Caesar and appointed Antony Master of Horse. Traditionally this post was occupied by the deputy of a Roman dictator. In this case it was a highly illegal appointment, but it gave Caesar's rule, and that of his deputy, a thin veneer of respectability.

While Caesar had taken the title of Dictator, under Roman law it was a temporary position, lasting a maximum of six months, and while the recipient remained at Rome at that. Just as Caesar was not entitled to still call himself Dictator, no one, neither he nor another consul, could bestow the title and powers of Master of Horse on Antony. Those powers, of martial law, made Antony absolute ruler of Rome in Caesar's absence, answerable to no one but Caesar. And how Antony intended enjoying those powers.

First discharging the Pompeian prisoners once he landed back in Italy, he had distributed Caesar's previously rebellious legions. The 25th, 26th, and 29th went into camp in Puglia. The 11th and 12th had overcome their rebelliousness once separated from the strike's ringleaders in the Spanish legions and had marched to Illyricum with General Cornificius, with orders from Caesar to tackle Pompeian supporters and local partisans who had taken over the main cities and towns of today's Croatia. This was the mission that Antony's brother Gaius had set out to accomplish the previous year with the amphibious landing that had gone disastrously wrong and resulted in the seventy-five hundred men of his landing force going over to Pompey.

This time the two legions sent to secure Croatia had taken the overland route. They would be joined a little later by retired lieutenant general Aulus Gabinius. This was the same General Gabinius who had restored Ptolemy XII to the Egyptian throne. Exiled by the Senate six years before for extortion, he had been recalled by Caesar, and now, after Caesar received intelligence—false, as it turned out—that republican generals who had escaped after Pharsalus were regrouping their forces in Macedonia, Gabinius had the job of eliminating opposition forces in Illyricum. Arriving with two legions newly levied in Italy earlier that year, the 34th and the 35th, Gabinius combined them with the 11th and the 12th and took command of difficult operations to take Croatian cities and towns, some of which remained loyal to the republican Senate while others had made a bid for independence. Gabinius would die from ill health in the costly campaign, which General Corfinius would eventually succeed in completing.

As for the men of the still defiant 7th, 8th, 9th, and 10th Legions, Antony led them up the Appian Way to Rome. Installing the four legions in a camp on the Field of Mars outside the city walls, he told their legionaries that only Caesar could resolve their continued demands for discharge and bonuses. Until Caesar completed his business with Pompey in the East and returned to Rome, he told them, they would have to stay where they were, or risk being branded deserters, a crime punishable by death.

Antony then set up residence in Pompey the Great's mansion in the Carinae or Keels district of Rome. This was a vengeful act the "feckless nobody" took great pleasure in, for he had known full well how Pompey despised him. The Master of Horse now spent his time enjoying himself, becoming a "night liver," eating long, luxurious dinners with his friends and favorites, drinking all night, and bedding any woman he pleased. It was even suggested that he also had an eye for pretty boys. He spent the daytime sleeping, and walking off his binges.

When Caesar's supporters at Rome began arguing among themselves, Antony made no attempt to intervene, just left them to it. He was having too much fun to be bothered with the petty affairs of government. First-century Jewish writer Josephus would describe Antony as "one that openly indulged himself in such pleasures as his power allowed to him."

Antony was merely reverting to type. As a young man, he and his best friend, Gaius Curio, had led just such an indulgent life together. In those days Curio had to borrow heavily to keep up with his friend. In the end, Curio's father had banned Antony from his house because he considered him a bad influence on his son. But Curio had acquired a taste for the high life under Antony's tutelage and continued to live well above his means until, in 50 B.C., after both he and Antony had been elected Tribunes of the Plebs, the debt collectors began to increasingly knock on his door.

Curio had initially supported Pompey in the Senate, but when Caesar discreetly paid off his huge debts after being approached to do so by Antony, Curio switched sides—this was the price of having his debts cleared up. When, in January 49 B.C., neither Antony nor Curio had been able to push Caesar's demands through the Senate and they had both fled to him after he crossed to Rubicon, he had rewarded them with military appointments—Antony commanding half the troops in his initial advance down through eastern Italy, Curio commanding four legions made up of mostly former senatorial troops whom Caesar had subsequently sent to occupy Sicily. Now Curio was dead, killed by senatorial forces, along with the men of the 17th and 18th Legions, after he had attempted to invade North Africa from Sicily for Caesar in the summer of 49 B.C. But Antony was very much alive, and enjoying the fruits of his support for Julius Caesar.

Orator and senator Marcus Cicero knew Antony well. Having eventually sided with Caesar after initially supporting Pompey, Cicero was now bitterly regretting his decision as he contemplated the poor character of many of the other men who supported Caesar, some of them with criminal records, others, rank opportunists. Antony in particular he considered "odious." Even many of Caesar's hard and fast supporters disliked Antony, considering him lazy, self-indulgent, and self-opinionated. Most kept such thoughts to themselves, knowing that no one could hold a grudge or enjoyed his revenge more than Mark Antony.

Before they'd parted at Farsala, Caesar had briefed Antony on his plan to go after Pompey wherever his flight might take him, while Antony took control back at Rome. Caesar would have told him that Marcus Brutus thought that Pompey could head for Egypt to call in the debt he felt was owed him by Ptolemy XIII and his sister Cleopatra. Antony had met both young Egyptian royals when he was a twenty-eight-year-old colonel stationed in Egypt in 55 B.C., following the restoration of their father to his throne by General Gabinius's legions. Antony had by that time already gained mild fame as the fearless hero of the Roman siege of the Jewish fortress of Alexandrium in Judea. "Mark Antony fought bravely and killed a great number," Josephus was to write of the siege, "and seemed to come off with the greatest honor."

Cleopatra, plain second daughter of the king of Egypt, had not made an impression on Antony in 55 B.C. Aged just thirteen or fourteen when they met at the royal court in Alexandria, she had been, according to Plutarch, unworldly and naive back then. There is no record of what Antony thought of her at the time, nor of what she thought of him. Neither could have guessed how their lives and deaths would become intertwined over the next eighteen years.

Happily ensconced at Rome, living a life of leisure, Antony would play no part in Julius Caesar's life-and-death struggles in the coming months and years. Nor would he attempt to help him once the news reached Rome that Caesar was in trouble in the East. Not that Caesar ordered Antony to send him help, even though, with increasing desperation, he ordered other subordinates, those in the East, to send him reinforcements and supplies. And, if ordered to do so, Antony no doubt would not have hesitated to obey.

But should Caesar perish in the East, then Antony, his duly appointed deputy, had the position, the troops, and the ambition to step up and take his place as ruler of the Roman world.

VII

SAILING INTO HISTORY

G ripping onto the rails, the rigging, the masts, and their comrades, the men of the 6th Legion stood on the unsteady decks of the warships of the small fleet as they plowed through the eastern Mediterranean swell. Above them, the leather mainsails of the battleships and heavy cruisers billowed, filled by the seasonal trade winds from the north, the Etesians. In the ships of the little fleet, belowdecks, under seasick soldiers' feet, oarsmen worked at banks of oars that rhythmically dipped and rose to the beat of the *kalustes*, timekeepers who relentlessly pounded out the rowing pace with wooden mallets on wooden blocks. It was the fall of 48 B.C., and Julius Caesar, backed by the men of the 6th Legion and a small number of other troops, was taking a large gamble. He was heading for Egypt in search of Pompey the Great.

After leaving the Farsala plain back in August, Caesar had ridden hard for Macedonia, driving his cavalry to make as many miles each day as their mounts would allow. In Macedonia he had found that while Pompey had issued orders for the drafting of troops in the region, he himself had never appeared there. Caesar hurried to the Hellespont, the modern Dardanelles. He was ferrying his cavalry across the strait to the province of Asia in small boats when a squadron of republican warships came up. The officer in command of these ships was Lucius Cassius, no relation to Brutus's brother-in-law, the General Gaius Cassius of Battle of Carrhae fame, who had become one of Pompey's admirals. Appian suggests that this junior commander Cassius had been sent to King Pharnaces of the Bosporan Kingdom by the Pompeians seeking support, and he was on his way to complete that mission when he ran into Caesar crossing the Dardanelles.

The number of ships Commander Cassius had with him is put at ten to seventy by Roman writers. From later events it is clear that Cassius had fourteen biremes or triremes detached from the Senate's seventy-ship Asiatic Fleet commanded by Admiral Decimus Laelius. Commander Cassius, with his fourteen light cruisers, changed sides to Caesar there at the Dardanelles. Giving Cassius the task of fetching him more warships from the island of Rhodes and meeting him with those vessels at the port of Cnidus on the southern coast of Turkey, Caesar had continued his march into the Roman province of Asia.

At cities and towns throughout the province Caesar received such a warm welcome from the locals that he reduced their taxes by a third. At Ephesus he frightened away Pompey adherent Titus Ampius Balbus, a former praetor who'd planned to rob the city's famous temple of Diana, and for this Caesar received the grateful thanks of the people of Ephesus. At Tralles the inhabitants proudly showed Caesar a statue they had recently consecrated to him. At the large city of Pergamum, close to the present-day town of Bergama, he was told that on August 9, the day of his victory at Farsala, the sound of drums had inexplicably come from deep within the holiest sanctums of the city's ancient Greek temples.

At Pergamum, too, Caesar's small staff was joined by a local nobleman, Mithradates of Pergamum. Likely to have been in his late twenties at this point, he was reputedly a son of Mithradates VI, King of Pontus, famous as Mithradates the Great and previously Rome's formidable enemy in the East on and off for half a century. Mithradates the Great had several wives and numerous children, although some historians suggest Mithradates of Pergamum's father was actually a noble named Menodotus and his mother a princess from Galatia who may have become a wife of the Pontic king, which would have made the younger Mithradates the king's stepson.

Either way, he had been plucked out of the city of Pergamum as a child by the elder Mithradates, who at the time controlled all of Asia—because of the boy's royal blood, according to Caesar's staff officer Aulus Hirtius, who did not elaborate. The boy had been raised in Mithradates the Great's court and treated by the king like a son, until the elderly monarch was defeated by Pompey and then murdered by his eldest son and heir, Pharnaces II.

Well educated, intelligent, a skilled and courageous soldier, according to Hirtius, and probably ruggedly handsome, as Mithradates Sr. had been in his youth, young Mithradates had a high standing among the elite of Pergamum at the time Caesar arrived in the city. All that the young Mithradates lacked were a fortune and a kingdom of his own. Looking for both, he threw in his lot with Caesar, who welcomed him into his entourage for the continued pursuit of Pompey.

Here at Pergamum the 6th Legion caught up with Caesar, as did, shortly after, the men of the five cohorts of the 28th Legion who had marched from Achaea in southern Greece. Adding the legionaries to his cavalry, Caesar led his small force of four thousand men down to the coast, to the city of Cnidus. Sitting on an island linked to the mainland by a small causeway at what today is Cape Kriyo, this prosperous trading city founded by Greeks three hundred years before and that had once been controlled by the Ptolemies of Egypt, had two excellent harbors: one for merchantmen, the other for warships. Here, at Cnidus, Caesar was joined by Admiral Cassius.

In addition to his fourteen Asiatic cruisers, Cassius brought ten heavy cruisers from the island of Rhodes, the latter squadron commanded by the Rhodian admiral Euphranor. The Greeks of Rhodes were famous as ship-builders, seafarers, and businessmen. Their large mercantile fleet, originally developed to export Rhodian wine around the Mediterranean, had diver-sified to carry Egyptian grain, pitch, and lumber from Macedonia, marble from Paros, and honey, olive oil, and pottery from mainland Greece. In tandem with the expansion of her merchant shipping, Rhodes had built an efficient navy to defend the shipping lanes and to protect wealthy Rhodes itself. Rhodes's sturdy warships were considered the finest afloat on all the Mediterranean.

This was why both Pompey and Caesar had sought Rhodes's aid. Greeks in general were considered by Romans to be thinkers, not fighters, but Rhodian sailors were the exception. Euphranor had a reputation as a skillful naval commander and for, in the words of Caesar's staff officer Colonel Hirtius, a "nobility of spirit and courage" that "challenged com-parison with our own [Roman] people rather than merely with the Greeks."

In late September, while at Cnidus, Caesar received news that Pompey had been spotted at Cyprus, from where, it was said, he had recruited two thousand slaves and sailed due south, for Egypt. Caesar had an impatient streak that impacted on all the major political and military decisions of his life. Now, worried that Pompey might win the support of the Egyptians unless he intervened, Caesar wondered whether he should continue to wait to be reinforced by General Domitius—as yet there was no sign of the 27th Legion or the former POWs Caesar hoped had been signed up by his officers back at Farsala. Caesar was sure he would be too late if he went overland to Egypt, a journey that would take weeks. The Etesian winds were blowing hard and strong down from the north, as they always did at this time of year, making a fast sea voyage to Egypt very tempting. Yet Caesar had only just enough shipping to carry the few troops now with him.

The welcome he had received along his route since he left Farsala had convinced Caesar that now that he had defeated the legendary Pompey the

Great, he could rely on his name alone to win his way. Of the decision he now made, he was later to explain, "Relying on the fame of [my] exploits, [I] had not hesitated to set out with weak forces, thinking that all places would be safe to [me]."

Caesar embarked the men of the 6th and the 28th Legions together with his eight hundred cavalry and their mounts and equipment aboard the twenty-four warships he now controlled. Some of these massive battle cruisers were of the *quadrireme* and *quinquereme* classes. The latter, based on the standard warship of the Carthaginian navy of a hundred years before, was some 120 feet long with a beam of 14 feet. Like all ships of the era, it didn't use the overlapping clinker construction method of today but had been built with its timbers nailed edge to edge over a framework—the carvel method.

The classical warship was steered not by a single rudder, but by a pair of steering oars protruding over the stern on the port and starboard sides. Both steering oars were connected by a mechanism of beams, so that a single helmsman could stand amidships in the stern and steer the ship by pushing the steering beam to left or right. Although it was equipped with a single demountable mast and square mainsail, the warship's principal motive power was provided by 270 oarsmen in several banks of oars below-decks. In battle, the *quinquereme* carried 120 marines for close-quarters ship-to-ship fighting and boarding operations, but for this voyage there were no marines; there was room enough only for Caesar's soldiers and horses to be crowded on deck.

Not only did Caesar possess a limited number of troops for this venture, he also was limited in the number and quality of his officers, having left all his experienced generals back in Greece. Replacing General Cornificius as his quaestor or chief of staff he had promoted a young tribune who had yet to distinguish himself in combat. Brigadier General Tiberius Claudius Nero was only in his early twenties, but Caesar, who had been disregarding republican law as a matter of course since taking control at Rome and making appointments as he saw fit, had ignored the legal requirement that a quaestor be age thirty at a minimum.

Two years back, Nero had courted Marcus Cicero's popular daughter Tullia. Cicero quite liked the young man, and after Nero had spoken with him and sought Tullia's hand in marriage, Cicero, who was then in Cilicia completing his term as governor, had sent clients to Rome to see his wife, Servilia, and Tullia to propose a match. To Cicero's surprise Servilia had written back to say that while she and Tullia had found Nero attentive and engaging, Tullia had given her heart to another—Publius Dolabella, the same Dolabella who later wrote so overconfidently to Cicero from the trenches at Durrës. Dolabella and Tullia had been married that same year, 50 B.C.

By the time young General Tiberius Nero was efficiently cramming Caesar's men and equipment aboard the warships docked at Cnidus, he was still single. Destined to survive the desperate times that lay ahead for Caesar and his companions, within a few years he would marry Livia, beautiful daughter of former major general Marcus Livius Drusus Claudianus. Livia would bear Tiberius Nero two children, Tiberius and Drusus, before divorcing Nero and marrying Rome's first emperor, Augustus. For a time Tiberius Nero would raise the boys on his own, but he would die when they were still quite young, and Augustus would adopt them. Tiberius, General Nero's eldest son, would one day become Augustus's heir and Rome's second emperor. Drusus would marry a daughter of Mark Antony and have two sons, Germanicus and Claudius. Claudius would become Rome's fourth emperor. Germanicus Caesar would become one of Rome's greatest heroes, while his son Gaius (Caligula) and his grandson Nero would each become emperor of Rome. But in 48 B.C., as Caesar's little fleet made its way toward Egypt, no one could have imagined the impact the young quaestor's descendants would have on Roman history.

Of Caesar's other officers on the Egyptian expedition we know little. While his loyal staff officer since the conquest of Gaul, Colonel Aulus Hirtius, didn't accompany him to Alexandria, Hirtius is credited by most historians with writing *The Alexandrian War*, one of the chapters attached to Caesar's memoir of the civil war to round it out—Caesar's personal account stops in the middle of his time in Egypt.

"I myself did not, as it happens, even take part in the Alexandrian and African campaigns," Hirtius in 44 or 43 B.C. wrote to Lucius Cornelius Balbus, Caesar's former chief of staff and subsequently publisher of his writings. "Although they are partly known to me from conversations with Caesar, it is one thing to listen to accounts that captivate one with the novelty and remarkable nature of events described, but quite another to listen with the aim of putting them on record."

But put them on record he did, collating a number of eyewitness accounts of Caesar's Egyptian, Pontic, African, and Spanish campaigns, and almost certainly personally writing much of *The Alexandrian War*. From the perspective of the events described in *The Alexandrian War*, one of Hirtius's sources had to be a senior staff officer who was at Caesar's headquarters at Alexandria, while one or more officers who served with the fleet would also have provided him with accounts of naval actions—

accounts that Hirtius managed to jumble somewhat in his rush to meet Balbus's persistent requests for Caesar's memoirs to be quickly rounded out for publication.

Hirtius was in his late twenties or early thirties. Deeply superstitious and religious, he often invoked "the immortal gods" in his writings and gave them rather than generals credit for influencing the fortunes of war. He considered himself a man of letters and a gourmet, and was in regular correspondence with Cicero, who made fun of him to others and was not impressed with his editing of or contributions to Caesar's memoirs. While Hirtius was present at Caesar's side for several major battles, he himself didn't shine as a soldier during this period nor later as a general when military command devolved upon him.

Twenty-eight-year-old Colonel Gaius Asinius Pollio, on the other hand, was a dashing officer. It's probable that he went to Egypt with Caesar, most likely as commander of his cavalry—he had commanded cavalry for Caesar previously—and he may have been Hirtius's headquarters source. Pollio had crossed the Rubicon with Caesar, after which he'd been sent to Sicily as commander of Gaius Curio's mounted units and had boldly seized Sicily from Cato the Younger. After Curio had so disastrously invaded the province of Africa and was in the process of losing his legions and his life to prorepublican forces beside the Bagradas River, Pollio had been bringing up his cavalry, arriving too late to save either Curio or the 17th or 18th Legions. Pollio had been one of the few to escape back to Sicily, from where he had hurried to find Caesar in Italy and give him the news of the bloody defeat of Curio and his army. Pollio was absolved from any blame for the disaster in Africa—Caesar laid all the blame at the dead Curio's feet. Pollio was thereafter constantly at Caesar's side.

One member of Caesar's staff who we know definitely accompanied him on this Egyptian expedition was the senior secretary Apollonius, whose participation was recorded by Cicero. Of Greek extraction, Apollonius had been a freedman, a former slave, in the service of Publius Crassus, one of Caesar's most successful generals in Gaul who had later been killed by the Parthians along with his father at the Battle of Carrhae. Cicero later made Apollonius a client; Apollonius had been a member of his staff when Cicero was governor of Cilicia. Cicero was to commend his loyalty and good sense during that period.

Apollonius subsequently joined Caesar's staff in the East. "I know him to be a scholar, much devoted to liberal studies since boyhood," Cicero would write in a recommendation to Caesar. Apollonius, a big fan of Caesar, even had plans to write a biography of the great man. Cicero was to later note that, in Alexandria, Apollonius not only served Caesar with zeal and fidelity but also "saw military service" there at Caesar's side—so desperate would the situation in the Egyptian capital become for Caesar and his men that his secretary would be forced to lay aside his pen and take up a sword.

On September 28, having bestowed Roman citizenship on all the delighted inhabitants of Cnidus, Caesar had sailed just as dusk was falling. As the two dozen galleys containing the small expeditionary force pulled away from Cnidus, they left the locals wondering where they were heading. Caesar was notorious for keeping his cards close to his chest and not revealing his plans to even his closest confidants. Nor did his deadpan expression or body language betray his thoughts or attitudes. He was like a house without windows; no one could look in and see what was going on inside.

True to form, Caesar didn't tell his own men where they were going as they departed Cnidus. All he would say to the officers in charge of the other ships of his convoy was that by night they should follow the lantern that hung from the high, curved stern of his ship, and by day his consular standard, which flew in the same place. Once they were out of sight of land, and out of sight of enemy agents who might guess his destination from the direction he took, Caesar ordered the helmsman of his flagship to set a course for Alexandria. A direct course.

To sail directly to Egypt from southern Turkey was in those days considered very risky, even insane, by merchant skippers. Shipping of the day usually "coasted," following the coast all the way around the Mediterranean from departure point to destination. This was primarily because navigators had neither instruments nor charts to work from. For a mariner to head into the open sea and put the shoreline out of view meant relying on the stars to guide him. It also meant that if a storm sprang up he would most likely be too far from land to seek shelter and could founder.

The men of the 6th Legion would not have been happy about this voyage across the open sea. Perhaps some of their centurions had served in the East before, and one or two may even have been in General Gabinius's army that invaded Egypt, but as far as the rank and file were concerned, they were heading for a place they knew only from stories, the most southerly place they had ever been in their lives.

That was, if they survived the journey! To Romans, a voyage across the open sea, far from land, only invited disaster. And if their ship went down, they were done for. Few Romans could swim, especially not those among the lower classes. No Roman considered swimming a pastime, let alone a joy or a sport. Caesar himself could swim; Suetonius says he had been known to swim swift-flowing rivers, sometimes unaided, sometimes using an inflated pig's bladder as a buoyancy aid. But, as with most things, Caesar was the exception. The only place most Romans could tolerate water was in the bathhouse. So the idea of spending days on end on a bucking, standing-room-only crossing of the Mediterranean with water on every horizon was both unnatural and frightening to the legionaries. Many a prayer to Neptune the sea god and to personal deities would have been uttered at various times during this voyage.

The warships did have the advantages of their solid construction and of their oars. Cargo ships were equipped with sails alone, so could only go where the winds blew them. A warship, with its banks of powerful oars, was less reliant on the wind. But because oarsmen couldn't row forever, it was still always preferable to use the sails where possible.

As the men of the 6th had set sail for their unknown destination, there would have been much talk in their ranks about what Pompey might do once they caught up with him, and what Caesar would do. Caesar had gained a reputation for clemency in these early days of the war, and would soon write to Mark Antony and others at Rome that the greatest pleasure he had gained from his victories to date had come from granting the lives of his defeated adversaries. But, the men would have wondered, would he be so generous when it came to Pompey? None of them knew that on the same day they set sail from Cnidus, Pompey's luck had run out and he had lost his life to the treachery of the Egyptians of Pelusium.

Caesar, on the other hand, was famous for his luck. He had hoped his luck stayed with him as he chanced the open-sea crossing to Egypt, and sure enough, the Etesians blew strong and uninterrupted, yet not so strong that they threatened the safety of Caesar's little fleet.

After three full days at sea, the Egyptian coast was sighted. Then Caesar's luck faltered a little. As, in the early evening, the ships turned to run along the coast toward Alexandria, dropping their sails and reverting to oar power, one of the ten Rhodian cruisers strayed too close to the shore. These big ships had a draft of less than five feet, enabling them to work close to shore, but this vessel was caught by the north wind and driven onto the rocks, where it was wrecked. There seem to have been few if any casualties; apparently the passengers and crew were taken on board the other ships for the last leg of the journey.

As October 2 dawned, the men of the 6th Legion and their fellow travelers from the 28th Legion donned their helmets and prepared their equipment as the twenty-three cruisers powered along the Egyptian coast.

Before long, the city of Alexandria came into view, and legionaries who had laid bets on their destination would have claimed their winnings with a grin or paid up with a grimace.

Questions would have now filled their minds. Had Pompey reached Egypt ahead of them? How would the Egyptians receive them? Would they support Pompey? And if so, would they fight?

VIII

EGYPTIAN RESISTANCE

A pproaching Alexandria in the night, Caesar's fleet would have been guided by the city's famous lighthouse, the Pharos, one of the seven wonders of the ancient world, whose light could be seen 50 miles out to sea. Sitting on an island just off the city, this massive 440-foot stone tower had been built for King Ptolemy II in about 280 B.C. by the architect Sostratus of Cnidus, and was a welcome sight for seafarers bound for the Egyptian capital.

In daylight on October 2, Caesar's ships warily made their way past Cape Lochias and into Alexandria's eastern harbor, the Great Harbor, with the troops on deck fully armed and ready for action. With oars rising and dipping at a slow, measured rate, one by one the cruisers entered the deep navigation channel on the western side of the harbor entrance and slid close by the Pharos, named for the low, rocky island on which it sat. From the decks of their ships the soldiers of the 6th would have craned their necks to eye with wonder the lighthouse rising hundreds of feet beside them at the harbor entrance.

Its white marble gleaming in the Mediterranean sun, the structure consisted of three stages: the bottom square, the middle octagonal, the top cylindrical, with a broad ramp spiraling around all three stages to the top, where a huge oil lamp glowed at night. Larger-than-life marble statues of Egypt's past Ptolemaic rulers stood around the lighthouse's base. Many centuries later the Pharos lighthouse would be toppled by an earthquake. Today, no trace of it remains; its site is occupied by a fort built by Arab occupiers in later times.

This massive navigational aid was indicative of the importance of the city for which it acted as a beacon. At this time Alexandria was the second city of the Western world after Rome, a prosperous center of trade, government, and education, with a population estimated at three hundred thousand people. Not only did Alexandria act as the point of export of goods coming down the Nile from the interior of Egypt and countries beyond, but also the lands flanking the Nile were among the most fertile in the world, making Egypt a major agricultural exporter.

In those days, lush farmland extended across parts of Egypt that today are sandy wastes. Over the centuries, poor agricultural management would turn farmland into desert. But in Caesar's day Egypt produced vast quantities of grain and olive oil, much of which it sent to Rome. In fact, Rome depended on Egypt and the Roman province of Africa farther west along the Mediterranean coast for its grain supply, the source of Romans' daily bread.

In terms of physical beauty, Alexandria was unrivaled by other classical metropolises. The 284-year-old city, sandwiched between salty Lake Mareotis and the sea, had been designed by Dinocrates, Alexander the Great's personal architect. It was named after Alexander, who personally chose this as the ideal place for a naval base that could control both the eastern Mediterranean and the Nile River. On a site partly occupied by the 1,500-year-old village of Rakotis, architect Dinocrates had laid out the city in a grid pattern, with broad streets dissecting uniformly at right angles, the same precise design used by all Roman legionary camps. In most other cities of the classical world, including Rome, the streets followed natural contours and tended to wind and snake unpredictably. Alexandria's planned straight, wide thoroughfares gave the city a grandeur that neither Rome nor Athens would ever possess.

Alexandria was, like all cities of the time, surrounded on its land sides by high stone walls equipped with guard towers. There was no gate in the western wall. Two gates in the southern wall gave entry from Lake Mareotis, while the city's principal street, the Canopic Way, a grand one-hundred-foot-wide stone-paved avenue, ran roughly west to east, to the Canopic Gate, Alexandria's main entry point, in the city's eastern wall. A road ran from the Canopic Gate to the town of Canopus, twelve miles farther along the Egyptian coast to the east. Canopus, as it was known to the Romans— it was called Kanopos in Greek, while the Egyptians called it PeGewat— was a famous center for the production of Egyptian medicinal preparations and cosmetics much sought after by the elite of Rome, and had been Egypt's principal Mediterranean port prior to the construction of Alexandria.

Intersecting the Canopic Way on the western side of the city was the Street of the Soma, toward the southern end of which Alexander the Great's tomb had reputedly been located. Close to the intersection of the Canopic Way and Street of the Soma, and extending north toward the sea along the Street of the Soma, was the Mouseion, Alexandria's renowned academy of arts and sciences.

The massive Alexandrian academy incorporated the Great Library of Alexandria, repository of seven hundred thousand volumes penned in Greek and the other principal languages of the ancient world by the greatest minds for centuries past—the mathematicians, the astrologers, the doctors, the philosophers on whose thoughts and theories classical learning was based. Attracted by the financial patronage of the Ptolemies, great men such as the mathematician Archimedes, the philosopher Plotinus, and Ptolemy the geographer had over hundreds of years come to Alexandria to think, to discuss, to write. Here, Eratosthenes had calculated the circumference of the Earth; the physician Herophilus had pioneered the study of anatomy; and Euclid, one of the ancient world's greatest mathematicians, had postulated about geometry and written his groundbreaking *Elements*. To this academy now came students from all parts of the Western world, to read the great books and to learn from the greatest practitioners in their fields then alive.

At the eastern end of the city, north of the Canopic Way and extending toward the harbor district, a vast royal complex spread. It incorporated the palace of the Ptolemies; guesthouses; the royal treasury; and, on the southern side of the main thoroughfare, a large half-moon-shaped Greek theater where the wealthy were entertained with plays, music, and mime. Throughout the city, magnificent Greek-style buildings of graceful arches and finely hewn pillars rose up in crafted masonry—marketplaces, temples devoted to the Egyptian and Greek gods, gymnasia where people gathered for meetings, education, and court sittings.

In the back streets more humble structures housed private houses, apartment buildings, workshops, and street-front shops. There was little visible use of timber in any of Alexandria's construction, and roof tiles, a common sight in Rome and throughout the Roman Empire, were here nowhere to be seen. Some Alexandrian roofs were clad in rough-cut stone, but many were flat and covered in flagstones, allowing the occupants of houses and apartment buildings to come out onto their rooftops at the humid height of summer and sit and enjoy a cooling breeze blowing in off the Mediterranean.

A hundred years later, a senior Jewish priest and leading resident of the city, Philo of Alexandria, was to say that Alexandria was divided into five precincts, each named after the first five letters of the Greek alphabet—Alpha, Beta, and so on. In Philo's time, two of these Alexandrian precincts were also called the Jewish Quarters, because the majority of their inhabitants were Jews.

Egypt had a large Jewish population, as it had for many centuries past. Philo was to write that in his day the Jews who inhabited Alexandria and the rest of Egypt from Libya in the west to Palestine in the east to Ethiopia in the south numbered "not less than a million of men," suggesting a total Jewish population in Egypt of more than four million men, women, and children. Philo says that there were two distinct and separate classes of inhabitants of Alexandria: Egyptians and Jews. He also quotes the geographer Strabo as saying that in neighboring Cyrenaica in the first century B.C. the Jews were the lowest of four classes of inhabitants.

Nonetheless, Jews were allowed to practice their religion at synagogues in the Jewish Quarters of Alexandria, and their justice was administered by their own chief magistrate, although they did observe Egyptian laws as well as Jewish law. They also worked industriously in the city as merchants and operating workshops that turned out all manner of manufactured goods.

This was the city in which Julius Caesar and his small force landed in October 48 B.C. As their warships docked and gangways were lowered, the men of the 6th and 28th Legions poured ashore to secure the dock area, scattering the locals working at the dockside, who made a hurried withdrawal.

Caesar himself then stepped ashore, dressed in shining armor and flowing red commander's cloak, the *paludamentum*, and with a red sash tied around his middle and tied in a bow—his general's insignia. He was immediately preceded by his official attendants, his lictors. As a current and former consul he was entitled to be attended by twelve lictors, each one carrying a *fasces*, a bundle containing rods and an ax bound with red tape, symbol of the Roman magistrate's power to punish and execute. In Caesar's case, too, laurel would have been wound around each *fasces*, signifying that during his military career his troops had hailed him as *imperator*. This was the greatest title that could be bestowed on a Roman general, and Caesar headed his correspondence with it—"CAESAR IMP," his letters would begin.

Caesar had hardly set foot on Egyptian soil before he heard the clamor of approaching voices and saw men running toward the docks. Soldiers of the Egyptian city guard, apparently unarmed, or lightly armed, but in a very agitated state, surged around the legionaries who lined the dock perimeter with raised shields. The Egyptian soldiers shook their fists at Caesar and angrily called out to him in their native tongue. From this Caesar gleaned that the Egyptians were affronted by the sight of his *fasces*. Only their sovereigns had the power over life and death in Egypt, they said, and this display by the Roman general was a slight on King Ptolemy's royal dignity.

Caesar seems to have been surprised by the audacity of this protest. After all, he had recently marched through Macedonia and Asia preceded by his lictors and been hailed wherever he went. But he was unmoved by the rude reception just the same. He continued on his way. With his legionaries pushing the mob back, Caesar and the tall German troopers of his bodyguard proceeded to the royal palace. Once Caesar had entered the palace the disturbance outside subsided, and the Egyptian troops went unhappily back to their quarters.

Striding into the palace, Caesar announced that he had come to see King Ptolemy XIII and his sister Cleopatra VII, only to be informed by haughty palace staff that his troops must disarm inside the palace and that brother and sister, their king and queen, were at war with each other. Ptolemy was with his army at Pelusium, Caesar learned, and Cleopatra and her lesser force were camped not far away from that city.

Caesar was now also informed that news had arrived from Pelusium that Pompey the Great had been killed on the beach there four days earlier, as he went to step from a boat and meet with Ptolemy. This news was both shocking and sobering to Caesar. Certainly he was surprised that Pompey, long his ally and lately his enemy, was so unexpectedly dead, but more than that, he was shocked by the meanness of his death and the Egyptian treachery that had brought it about. Some classical authors were to suggest that he even shed tears at the news. And he was sobered by the realization that a great name was no protection as far as the Egyptians were concerned, and that with so few troops around him he, too, might be considered vulnerable by these untrustworthy people.

At this point, Caesar and his men could simply have boarded their ships once again and sailed away. After all, the object of their pursuit no longer existed; Pompey was dead. But now that he was in Egypt, Caesar pursued another agenda. And, as usual, he didn't share his intentions or motives with anyone. Later writers would speculate that Caesar lingered in Alexandria to dally with Cleopatra. But Caesar had never met the young woman, who, at that time, had no great reputation as a seductress. Plutarch was to write of Caesar's dalliance in Egypt, "Some say it was both dangerous and dishonorable, and in no way necessary."

In fact, as was to become apparent, Caesar's motives for hunkering down in Alexandria were financial. Revolutions run only so far and for so long on ideology. In the end, revolutions require resources. And Caesar's resources were as low as they had ever been. Cassius Dio quotes Caesar as saying, "There are two things that create, protect, and increase sovereignties—soldiers and money—and these two are dependent on each other."

According to Dio, Caesar had added, "In case either were lacking, the other would also be overthrown."

Caesar's need for money extended beyond the cost of equipping, feeding, and paying the salaries of his troops—and these expenses were substantial enough. At the outset of the civil war, Caesar had promised every one of his legionaries 20,000 sesterces each, and every citizen of Rome 300 sesterces, once he had gained power. At this time, assuming the troops who had mutinied after Pharsalus continued to march for him, which they must if he was to win the civil war, he had about 165,000 legionaries in 34 legions on his payroll, from Spain to Gaul to Illyricum to Italy to the East. And somehow he had to find the money to pay every one of them those 20,000 per head.

For, as they had already shown, even his best legions would not support him if he failed to keep his promises. He recognized, better than anyone, that it would be pointless to win the civil war only to be deposed by his own troops when he couldn't come up with the money he had promised them.

Following the Battle of Pharsalus, Caesar had demanded money from the potentates of the East to allow him to continue the war, but so far little had been contributed. Here in Alexandria stood the treasury of the Ptolemies, containing what was said to be the single greatest fortune in the world, worth billions. Motivated by money, Caesar was determined to convert Egypt into a pliant and generous ally. That task would, to his mind, not be difficult, bearing in mind that he would be dealing with children, albeit children of royal blood.

Two of those royal children were then in residence at the palace: fifteen-year-old Arsinoe, youngest daughter of King Ptolemy XII, and eleven-year-old Ptolemy XIV, the late king's youngest son. Caesar virtually ignored this pair, as he directed his attention to their elder siblings. Ordering his troops to occupy quarters in a small part of the palace complex adjacent to the royal theater, Caesar also instructed Commander Cassius to quickly reprovision one of his cruisers and then set off back to Asia with all speed. Cassius was to locate the 27th Legion and the legions made up of Pompey's former troops recruited after Pharsalus, the units ordered to march to Asia with General Domitius. Commander Cassius's instructions were explicit and urgent: General Domitius was to have these reinforcements brought to Caesar here at Alexandria without delay.

Cassius was told to say that Caesar could not leave the city because he was, in Caesar's own words, "detained at Alexandria by the Etesian winds, which are most adverse for those sailing from there." This ignored the fact that Cassius would do just that, sail against the northerly winds, using his rowers to follow the coast all the way up past Syria to Asia if need be, as Cassius was about to do. Cassius would also take correspondence from Caesar to Antony and others at Rome.

Cassius was able to up anchor and sail without hindrance from the Egyptians. Once Cassius had set off, Caesar, who had taken up residence in a guesthouse in the royal compound that had been allocated to him by the palace staff, a guesthouse also close to the royal theater, composed a note to young King Ptolemy. The quarrels of the Egyptian royal family, said his letter, concerned both the Roman people and himself as their consul, and he had all the more duty to act in this affair because it had been in his earlier consulship that an alliance had been forged between Ptolemy XII and the Senate and people of Rome, by a law and a decree of the Senate.

He had decided, he announced in the letter, that King Ptolemy and his sister Cleopatra should dismiss their respective armies and settle their quarrels by submitting them to him for judgment rather than by force of arms, as the old treaty of friendship between Rome and Egypt provided. Messengers then hurried away down the coast to deliver Caesar's message to the king at Pelusium.

As the days passed, with Caesar waiting for a reply from young Ptolemy, large crowds of Egyptians gathered throughout the city to protest the Roman presence. When Caesar sent troops to disperse the crowds, riots broke out. This went on for several days in succession, and the mobs were only finally broken up when Caesar's legionaries resorted to using their weapons. Egyptians put up sporadic resistance, and in the process several of Caesar's men were killed. Caesar's troops had restored order in the city by the time messengers arrived back from their journey to Pelusium to say that King Ptolemy was on his way to Alexandria to meet with Caesar.

Leaving his army at Pelusium, with General Achillas in charge of the troops, Ptolemy returned to his capital within days, accompanied by an entourage that included his tutor and chief adviser Pothinus the eunuch and his rhetoric master Theodotus. No defining image of young Ptolemy survives, but his Ptolemaic predecessors tended to have curly hair, a hooked nose, small ears, and a jutting jaw, and perhaps he inherited those same characteristics. Caesar's staff officer Colonel Hirtius was to say that Ptolemy was physically weak, indicating he was short and slight. At sixteen he was considered legally an adult by the Romans, but whether he had the intelligence and maturity of a full-grown man, or whether his thinking and decisions were dominated and manipulated by his advisers, Caesar had yet to determine.

Caesar received the king in his own royal palace, but graciously, respectfully. To begin with, he found the young monarch and his minions cool. The confidence of the Egyptians was high after the assassination of Pompey. That confidence had been boosted when, two days after Pompey's murder, another Roman general had stepped ashore at Pelusium and fallen into Egyptian hands. This was General Lentulus, the 6th Legion's divisional commander at the Battle of Pharsalus. Lentulus had gone to Rhodes seeking aid for Pompey, but the Rhodians had already decided to support Caesar and so sent Lentulus packing. The Egyptians had quickly grabbed General Lentulus and slapped him in irons. They were keeping Lentulus a prisoner for the time being, thinking they might be able to use him as a pawn in their negotiations with Caesar.

As the interview in the Alexandrian palace unfolded, Caesar was appalled when Theodotus produced a sack that he said contained the head of Pompey the Great. The head had been roughly severed by Colonel Septimius with several blows of his sword in the boat that had taken Pompey ashore at Pelusium on September 28. Caesar refused to look at the head, ordering that it be interred in a shrine he wished built for Pompey outside the city. Appian says this was subsequently done, with the structure erected being called the shrine of Nemesis; it was pulled down by the Jews of Alexandria 150 years later during an insurrection against the emperor Trajan.

Caesar did accept Pompey's signet ring when Theodotus offered it. This ring bore Pompey's seal of a lion with a sword in its paw. It was a seal Caesar knew well—many was the letter bearing that seal that Caesar had received from Pompey over the years, when they had been friends, and later, when correspondence had flowed between them in the early weeks of the civil war when Caesar still thought a settlement possible and envoys had shuttled between the pair.

Saddened by the gory reminders of Pompey's cowardly murder, but focused on his goals, Caesar now made it clear that he was here in Alexandria to act as a judge who would settle the dispute between Ptolemy and Cleopatra. As proof of his right to act as the arbitrator of Egyptian affairs, Caesar produced a copy of the will of Ptolemy XII. One copy of this will had been held by Pompey the Great at Rome, while another had been kept at the palace at Alexandria. While Caesar had been waiting for the young king to arrive from Pelusium, he'd had his staff, no doubt led by his secretary Apollonius, unearth the Egyptian copy at the palace. In this will, which Caesar commanded be read aloud to the young man, Ptolemy XII called on the Roman people, by all the gods and in conformance with the treaties he had made at Rome, to ensure that his last wishes were carried out. This, said Caesar, was his authority to mediate in the affairs of the Egyptian royal house.

Young Ptolemy could not argue with this; he had acceded to the Egyptian throne on the terms of that same will. But Ptolemy and his advisers Pothinus and Theodotus were determined not to allow Cleopatra to regain her former place, and the king protracted his discussions with Caesar for day after day, at the same time refusing to dismiss his army. In the meantime, Caesar came to hear that Ptolemy's adviser Pothinus was complaining indignantly to other members of the king's council. Who did this commoner Caesar think he was? Pothinus was saying. How dare he summon their king, a Ptolemy, to plead his case!

At their next meeting, Caesar informed Pothinus that he was calling in the loan he had given to Ptolemy XII at Rome some years before. According to Plutarch, this loan amounted to 70 million sesterces. But, said Caesar, when a look of dismay no doubt came over Pothinus's face, he had decided to will 30 million of that to his heirs. So, he said, he was only demanding 40 million at this time, to maintain his army.

Pothinus had no intention of parting with the money. "You had better go and attend to your other affairs of greater significance, Caesar," Pothinus arrogantly retorted, so Plutarch records. "You will receive your money at another time, with our thanks."

"I do not need Egyptians to be my counselors!" Caesar exploded before he dismissed Pothinus from his presence.

After this, Pothinus pleaded poor, ordering that all the king's gold and silver plate be hidden. Pothinus was now served his meals on dishes of wood and earthenware. His gold and silver had to be sold, Pothinus claimed, because the royal treasury was in debt and in no position to repay Caesar's loan. Keeping up the pretense of poverty, Pothinus instructed the Egyptian quartermaster to dole out musty grain from the royal granary to Caesar's troops when Caesar asked that his men be provided with provisions. When the legionaries of the 6th Legion complained, Pothinus cynically told them they would have to make the most of what they were given, since they were being fed at the cost of another—the king of Egypt.

Seeing that he was making no headway with the king and his advisers, Caesar decided to bring a third player into this drama. Briefing an envoy to secretly make his way along the coast, he ordered him to locate Ptolemy's sister Cleopatra and summon her to Alexandria for a reconciliation with her brother and a return to her previous position as coruler of the kingdom of Egypt. And the scene was set for a dramatic new twist in the tale.

IX

THE KIDNAP

T he message from Caesar was a godsend to Cleopatra. The twenty-one-year-old desperately needed a new champion, and a Roman champion at that. But reaching Caesar would be no easy task. If she fell into Egyptian hands, she could expect no mercy from her brother and his entourage. So, taking just one adviser with her—Apollodorus, a native of the Roman province of Sicily, a freedman of Greek extraction—Cleopatra hired a small boat to conduct her secretly along the coast to the Egyptian capital.

Several days later, Cleopatra's little boat slipped unnoticed into Alexandria's Great Harbor in the fading light of sunset. The craft tied up not far from the royal palace, and as darkness was descending, Cleopatra and Apollodorus climbed up onto the dockside. All industry within the city ceased at nightfall, to resume again at dawn the next day, so in the dark and with the streets soon deserted, Cleopatra could reach the palace unnoticed. But gaining entry into the palace, with its Egyptian guards, was another thing.

At first Cleopatra was stumped as to how she might get past the sentinels. But her agile mind soon devised a solution to the problem. Apollodorus, a large man apparently, had brought his bedding with him, so Cleopatra lay full length on the bedding and commanded Apollodorus to wrap her up in it and tie the ends. The freedman then hoisted the bedroll onto his shoulder and proceeded to the palace gate. There he informed the guards that he had a gift for General Caesar, and they let him enter.

When Apollodorus reached the guesthouse within the palace compound where Caesar was staying, he told the Roman legionaries on guard that he had a gift for Caesar from Queen Cleopatra, and the centurion of the guard also let him pass, until Apollodorus was escorted into Caesar's presence. With Caesar's staff and men of his German cavalry bodyguard looking on, Apollodorus lay the bedroll on the floor in front of a curious

70

Caesar, untied the ends, and unraveled the coverlet. To the amazement of all the Romans, Cleopatra emerged from the bedding, came to her feet, and stood, smiling, before Caesar.

Few images of Cleopatra survive. Those that do exist show a woman with a long, bent nose, narrow eyes, large mouth, small chin, elaborately braided hair in the ancient Egyptian style, and small but pronounced breasts. She was, by all accounts, quite plain. But she made up for her lack of physical beauty with other qualities. Like all the Ptolemies, Cleopatra's ancestry was not Egyptian but Greek. Greek was the language of the Egyptian court, and Cleopatra was the only member of the Egyptian royal family to bother to learn Egyptian, the language of their people. In fact, she was a talented linguist, fluent in many of the languages of the East, including Hebrew and Parthian. And, of course, she spoke Latin like a native. Plutarch was to say that it was a mere pleasure to hear the sound of her voice, with which she could effortlessly pass from one language to another, "like an instrument of many strings."

Cleopatra also had other talents. She was able to quickly assess all with whom she dealt, and to cut her cloth to fit each. If a man quoted Greek poetry to her, she could quote the finest Greek poetry back. If a man told her a coarse soldier's joke, she would tell him an equally lewd joke in return. She could drink all night and play dice like a man, but equally she could charm and seduce as only a woman could. Plutarch was to write that while Plato had said there were four kinds of flattery, Cleopatra possessed a thousand. "The attraction of her person, combined with the charm of her conversation and the manner that attended all she said and did, was something bewitching," said Plutarch of the young queen.

And here now, having made an unforgettable entrance, stood the bewitching Cleopatra, petite and alluring. Caesar was delighted by her clever use of the bedroll—Plutarch says that he was immediately captivated by both the cleverness and the boldness that Cleopatra had displayed in coming up with such a ploy.

The Romans had a saying, "The traveler with an empty purse sings in front of the highway robber." And Cleopatra, now a nearly penniless traveler on Egypt's royal road, put on a superlative performance in front of Caesar. Plutarch was to write that he was soon overcome by her charm.

But if Cleopatra believed that she could charm Caesar into installing her as sole ruler of Egypt and to then go away to continue his prosecution of the Roman civil war, she was in for a shock. Caesar had his own ideas on how Egypt would be ruled in the future, and while he had a role in mind for Cleopatra, it was not that of a solo star. For the moment, Caesar gave orders for Cleopatra and Apollodorus to be lodged within the palace complex.

Many historians have assumed that from that first night, Cleopatra made herself at home there at Caesar's guesthouse, within the royal compound south of the Canopic Way. Later outcomes point to a different turn of events. After ordering a strong guard to be provided for Cleopatra, it seems that in the early hours of the morning Caesar sent her across the Canopic Way to take up residence once more in the wing of the palace that had been her home prior to her ejection by Ptolemy's people. As she settled into her old quarters, a guard of Roman troops took up positions outside, with orders to let no one make contact with her without Caesar's permission. Almost certainly, Caesar chose the 6th Legion to provide Cleopatra's guard. The youths of the 28th Legion were too callow and unworldly for such a delicate task. The German troopers of Caesar's bodyguard were too coarse; besides, they weren't Roman citizens, so to place them over Cleopatra would have been a rank insult to the young queen. The tough, no-nonsense veterans of the 6th would have been the ideal men for the job.

The transfer of Cleopatra to the main palace would have been done by the legionaries with as much courtesy as circumstances allowed, but as the hardened soldiers of the 6th Legion took up guard duty outside her door, Cleopatra knew that even though she had come to Caesar of her own will, and the Roman troops outside her door were supposedly there for her protection, she was now very much Caesar's prisoner. She would have felt a measure of relief, knowing the legionaries keeping her under lock and key had orders to prevent any attempt on her life by her brother's adherents. But she knew that if she was to achieve her ambition of getting rid of her brother and becoming sole ruler of Egypt, she would have to use all her wiles and all her charms on Julius Caesar.

Caesar, meantime, moved quickly to exploit the fact that he now had Cleopatra in his power. That same night—sometime before dawn, according to Cassius Dio—Caesar sent a message to Ptolemy XIII, informing him of Cleopatra's presence in Alexandria and of his wish to reconcile brother and sister. It was his fervent desire, he said, that Ptolemy and Cleopatra once more rule Egypt jointly, as their father had wished and decreed. This was despite the fact that Caesar knew that Cleopatra and Ptolemy now despised each other. The early morning message from Caesar would have surprised and enraged Ptolemy and his clique. The sudden change in circumstances would require a tactical reevaluation by the Egyptian leadership.

The next day, surrounded by Roman troops, Caesar brought Ptolemy and Cleopatra together in the palace and succeeded in wringing an agreement from the reluctant Ptolemy that his sister—who cunningly gave the impression that she was all for the idea—could once more rule beside him as his colleague in power. Cleopatra would have set her mind at using all her charms to convince Caesar to dump her brother. Ptolemy, meanwhile, still harbored ambitions of getting rid of Cleopatra as soon as Caesar was out of the picture.

Before an assembly of the Egyptian court, Caesar now announced that under the terms of the will of Ptolemy XII he, as a consul of Rome, had successfully arbitrated the dispute between Ptolemy and Cleopatra and as a result they would once again rule jointly as king and queen, as their father had wished. He also announced, according to Dio, that their younger siblings Princess Arsinoe and Ptolemy XIV would rule over the island of Cyprus, of which Rome had taken control during their father's reign.

In acting as the arbitrator, Caesar was giving legitimacy to the will of Ptolemy XII. But, in turn, he was affirming the legitimacy of his right as a consul of Rome to determine who should rule Egypt. It was a clever strategy, but not one that suited either Ptolemy or Cleopatra. While, for now, both played along, neither had any intention of allowing this return to joint rule to be a long-term arrangement.

Plutarch says that Caesar then put on a dinner to celebrate this reconciliation of brother and sister. While the dinner was in progress, Plutarch says, some of the Egyptian guests drank too much. One of Caesar's servants, his barber, "a busy listening fellow," according to Plutarch, and who came across as timid and unthreatening, had an ear for all that was said around him. The barber overheard dining couch talk of a plot between Pothinus and the absent General Achillas of the Egyptian army to kill Caesar. When the barber informed his master of what he had heard, Caesar quickly had an armed guard put on the dining hall. Caesar, who was not a heavy drinker, sat up all night, pretending to drink but on his guard against the assassination attempt.

Within a few days, it was reported to Caesar that the Egyptian army was on the move. Leaving a garrison at Pelusium, General Achillas was marching most of his twenty thousand infantry and all of his two thousand cavalry toward Alexandria. In his memoirs, Caesar wrote that his own force was much too small for him to consider confronting the Egyptian army in the open outside the city, something he would have done had his troop numbers been greater. His only alternative, he said, was to stay where he was in the city and try to learn what Achillas's intentions were. He called his troops to arms.

Yet, Caesar did more than that. Much more. The approach of the Egyptian army forced him to take drastic action to secure both his political and his military positions. We know from Caesar himself the outcome of what he did next; the exact methodology has always remained a mystery, until now. Throughout his career Caesar demonstrated a talent for doing the unexpected, for catching his opponents off guard. Several times, for example, he conducted hazardous amphibious invasions in winter, when the other side was expecting him to wait for spring and more favorable weather conditions.

But his most effective tactic was the use of night operations. At critical points in his military campaigns, Caesar conducted night marches to take the enemy by surprise. More than once, he had his legions build a marching camp for the night, and then, in the early hours of the morning, he led them quietly out of camp and covered a number of miles in the darkness, sometimes to put distance between sleeping pursuers and himself, at other times to suddenly appear on the enemy's doorstep come the dawn. It seems that here in Alexandria this October night, he again employed darkness to his advantage.

Roman legions changed the watch every three hours during the night, when a fresh contingent of sentries would replace those of the old watch. Over the several days since Cleopatra had been installed at the royal palace, the Egyptian palace guards became accustomed to the Romans following their change of watch routine. Every three hours each night they would have seen a new detachment of 6th Legion men march in to replace those of the old watch. This particular night was no different. In the early morning hours, as a Roman trumpet sounded the change of watch from Caesar's guesthouse south of the Canopic Way, the legionaries of the new guard made their way into the main palace compound, probably via a small gate controlled by the Roman sentries. And the Egyptians on guard in their towers and on the walls would have thought nothing of it.

The size of the guard allocated by Caesar to Cleopatra would have been no less than century strength—a hundred men. So at least a hundred soldiers of the 6th Legion made their way to Cleopatra's quarters. But instead of the men of the old watch retiring to their quarters at Caesar's guesthouse, they combined with the new guard contingent. Just such a plan had probably been in Caesar's mind when he had installed Cleopatra in her old quarters with a legionary guard. Now two hundred legionaries swept through the marble halls of the palace of the Ptolemies.

We know that King Ptolemy's bodyguard was made up of spearmen, probably men handpicked from the Egyptian army for this prestigious role. But their elite status counted for nothing when confronted by Caesar's characteristic use of the tactic of surprise. Before they could react, sleepy Egyptian sentries posted outside the door to King Ptolemy's quarters were quickly overpowered. Caesar's account of these events makes no mention of casualties, and it seems that surprise was complete and not a drop of blood was spilled. The door to Ptolemy's bedchamber crashed open. As the young king awoke with a start, his bed was surrounded by legionaries with drawn swords.

"Get out of bed!" a centurion would have snapped. "You are coming with us!"

Ptolemy, accompanied by a few servants and key advisers, was herded out of the main, northern compound of the royal palace and across the Canopic Way to the guesthouse being used by Caesar as his headquarters. At the same time, his siblings Arsinoe and Ptolemy Jr. and a few attendants also were being hustled at swordpoint through the night from their palace quarters to the guesthouse by businesslike legionaries.

Cleopatra, too, would have received a rude awakening and been informed by a stern-faced centurion of the 6th that she was being moved to new quarters. And when she asked why, she would have been gruffly informed, "You and your brothers and sister are now hostages of Gaius Julius Caesar." The centurion would have added with satisfaction, "We have kidnapped the entire Egyptian royal family."

Cleopatra and the other three young royals were allocated cramped quarters at Caesar's headquarters, with Roman troops on the doors. Ruffled and in shock, teenaged King Ptolemy was brought before Caesar, who informed him that he and his siblings were all now his "guests." Caesar then instructed the king to immediately send leading men of his court as envoys to Achillas, to ask him what he was up to. As his envoys, Ptolemy nominated two men from his inner circle who had been very influential in his father's court and who in the past had gone to Rome as Egyptian ambassadors. These men, Dioscorides and Serapion, were briefed on their mission. The pair then hurried to the city's Canopic Gate with an entourage of servants, to meet the approaching army in the name of King Ptolemy and Queen Cleopatra.

The Alexandrian city guards, meanwhile, were in a quandary. No attempt was made to launch an assault on the compound occupied by the Romans to free King Ptolemy, by either his remaining bodyguards or the men of the city guard. No doubt they lacked leadership in the vacuum left by the kidnap of Ptolemy and his senior advisers. Besides, the Romans outnumbered the Egyptian troops then in the city, and there also would have been a fear that their king would be harmed if they did try offensive action. All the city guards could do in the wake of the kidnap of all the members of the royal family was to close the outer gates to lock down Alexandria. Now, when the ambassadors of their king and queen sought to leave the city on royal business, the guards had no choice but to allow them to depart.

Dioscorides and Serapion hurried east, and encountered the Egyptian army on the march in the Nile Delta. When the two envoys were brought into General Achillas's presence, knowing they would have come at Caesar's instigation, he didn't even give them the chance to open their mouths to explain why they were there. He ordered them arrested and put to death at once. The pair was dragged away. One of the envoys was killed immediately, apparently having his throat cut. From what Cassius Dio was to write, it was the ambassador Serapion who died.

The other ambassador, Dioscorides, also had his throat slit and was left for dead. But after General Achillas's murder squad had departed, Dioscorides's servants found that he was still alive. Pretending he was dead, they quickly carried Dioscorides away, as if to conduct his funeral. They then bandaged his wound and brought him back to Alexandria, where he was able to inform Caesar of what had taken place.

The Romans considered envoys inviolate, although Caesar himself had once, in Gaul, ignored the neutrality of German ambassadors and seized them. That act of expediency on Caesar's part had caused Cato the Younger to rise in the Senate and demand, in vain, that Caesar be handed over to the Germans for violation of the laws of neutrality. Now Achillas's brutal response to the sending of envoys gave Caesar a very good idea what the Egyptian general's attitude and intentions were.

Achillas's actions suited Caesar just fine. In murdering one of his own king's emissaries and almost killing the other, Achillas had seemingly set himself against the king. Caesar was to write in his memoirs that apart from the fact that the king's name carried great weight with his people, far more so than that of Cleopatra, who had no popular following to speak of, Caesar wanted it to appear to the Egyptians that this conflict now flaring up between the Egyptian army and Caesar was not at the initiative of the king but was the idea of a few "ruffians," namely Pothinus and Achillas. And in that respect Achillas played right into Caesar's hands.

Not that Achillas would have been concerned about the semantics of the situation now developing. Clearly, he was undaunted by Caesar's reputation. Achillas had a formidable army that significantly outnumbered Caesar's legionaries. Not that he had any fear of legionaries; Achillas knew that in the previous year, Caesar's general Curio and two legions of Italians had been wiped out in Africa by native troops, proof to Achillas and the soldiers of his Egyptian army that Roman legionaries were not supermen. The Egyptian army continued its advance on Alexandria.

Meanwhile, knowing that Egyptian troops were fast approaching, a number of men in Caesar's force were by this time wondering why they were still in Alexandria. Pompey was dead, so what was the point of staying here? Some suggested that Caesar had fallen for Queen Cleopatra. Other legionaries would have said that in that case, why didn't he just sail away with her and take them with him? Hearing of these mutterings in the ranks, Caesar sent a message to his men via their officers. He would soon be ordering all his men to board their ships and to leave this inhospitable place. In the meantime, they should be patient, do their duty, and trust that he knew best.

Within days, General Achillas and his army marched up to the city walls from the east; and the Egyptian guards at the Canopic Gate enthusiastically sprang to operate the giant wheels that opened the big wooden gate—it was, apparently, like the gates of Rome, a single wooden gate that, in the open position, was raised up into the gate tower.

As the Egyptian army marched into the city via the Canopic Gate, Caesar ordered his troops to their posts around the small perimeter he had set up surrounding the part of the royal palace he occupied. At the same time, he instructed his friend Mithradates of Pergamum to immediately take one of the Asiatic cruisers and head for Syria and Cilicia, to seek backup. It is quite possible that Caesar now had doubts that Commander Cassius had fulfilled his earlier orders to bring reinforcements, that he feared Cassius had deserted him once it was clear his situation was tenuous. Caesar also seems to have doubted that the former Pompeian POWs had turned up in Asia as he had ordered.

Caesar's instructions now ignored Cassius's earlier mission. Those instructions were specific: Mithradates was to round up as many additional warships as he could from Syria, Cilicia, and Rhodes, and he was to have them bring him reinforcements. Mithradates carried letters from Caesar to leaders throughout the region containing detailed demands for their military support. Auxiliaries were to be put together and dispatched to Caesar's aid. Corn was to be sent to him. Artillery was to be collected from all quarters. Archers were to be brought from Crete. And Malchus, king of Nabatea, on Palestine's southeastern border, was to send his renowned cavalry.

One of Caesar's letters was addressed to Hyrcanus bar Alexander, Jewish high priest at Jerusalem, recognized by Rome since Pompey's heyday as ethnarch, or chief magistrate, of the Jews of Palestine. In his letter, Caesar urged Hyrcanus to join a relief column led by young Mithradates, taking with him all the financial and physical support he could muster from among the Jewish people of Palestine. As Mithradates sailed off, all Caesar's hopes were now pinned on the success of his mission. Without reinforcements, and so thoroughly outnumbered, Caesar knew that he would fail at Alexandria. And he could not afford to fail.

Achillas, whom Caesar describes as "signally audacious," was to prove very adept at the sort of tactics needed in a battle within the confines of a city. On the day of his army's arrival in Alexandria he had very clear military goals: seal Caesar off in the city, and then eliminate him. As he entered Alexandria, Achillas divided his army in two. One force had orders to push through the city to the harbor and secure the docks, preventing Caesar's escape. The other was to launch an assault on the guesthouse where Caesar was staying.

Caesar, on the other hand, knew that his future depended on maintaining a strong defensive position within the city while at the same time retaining contact with the harbor, where his warships were still at anchor, to preserve a route for supplies to reach him in the city. The Egyptian troops reached the docks too late to prevent Mithradates from sailing on his mission to secure reinforcements—in the streets around the docks, they ran into the bulk of Caesar's legionaries, most likely the men of the 28th Legion, who were able to hold the Egyptians back while Mithradates's cruiser cleared the harbor.

Meanwhile, the second Egyptian force launched a determined attack in the direction of Caesar's quarters, aiming to free King Ptolemy. Caesar says that he stationed several cohorts in the streets around the house. These were almost certainly the two cohorts of the 6th Legion. The tough Spaniards, spoiling for action after weeks of inactivity, stopped the Egyptians in their tracks. The legionaries then pushed the Egyptian attackers back from the vicinity of Caesar's quarters, where the royal Egyptian hostages would have been guarded by a detachment of Caesar's dismounted cavalry.

Caesar himself was at the docks. This, he later wrote, was where the most serious struggle took place that day. Achillas and his men, repulsed in their first attack at the waterfront, came again, determined to get through to seventy-two Egyptian warships docked in the city's Inner Harbor, the so-called Harbor of Eunostos to the west, which was separated from the Great Harbor by a narrow, man-made causeway.

This causeway was called the Hepstadion because it was seven stades long—about fifteen hundred yards. There was an arch at each end of this causeway, the one at the island end to the north being the larger, with a wooden bridge over each arch. While small craft could pass beneath them, these bridges could be raised to allow warships to pass from one harbor to the other. If the Egyptians could bring these warships into the conflict they would be able to attack Caesar's ships with the aim of securing the Great Harbor and so cutting off Caesar from the sea.

Of the ships in the Inner Harbor, fifty were Egyptian battleships of the *deceres* class and heavy cruisers of the *quadrireme* and *quinquereme* classes that Gnaeus Pompey had taken to Greece in support of his father the previous year. After ranging along the western coast of Greece, sinking scores of Mark Antony's transports, young Pompey had landed to join his father. Once the Egyptian commander of the warships learned of Pompey's defeat at Farsala he did not participate in the evacuation of senatorial troops from the Buthroton area but instead brought his ships back home to Alexandria.

The other twenty-two ships in the Inner Harbor were lighter craft, although all were decked so were larger than frigates. This smaller squadron consisted of the warships that normally guarded Alexandria. Caesar says that all seventy-two vessels were in tip-top condition and fully fitted out, ready for battle. The barefoot Egyptian seamen and marines who manned them were all quartered ashore, and Caesar had been able to get his men into position at the docks in time to prevent these crews from reaching their vessels.

Soon there were a number of separate fights in different streets near the docks. Neither side was able to come to grips with the other, fighting shield to shield just ten or twelve men abreast in the narrower back streets, and casualties on both sides were only minimal. Nor, in the confines of the city streets, could either side employ its cavalry with any effect. Caesar was a great proponent of cavalry and always employed them with skill. Conversely, several times during his career he came close to losing a battle and his life for lack of cavalry. He had made a point of bringing his cavalry horses with him on this expedition, but for now, unable to use them for reconnaissance work or for a galloping charge, he had no choice but to employ his troopers as little more than mobile infantry who would dismount and go into action on foot.

For a time the fighting around the docks was stalemated, with neither side able to gain an advantage. But gradually Achillas's greater numbers told, and some of his men were able to press around Caesar's containment line toward the Egyptian warships. Seeing that the enemy would soon regain control of their ships, Caesar ordered that the ships be set alight, to prevent them falling into Egyptian hands and so keeping his lines of communication open via the sea.

The north wind was blowing forcefully as the first fires were lit. Tinder-dry vessels were soon blazing from stem to stern. Flames leaped to adjoining ships. Before long, the entire Inner Harbor northwest of the city was one mass of flames. But the fire didn't stop there. Driven by the wind, the flames spread to dockyards along the shoreline where a number of vessels were drawn up out of the water. Forty of these dry-docked warships also caught fire. From the dockyards, the flames spread to buildings lining the shore. Shipbuilders' workshops, grain warehouses, and the residences of seamen and dock workers close to the harbor in the northwest of the city were soon ablaze. The fire began to creep along the Street of the Soma.

Precisely what happened next is unclear, but before long the fire spread to part of the Great Library of Alexandria, which was filled with its precious papyrus volumes. Some ancient authorities would claim that the entire library of seven hundred thousand volumes, greatest in the world, was razed to the ground by this uncontrollable fire. Others state that part of the library was gutted and that perhaps one hundred thousand volumes were destroyed. Whatever the number of books involved, all were irreplaceable.

Caesar's original object had been achieved. Seventy-two Egyptian warships in the Inner Harbor were either burned to the waterline or sunk, the destruction also eliminating their artillery and ammunition. Another forty warships had been totally destroyed ashore. But history would soon forget the military objective. Blame for the destruction of the world's greatest collection of literary works would rest heavily on the shoulders of Julius Caesar forevermore.

While Achillas's troops were distracted by combat, and by futile efforts at firefighting with bronze and leather water buckets at the Inner Harbor and at buildings toward the northern end of the Street of the Soma, Caesar, at the Great Harbor to the east, had his own warships load several hundred men, perhaps from his cavalry, and these were rowed across the Great Harbor to the Pharos lighthouse. Meeting no opposition, these troops scrambled ashore and occupied the near-deserted lighthouse.

Here at the Pharos, Caesar's landing party either set up artillery brought ashore from Caesar's ships or took control of existing catapults that could command the harbor entrance. While the distance from the Pharos to Cape Lochias was a little over half a mile, shallows extended much of the way from the mainland shore, so that the navigation channel ran close by the point where the lighthouse stood. From here, this detachment of Caesar's could control who came and went via the Great Harbor and so could guarantee access to the reinforcements and supplies that Caesar was banking on receiving by sea.

As night fell and the fires continued out of control to the northwest, Caesar gave his troops no rest. While the enemy was occupied with the fire, the Roman commander had his men toil at creating a defensive cordon around the part of the city he occupied. His troops now controlled one of Alexandria's five precincts, while General Achillas's troops occupied the other four.

Caesar's area of control included that portion of the royal palace south of the Canopic Way where his guesthouse was located, together with the adjacent Greek theater. In the event that his troops were pushed back from the outer defensive positions, he could withdraw to the theater, with its high, thick stone walls, for a last-ditch stand. In the meantime, the theater became his headquarters. Here his troops assembled at sunup for Daily Orders, here men were engaged in the manufacture of ammunition, here the wounded were brought.

The Egyptian forces occupied buildings on Caesar's eastern and western flanks. A marsh lined his southwestern perimeter, with the Egyptians manning the city wall that bisected the marsh. Opposition forces also occupied the buildings north of the Canopic Way all the way to the harbor.

The fire at the Alexandrian docks and northwestern part of the city burned all night. From their vantage points on walls and rooftops as they toiled at building defenses, men of the 6th Legion would have watched as an awesome red-orange glow illuminated the north and west of the city through the hours of darkness. Come the morning, a smoky gray cloud would have hung over Alexandria, with the air filled with wafting cinders and the smell of a singed city, and the rising sun glowing an eerie orange through the hazy smoke.

With all the men of the 6th Legion thrown into the street fighting and the subsequent construction of defensive works, the task of guarding the Egyptian royals had fallen to members of Caesar's cavalry. King Ptolemy and Queen Cleopatra had been under tight Roman guard all through the night, for they were vital to Caesar's plans for the future of Egypt. Less attention had been paid to Ptolemy's younger siblings, and come the morning Caesar was informed that in all the confusion of the previous night, Princess Arsinoe and her tutor Ganymede had managed to slip by her cavalry guardians and escape. This Ganymede was named after a figure from Greek myth—the original Ganymede had been a son of the king of Troy, and because of his extreme beauty had been kidnapped by the gods to become their servant. Quite possibly then, Arsinoe's tutor, in addition to possessing a learned mind, was a handsome man.

At the time, the escapes of Arsinoe and Ganymede seemed minor irritations and nothing for Caesar and his troops to be greatly concerned about. But fifteen-year-old Arsinoe was intelligent and ambitious. Encouraged by the wily Ganymede, she saw her opportunity to grab power now that her brother and sister, the king and queen, were prisoners of the Romans. After escaping Roman custody Arsinoe found her way to the Egyptian lines and had herself taken to General Achillas's headquarters. Here she volunteered to act as the focal point of Egyptian resistance to the Roman invasion, an offer that Achillas gladly accepted. Now the Egyptian people could be encouraged to fight behind the standard of a member of their own royal family, not merely the "ruffians" that Caesar had previously alluded to.

To extend and secure the perimeter of the sector of the city he now occupied, Caesar ordered his small force to barricade the streets around it and block off entrances to buildings along the demarcation line. The industrious men of the 6th Legion quickly built a battering ram, which was suspended on a frame on wheels, and using this, they battered down internal walls to create building materials for their barricades and to establish clear lines of fire.

So rapid had the Egyptian assault been the previous day that few residents of the part of Alexandria now occupied by the Romans had time to flee. Most had been trapped inside the cordoned-off area with Caesar's men. Now the locals encouraged the Roman occupiers and offered them assistance. Residents and Romans alike were in the same proverbial boat. Completely surrounded within the city of Alexandria, for the time being the civilians would have to rely on what supplies they had stockpiled and hope for a rapid end to hostilities.

Many legionaries of Caesar's small force would have assessed their situation with furrowed brows. They were now cut off from the outside world, surrounded, and outnumbered more than five to one, with enough provisions to last perhaps a few weeks. No relief could be expected to come to them overland—not in time to save them from starvation, anyway. Supplies and reinforcements could only reach them by sea. Even that was a tricky proposition. Sure, Caesar had burned more than 110 Egyptian warships, meaning that the Romans' own relief ships should be able to reach Alexandria without being intercepted by the Egyptian navy, which had been virtually eliminated overnight. And yes, Caesar had his own cruisers at anchor in the Great Harbor, and a contingent of his soldiers held the Pharos lighthouse. But how were the supplies to be gotten to the trapped men once they reached Alexandria? Egyptian troops now occupied the buildings between the Roman sector and the harbor.

When supplies did arrive, as Caesar assured his men they would, Caesar's troops would have to make a drive from their lines down the streets to the harbor, under fire from the rooftops, to link up with the men landing with the supplies, and then run the gauntlet all the way back, carrying the supplies.

The old hands of the 6th seem to have been reasonably pragmatic about their situation. But already there were rumblings of revolt among the ranks of the young Italians of the 28th Legion. Pessimists among them would have been spouting the old Roman proverb "Bad beginnings have bad endings" as they began to openly question the wisdom of trying to hold this corner of the Egyptian capital. They pointed out that they had ships in the harbor. Why couldn't they simply break out from their current position, reach the ships, and sail away from this damnable place?

X

CAESAR'S BABY

L ucius Caienus was a soldier of the 6th Legion. On his gravestone would be inscribed, after his name and before the name of the unit in which he had served his Roman army enlistment, the fact that he had been a *velite*. This reference to velite must have been stipulated in his will, and been carried out by his executor—in which case, Legionary Caienus seems to have been very proud of that title, one that had fallen into disuse long before his death.

In times past, the velites had one of four classes of citizen serving in a Roman legion. In the centuries before Caesar's time there had been just four Roman legions, I, II, III, and IIII (the legion number 4 was always written IIII, not IV). The men of these legions were conscripted into service at Rome annually—the name "legion" comes from the Latin word *legio*, meaning conscript. Every spring, the two consuls for the year took out the muster rolls and summoned the citizens of Rome to serve in the four legions, with each consul commanding two legions in the field. Late each October, the legions were disbanded and the men sent home.

When Rome had to go to war, her four legions were reinforced by units provided by her Italian allies: the Marsi tribe from just outside Rome sent their unit, the Martia Legion, named for Mars, the god of war, the Picenians of eastern Italy sent the Valeria, the "Powerful" Legion, and so on.

In these legions' battle formations, the velites formed the first line. These were lightly armed men who acted as skirmishers. Their task was to disrupt the enemy before they reached the heavy infantry of the second line. On the march, the velites served as scouts, spies, and foragers. But by Caesar's time the velites had been phased out, having been replaced in the light infantry role by auxiliaries—noncitizen soldiers provided by Rome's allies.

When Caesar sailed to Alexandria, he did so without any auxiliary light infantry whatsoever. This meant that once he and his four thousand legionaries and cavalry troopers were encircled in the city, he was devoid of troops he would normally use in the skirmishing role. The fact that Legionary Caienus proudly had the title velite inscribed on his tombstone suggests that at Alexandria Caesar pulled out a small number of men from his legionary cohorts, handpicking them in the same way he chose his centurions, and assigned them the velite role. Certainly he needed men who were quick on their feet to conduct night patrols and keep an eye on Egyptian activities, and to run messages to and maintain contact with his sailors at the harbor.

Another task that fell to these scouts would have been foraging fodder for about nine hundred horses used by Caesar's cavalry and officers. Caesar's intent was to eventually break out of the city once the hoped-for reinforcements arrived, and then draw the Egyptians into battle in the open, when he could use his cavalry to best advantage. For this reason he didn't even contemplate sacrificing some of his mounts—not to cut down on the quantity of horse feed he would require, nor to provide horsemeat for his men.

Not that the legionaries would have appreciated being given horsemeat to eat; their dietary staples were bread and olive oil, with meat used only as a supplement. There would be times in the future when legionaries would go on strike when the grain supply ran out and they were offered meat in its place.

At Alexandria, Caesar kept his horses fed in a novel way. At night, his foragers crept from their lines to the marsh that occupied his southern perimeter. Under the noses of Egyptian guards on the city walls nearby, these foragers cut weeds from the marsh and brought them back inside their lines. In daylight, these weeds were laid out in the sun, on pavements and rooftops in the Roman sector, and dried out. Fortunately for Caesar and his troops, the horses ate this feed and survived.

But this was the least of the Romans' worries, for the Egyptians were determined to defeat Caesar and his little army within the city. And as the men of the 6th Legion and their fellow Romans soon discovered, the troops facing them were no pushovers. Even Caesar was to concede that the Egyptian army "appeared by no means contemptible either in numbers or in the quality of the men or their military experience." These men weren't all Egyptian. In fact, many were foreigners, and there was something of the quality of the latter-day French Foreign Legion about the Egyptian army that now confronted Caesar's troops.

In addition to General Gabinius's former Roman troops, who apparently made up the bulk of the Egyptian army's middle-ranking officers, the men of this army were a mixed bag from throughout the East. Chief among them were Cilicians, men from the Roman province of Cilicia in present-day Turkey, who had two decades earlier plied the Mediterranean as pirates. They had done so in such numbers—there had been tens of thousands of them—that these Cilician pirates had paralyzed Roman maritime trade in the East for years. Pompey the Great, authorized by the Senate to use all necessary means to terminate this pirate threat to free up Roman trade, had loaded his legions aboard 270 warships, trained them as marines, and had gone after the buccaneers on the high sea. He had soon drawn the pirates into battles in which the better-trained, better-equipped legionaries had invariably come off better in boarding operations.

This tactic hadn't eliminated the pirate menace, but the buccaneers from Cilicia soon discovered that nine times out of ten when they put to sea, Pompey's pirate-busters would appear on the horizon. Pompey had then employed a tactic for which he was renowned: he cleverly terminated a military problem with a financial solution. Often he very effectively bribed the officers, advisers, or family members of his enemies to murder their generals—both Mithradates the Great and General Sertorius in Spain had ultimately perished in this manner. This time Pompey bribed the entire pirate community to give up the sea and settle on land he gave them in Cilicia.

Skeptics in Rome had been sure this scheme would fail, but twenty thousand pirates had taken Pompey's offer of a pardon, a bounty, and a plot of land, had sunk their ships, and taken up the plow, becoming model settlers. But not every pirate chose to become a farmer. Some of these Cilicians who were not prepared to lay down their swords had gone in search of gainful employment of their fighting skills elsewhere. In Egypt they had found recruiting officers only too willing to sign up tough men who would fight for any master for money.

In the same way, bandits operating in Syria who had been driven out of their country by Rome's legions had come south and joined the Egyptian army. And escaped Roman slaves from throughout the East knew that if they reached Egypt they would be welcomed into the Egyptian army's ranks as fighting men. Likewise, the escaped slaves of wealthy Egyptians were signed up, no questions asked.

Caesar says that the sense of brotherhood among these Egyptian troops was so strong that if a runaway slave in the army's ranks had in the past been identified and arrested by his master, the man's comrades in arms had banded together and rescued him. A threat of violence to any one of them, Caesar was told, was considered a threat of violence to them all.

This esprit de corps had kept the Egyptian army welded together for decades. But their loyalty was to themselves, first and foremost, and to whoever paid the best. Many of these men had served Cleopatra's older sister Queen Berenice and then, for money, had not resisted the restoration of King Ptolemy XII when Gabinius's legions came marching down from Syria. In the past these troops had successfully demanded the execution of royal favorites they disliked, had succeeded in plundering the homes of certain rich Alexandrians, and had even besieged the royal palace to demand a pay raise.

Now the men of the Egyptian army were being driven by this long-established comradeship and a haughty pride, by a dislike of foreign invaders, and by competing pledges of big bonuses being offered by both Princess Arsinoe and General Achillas, for Arsinoe was not content to be merely a figurehead and to let Achillas run things. Encouraged by her tutor Ganymede, she was intent in taking total control. Recognizing this, Achillas was trying to buy the continued loyalty of his men and sideline the teenager.

Caesar was amused to learn of this competition for the loyalty of the troops on the other side. But he was not amused when several Egyptian prisoners were brought to him. These men had been intermediaries between King Ptolemy's adviser Pothinus and General Achillas. Betrayed by members of Pothinus's retinue, the intermediaries were caught red-handed carrying a message from Pothinus to Achillas urging the Egyptian general not to slacken in his efforts to defeat the Romans and not to lose heart. This was all the evidence Caesar needed to rid himself of a sinister snake in the grass and a major detrimental influence on young King Ptolemy. Caesar immediately had Pothinus arrested, and ordered his execution. A burly German trooper of his bodyguard would have soon after cleaved the kneeling Pothinus's head from his shoulders with a blow from his sword.

Probably in reprisal for Pothinus's execution, Achillas had his Roman prisoner General Lentulus, former commander of the 6th Legion, also put to death. Achillas was determined to win this contest with Caesar, and as soon as a drawn-out siege became apparent, Achillas dispatched envoys and recruiting officers to every part of the kingdom of Egypt to draft men into militia units for the war against the Romans. Some of these militiamen were used to bolster garrisons at outlying centers such as Pelusium, but most were hurriedly marched to Alexandria to join operations there. Every adult male slave in Alexandria also was drafted and armed for the duration.

By this means Achillas more than doubled and perhaps quadrupled the number of men he had under arms in Alexandria, and this enabled him to use the militia to man the strung-out defense line that zigged and zagged through the city while the Egyptian army's regulars were based at several points in the most densely populated parts of the city as rapid reaction forces, to be deployed in offensive action when weaknesses in Caesar's defenses were detected, or to counter assaults by the Romans.

Vast quantities of ammunition were brought into the city by the Egyptians, along with stone-throwing and arrow-firing catapults. Achillas also set up huge workshops in the suburbs to manufacture weapons, ammunition, and siege equipment. The Egyptians had excellent engineers and stonemasons in their ranks, and they flung up barriers blocking off every street and alleyway around the Roman sector. The tallest of their siege walls were forty feet high and used smooth, dressed blocks of stone so they could not be climbed. In the lower-lying parts of the city Achillas's engineers built giant stone guard towers ten stories tall; from these they could keep an eye on movements in the Roman sector. Other towers they built in wood; these they put on wheels, then hauled them, using manpower and horsepower, from one part of the encirclement to another as and when needed.

Colonel Hirtius gives credit to the Alexandrians engaged in the fighting against the Romans for being both intelligent and quick-witted. As soon as the Romans came up with some initiative or other, Hirtius was to write, the Egyptians would immediately copy it, until the Romans began to wonder whether they weren't imitating the Egyptians, not the other way around.

Hirtius noted that the opposition also developed novel tactics of their own. One of these was directed at the Roman ships anchored in the Great Harbor. The existence of these vessels and their control of the Great Harbor were sore points for the Egyptians. At first they attempted to send boatloads of troops through the two arches from the Inner Harbor to the Great Harbor to board the Roman cruisers, but the crews of the warships were ready for them, and as the boats came through the arches they were drilled by the concentrated artillery fire of all of Caesar's cruisers, to devastating affect.

With their boarding parties suffering heavy casualties and many small boats sunk, the Egyptians tried a new variant on the same theme, sending burning boats through the arches, hoping they would set fire to the ships of the Roman squadron. But adverse winds and more accurate Roman artillery fire ended that tactic before it could cause any damage. Cassius Dio indicates that these initial failures didn't prevent the Egyptians from trying to employ fireboats again later.

Caesar extended the defensive line in his sector here and there, where he felt it was needed. He was especially anxious to secure his southern flank all the way to the marsh, with its supply of unlikely horse fodder, a flank he only partly held to begin with. Using aggressive operations, he demolished buildings and sent assault teams that drove out Egyptian occupiers in the south of his sector, until there were no enemy between him and the marsh. Not realizing how important the marsh and its contents were to Caesar, the Egyptians seemed to be not overly concerned at being driven out of this area, for they still occupied the city wall overlooking the marsh and so still hemmed in the Romans.

Every day, the Egyptians held large public meetings in various parts of Alexandria to keep up the spirits and the resolve of their people. An account of one of these meetings was to reach Caesar's staff officer Aulus Hirtius, from someone who attended it. Hirtius wrote that the speaker—perhaps General Achillas himself—reminded the people of Alexandria that first General Gabinius had invaded their country several years back. Now, he said, Caesar had come with his army. Yet, "the death of Pompey has done nothing to prevent Caesar from lingering here. If we don't drive him out, the kingdom will be turned into a [Roman] province."

To instill a sense of urgency in his audience, the speaker urged his listeners to act quickly to defeat Caesar. The Egyptians knew that Caesar had sent for aid, but the speaker said that the stormy weather now setting in across the Mediterranean meant that the Romans were cut off here for the time being and unable to receive reinforcements by sea. They must defeat Caesar now, he said, while he was isolated. His audience would have gone away nodding in agreement.

Throughout his career, Julius Caesar was notorious for his good luck. And it was now that the goddess Fortune smiled on him once again. The rivalry between Princess Arsinoe and General Achillas had escalated and become lethal. Their competition had split the Egyptian partisans down the middle: the multinational army supported their general, a fighting man, while the members of the militia, being Egyptians all, swung behind their princess. With each leader trying to outdo and outsmart the other, both began to plot the overthrow of their opponent so they would have total command for themselves.

Finally, weeks into this damaging internal conflict, with the help of her tutor Ganymede, Arsinoe was able to terminate the rivalry by organizing the murder of General Achillas, apparently by bribing his guards. With Achillas out of the way, Arsinoe quickly assumed supreme command of all Egyptian forces, giving command of the regular army component to Ganymede.

The fact that the able and determined Achillas was no longer their chief adversary was a definite plus for Caesar and his troops, and a lucky break. Yet Ganymede was no fool. Although he had no military experience, he was extremely shrewd, and even more ruthless than his predecessor. To quell any unrest in the ranks of the army on the death of their general, and knowing that these troops spoke only one language—the language of money—he immediately increased the amount of the bonuses being offered to the troops if they defeated Caesar.

Then, at a council of war not long after taking command of the army, Ganymede proposed a novel way of forcing the Romans to either quit Alexandria or surrender. He reminded the other members of Princess Arsinoe's Egyptian war cabinet that the water supply for much of the Roman sector of the city ran through part of Alexandria under Egyptian control. Here, said Ganymede, was a weapon they could and should use against the enemy.

Alexandria's main source of freshwater was the Nile River, and a long, man-made watercourse, the Alexandrian Canal, ran from the Nile east of the city, then along its southern boundary, to enter the built-up area from the west. From that entry point a network of many smaller open channels cut into the bedrock beneath the city, and clay pipes laid by the city's original builders conducted the water to storage cisterns throughout the city's five precincts. There were some wells in private houses in the Roman sector, but the majority of the water being used by the invaders was delivered via this canal system. The drinking water delivered into Alexandria by this system was by no means perfect. Unlike Rome's water, which was channeled many miles to the hilly city from distant lakes and springs by a number of aqueducts, and which was delivered reasonably clean to the population via many fountains spread throughout the city, Alexandria's canal water was muddy and turbid.

Even in those times it was known that unclean water was not healthy, and in the words of Colonel Hirtius, Alexandria's water gave rise to many different illnesses. "But the common people had no choice but be content with it," said Hirtius. In the same way, the men of the 6th Legion and their fellow legionaries had to use this muddy water for drinking and washing. Remarkably, there is no record of dysentery or other similar hygiene-related illnesses or gastrointestinal problems affecting the Roman troops to any extent during this affair.

Water was life, and Ganymede won agreement from his war council to poison the water supply to the Roman sector to force the Romans out. It is probable that General Achillas had thought of this early on, but as poisoning the Romans would also mean poisoning the thousands of Alexandrians also trapped in that part of the city with the invaders, he had decided against that option. Ganymede had no such qualms.

Ganymede wasted no time setting the scheme in motion. First he had all the water channels leading into the Roman sector blocked off. That was the easy part; there were still wells in the Roman sector to counter. To do this, Ganymede had his engineers construct large water pumps operated by handturned wheels, and with these he gradually pumped vast quantities of seawater from the Inner Harbor into the city. The Roman sector occupied lower-lying ground than that flanking it, and from the higher ground Ganymede quietly poured the seawater toward the Roman positions each night, hoping it would contaminate the enemy's wells.

Before long, the Roman troops occupying the area nearest the influx of seawater began to taste salt in the by now rationed water they were drawing from the few wells in their part of the town. Much discussion took place among the legionaries as to how this increasing salinity was occurring, but no one could come up with an answer—especially when soldiers stationed lower down in their sector said their water was unchanged. Within a few days, water from the northernmost wells was completely undrinkable, while that from wells farther south had become increasingly brackish. The morning that this became apparent, young men of the 28th Legion panicked, sure that either through some natural phenomenon, or the work of the gods, or an Egyptian ploy, their water was being poisoned, and it would only be a day or two before there was no more water left for the Romans to drink.

It was then that panic turned to near mutiny. Some men of the 28th were convinced that the water had been turned bad by divine intervention. More still were sure that the locals trapped in the Roman sector with the legionaries had poisoned the water and were secretly working with the Egyptians on the other side of the defenses to defeat the Romans. Even a number of Caesar's officers had doubts about the trustworthiness of the locals. "If I had to defend the Alexandrians as being neither deceitful nor foolhardy," Colonel Hirtius would later say, "I would be merely wasting so many words. In fact, when one gets to know both the nation and its nature, nobody can doubt this breed is most likely to be treacherous."

The experienced men of the 6th Legion were more philosophical about the situation. They had, after all, been through plenty of desperate situations during their seventeen years in uniform, and had always managed to survive. They had signed up for service with Caesar for one very pragmatic reason: profit. And they knew that Alexandria was reputedly the richest city in the world. They would have told themselves that if they didn't lose their heads, and once they defeated these stubborn locals, they would find themselves rich men. They had gone through situations where they had been deprived of water before now, most recently with

General Afranius in eastern Spain before he'd surrendered them to Caesar. They had survived that drama; they would survive this one.

Just the same, they wouldn't have kidded themselves that this was going to be easy. These Egyptians were, in Suetonius's words, "well-equipped and cunning." The men of the 6th accepted that. The Romans had a saying, "Where honey is, there are bees." So the men of the 6th would take the stings in their stride; the honey was within their grasp. And while Caesar refrained from panicking, they would refrain from panicking.

When Caesar was brought the news of the upheaval among his own officers and men, and being acutely aware that the troublesome 28th Legion represented something like 60 percent of his manpower, he decided to take the bull by the horns and promptly called an assembly in the royal theater. After the revolt of all his own legions following the Battle of Pharsalus he was tired of revolts in the ranks, and he went to the assembly determined not to budge from his strategy of holding on at Alexandria until Roman reinforcements arrived. The potential rewards were far too great to pull out now. The downside did not even bear thinking about.

There, in the early evening, standing on the theater stage in the light of fluttering oil lamps and torches before the majority of his men of the 6th and 28th Legions, Caesar told them quite emphatically that departure from Alexandria was not an option. As he was to later confide to Colonel Hirtius, he acknowledged that the fighting in Alexandria took place amid great dangers, but to his mind rumors had made those dangers even greater than they were. Now he would counter rumors and revolt by focusing his men's attention on a remedy to the latest danger. He instructed his centurions to cease all ongoing operations. "You will have the men devote themselves to digging wells," he commanded the officers. "They will work continuously through the night."

This solution hadn't occurred to the rebellious rank and file. It was such a simple answer to the problem that every man gladly took up his digging tools and enthusiastically began digging in basements, courtyards, even in streets and alleys. With each cry of success from one digging site or another as water was found, the digging parties were driven to greater efforts through the night. When the sun rose the next morning and the troops lay down their tools, scores of new wells had generated new sources of untainted water. The crisis had been overcome.

Caesar, who was as much an engineering genius as a brilliant general, had probably thought of this simple and expedient resolution himself. Then again, he seems to have been the recipient of local knowledge throughout his stay in Alexandria. One of his sources of local knowledge would have been the Egyptian queen, Cleopatra. From the moment the kidnapping of all four surviving members of the Egyptian royal family had been accomplished and she had lodged under Caesar's roof, Cleopatra had set about winning Caesar's confidence, his support, and his heart. She may have been young enough to be his daughter, but she was by now regularly in Caesar's intimate company. So intimate, that before October was at an end Cleopatra had fallen pregnant—with Caesar's child.

Two days after the night-long well-digging exercise, a courier slipped through the Egyptian lines with a message for Caesar: Roman reinforcements had arrived by sea from Asia and were just miles away, down the coast.

XI

DEFEAT AND CASTRATION

I n Caesar's opinion, Lieutenant General Gnaeus Domitius Calvinus
was one of his best generals. Certainly he had shown that he was
an energetic commander who did not hesitate to act when he had
to. A consul in 53 B.C., Domitius, now in his late forties, had skillfully
commanded Caesar's forces in Macedonia prior to the Battle of Dyrrhachium, causing great difficulties for Pompey's father-in-law, Scipio, and
the two legions he'd commanded there. Domitius had subsequently been
given command of Caesar's center at the Battle of Pharsalus, where, after
Pompey's wings had been hammered, the ultimate victory had been made
possible when the inexperienced senatorial troops in Pompey's center gave
way.

Following Pharsalus, Caesar had appointed Domitius governor of the
province of Asia in western Turkey, replacing the previous republican
appointee, additionally giving him overall command of all Roman territories in the East for the time being. He had also ordered him to bring to
Asia the 27th Legion and those of Pompey's troops who changed sides
after their defeat on the Farsala plain—other than the 6th Legion.

Domitius had subsequently reached Asia with the 27th, 36th, and 37th
Legions some little time after Caesar had sailed from Cnidus for Alexandria,
and Domitius put these units into winter camp there while awaiting further orders. But Domitius had not been in Asia long before he received
disturbing news from the northeast. The elderly King Deiotarus, ruler of
Armenia Minor and Gallograecia, and for many years a friend of Pompey
and a firm Roman ally, came to General Domitius in Asia to warn him
that a foreign monarch had crossed the Black Sea from today's southern
Ukraine and made an amphibious landing in Armenia Minor with a powerful army. That army had quickly marched down into the kingdom of

Cappadocia and was threatening to swing west and occupy Pontus, a Roman province.

The monarch in question was King Pharnaces II, young ruler of the Bosporan Kingdom, and son of the late Mithradates the Great, king of Pontus. In 63 B.C., after Pompey had driven back Mithradates the Great's army, which had previously been fighting Rome for a decade with great success, the aging Mithradates had retreated to Panticapaeum, today's port city of Kerch in the Ukraine.

Kerch had been founded by the Greeks five centuries earlier as a trading center and was part of Mithradates' extensive Eastern empire. Several of Mithradates' sons had subsequently been kidnapped and taken to Pompey. One of these sons was Pharnaces II; another may have been Mithradates of Pergamum. According to third-century Roman historian Cassius Dio, who had access to earlier histories that have not survived to the present, young Pharnaces had then only recently achieved manhood—Romans were considered to come of age at fifteen.

Pompey had proposed to young Pharnaces that he return to Kerch and convince his people to overthrow old Mithradates before he brought about the destruction of them all at the hands of Rome. The teenaged Pharnaces had agreed and set off with a band of followers and Roman aides. Old Mithradates had heard that his son was leading a small force against him, and sent part of his Gallic bodyguard to arrest him.

But, like Napoleon Bonaparte after his return to France from exile on Elba in 1815, Pharnaces was able to talk the French soldiers sent to arrest him into joining him. When the prince reached Kerch, the city had gone over to him. His father, locking himself away in his palace, had poisoned his wives and remaining children but failed in his bid to kill himself when the poison ran out. He finally convinced one of his loyal Gallic bodyguards to kill him. Pharnaces had then surrendered Kerch to the Romans.

With Mithradates the Great out of the way, Pompey had been able to carve up the brutal king's former Eastern empire. To young Pharnaces, as his reward for removing his father, Pompey had given the prosperous Bosporan Kingdom, one corner of his father's former large realm, to rule over as a client of Rome. Since then, based at his capital, Kerch, Pharnaces had spent the past fifteen years maturing, consolidating his power base, and building an efficient army—supposedly in support of Rome's interests. But Pharnaces was known to have ambitions to expand his realm into areas in the East that had once been ruled by his father, most notably Pontus, his family's hereditary kingdom, which Pompey had turned into a Roman province.

When Pompey's fleeing generals had gathered in western Greece following the Pharsalus defeat in August 48 B.C. and had decided to withdraw their surviving troops to Africa, they had ordered a senior officer to sail to Kerch to see Pharnaces, who was now about thirty-one and firmly established in his little realm on the Black Sea. It was this senatorial officer's task to urge Pharnaces to invade Pontus, behind Caesar's back, in support of Pompey, to whom, it was felt, Pharnaces should feel indebted for his throne. This tactic was designed to keep Caesar's troops busy in the East while the senatorial forces regrouped in North Africa.

Pompey had previously sent to Pharnaces asking for troops for the fight against Caesar in Greece, but Pharnaces had declined, because he could see no advantage to himself. But this request from Pompey's subordinates, if it indeed reached Pharnaces, was a different matter. One way or another, Pharnaces learned that Pompey was on the run, with Caesar in hot pursuit, and he saw an opportunity to lay claim to part of his father's former domains in Turkey and Armenia and expand his own little empire while Rome's back was turned. It hadn't taken Pharnaces long to launch the invasion the Roman republican leadership had wanted him to undertake as a diversion.

Caesar, before he'd left Asia, had written to all the Roman allies in the East, instructing them to send him money to fund his continued military operations, in compliance with their treaties with Rome. But, King Deiotarus of Armenia Minor now told General Domitius, it was a disgrace to the Roman people and brought dishonor to both the victorious Caesar and himself that the kingdoms of Rome's allies and friends had been permitted to be occupied by a foreign invader.

"Unless we are freed from this menace," the *Alexandrian War* section of Caesar's memoirs says Deiotarus told General Domitius, "we can't carry out orders and pay the money promised to Caesar."

At almost the same time that General Domitius heard of Pharnaces' invasion, Commander Cassius landed in Asia with Caesar's order to urgently send reinforcements to Alexandria. General Domitius found himself in the proverbial cleft stick. He had to send Caesar reinforcements, but he knew that neither Caesar nor history would forgive him if he were to let Pharnaces devastate the Roman East with what was, by all reports, a sizable and well-equipped Bosporan army. There was also the problem of how Domitius was going to get reinforcements to Caesar, as he had no shipping.

General Domitius sent envoys to track down Pharnaces and deliver a message ordering him to withdraw from Armenia and Cappadocia at once and not attempt to take advantage of Rome's civil war to further his own ambitions. At the same time, Commander Cassius set sail again, this time with instructions from Domitius to round up shipping. Cassius soon pulled together a small convoy of transports supported by eight warships from Pontus and five from Lycia.

The Pontic flagship was a *quadrireme* heavy cruiser, and it was supported by several *bireme* light cruisers plus *liburnians*—small open, fast frigates propelled by some seventy oars with two men to each. The Lycian ships were all frigates. At Admiral Cassius's direction this little fleet arrived in Asia to provide transport for Domitius's Alexandrian relief force.

Domitius had decided to send Caesar two of his three legions, retaining one, the new 36th, which he would combine with other local forces to counter the threat posed by Pharnaces. The few transports organized by Cassius—perhaps thirty at most—could accommodate only one legion, so Domitius embarked the 37th Legion together with a cohort or so of picked local auxiliaries plus grain, ammunition, artillery, and other supplies, and ordered the little fleet to sail across the eastern Mediterranean to Egypt to relieve Caesar. At the same time, because he had no more shipping, he ordered the 27th Legion to march overland from Asia via Syria and Palestine to also join Caesar at Alexandria.

King Deiotarus maintained two infantry legions that he had withdrawn into Cappadocia from Armenia Minor ahead of Pharnaces' advance, and these he now handed over to General Domitius' command, together with a hundred of his best cavalry. These two infantry units, the so-called Deiotaran Legions, made up of men from Armenia and central Turkey, had been organized and equipped in Roman fashion and trained by Roman officers. They had been in existence for "several years," according to Caesar's staff officer Colonel Hirtius—it would have been at least three years, for in 51 B.C., when Marcus Cicero was governor of Cilicia, one or both Deiotaran units had marched with Cicero's two Italian legions, the "Cilician Legions" that had formed the basis of Pompey's Gemina at Pharsalus. In the second half of 51 B.C. the Deiotarans had campaigned with Cicero's legions in Cilicia, first against a Parthian advance force, sending it retreating from whence it had come, then successfully laying siege to, overrunning, and pillaging the fortified mountain town of Pindenissum, which had been the stronghold of Cilician rebels for as long as anyone could remember.

Adding the two Deiotaran legions to the 36th, Domitius marched for Cappadocia, thinking, according to Colonel Hirtius, that his order to Pharnaces to get out of Cappadocia and Armenia would carry more weight if he advanced Roman forces toward the invader. At the same time, Domitius

sent officers throughout the region to muster as much local military support as possible, telling them to meet him at the town of Comana in Pontus, near present-day Tokat. Domitius sent Major General Publius Sestius
galloping ahead to Pontus to fetch a new legion that had just been hastily
recruited there among Roman citizens by Domitius's chief of staff, Brigadier General Gaius Plaetorius. Colonel Quintus Patisius was dispatched to
Cilicia for auxiliary troops. General Domitius also commandeered a hundred cavalry from King Ariobarzanes of Cappadocia, a Roman ally.

When Pharnaces first received General Domitius's instruction to withdraw from the territory he had occupied, he had learned from the Roman
envoys that Domitius commanded a force that included four Roman
legions and the two Deiotaran legions. Pharnaces was no fool. In fact, he
was extremely shrewd. He would have done the math and calculated that
his adversary could confront him with some thirty thousand heavy infantry. The size of Pharnaces's army has not come down to us, but it probably
consisted of about twenty thousand men.

So Pharnaces withdrew from Cappadocia, back up into Armenia Minor.
But when he learned that Domitius had only retained two of his four
Roman legions and was sending the other two to Caesar in Egypt, he set
up a military camp in Armenia Minor near the city of Nicopolis.

Its name meaning "City of Victory," Nicopolis had been established by
Pompey the Great in about 66 B.C. as a colony of wounded and time-
expired veterans who had served in his legions in his war against Mithradates the Great, and it had swiftly attracted settlers from throughout the
region. A century or so later, the Nicopolitans, under pressure from Parthian invaders, would abandon their city and migrate to Cappadocia.

From Nicopolis, Pharnaces sent General Domitius a message. He intended retaining control of Armenia Minor, he said, because it had previously been part of the realm of his father and his ancestors, earlier kings
of Pontus. But, he said, he was prepared to keep the question of his long-
term rule over Armenia Minor open and would submit to Caesar's decision in the matter.

Domitius had no intention of letting Pharnaces remain in occupation
of Armenia Minor—which had been assigned to King Deiotarus by the
Roman Senate following the death of Pharnaces' father. Domitius decided
he would have to use force to eject the invader, and sent Pharnaces a curt
message to say that the matter of who controlled Armenia Minor was not
"open" for discussion, and insisting that Pharnaces return home at once.

The forces that Domitius had sent for quickly assembled at Comana,
and from here he set off to confront the enemy in Armenia. To get there
he marched his force along the wooded Taurus Mountain ridge that sepa-

rated Cappadocia from Armenia and that led from Comana all the way to Armenia Minor. This route was preferable to the easier lowland route because it eliminated the potential for ambush in mountain passes, and enabled Domitius to send down into Cappadocia for supplies en route.

Domitius's approach was no secret to Pharnaces. He sent ambassadors to meet him in the mountains, ambassadors who offered the Roman general expensive gifts and asked him to put up peace terms for their royal master's consideration. Domitius sent back the royal trinkets, accompanied by the message that he was only interested in recovering the prestige of Rome and the territory of her allies. Pharnaces, now learning that only a single Roman legion containing experienced troops marched with Domitius, and scornful of the hastily recruited and untried Pontic recruits and King Deiotarus' native legions, prepared for war.

By a series of long forced marches, the Roman column followed the ridge route and quickly entered Armenia Minor from the west. Scouts told Domitius that Pharnaces was not far away. Seven miles from the town of Nicopolis, Domitius halted and built a fortified camp in the hills. Nicopolis lay on a plain with tall mountains flanking it on two sides. To reach Pharnaces' Bosporan army, which had by this time occupied the town, Domitius would have to come down out of the mountains and enter the plain via a narrow pass.

The proactive Pharnaces laid an ambush in this pass, using a detachment of picked infantry and all his numerous cavalry. To screen his ambushing force, he also had a large herd of cattle spread through the pass and the rolling fields below it, and forced farmers and residents of Nicopolis to go up into the pass and pretend to be tending the cattle, and farming. He reasoned that this way Domitius would either not suspect an ambush or would allow his troops to scatter to round up the cattle as booty. Either way, when he sprung his trap he would have the Romans at a disadvantage. All the time, he kept sending new deputations to Domitius seeking peace, to keep him off guard.

But Pharnaces outsmarted himself. Domitius was not in a hurry to give up the advantage of high ground, and while Pharnaces continued to send him envoys and held out the hope of a peaceful solution, he kept his troops in the camp in the hills. As days passed like this in stalemate, and with Roman scouts likely to stumble on his ambush at any moment, Pharnaces withdrew his ambushers and recalled his envoys.

The next day Domitius came down out of the hills and moved his force closer to Nicopolis, camping on the plain within sight of the enemy. While the Roman troops were busily building a new camp, General Domitius's attention was drawn to the enemy position—Pharnaces' army was moving out from the town and forming up in the open in battle order. Pharnaces had his well-drilled troops line up in a battle formation that involved a single, straight, uninterrupted front line of infantry from one side to the other. Behind the front line, on each wing and in the center, three bunched lines of reserves formed up, with a single reserve line linking the three main reserve concentrations.

To counter this fancy formation, Domitius lined up part of his force in battle formation in front of the camp ramparts while the remaining men increased their efforts to finish building the walls and ditches of their new camp. Neither side attempted to launch an attack, and through the afternoon the opposing troops stood in their ranks behind their standards, eyeing each other across the plain until, as sundown approached, the Romans completed their camp and the Bosporan army marched back to its camp, allowing Domitius' men to also withdraw behind camp walls.

That night, Pharnaces' wide-ranging cavalry patrols intercepted Roman couriers bringing dispatches for General Domitius. These dispatches had come from Mithradates of Pergamum, whom Caesar had urgently sent from Alexandria to find the reinforcements he had originally ordered Cassius to round up. Mithradates—Pharnaces' half brother—had landed in Syria after leaving Alexandria ahead of the Egyptian assault on Caesar and sailing around the coast. Apparently basing himself at Laodicea, principal port of Syria, and a city strongly behind Caesar, Pharnaces' brother had sent messages to all quarters seeking the reinforcements that Caesar so desperately needed.

When Pharnaces read the dispatches from Mithradates intended for General Domitius, he learned for the first time that Caesar was trapped in Alexandria and in extreme danger. Mithradates was as yet unaware that Commander Cassius had done his job and that the 27th and 37th Legions were now on their way to Egypt, with the 27th yet to reach Laodicea overland. He ordered Domitius, on Caesar's behalf, to immediately send Caesar reinforcements and to himself move closer to Alexandria with those forces he retained.

Pharnaces now cunningly released the couriers and permitted them to deliver the dispatches that he had just read to Domitius. Pharnaces's strategy now was to spin out the time, to put off a full-scale battle, until Domitius had no choice but to pull out and head south in aid of Caesar, as he had been ordered to do in these latest dispatches. In this way Pharnaces could have Armenia Minor without a fight.

To strengthen his defensive position and deter Domitius from considering an attack, Pharnaces now had his men dig two parallel trenches, each four feet deep, running out from the part of the town that offered easiest access to the Romans, and lined up his infantry on the ground between the trenches, placing his cavalry at either end of the trench lines.

Colonel Hirtius says that Domitius was more worried about Caesar's position than his own, but he was not prepared to negotiate terms with Pharnaces after having rejected giving him terms before. Even worse to the proud Domitius would be for him to approach Pharnaces with terms for a settlement that would allow him to go south secure in the knowledge that Pharnaces would not occupy Pontus behind his back, only for Pharnaces to reject his approach.

On the morning of a fine fall day, having decided that he would have to deal with Pharnaces before he did anything else, General Domitius led his troops out of the camp on the plain outside Nicopolis and formed them in battle order.

The men of the 36th Legion, former Pompeian troops, had at least experienced combat at Farsala, even if they had lost the battle, and so, considering them his most experienced troops, Domitius placed the 36th on his important right wing. The left wing he assigned to the Legio Pontica. Most of the men of this Pontic Legion, Roman citizens from Pontus, were raw recruits, having been in uniform for only weeks. But it is highly likely that several cohorts of this new legion were actually retired veterans of the old Valeria Legion, which had served in the East under Pompey and been discharged by him here and given land grants in Pontus. Under their discharge agreements, retired legionaries were required to serve a total of four more years as reservists if and when required, and it is more than likely that the Valerians had been recalled to help bring the Pontic Legion up to strength. On the negative side, while these recalled veterans had significant experience—having fought Pharnaces' father, Mithradates the Great—all were now in their forties at least and had not thrown a javelin in anger in a decade.

Domitius would have deployed the legions on the wings in the standard Roman battle formation of three lines, splitting their cohorts four-three-three through the three lines, as Caesar did. He placed King Deiotarus's two legions in his center. Because he had no great confidence in these native units, he bunched them tightly. The aged king himself was not present. Domitius held the auxiliary cohorts from Cilicia in reserve. For cavalry, he only had two hundred men, a hundred supplied by Deiotarus and the hundred Cappadocians. He would have placed a hundred troopers on each of his wings, under the direction of his commander of cavalry, Colonel Quintus Atius Varus.

Seeing that the Roman general meant business, Pharnaces decided that he would give battle, and lined up his troops between the trenches, in the formation he had used previously. But this time, while the reserve lines took up their positions between the two trenches, Pharnaces placed his front line in advance of the trenches. Once again, he split his cavalry between his wings. His mounted troops significantly outnumbered the Roman cavalry; Pharnaces possessed perhaps a thousand cavalrymen. Where they came from we don't know, although it's possible many of them were Sarmatians. Pharnaces' aggressive Ukrainian neighbors, the Sarmatians were the original inhabitants of his Bosporan Kingdom. They were expert horsemen who excelled as heavy cavalry, wearing fish-scale-style metal armor and sporting long lances.

The nature and origins of Pharnaces' infantry also are unknown. We do know that his army had been together for a number of years, fighting numerous battles, and had never been beaten in all that time. Pharnaces would have used his father's large army as the basis of his military, retaining the best officers and soldiers when Pompey demobilized the surrendered army in 63–62 B.C. Mithradates the Great had employed mostly Greek officers, plus a few Romans who had defected to him. Much like the men of the Egyptian army facing Caesar now in Egypt, many of Pharnaces's rank and file would have been mercenaries, men from throughout the East and perhaps as far afield as Gaul (the men of his father's bodyguard unit had been Gauls) who had voluntarily signed up with him for profit, not for patriotism. It's likely a few former Cilician pirates also marched for Pharnaces, as they did for the Egyptians; the pirates had been allies of Pharnaces' father.

The Bosporan unit names and strengths are not recorded. Pharnaces' father, Mithradates the Great, was named for the god Mithra, who, through much of the East, was worshiped as the god of the sun, justice, contract, and war. Typically, the Romans, who tolerated the worship of many Eastern gods, incorporated Mithra into their pantheon, and a temple to him was built at Rome. Later, the Christian church would appropriate Mithra's birthday, December 25, as the day on which the nativity of Jesus Christ would be celebrated. It's thought that Mithradates worshiped Mithra; his allies the Cilician pirates certainly did. If his son Pharnaces was also a follower of Mithraism it's probable he appropriated its symbols for his army.

The white bull, Mithraism's key symbol, is likely to have been his emblem, while his troops marched behind standards bearing the four elementary symbols of Mithraism—the raven (air), the lion (fire), the serpent (earth), and the mixing bowl (water). Perhaps his units were named in the same manner. The moon also was an important symbol to followers of Mithra, for in their legend of creation, after Mithra sacrificed the white bull from which all things subsequently grew, the bull transformed into the moon. It's possible that a quarter-moon emblem appeared on the shields of Pharnaces' soldiers.

The arms carried by most of Pharnaces' infantry were apparently similar to those of the Romans—throwing javelins and swords, not the long spears used by Greek phalanxes in the past and by the tribes of Germany. The East produced the best archers of the ancient world, and it's probable that Pharnaces had companies of bowmen among his reserve units.

As for Pharnaces himself, apart from his approximate age we know that he had at least one wife—probably several, as his father did—and a daughter and a very young son named Darius. He would have spoken Greek as his primary language, for all the cities of the Bosporan Kingdom were peopled primarily by people of Greek extraction. He would have been raised by Greek tutors, and his learning would have been remarkably similar to that of his Roman adversaries. He is likely to have been square jawed, and clean-shaven in the Greek and Roman fashion—as his father had been and as several rulers of the Bosporan Kingdom were.

As the Romans later learned, Pharnaces consulted auspices prior to battle, just as they did. In the predawn, General Domitius would have attended the sacrifice by Roman augurs of a bull, dedicated to the Roman war god, Mars, as all Roman generals were expected to do prior to a battle. He would have obtained favorable omens—Mars was with the Romans, the augurs would have assured Domitius. In the same way, Pharnaces would have presided over the sacrifice of a bull in the early morning hours. With the entrails of the animal clear and unblemished, a good sign, Pharnaces would have proceeded to battle confident that Mithra smiled on him and his army this day.

The two armies stood in their battle formations, facing each other across the plain, with less than half a mile separating them. There would be no pointless standoff between the two armies today—at almost the same instant, Domitius and Pharnaces each ordered their armies to charge. In the midst of the Roman army, wearing his armor and scarlet general's cloak and surrounded by his staff, General Domitius nodded to his personal standard-bearer. His purple standard bearing the twelve *fasces* of a consul dropped, trumpets sang out through the ranks of some sixteen thousand or seventeen thousand men, and with an exultant roar the men of all three Roman lines advanced at the run.

A similar catalyst sent the Bosporan front line charging forward, but Pharnaces' cavalry on the wings and the reserves behind the lines held their positions, as they had been ordered. The Roman cavalry also remained stationary, as their general awaited the ideal opportunity to insert them into the action. As the infantry dashed forward, both sides let fly with their javelins, on the run. Then, at the last moment, just as the two front lines were about to ram into each other, the Bosporans let out a blood-curdling battle cry. A moment later, the two sides collided with a roar in a mass of clashing shields and slashing swords.

General Domitius had decided his strategy in advance of the battle. He had passed on instructions accordingly at a full assembly of the troops in camp that morning, before the legions had marched out to do battle. He didn't want to attempt to cross the Bosporan trench lines; that would break up his battle formations and leave his men vulnerable. So, while the Deiotarans kept the Bosporans occupied in the center, the 36th and Pontic Legions were under orders to run around the outside of the trenches and then sweep in on the flanks of the reserve behind the trenches.

On the Roman right, the 36th Legion charged into the Bosporan cavalry standing just outside the trench lines. Their charge broke up the mounted formation; Bosporan troopers dispersed in disorder. The 36th could have then swung into the left flank of the Bosporan reserve infantry, but the tribune leading it chose instead to lead his men all the way to the town walls. From there the 36th wheeled around, crossed the trench behind the Bosporan reserves, and attacked them in the rear.

On the other wing, Bosporans met the charge of the Pontic Legion in the open, stood their ground, and brought the mostly inexperienced Roman troops to a shuddering halt. So the commander of the Pontic Legion drew his troops back. The Bosporans, fearing a trap, did not follow them. The Pontic Legion re-formed, then launched a fresh attack, this time heading toward the first trench, planning to negotiate the trench and then attack the enemy beyond it. This was a disastrous error. While, in normal circumstances, a man could jump into the four-feet-deep ditch and clamber out of it again on the other side on his own or with a helping hand from a comrade, it was a different story when that man was under attack from above.

The Bosporans quickly swarmed up to the trench and launched spears, arrows, and stones at the Roman legionaries as they struggled to get across it. To the men of Pharnaces' right division—no doubt his best, as units on the right wing of a battle line invariably were in these times—it would have been like a turkey shoot.

In the center, the men of the two Deiotaran legions met the Bosporan charge, came to a standstill, then buckled as the enemy pushed forward again. Many Deiotarans began turning and streaming from the field in panic, leaving comrades to be mowed down. Their Bosporan opponents, being well disciplined, instead of giving chase, saw that their fellows on their left were under sustained attack from the 36th Legion and in trouble, and turned to give them support.

With the Pontic Legion pinned down at the trench and taking very heavy casualties, many Bosporan troops on that wing were pulled out and also sent to aid Pharnaces' embattled left. The 36th Legion soon found itself under attack from almost the entire Bosporan army. Colonel Hirtius, quoting an eyewitness, was to say that the 36th bore the brunt of this attack bravely. But before long the legion was surrounded.

The men of the 36th were all former republican troops, from a variety of Pompey's legions, and some of them would have been highly experienced soldiers. But they suffered from the fact that the 36th had been thrown together, and its men had yet to develop an esprit de corps. Heavily outnumbered, seeing the Deiotarans in the center of the Roman line flee, and seeing the Pontic Legion being carved up on the other wing, they could only think about survival. Orders rang out for the 36th to form an *orbis*, the Roman army's circular formation of last resort.

The men of the 36th obeyed with good discipline. Then, with their standards in the center of this ring, the 36th gradually withdrew in a practiced maneuver, fighting all the way, toward the hills. Seeing this, Pharnaces ordered his troops not to follow the Romans into the foothills, where the 36th, which continued to maintain its discipline, would have the advantage of high ground and could launch an effective counterattack.

At the same time, given a respite by the enemy's concentration on the 36th, survivors from the Pontic Legion were able to escape the deadly trench, now the grave of thousands of their fellow recruits, and flee from the battlefield. Accompanied by his cavalry, General Domitius also withdrew into the hills, abandoning his camp to the enemy.

The Battle of Nicopolis was over. It had resulted in a resounding success for Pharnaces and his Bosporans—a "notable victory" according to historian Appian—and a bitter defeat for Caesar's deputy. Precise casualty figures are unknown. As General Domitius's subordinates were able to round up surviving troops in the hills and regroup with their commander, the losses were tallied. The Deiotarans had lost more than half their number, men who had either been killed or were still running. The Pontic Legion had lost about two-thirds of its men. The 36th Legion had fared best of all, losing just 250 men in the battle. All told, Roman losses would have approached 9,000. Included among the dead were a number of tribunes, young colonels of the Equestrian Order who had perished leading their legions and cohorts, several of them from Rome's best families—"men of distinction and renown," according to Colonel Hirtius.

During the afternoon, Domitius led his bloodied, regrouped units back the way they had come, along the mountain ridge toward Cappadocia. From Cappadocia he would retreat all the way back to Asia, to lick his wounds and reequip, and to try to restore the confidence of his remaining troops. In doing so, he left the East open to Pharnaces and his victorious army.

Pharnaces was delighted with himself. He had just emulated his famous father and defeated a Roman army, and with only minimal casualties. The way lay open for him to consolidate his control over Armenia Minor and to advance unopposed into Pontus, which had always been the objective of his invasion. After looting and burning Domitius' abandoned camp, he led his army across the mountains into Pontus. Over the next few weeks Pharnaces' army stormed and looted scores of wealthy Pontic towns and cities that shut their gates to him, as he took full control of the province and as his troops glutted themselves with pillage, rape, and destruction. Colonel Hirtius says that Pharnaces behaved "as a conqueror and cruel despot" throughout the conquest of Pontus.

According to Appian, at the city of Amisus in Pontus, which held out against Pharnaces for some time until his troops succeeded in storming it, Pharnaces sold the entire population into slavery, castrating all the boys of the city. Hirtius indicates this practice of castration was more widespread, inflicted by Pharnaces throughout Pontus on "those men whose beauty recommended them" to such a punishment—a punishment more wretched than death, in Hirtius's opinion.

With little effort, Pharnaces had recovered his hereditary kingdom. Made arrogant by his success at the Battle of Nicopolis and the easy conquest of Pontus, and knowing from the captured Roman dispatches that Caesar was in dire straits in Egypt, he could see no reason why he could not use his army to spread his sovereignty throughout the East, the way his father had. These Romans, he would have declared to his celebrating followers, weren't the mighty soldiers they were cracked up to be.

XII

REINFORCEMENTS

No one at Alexandria yet had the slightest idea that a Roman army led by one of Caesar's generals had been defeated in Armenia Minor. As the siege of Caesar's 6th and 28th Legions continued unabated in the Egyptian capital, the possibility of Roman reinforcements reaching Caesar would have increasingly exercised the minds of the men on either side—for both sides knew that if reinforcements were to reach the Romans, Caesar could be in a position to lift the siege and take the offensive.

With this in mind, Ganymede, the new commander of the Egyptian army since his mistress, Princess Arsinoe, had engineered the permanent removal of General Achillas, now set out to galvanize the dispirited members of the Egyptian royal council with a powerful speech. This speech by one of the Egyptian leaders was again chronicled verbatim by Colonel Hirtius—suggesting that its contents were later related to Hirtius by someone who had been present at the meeting in question. From later events it is not impossible—in fact, it is quite likely—that these details were subsequently provided by Ganymede himself.

In this speech, Ganymede showed a good tactical mind and considerable skills in the areas of improvisation and organization. Yes, Ganymede acknowledged to his fellow council members, the Egyptian forces had lost more than 110 ships during the disastrous fires lit by Caesar's men, but that should not discourage the Egyptians from making the water a battleground.

"Alexandrians are seafaring men," he went on, "with many of you receiving daily training in sailing since childhood. The sea is natural to you and a part of your everyday lives. You should be taking advantage of your skills in building and sailing watercraft to achieve your earlier ambition, curtailed by the fire, of denying the sea to Caesar and preventing reinforcements and supplies reaching him over water."

There were many calls of agreement and nodding heads in his audience.

"It is merely a matter of using your native intelligence and the resources of Alexandria," Ganymede assured his listeners. "For one thing," he said, "we still have a number of small craft we can employ, if only in the harbor."

As his listeners agreed with him, Ganymede continued, pointing out that a flotilla of light frigates of fifty oars or so was stationed at the seven mouths of the Nile, where the great river entered the Mediterranean. The usual task of these frigates was that of collecting customs duties. But what was the point of customs duties when Alexandria was occupied by an invader and the city was in need of warships? Ganymede declared that these vessels should be immediately recalled to Alexandria and pressed into military service.

Then he reminded his colleagues that there were many old, abandoned ships, now mere hulks, sitting in royal dockyards attached to the palace, at the so-called King's Harbor, a small, walled-off dock on the northeastern side of the Great Harbor. Although these ships had not been near the water in years, they could and should be resurrected by the Alexandrians, Ganymede said, using their boat-building skills, and sent against Caesar's ships. All this made a great deal of sense, and there was much enthusiastic agreement from the reinvigorated members of the Egyptian council.

Fired up by their new general, the Egyptians quickly recalled the customs boats from the mouths of the Nile and inspected the hulks in Alexandria's royal dockyards. It became apparent that several dozen ships in the royal dockyards, including heavy cruisers, might be repaired sufficiently to be pressed into service against the Romans. After all, Ganymede told his colleagues, it wasn't as if they had to prepare these craft for a long sea voyage. They would only be used in the harbor.

It was soon found that in Alexandria's hot climate, the timbers of the old ships had remained in remarkably good condition, and only minor repairs would be needed on the hulls. It was decided not to bother with masts or sails, and to rely on oarpower alone. But even this presented a problem: none of the hulks was equipped with oars. And the Egyptians had used the last of their spare timber building a wooden barrier along the front of the docks of the Great Harbor to prevent Caesar's twenty-one cruisers from getting in close to shore and using their artillery against the Egyptians holding the docks. Now someone suggested removing the roofs of city colonnades, gymnasia, and public buildings and stripping them of their rafters to provide the timber they needed for oar manufacture. The idea was immediately seized on. Without letting up on the military operations against the Romans around the perimeters of the encircled Roman sector, large Egyptian work parties repaired ships, while others spread through the city, dismantling roofs with enthusiasm and energy.

On the other side of the battlements, two days after they'd dug the new wells in their sector of Alexandria, the news that Roman reinforcements were close by came as a great relief to Caesar and his men. To the legionaries of the 6th, the tidings, delivered via a small rowboat that slipped into the Great Harbor at night without the Egyptians knowing, vindicated their belief that Caesar knew best. And it was news to make the panicky youngsters of the 28th eat humble pie. The questions now were: How many men were coming to their relief? From which units? And when would they arrive?

Caesar knew some of the answers to these questions. The reinforcements consisted of some five thousand former Pompeian legionaries of the new 37th Legion who had signed up on the Farsala battlefield, plus a small contingent of auxiliaries. Commander Cassius had not let Caesar down— the reinforcements had been sent by General Domitius from Asia as a result of Cassius's mission. As to when these extra troops would reach Alexandria, that was a trickier question to answer, as the convoy was stranded.

The 37th Legion's convoy of thirty or so merchantmen and an escort of thirteen warships of various types had chanced the last leg of its journey across the open sea, and had made landfall too far to the west. The vessels were now anchored in a sheltered cove some miles from Alexandria, on the Libyan coast, unable to make any further progress because of a strong east wind blowing in their crews' faces. The message that Caesar received via the ship's boat sent from the convoy commander also informed him that the reinforcements were suffering from a lack of freshwater and would soon be in no shape to fight anyone if water was not soon found for them.

With reinforcements so frustratingly near, yet still out of reach as the wind blew hard from the east without relent for days on end, the impatient Caesar decided that he would tow the relief convoy all the way into the Great Harbor if he had to. In the night, taking just a few staff members with him, he stole out of the Roman sector of Alexandria and slipped along silent cobbled streets to the docks, then took a small boat out to one of his cruisers anchored in the harbor.

With the dawn, Caesar sailed from the Great Harbor, leading all twenty-one of his warships out to sea. The Roman flotilla then set a westerly course, with the wind behind it, to follow the coast toward the Libyan cove where the relief convoy was sheltering. On shore, the bemused Egyptians, seeing the Roman ships depart and then turn west and hug the coast as they headed for Libya, but not having the slightest idea what they were up to, ordered a cavalry squadron to shadow them along the coast.

At a coastal village called Chersonesus, Caesar, conscious of the water problems of his reinforcements and the limited water supply he had back in Alexandria, put in and landed some of his seamen with water amphorae and orders to fill them and then quickly return to their ships. Most did as they were told, using the town's wells, and his ships' holds were within several hours loaded with water-filled jars. But one band of oarsmen decided they would loot the place while they were at it. These men strayed too far and walked straight into the hands of the skulking men of the Egyptian cavalry squadron, who had been watching proceedings from cover. The seamen were quickly taken prisoner.

Caesar didn't wait for the missing crewmen to return—there was much he had to accomplish before he ran out of daylight. So he continued along the coast minus the missing men. Meanwhile the seamen, prisoners now, revealed to their Egyptian captors under questioning that Caesar himself was aboard one of the ships. More importantly, they told their interrogators that Caesar had not brought any troops with him. A messenger from the cavalry unit was sent galloping back to Alexandria with this vital information.

As soon as he received this dispatch, Ganymede saw an opportunity to strike Caesar while he was at a disadvantage. By this stage the Egyptian work parties at the docks had managed to refloat and reequip four cruisers of the *quadrireme* class. In addition, as had been hoped, carpenters had succeeded in fashioning oars from rafters stripped from city buildings, and there were more than enough willing rowers to man them. The four cruisers and the former customs frigates were immediately loaded with heavily armed marines and dispatched from the Inner Harbor with orders to intercept the larger Roman formation. It was a risk to all on board to send the quartet of resurrected cruisers to sea, but if they could disrupt Caesar's plans—or better yet, deliver him a crippling blow—it would be worth the risk.

It was late in the afternoon when lookouts on Caesar's ships spotted the small Egyptian fleet making toward them from the east at high speed, with the wind behind it. Despite the fact that his ships outnumbered the enemy's, Caesar chose not to give battle. Instead, he steered his squadron into shallow water and ran most of his ships onto the beach. Colonel Hirtius ascribes to Caesar two reasons for avoiding a battle: he had no soldiers

or marines with which to fight, and the enemy knew these waters far better than his captains did and would be at an advantage if a battle extended
into the night, when Caesar's masters would be as good as blind.

Not all of Caesar's vessels could fit onto the small beach; a heavy
cruiser from Rhodes had to drop anchor some distance from the shore.
Occupying Caesar's right wing, the cruiser was several hundred yards from
the rest of Caesar's ships. Seeing this, the Egyptian commanders made a
beeline for the lone Rhodian cruiser. The Egyptian flotilla swept in, surrounded the ship from Rhodes, and began peppering it with missiles. The
plucky Rhodian crewmen put up a mighty fight, returning fire as best they
could, but, heavily outnumbered, it was obvious to observers on the beach
that they were doomed if left to their own devices. Their countrymen from
Rhodes couldn't stand by and let them be overpowered and wiped out,
and before long Admiral Euphranor and his colleagues spontaneously
launched their cruisers to go to their aid, without even conferring with
Caesar.

Seeing the eight Rhodians launching, a furious Caesar had no choice
but to commit all he had to the fray, or run the risk of losing more than
one cruiser. All the beached ships were heaved back into the water, their
crews scrambled aboard, oars dug into the water, bows came around, and a
course was set for the Egyptians.

Well in advance of the rest of Caesar's ships, the eight skippers of the
Rhodian ships, determined to help their own, quickly maneuvered into
attacking positions and went into action. The opening gambit in a classical sea battle was normally an attempt to ram and sink the opposition. All
warships of the era were constructed with a large pointed ram, nicknamed
a "beak," projecting from the prow. Most of a ship's beak was just below
the water's surface, and if it hit an enemy craft side-on with sufficient impact, this ram would either splinter timbers or force an opening between
planking below the waterline. If the hole created was large enough, the
damaged ship would fill with water and sink.

In the fading light, one of the Egyptian cruisers either didn't see the
Rhodian ships coming to the rescue or was so determined to keep up its
attack on the moored ship it didn't attempt to get out of the way of the
Rhodian cruiser that bore down on it with its oars pulling at maximum
rate. With a sickening thud the Rhodian vessel plowed into the Egyptian
quadrireme broadside and came to an abrupt halt.

As missiles flew from the decks of both ships, the Rhodian oarsmen
backed water furiously, and with a creak of shattered timbers it disen-
gaged, its beak slipping from the hole it had driven in the Egyptian's side.

The Egyptian cruiser began to quickly fill with water, listing badly to one side. Those crewmen and marines who could swim—and in these times, few could—abandoned their posts and dove into the bay. Men who could not swim stayed with the ship, and most drowned when it went down.

A second Egyptian *quadrireme* was rammed by another of the attacking Rhodians, but after the Rhodian backed off, the damage proved insufficient to sink it. So several of Caesar's ships ranged close alongside the stricken Egyptian vessel, like wolves surrounding and hounding a wounded deer. Large, harpoonlike iron grappling hooks called *harpogos* were shot from catapults on the Rhodian decks. The hooks flew through the air with ropes trailing behind them, and connected with the stricken Egyptian cruiser's woodwork. The damaged Egyptian was snared, and reeled in like a fish on a hook. Cheering boarding parties of armed Rhodian sailors swarmed onto its deck. The ship's defenders were quickly overcome, and the cruiser was captured.

The two remaining Egyptian cruisers lost so many of their marines to missiles from the Roman ships that they pulled out of the battle and fled east, with their decks awash with blood. The open Egyptian frigates received frightening numbers of casualties from the missiles launched by the much larger Roman ships as they towered beside them, and they, too, turned tail and ran for home.

With night falling, Caesar chose not to give chase. None of Caesar's ships had been lost, and casualties among his crews were comparatively light. With his oarsmen and sailors exhilarated at their success against the Egyptian marines, he spent the night there in the lonely Libyan bay. Nothing more is heard of the captured Egyptian *quadrireme*, and it seems it sank in the night.

Next day, as soon as it was light, Caesar continued on along the coast to the west and located the anchored fleet of Roman transports and their thirteen escorts. He shared his water with the reinforcements; then, with most of the thirty-four oar-powered warships of his now enlarged navy taking a transport in tow, and with sails lowered, he set off back to Alexandria against what was now a gentle easterly breeze. The few now greatly outnumbered Egyptian warships, which had returned to Alexandria the previous night, did not venture out to contest Caesar's return. Later that day he was able to tow his heavily laden transports past the Pharos lighthouse and his cheering, waving troops who occupied it, into the Great Harbor, where all his ships dropped anchor.

Now that Roman reinforcements had arrived, a new phase in the Battle of Alexandria was about to begin.

XIII

TAKING THE ISLAND

Caesar's ships lay at anchor in Alexandria's Great Harbor. Instead of sending his reinforcements from the 37th Legion and their few auxiliary companions ashore, Caesar kept them on board ship, spreading them out between the merchantmen and all the vessels of his now sizable fleet of thirty-four warships. There was neither the room nor the necessity to house them with the 6th and 28th Legions ashore in Alexandria's occupied sector.

The reinforcements had brought grain with them, Caesar had sourced some water for them en route to locating them, and they could shelter under the leather tarpaulins that the crews stretched over the decks at night to provide warmth and to collect rainwater. In this way Caesar could use the fresh, newly arrived troops as marines if another naval battle developed, while reserving the more experienced 6th and the 28th for tasks on land.

Another factor also came into play. Throughout Caesar's career as a general, whenever one of his units let him down he invariably turned his back on it and called on other units to take the forefront in future battles. The 28th Legion had let him down through its mutinous questioning of his orders and the wisdom of staying in Alexandria. Worse, its men had panicked over the sabotaged water supply when the veterans of the 6th had not. He would not forget the way the 28th acted; and when it came to the next phases of his Alexandrian campaign, it would be relegated to guard duty around the Roman sector while the newly arrived 37th and the trusty 6th were allocated the more dangerous missions, the missions that could only enhance their reputations and status.

On Caesar's return to Alexandria the Egyptians immediately commenced offensive operations against the newly arrived vessels. From time to time previously they had sent fireboats from the Inner Harbor through the two arches in the Hepstadion, the causeway linking Pharos Island with the mainland, aiming to set alight Caesar's warships anchored in the Great Harbor, and now they resumed the same tactic. To protect his precious warships against this kind of attack, Caesar seems to have placed his cargo ships around the outside of the anchorage, like wagons circled against an Indian attack in more recent times, with the more valuable warships moored inside the circle.

This time the Egyptians had success with their small-boat tactics. The fact that the warships were inside the ring worked for the attackers— artillery on the warships couldn't lower their elevation to fire at the small craft once they were close alongside the merchantmen. Soon, burning Egyptian small boats were banging alongside Roman cargo ships, with their flames licking the woodwork and racing up into the rigging of the tubby "round ships," as they were called. Fires ignited by the burning small craft caught and spread. According to Cassius Dio, several of Caesar's merchantmen were burned to the waterline in this way, while others were captured after their crews and passengers abandoned them in fear of the fires. The captured Roman cargo ships were victoriously towed away to the Inner Harbor.

The Egyptians now also had maritime success of another kind. Within a few days of Caesar's victory in the naval contest down the coast, and "against all expectations" of the Romans, says Colonel Hirtius, the Egyptians deployed dozens of warships in the Inner Harbor. These were the remaining ships that Ganymede's work parties had been laboring to resurrect when the first four had been sent against Caesar. From high points in the city Caesar's amazed troops were able to see five quinqueremes, twenty-two quadriremes, and at least four smaller biremes undertaking rowing trials on the Inner Harbor just days after the battle off the Libyan coast.

This unexpected development alarmed everyone in the Roman camp, including Caesar, who realized that the enemy once again possessed the capacity to cut off his continued supply by sea. As usual, Caesar now took the initiative. He ordered preparations for a naval battle to destroy the Egyptian fleet, calling on the men of the 37th Legion to select some two thousand of their number to serve as marines in the coming struggle. The rest would be transferred to the merchantmen to sit out the battle.

There was something of a double-edged sword about this request from Caesar. It was great honor to be asked by the commander in chief to take the lead in the upcoming operation. But legionaries considered marines their inferiors. Marines were invariably freedmen, former slaves, and were not Roman citizens, which put them low in the Roman social order, well below citizen soldiers of the legions. Like legionaries, marines signed up for long-term paid enlistments, but their enlistment periods lasted considerably longer than those of legionaries, and they were paid much less. Because ships' decks were often wet, and in battle sometimes awash with blood, marines served barefoot, to ensure a better footing. Even when they were on land they went without shoes. For proud, status-conscious Roman legionaries, to be called on to serve as marines was asking a great deal of them. And this was why Caesar asked the men of the 37th to choose those among them who must swallow their pride, remove their footwear, and find their sea legs. But choose they did.

When, a day or so later, all was ready, and with the chosen men from the 37th Legion aboard his cruisers and frigates ready to go to war as marines, Caesar boarded his flagship. He was very conscious of the fact that although the 37th Legion had provided the marines he had asked for, the men were not enthusiastic about it. Before any battle, if time permitted, Caesar always gave a speech to his troops, to fire them up, as was the custom of the times. He knew that on this occasion that speech would be particularly important.

Before the order to sail was given, the captains of all thirty-four of his warships and officers of the 37th Legion were summoned aboard Caesar's flagship. Once on board, they heard him give a speech to the soldiers and crew on his own vessel. Surrounded by these officers and his staff, he told the men crowding the deck around him and hanging from the rigging what he had been telling them for days, that if the Egyptians came off better in a naval contest they would have mastery of the sea. If that were to happen, he reminded his listeners, neither sea nor land offered the Romans a way of escape.

"It seems a hard and pitiful state of affairs," Caesar said, "that a mere handful of you should be struggling for decisive victory and the safety of us all. If any one of you fails in spirit or courage, the remainder will have to look out for themselves without having had the opportunity of fighting on their own behalf."

Having reminded his temporary marines of the responsibility they bore, for the fate not only of themselves but also of all those who must wait behind, Caesar gave his officers their individual instructions. They then returned to their ships, where they repeated Caesar's message to their own men.

Colonel Hirtius was to say that the men in the ranks impressed the same point on their colleagues—about so much depending on so few. Some of them had volunteered for this fight in the unaccustomed role of marine; others had been nominated by the ranks to take part. Either way,

Hirtius would note, they had an obligation not to let down the men who were staying behind and relying on them to succeed. And they knew it. In very emphatically imparting this responsibility to them, Caesar was cleverly sidestepping the matter of service as marines. Now all that mattered was not letting down the team, or themselves, or Caesar.

The two anchors on Caesar's cruiser came rattling up from the harbor floor. On command, oars jutted from the rowing ports along both sides of the flagship, then bit into the water. To the slow beat of the timekeeper's mallets, the oars mechanically dragged through the water, and the Rhodian warship began to make its way toward the harbor entrance, with Caesar's standard fluttering in the breeze. Behind, the thirty-three other ships of Caesar's augmented battle fleet followed, leaving the merchantmen riding at anchor, with, from their decks, their 37th Legion passengers watching their comrades go to meet their destiny. Some of the men left behind would have been waving, cheering, and applauding their departing colleagues. Others, their arms folded, would have been silent and apprehensive as they watched the fleet leave the Great Harbor.

Turning left once they cleared the harbor, and sailing around Pharos Island, the Roman ships approached the Inner Harbor from the west. The Egyptians quickly saw that the Romans meant to do battle, and their ships promptly prepared to meet them. With trumpets summoning them to their battle stations, and amid an air of excitement and anticipation, thousands of Egyptians ran along the docks to join their ships—sailors, rowers, and marines—yelling encouragement to one another. The men who were to serve as marines in this action had been carefully chosen from among their countrymen for the valor they had shown to date in this war with the Romans. Untying from the docks or upping anchor, the Egyptian ships swiftly moved to take up their appointed positions in their battle lines. Both sides were full of confidence according to Colonel Hirtius, as their ships formed up, facing each other.

Entrance to the Inner Harbor from the west was made difficult by extensive shoals, through which there was only a narrow, deep-water passage, which could prove treacherous in all but the calmest conditions. This was why the Egyptians had created the arches in the causeway that allowed craft to enter the Great Harbor from the Inner Harbor. The opposing fleets formed up on either side of these shoals, the Egyptians inside the Inner Harbor, the Romans outside, in the open sea.

The Egyptians placed their twenty-seven principal ships in a front line, with their frigates forming a second line behind them. They also brought out a large number of small boats equipped with quick-firing catapults, their crews armed with bolts dipped in tar and holding burning firebrands. Caesar assigned his nine powerful Rhodian heavy cruisers to his right wing, and the eight cruisers and frigates from Pontus to his left. He left a gap of a little under half a mile between these two squadrons. Behind this front line he placed his lighter ships from Asia and Lycia. Prior to upping anchor he had given each skipper in the second line a particular ship in the front line that he was to shadow and support. Caesar himself was aboard a Rhodian ship on the right.

If there was going to be a battle, one side or the other would have to send ships through the narrow channel in the shoals to reach their opponents, but for some time the two sides faced off across the shoals with neither commander prepared to commit vessels to the channel, each knowing that once through, they could be cut off on the other side of the shoals.

In the city, the men of the 6th Legion and their comrades of the 28th had taken up vantage points on rooftops and at high windows in their sector, so they could watch what took place in the Inner Harbor. Throughout the city, Egyptian soldiers, militia, and civilians did the same, making themselves comfortable, as if preparing to watch a sporting event. On both sides, men offered prayers and vows to their gods in hopes of bringing victory to their men out on the water.

For perhaps an hour, nothing happened. The ships of both sides did not advance, with their oars only occasionally moving to maintain their positions. Finally, tiring of the standoff and impatient to come to grips with the Egyptians, the Rhodian commander, Admiral Euphranor, set his cruiser in motion and came around alongside Caesar's flagship.

"It seems to me, Caesar," the Rhodian admiral called across the strip of water separating the two warships as they wallowed just yards apart, his words being noted by an officer at Caesar's side, "you're afraid that if you enter the shoals with your leading ships you might be forced to fight before you can deploy the rest of the fleet." He pointed to the ships of the Rhodian squadron. "Leave it to us. We'll bear the brunt of the fighting while the rest are following up. We won't let you down. We're ashamed and indignant to watch those people flaunting themselves before us any longer."

So, praising Euphranor's valor and enthusiasm, and knowing that the Rhodian would probably launch into the attack whether he approved or not, Caesar agreed to Euphranor's plan and gave him permission to take four of his cruisers through the channel to engage the enemy. After wishing Euphranor luck, he signaled for the rest of the fleet to follow his lead when he gave the signal for an all-out attack.

As Euphranor's four cruisers filed through the channel one by one, Caesar held back. Once inside the Inner Harbor, Euphranor's ships moved to left and right and formed up in line abreast. The ships of the Egyptian front line began to move forward. All of the Egyptian cruisers closed around the Rhodians like jackals. Then four of their number increased to attack speed, and each charged one of the four waiting Rhodians. Euphranor and his three fellow Rhodian masters were experts at this game. Seeing an enemy ship bearing down on them, they were able to issue orders that brought oars on one side or another into action and that accordingly brought their bow around so that they were always facing the enemy head-on.

If, as the captain of a classical warship, you couldn't catch your opponent broadside, your second objective was to charge him from front or rear, and then run alongside him with your own oars withdrawn at the last moment, using your hull and your momentum to run over his projecting oars on one side. If you did this correctly, you would crush the other ship's oars like matchsticks, leaving him as powerless and immobile as if you had lopped off a man's leg.

But Euphranor and his trio of fellow skippers were all able to maneuver so that they met the Egyptian attacks head-on. With shuddering crunches all eight cruisers collided and came to a dead stop. Then their oars began to dig and pull, and all the adversaries reversed away, launching missiles as they went. No critical damage had been done to the ships of either side. As the combatants separated, another four Egyptian cruisers charged the Rhodians. Again Euphranor and his colleagues were able to swing their prows around and meet the attacks head-on, and again the Egyptians smashed into the Rhodians with almighty thuds. It was like pairs of mountain rams butting each other.

Caesar had held back long enough. Seeing the two sets of cruisers exhausting their crews without result, he raised his battle standard high and set his own Rhodian cruiser in motion. Soon he was leading the remainder of his fleet through the channel to the other side of the shoals, and his ships were fanning out to follow their individual orders. In response, the rest of the Egyptian ships moved forward to meet the Romans.

As the newly arrived craft filled the confined space of the Inner Harbor, there was no room for high-speed ramming. It was now just a matter of getting alongside an enemy and boarding him. No science was required, no seafaring skill was called for. And the advantage of numbers was nullified by the fierce determination of a few.

Some battles, the Romans said, were won more by Mars than by Minerva—more by courage than by skill. According to Colonel Hirtius, victory on the Alexandrian harbor all came down to courage—plus, he said, the knowledge on the Roman side that defeat was not an option. If Caesar could not gain control of the harbor, he was doomed. The Egyptians, on the other hand, could always console themselves with the thought that even a loss in a battle here did not mean they had lost the war. And that heightened desperation level seems to have made the difference as the Roman troops of the 37th Legion, equipped with swords and axes, swarmed aboard enemy vessels.

Three Egyptian biremes were sunk by boarding parties, and another was captured. One of the largest of the Egyptian cruisers, a quinquereme, also was captured. The rest of the Egyptian ships turned and fled back toward the docks. When Roman ships gave chase to the fleeing Egyptians, passing close by the island of Pharos on their left, they came under heavy covering fire from Egyptian forces occupying piers and waterside buildings on the island's southwestern shore, and were forced to withdraw to avoid a hail of heavy stones and burning darts with smoky tails. The battle had ended.

Not a single Roman ship was lost in the engagement. As Caesar led his victorious craft back through the shoals and around Pharos Island to the Great Harbor, he would have been thinking seriously of another waterborne raid on the Inner Harbor to finally eliminate the still substantial Egyptian fleet, whose capital ships outnumbered his own. But, as his officers would have pointed out, the Egyptian forces occupying most of Pharos Island effectively protected the Inner Harbor.

Another Egyptian fireboat raid through the causeway arches soon after the Roman ships returned to anchor in the Great Harbor, although unsuccessful, would have made clear, too, how vital it was to seal off the causeway. While Caesar had a toehold on the island with troops occupying the lighthouse on the eastern tip, that was not enough to control the island as a whole, and he decided that before he did anything else he must occupy both the island and the causeway.

According to legend, the low, rocky Pharos Island had, prior to the coming of Alexander the Great, only been home to a colony of seals. Now it housed a suburb of Alexandria that was in effect a large town, with, in peacetime, a population of twenty-five thousand or more, many of them sailors, fishermen, and shipbuilders. The island's buildings mirrored those of downtown Alexandria, except they were not as high—the tallest were only thirty feet tall, according to Hirtius. Philo of Alexander was to say that there was no Jewish population on Pharos Island, but once a year the Jews of Alexandria crossed to the island for a festival to celebrate the first translation of the commandments of Moses into Greek, which had taken place on the island. Many other Alexandrians also attended this annual festival.

By this stage in the fighting at Alexandria between Caesar and the Egyptians, now several months old, some of the women, children, and elderly of Pharos Island would have evacuated to the mainland, leaving their menfolk to serve on the Egyptian warships and as militia holding the island in conjunction with the regular army. Yet, despite the dangers, many civilians still occupied their island homes.

Caesar made preparations to take the island, selecting ten legionary cohorts comprising four thousand men for an amphibious landing, backed by handpicked members of the auxiliary reinforcements and those men among his five hundred Gallic cavalry troopers whom he thought would be suited to act as infantry. Most of the legionaries chosen for this operation would have come from the 37th Legion, as they were already on the ships in the harbor. But it seems that to lead the operation Caesar had one or both cohorts of the 6th Legion make a dash from their position in the occupied zone and join their comrades in the harbor.

Within days of the naval engagement in the Inner Harbor the Roman operation to take Pharos Island was under way. It began with Caesar's larger warships attacking the island from the northern, seaward side with missile fire. Once some Egyptian defenders had been drawn off to counter this attack, Caesar launched his infantry against the southern side. He personally directed this landing operation from the deck of one of his warships. For the landing he had assembled scores of ships' boats and fishing boats. These landing craft came under sustained fire from the rocky shore and the rooftops of buildings lining the shore. At the same time, the Egyptians sent five warships and a number of smaller craft from the Inner Harbor via the causeway arches, and these skillfully maneuvered to keep the Romans from making a landing.

Another problem encountered by the Romans was a natural one. The water around the steep, craggy shoreline of the island on the Great Harbor side was found to be quite deep—too deep for troops to jump overboard from their landing craft without submerging. Finally, one boatload of legionaries, improvising a sounding rope to determine the depth, managed to find a spot beside the forbidding rocks where it was shallow enough for them to jump overboard. Into the water they went, and from there they clambered onto the rocks.

From this point these troops were able to climb the rock face and reach flat, solid land. Other boats quickly followed their example and landed troops at the same place. When they saw Roman troops successfully making a landing, Egyptian militia formed up on level ground in their path to prevent their expanding their foothold. The panting, waterlogged, sweating legionaries who'd made it ashore formed up in their units; then, apparently led by the men of the 6th, they made a determined charge—so determined that it scattered the defenders. Seeing this, the remaining civilians on the island abandoned their homes in terror and fled en masse in the thousands across the causeway to the city and safety behind Egyptian lines.

To counter this landing on Pharos Island, Ganymede had Egyptian marines quickly mobilized. These men landed on the southwestern end of the island, from ships in the Inner Harbor, and once on Pharos they hurried to throw back the Romans now streaming ashore at the opposite end. The Egyptian reinforcements hastily occupied buildings in the Romans' path and took up defensive positions on their flat roofs, preparing to rain down javelins, stones, and slingshot on the Romans.

The legionaries had not come prepared with scaling ladders or other assault equipment, but this didn't prevent them from taking one building after another. Again it seems that the 6th Legion was to the fore in this gritty, determined offensive, its troops moving from house to house, securing one before attacking the next, fighting their way upstairs to the rooftops and slaying the defenders, leaving bloody bodies in heaps as they progressively cleared building after building.

Terrified Egyptian marines, seeing and hearing their comrades in neighboring houses being methodically and ruthlessly slain by the veteran legionaries as one building after another fell to them, lost their earlier courage. Many panicked. Terror robs men of reason and judgment, so Colonel Hirtius was to observe, and this proved to be the case now. Some of the Egyptians threw away their weapons, cast off their armor, and dove from the tops of harborside buildings into the water and swam to the mainland—a distance of three-quarters of a mile in Hirtius's estimation. Many more surrendered to the unstoppable Roman troops rather than fight or die.

All of Pharos Island fell to the Roman invaders, and with barely a casualty in their own ranks. In the process, the legionaries killed a number of Egyptian fighters and took another six thousand prisoner. It seems that these Egyptian prisoners were kept on the island, guarded by the auxiliary troops, with the intent that they would be sold into slavery once the war was over. As their reward, Caesar let his long-suffering men loot the island's deserted houses and public buildings for an hour or two. In other places, at other times, Caesar's army was invariably trailed by an entourage of merchants and prostitutes. The merchants would set up for business in the center of the legions' camps and buy the soldiers' booty from them, and the prostitutes would soon after relieve the legionaries of much of their profit. Caesar never prohibited fraternization between his soldiers and whores and local women. "My soldiers fight just as well when they are stinking of perfume," Suetonius quotes him saying more than once. With neither women to carouse with nor merchants to deal with, on this occasion Caesar's legionaries could do no more than pile up their loot and make plans to sell it after they had won this Alexandrian campaign.

Once his men had pillaged all they could carry and made their booty piles, their commander had them demolish buildings along the waterfront on the southern side of the island. During the afternoon they used stone from the demolitions to build a fort commanding the causeway arch nearest the island and to fill in the opening beneath the bridge over the arch, making it impassable to shipping. The Egyptians had begun to build a fort at the other end of the causeway, the city end, to protect the second, smaller arch. That night, leaving a mixed force of eighteen hundred men from various units, not including the 6th Legion, occupying the fort at the island end of the causeway, Caesar took the remainder of his assault troops off in small boats.

With the Egyptians still controlling the city end of the causeway and controlling one arch through which they could still launch attacks on the Great Harbor, the following day Caesar initiated a new attack, this time against the Egyptians' causeway fort. While he himself supervised the operation from a frigate in the harbor, the eighteen hundred men on shore advanced down the causeway from their new Pharos Island fort while Caesar's warships unleashed a barrage of bolts, arrows, and stones against the unfinished Egyptian fort.

The covering fire was so intense that the Egyptians at this position were forced to vacate their position and retreat to the city, allowing Caesar's troops moving down the causeway to easily occupy the incomplete fort. Caesar ordered these troops to then fill in the archway with rocks, as they had at the far end, and to build a barricade in the water on the western side of the arch. Caesar had his vessel tie up beside the causeway, and he then climbed up onto the causeway itself with members of his staff to personally supervise this engineering work.

After the Roman troops had been carrying rocks from demolished buildings on Pharos Island along the causeway to the bridge for an hour or so and dropping the stones into the water, the Egyptians mounted a counterattack. Massing troops and artillery at the city end of the causeway they opened up a heavy barrage of missiles on the legionaries working on the causeway. At the same time they sent men in small boats ranging along the western side of the causeway. Seeing this, a number of Caesar's smaller ships, his undecked frigates, put in to the causeway, and their crews clambered up onto the causeway, some men intending to watch the battle at the southern end, while others soon became actively involved in the melee by raining stones and slingshot down on the Egyptians in the small boats on the far side of the causeway, driving many of the boats away.

Ganymede, the Egyptian commander, now saw an opportunity to embarrass Caesar. While the Romans' attention was focused on the southern end of the causeway, the Egyptians ferried a number of troops across the Inner Harbor and landed them on the island near the northern end of the causeway. When the seamen on the causeway saw Egyptians advancing down the causeway toward them from the direction of the island, and saw Caesar himself then withdraw to his ship, they lost their nerve and ran back to their own vessels.

As the Egyptians came dashing up to them, waving their weapons and yelling triumphantly, the sailors tumbled in terrified disorder down the side of the causeway and crushed together to board the nearest vessels. Crewmen still on board, seeing so many men trying to get aboard at once, and also seeing the Egyptian troops close behind, hauled in their gangways and began to push off. Desperate men, most of whom couldn't swim, clung to the sides of ships, which soon became overloaded. One after the other, Roman vessels rolled over and capsized, or simply sank, there beside the causeway, beneath the weight of too many passengers.

The mayhem caused by this disaster, with all the yelling and cursing and screaming from the seamen and their attackers, caused the eighteen hundred Roman troops at the southern fort to look around in alarm. As it was, they were taking casualties from the heavy Egyptian artillery fire, and now, fearing they would be cut off on the causeway, with Egyptians at both ends, and seeing their ships pulling away, they deserted the unfinished fort and dashed for the last ships, including Caesar's, calling out for their comrades not to go without them. These soldiers came slithering down the side of the causeway in disarray, and tried to get aboard the last vessels before they departed.

Caesar, who had already seen several frigates go down, and confronted by the sight of heavily equipped soldiers clinging onto the side of his own ship, and feeling it begin to list alarmingly, quickly removed his helmet, armor, and sword belt, and dove into the water, as did his staff around him. The ship soon rolled over on its side and sank like a stone, taking all on board with it. Caesar, being a strong swimmer, swam out to the nearest small boat and was hauled aboard, before being transferred to one of the larger warships anchored some distance away.

Hirtius, Appian, and Suetonius all describe this incident. Suetonius, in his account, wrote that Caesar swam with documents in one hand and dragging his valuable general's cloak, his *paludamentum,* with his teeth. Suetonius wrote that the cloak was purple, but it was only in Suetonius's time, the imperial era, that commanders in chief wore purple cloaks. In Caesar's day it was still a scarlet cloak. Appian and Dio say that Caesar eventually had to discard the cloak, and that the Egyptians later fished it out of the harbor and displayed it as a trophy, "as if they had captured him himself," says Dio.

The day ended badly for the Romans. Hirtius says that 400 legionaries died in the harbor and on the causeway—some tried to make a stand, seeing the chaos in the water, only to be overwhelmed and killed by Egyptians who attacked along the causeway from both ends. About 450 sailors also perished. The Roman losses would have been even heavier had Caesar not sent small boats from his fleet to the scene of the disaster beside the causeway, where, under fire from Egyptians all along the causeway, the crews valiantly plucked soldiers and sailors from the water where they were trying to swim for it, and from the hulks of overturned Roman frigates.

It was an unmitigated defeat for Caesar and a badly needed victory for the Egyptians, who retook the causeway, occupied both forts, and unblocked the two archways, then reopened them to navigation. As a result, they could continue to launch attacks on the Great Harbor from the Inner Harbor. It also seems that they reclaimed all of Pharos Island but the lighthouse and freed from captivity the six thousand prisoners being held there by the Romans.

There would have been great celebrations in Egyptian quarters that night. Caesar's men had been dealt a morale-sapping blow, had been driven into retreat, and had suffered heavy casualties, including almost a thousand dead. The Romans also had lost a number of ships, sunk in the harbor. And Caesar, whose string of successes so far in this conflict had been brought to an abrupt end at the causeway, had himself been made to swim for his life. Here was clear evidence that Caesar could be beaten, so Ganymede would have told his people. Now it was just a matter of capitalizing on this successful recapture of the Hepstadion and Pharos Island, and finishing off the Romans.

XIV

RELEASING THE KING

T he old year had passed. It was now 47 B.C., or, according to the Roman calendar, A.U.C. 707, literally 707 years since the foundation of Rome. The bloody, ongoing conflict at Alexandria, now months old, had become a daily grind of infantry sortie and counter infantry sortie by either side, as each tested the defenses of the other. The Egyptians were full of confidence after regaining Pharos Island. Meanwhile, the pride of the Roman troops had been stung by their reverse at the causeway, and they were hell-bent on making up for it. Colonel Hirtius records that all three of Caesar's legions were now determined to show him they were his best troops, and, he wrote, rather than having to urge them to fight, Caesar had to restrain his legionaries from engaging in dangerous encounters that would only cause unnecessary casualties for little gain.

Caesar was biding his time, waiting for his next contingent of reinforcements. The approximately fifty-five hundred men brought by the reinforcement convoy had proven not to have been enough to tip the balance in his favor. With as many as eighty thousand men under arms, the Egyptians still significantly outnumbered his force, which, while bolstered by the 37th's arrival, still numbered less than ten thousand.

Caesar now knew, from the officers of the 37th Legion, that General Domitius had sent the 27th Legion marching overland from Asia to join him in Egypt. Having no idea about the Roman defeat at the Battle of Nicopolis, he also expected Domitius to himself be moving down toward Egypt with his other forces, as he had sent him orders to do via Mithradates of Pergamum. On top of that, Caesar held high hopes that young Mithradates would himself have pulled together a coalition of troops from Rome's eastern provinces and allies and that he was now bringing them to Egypt by sea or land. Until he received additional troops, Caesar knew he had to be patient—not an easy thing for the notoriously impatient Julius Caesar to do—and tread water.

Now, out of the blue, the Egyptians sent him a delegation to talk peace. Caesar never learned precisely what caused this unexpected development. Colonel Hirtius was to later speculate that perhaps the Egyptians simply could not see themselves being victorious against Caesar's troops. Alternatively, he was to write, they may have hatched a scheme with supporters of young King Ptolemy XIII who were being held with the king and his sister Cleopatra by Caesar. Or perhaps, Hirtius mused, the scheme had originated with the teenage king himself, and he had used secret agents to communicate with his people outside the Roman zone.

When Caesar met with them, the Egyptian envoys proposed that he return the boy king to them. They claimed that the Egyptian people were tired of the rule of the girl Arsinoe and her cruel associate Ganymede, and were ready to obey their king, Ptolemy. And, they said, they were sure that once he had resumed control of the Egyptian armed forces the king would enter into a relationship of friendship and trust with Caesar, that he would convince the Egyptians to lay down their arms and submit to Caesar.

This all came as a complete surprise to Caesar and his officers and staff. Those closest to Caesar were unanimous in arguing against releasing the king. They didn't trust the Egyptians. Even Caesar admitted to his staff that he was well aware this was a deceitful and lying nation they were dealing with. Yet, Caesar said to his companions, "It would be politic to grant their request."

As those around him vehemently opposed Ptolemy's handover, Caesar declared that if the king were released he felt sure he would remain loyal to him. This would not be the first time that Caesar had misjudged the loyalty of someone he thought on his side. It would be a characteristic of his career. Men he had known, trusted, and even loved fraternally for many years, such as his "son" Brutus, men who had served him loyally, such as General Labienus, his deputy in Gaul for nine years, had chosen the republic over him when it had come to the crunch in the lead up to the civil war, much to Caesar's surprise.

Hirtius says that Caesar went on to reason that if the Egyptians were foxing and wanted to make Ptolemy their war leader, then he would be happier to make war on a king than on "a horde of foreigners and runaway slaves."

Caesar sent for Ptolemy. When the young king was brought before him, Caesar urged him to consider the interests of Egypt and to have mercy on his own country, which had been shamelessly scarred by fire and destruction—all because, said Caesar, of the senselessness of the Egyptian people. He told the king he wanted him to bring his people back to their senses, and to show good faith to himself and the Roman people. Caesar then informed young Ptolemy that he trusted him so implicitly he would agree to the envoys' request and deliver him up to his own armed enemies.

Caesar then took the sixteen-year-old's hand and shook it, wishing him well. He was about to send him on his way, but at this, to the astonishment of Caesar and those around him, Ptolemy burst into tears. The young king begged Caesar not to send him away, saying the sight of Caesar was more dear to him than possession of his own kingdom.

Caesar wiped the youth's tears, and, obviously moved himself, said that in that case Ptolemy need not be concerned, for they would shortly be together again, as soon as Ptolemy had convinced the Egyptian people to choose the path of peace with Rome. Saying this, he sent the young man on his way, and Ptolemy was handed over to the Egyptians, taking along with him his personal attendants and several of his chief courtiers, among the latter being Theodotus, and Dioscorides, the ambassador who had been badly wounded by General Achillas and had by now recovered from his injuries.

Few in Caesar's circle had been in favor of releasing Ptolemy. What Cleopatra counseled we are not told, but in all probability it suited her to have her brother and rival out of the picture, and she may well have urged Caesar to release him to the Egyptians. She was already several months pregnant to Caesar and had chosen him as her latest protector and champion, although to the outside world the impression continued that she was being held a hostage still. In some respects she was—it must have been in Caesar's mind that even if Ptolemy proved untrustworthy and had to be eliminated, at least he still had the other ranking member of the Egyptian royal house in his power.

Hirtius says that many of Caesar's senior officers, his friends and staff members, his centurions and most of the common soldiers were convinced that Ptolemy had pulled the wool over their commander's eyes. They considered that on the one hand Caesar had been overly generous, while on the other the king was no different from any of his deceitful countrymen. His tears, they were certain, had been contrived. They knew that Ptolemy was "well trained in wiles," Hirtius was to comment cynically. But Hirtius himself would later claim that Caesar's decision had nothing to do with generosity. It was a shrewdly calculated move, Hirtius wrote. But he wrote that some time after the event.

As it turned out, the pessimists were proven right, and quickly so. As soon as Ptolemy rejoined his royal court, he enthusiastically assumed control of the Egyptian war effort against Caesar and urged Egyptian troops to complete his destruction. Arsinoe now meekly took a backseat as Ptolemy adopted Ganymede and Dioscorides as his chief military and civil advisers. Ptolemy urged his people to achieve victory over the Romans, but to do it quickly. Having been in Caesar's headquarters, he knew that the Romans were banking on receiving more supplies and reinforcements. He also knew that Caesar had good reason to believe that both were on the way to him.

The Egyptians were now beginning to receive reports of troops movements in Palestine. And, with the likelihood of another Roman supply convoy appearing over the horizon any day, the Egyptian battle fleet was now ordered to seal off Alexandria. Despite the fact that its refloated vessels had not been intended for deep-water operations, and a doubt hung over their serviceability and even their survivability once they were offshore, the fleet hurriedly put to sea.

Many of Caesar's troops were soon saying "I told you so" when, not only did the Egyptians increase their offensive activities around the Roman perimeter following the young king's release but also the Egyptian warships were seen filing out of the Inner Harbor via the narrow western channel to the sea, then sailing past Pharos Island and heading east. From tall buildings, the Romans watched the enemy ships head up the coast toward the mouths of the Nile. Caesar immediately realized the implications of the enemy move, and issued instructions for his own warships to prepare to sail in pursuit of the Egyptian fleet.

It probably occurred to him that the Egyptians had heard that another Roman convoy was on its way south and were sailing to intercept it. He also would have been acutely aware that this may be a trick designed to lure him away from Alexandria. Once before, at Durrës the previous year, he had been lured away from his army, only for the enemy to launch a well-prepared attack behind his back. That error had lost him the Battle of Dyrrhachium and almost lost him the civil war.

Caesar had learned several hard lessons during this civil war. One such lesson had come out of the Durrës deception, and he had been wary ever since of being lured away from the main conflict by a sideshow. The other lesson had stemmed from Curio's annihilation in North Africa—never again after that had Caesar sent a subordinate to do what he could do himself. This was why he had personally commanded the naval operations in and around Alexandria to date. On balance, the Durrës lesson seemed the most applicable here. So in case the Egyptians were indeed trying to lure him away from Alexandria before launching a major counteroffensive inside the city in his absence, Caesar gave command of the fleet to his chief of staff, young General Tiberius Nero.

In a flurry of activity and swirling water, Caesar's cruisers and remaining frigates upped anchor and rowed out of the Great Harbor, then turned right and headed east. As had previously been the case, selected men of the 37th Legion sailed with the fleet as marines. General Nero found the Egyptian fleet at anchor near Canopus, a dozen miles up the coast. The city sat beside, in the words of the Roman poet Virgil, "the Nile's lagoon-like overflow" into the sea. Here the Egyptians were indeed lying in wait for the next Roman convoy bound for Alexandria, which they expected to arrive at any time.

As in the past, Admiral Euphranor commanded Caesar's Rhodian squadron. Euphranor had previously proven impatient and difficult to manage, even when operating right under Caesar's nose. Now, no doubt with little respect for Tiberius Nero, an officer in his twenties without any naval experience, Euphranor didn't wait for orders. While the ships of both sides were forming up in battle lines, and before General Nero gave the order to attack, Euphranor took his cruiser charging straight at the enemy, no doubt expecting the remainder of the fleet to follow, as it had the last time he'd charged into the attack like this, off the Libyan coast.

With her banks of oars splashing and gyrating in unison like well-oiled machines, the big Rhodian cruiser powered through the water toward an Egyptian quadrireme. Taken by surprise by his solo attack, the Egyptian's master was unable to bring his bow around in time. Euphranor slammed into the Egyptian cruiser beam on with an impact that would have knocked all on board from their feet. With an ominous creaking and splintering of timbers from his opposite number, Euphranor then backed away. The Egyptian ship immediately began to sink. A cheer would have risen up from the men aboard the Rhodian flagship.

Meanwhile, other Egyptian cruisers were swarming toward the victorious Rhodian ship like vengeful bees. When Euphranor looked around for help, he saw that General Nero was holding the other Roman ships back. No one went to Euphranor's aid, says Hirtius. Perhaps, he suggested, it was because the other Romans commanders thought he could take care of himself. After all, he had been at the forefront of all the Roman naval victories during this campaign.

The renowned Rhodian skipper paid the price for his impetuosity and his disregard for his fleet commander. Trying to fight off several attackers at once, his ship was successfully rammed. The Rhodian flagship was soon taking water. It sank there off Canopus, in an indecisive action that produced no other result for either side other than the loss of a cruiser each. But Caesar paid a higher price, losing his best Rhodian commander—the rash, overconfident Admiral Euphranor went down with his ship and drowned.

XV

THE RELIEF COLUMN

Mithradates of Pergamum had kept his word to Caesar. After landing in Syria and, from the principal Syrian port of Laodicea, sending Caesar's dispatches on to General Domitius, he had met the 27th Legion, marching from Asia on Domitius's orders. Taking over the legion's command, and probably adding archers he'd recruited from Cyprus to the legion's column, Mithradates led the 27th as far as Ascalon, on the Idumaean coast of Palestine.

Ascalon was the last port before Egypt, and here Mithradates paused to consolidate his forces, sending out letters to various local leaders in the region, including the king of nearby Nabataea, summoning help for Caesar. It seems that the Nabataeans, who were superb horsemen, subsequently sent a sizable contingent of cavalry. But others weren't so forthcoming, and, fearing that his relief force was not strong enough to fight its way past the Egyptian garrison at Pelusium, Mithradates had sat there at Ascalon with the 27th Legion for weeks on end, waiting for more troops to materialize.

Ascalon was then a wealthy port city with a sizable Jewish population, and among those Mithradates approached to help Caesar was the Jewish community. Their leader was Antipater, an ambitious and charismatic Idumaean whose children included fourteen-year-old Herod, the future Herod the Great. Antipater had been a good friend to Rome during Pompey's heyday. When, ten years before, General Gabinius had marched his legions down from Syria to invade Egypt and reinstall Ptolemy XII on his throne on Pompey's orders, Antipater had provided auxiliary troops, money, weapons, and grain for the expedition.

With Pompey gone from the scene, the farsighted Antipater now recognized that even though Caesar was now in difficulties, his patronage, and through him Rome's continued patronage, was vital to his own future. Antipater had married Cypros, a highborn Arabian woman, and he had close ties to King Aretas of Arabia—some years back the king had sheltered their four children, including young Herod, while Antipater fought off a rival. Antipater also had good relations with the rulers of the small independent nations and city-states throughout the region that were allied to Rome, states such as Chalcis, which extended up into Syria from the Sea of Galilee. Quickly making contact with his powerful friends throughout the region after learning of Caesar's plight, Antipater urged them to join him in going to Caesar's aid.

By the end of February 47 B.C., Antipater had been able to attract large numbers of troops from Arabia and other allied states in the region, among them a significant number of cavalry, and these all joined Mithradates and the 27th Legion at Ascalon. At the same time, Antipater himself assembled three thousand well-armed Jewish foot soldiers, and took his place in Mithradates' army at their head.

Of equal importance, Antipater organized letters from the Jewish high priest, Hyrcanus bar Alexander, who also was the Jewish ethnarch, or chief magistrate, of Jerusalem. These letters were addressed to the Jewish elders of Egypt, calling on them not to support the Egyptians but instead to throw their support behind Caesar and provide him with money, provisions, and fighting men.

More reinforcements had been promised, but Mithradates, fretting that he had already delayed too long, decided to march on Egypt with the force he now had. With no shipping at his disposal, Mithradates had no choice but take the overland route. This meant having to fight his way past the Egyptian garrison at Pelusium.

In February, Mithradates's column entered Egypt and marched on Pelusium. The Egyptian fortress quickly closed its gates as Mithradates's army of perhaps twelve thousand men approached, and the Egyptian commander refused him passage.

While Pelusium dominated the narrow stretch of land between the Mediterranean and the Gulf of Suez, Mithradates could have marched on by. But he knew he would only have been inviting the strong Egyptian garrison originally posted here by General Achillas to emerge behind him, block his supply line and path of retreat, and attack him in his rear. Mithradates decided to lay siege to the Pelusium fortress and eliminate the garrison and the threat it posed.

Led by the Italian legionaries of the 27th, the attacking force swiftly encircled the fort with entrenchments. Once the fortress was cut off, Mithradates immediately sent his troops against the walls with battering rams. Through the day he regularly rotated his men working at the walls under cover of shields and mantlets—wooden siege sheds on wheels—frequently pulling out the wounded and the weary and replacing them with fresh cohorts.

When a breach was first made in the wall by a battering ram, it was a Jewish unit that achieved the success. Jewish historian Josephus writes that their commander, Antipater, personally pulled down part of the wall, opening the way for assault troops, which he then led as they poured into the city. Pelusium took just one day to storm and seize.

Leaving a garrison of his own at Pelusium to safeguard his back and guard his prisoners, Mithradates advanced into the Nile Delta. The Delta, named for the Greek letter whose shape it resembled, was then a lush paradise of wheat fields, vineyards, and orchards irrigated by the Nile and its numerous branches as they flared out to the Mediterranean. Here the Nile "swift parted into sevenfold branching mouths," in the words of the poet Virgil, and "with black mud fattens and makes Egypt green."

When the relief column approached a district known as Onias, or Onion, the large local Jewish community here initially resisted its passage. So Antipater, as a Jew, met with the Jews of Onias, and showed them the letters he carried from High Priest Hyrcanus. On reading the letters, the Jews of Onias came over to the invaders, who continued their advance. Once they heard about this, the Jews living in and around the city of Memphis, the pharaohs' capital of Egypt in centuries past, sent to Mithradates and invited him to come to them in peace. So Mithradates marched inland to the Nile proper and to Memphis, and there, the Jews of Memphis also joined his growing army.

News of the success and approach of the Roman relief force caused great alarm at the royal palace in Alexandria. This was the Roman relief force the Egyptians had been expecting to come by sea. A task force of regular soldiers and militia was swiftly put together and dispatched from the capital by King Ptolemy, with orders to deal with Mithradates and his troops before they could reach Caesar in Alexandria.

According to Colonel Hirtius, this Egyptian force had instructions to either destroy or delay the relief force. Delay would be good enough, in the opinion of the Egyptian leadership, for they felt sure they had Caesar on the ropes in Alexandria. Knowing his supply situation in the city was by now critical, knowing that many of his troops had previously been close to mutiny when their water supply was threatened, and feeling able to prevent convoys reaching him by sea with their larger navy, they were convinced it was just a matter of time before Caesar was forced to capitulate—if they could prevent reinforcements and supplies from reaching him overland.

There are several differing accounts of what followed. Colonel Hirtius, who went out of his way not to be critical of Caesar or his subordinates when he put together Caesar's memoirs, would have us believe that Mithradates had an easy victory over the Egyptian army sent to intercept him. The Jewish historian Josephus tells a different story, or, to be more precise, the complete story, about what happened:

Mithradates advanced the Roman relief force down the Nile from Memphis toward Alexandria with the river on his left, and in the third week of March made a fortified camp for the night on high ground near the river at a place known locally as Jews Camp. The army sent by Ptolemy approached from Alexandria, and, late in the day, the Egyptian advance party, without waiting for the vanguard of their army to link up with them, crossed the Nile, using riverboats. Overconfident and keen for glory, they immediately attacked Mithradates' camp.

Seeing that the attackers were concentrating on one sector of his defenses, Mithradates led a sally by a number of his troops, emerging from a rear gate of his camp, out of sight of the Egyptians attacking the wall on the far side. Coming up behind the enemy, Mithradates's troops surprised the Egyptians and killed a number of them. The remainder fled, using the boats with which they had come to withdraw back across the river. Here Hirtius's account of this episode ends with just the comment that the Egyptian survivors of the advance party linked up with their main expeditionary army, which launched a new attack on Mithradates.

As Josephus tells us, the day following the first skirmish at Jews Camp, the main Egyptian army crossed the river and built a fortified camp in the Roman style close by Mithradates's camp, before coming out onto the river flat and forming up opposite the Roman camp ready for battle.

According to the later Roman historian Cassius Dio, whose source is unknown, the commander of the Egyptian forces here was Dioscorides, the envoy of the king wounded by General Achillas months before. This means that young King Ptolemy and his general, Ganymede, remained back in Alexandria with the rest of the army.

Josephus says that Mithradates decided to accept the Egyptian invitation to fight and led his troops out, forming them in battle order. The men of the Roman force apparently had their backs to the river. Allocating the 27th Legion to his right wing, where he stationed himself, Mithradates gave the left wing to Antipater and his Jewish contingent, which, bolstered by the addition of the Jews of Onias and Memphis, would now have contained about the same number of men as the legion, five thousand to six thousand. The other allied infantry were placed in the middle of the battle line, with the cavalry split between the two wings as usual.

Both sides charged simultaneously. On the left, Antipater's Jewish fighters had a torrid time of it to begin with. Antipater himself was wounded more than once, but, ignoring his injuries, he led from the front, and fighting like a demon, he was able to drive back the Egyptians facing him.

Before long, the unrelenting onslaught of the Jewish troops had forced the Egyptians on the left wing to turn and run. Looking around, Antipater saw that on the right wing the 27th Legion was withdrawing under heavy pressure from a large number of Egyptians, taking numerous casualties in the process. Dead, mutilated, and wounded Roman legionaries lay all over the battlefield on the former Roman right wing.

Going to Mithradates' aid, Antipater led his Jewish contingent down the riverbank at the run and then swung in behind the Egyptians who were harrying the hard-pressed Mithradates and the 27th, plowing into the surprised Egyptians from the rear. Antipater personally fought his way through the Egyptians to reach Mithradates, who was surrounded and in danger of being overrun. Mithradates would later write to Caesar that Antipater saved his life there beside the Nile.

Antipater's fighting Jews didn't stop there. They drove the Egyptians from the battlefield and then overran their camp. It was a victory for the relief force, but a costly one. The 27th Legion lost eight hundred men killed in the battle and suffered an undisclosed number of wounded, while Antipater lost fifty to eighty of his men.

Egyptian losses were not recorded, but they were not sufficient to end the threat this force posed. Their commander, Dioscorides, rallied his troops, regrouped, and built a new camp downriver in Mithradates' path. Mithradates and Antipater retired to their own camp to patch up their wounded and take stock.

Both sides now sent urgent messages to their respective commanders in chief at Alexandria. Mithradates told Caesar of the Battle of Jews Camp and the mauling he had received, and informed him that the Egyptians still stood in the way of his now bloodied relief force and prevented him from reaching Caesar.

Dioscorides would have informed his young king that the Romans and their allies had been held at the Nile, but there was no telling how much longer they could be contained with the troops available.

Both sides called for urgent reinforcements from their commanders in chief.

XVI

BATTLE ON THE NILE

C aesar and young Ptolemy XIII both reacted in the same manner and at about the same time to the news from their commanders on the Nile. Ptolemy decided to set off from Alexandria, taking the bulk of his remaining forces to, in the words of Caesar's staff officer Hirtius, "check" Mithradates. Having dealt with the relief force, he would return to Alexandria to finally destroy Caesar. So the Egyptian fleet was summoned back to the capital from its position off Canopus, to quickly transport Ptolemy, Ganymede, and their troops to the Nile, where they would link up with Dioscorides and the second, bloodied Egyptian army currently standing in Mithradates' way, and then launch into a climactic and decisive battle. That was the plan, anyway.

Caesar also knew that his relief force was close, but bogged down. It was all or nothing for Caesar now. First, he chose a garrison to remain behind in the sector of Alexandria controlled by the Romans and provide a guard for his remaining hostages, Cleopatra and her little brother Ptolemy XIV. That garrison was made up of his auxiliaries and probably part of the 28th Legion, which had disappointed him until now. After saying farewell to Cleopatra, who was now close to six months pregnant, Caesar loaded the rest of his troops on board his ships, then sailed from the Great Harbor.

According to Cassius Dio he sailed at night, and he built large signal fires on his ships so the Alexandrians could see that he was leaving, then turned east up the coast, as if sailing for the Nile. But once he was out of sight of Alexandria, says Dio, Caesar extinguished the signal fires and turned about and slipped back past Alexandria and along the Libyan coast toward the west.

Hirtius says that Caesar didn't want to invite a time-wasting battle on the Nile between his forces and Ptolemy's navy, which he believed to be still stationed up the coast near the mouths of the Nile, and that was why he turned west. His primary objective was to link up with Mithradates of Pergamum, without a fight. A little way down the coast toward Africa he landed his men, and set off to march inland via a diagonal route, to link up with Mithradates at the Nile.

For the men of the 6th Legion and their comrades of the 28th and 37th this route march would have been a welcome change from the sedentary life they had been leading in the city. The Spaniards of the 6th had been cooped up in Alexandria for close to six frustrating months, and the prospect of a decisive pitched battle in the open, where the Roman legionary shone, would have been a welcome one.

Following Caesar's departure from the city, the Egyptian fleet returned to Alexandria, as instructed by their young king. Ptolemy quickly loaded most of his troops onto the ships along with arms and ammunition. Leaving his sister Arsinoe with a force of militia to garrison the city, and possibly also leaving Ganymede in charge at Alexandria—it is unclear whether Ganymede accompanied the king or remained at Alexandria—Ptolemy set off, believing that Caesar was somewhere ahead of him.

Ptolemy's route was the most direct, and he was using water transport, meaning his progress should be by far the most speedy. Once he reached the mouths of the Nile, Ptolemy collected a number of smaller, shallow-draft craft—hundreds of them, it would appear. There he off-loaded his troops from his cruisers and frigates onto the smaller river craft. This fleet of distinctive Nile riverboats, wherries with high, pointed sterns and prows, a single mast, and several oars each, their timbers brightly painted, according to Virgil, then made its way up the Nile to locate and join Dioscorides and his troops.

Although Ptolemy had the shortest, fastest route to travel, Caesar had a good head start of perhaps a day, with the result that both sides reached their respective Nile armies at much the same time on March 25.

As his two armies came together with hails of comradeship and cheers of joy, Caesar warmly greeted his faithful friend Mithradates, who would have sighed with relief at the sight of the man he had not seen since the previous October and had come to fear had perished in Alexandria. Caesar also embraced the Jewish commander, Antipater, and congratulated him for his feats and his valor in the battles at Pelusium and in the Delta.

Caesar also was delighted to welcome another Jewish leader, who had just joined Mithradates. Hyrcanus, high priest of the Jews, from Jerusalem, to whom Caesar had written the previous fall seeking help, had arrived to join Mithradates with another fifteen hundred Jewish troops, more than making up for the Roman losses at the Battle of Jews Camp. Whether these fifteen hundred men had previously made up Mithradates' garrison at Pelusium or whether Hyrcanus had brought them down from Palestine as additional reinforcements is unclear.

At the same time that Caesar united his forces, ten to twelve miles to the north of the Roman position King Ptolemy linked up with Dioscorides and the Egyptian holding force. During street fighting at Alexandria not long after the king had rejoined his troops, some among Caesar's men had called out jibes to the Egyptians, deriding Ptolemy's youth and physical weakness. But the Egyptians had rallied solidly behind their king, who, now that he had been freed from the overbearing influence of the arrogant Pothinus by Caesar's executioner, was displaying strong leadership qualities and excellent strategic skills.

Unloading most of his men onto the eastern bank of the Nile, and leaving a few selected units of archers and slingers on the boats in the river, Ptolemy chose a site for a new camp beside the river for his unified army. That site, close to an unnamed village, was, according to Hirtius, a naturally strong one. It was a sloping rise elevated above the river plain, with the river on one side, a marsh on another, and steep cliffs along the third, highest side, with a more accessible, gently inclining approach on the fourth side. The Egyptian army quickly set to work building fortifications around the rise, fortifying the nearby village, and building a wall linking the village and the camp on the rise.

The officers in charge of building the Egyptian fortifications borrowed from the Roman army textbook, as would be expected of the Romans, the so-called Gabinians, who officered the Egyptian units. A wall of earth at least ten feet high and three feet thick created from a ditch ten feet deep and three feet across ran around the camp's outer perimeter. But unlike the standard Roman legion camp, which had a gate in each of its four sides, there seems to have been just a single gate in the walls of the Egyptian camp, on the most accessible side. From this strong base, the king intended to watch Caesar's movements and choose an appropriate time to attack him.

While this construction work was under way at the Egyptian camp, Ptolemy dispatched cavalry to screen Caesar's approach, and, on March 26, Ptolemy received a report from cavalry scouts that the Roman army was marching down the Nile toward his position. From his scouts, the king learned that seven miles from the Egyptian camp Caesar's route of march would bring him to a river, a tributary of the Nile that diverted from it and angled across the Delta to enter the sea many miles from the mother river. This river was not wide, but it was deep, and its banks on either side were steep. An army reaching this barrier would have to pause to create a crossing of some kind. Seeing an opportunity to strike Caesar while he was at a disadvantage, Ptolemy dispatched all his cavalry and selected light infantry units to ambush the Romans while they were making the river crossing.

Marching north now, Caesar was determined to swiftly terminate this Egyptian war with a decisive victory here beside the Nile. In coming out to face him on the Delta, the Egyptians had played right into his hands; he much preferred a set-piece battle on open ground, as opposed to the restricting type of urban fighting he'd had to engage in at Alexandria.

Caesar was confident that with the combined forces now at his disposal he had both the quantity and the quality of troops he needed to do the job. In addition to Roman legionaries of the 6th, 27th, 28th, and 37th Legions, he had the forty-five hundred Jewish fighters of Antipater and Hyrcanus, most of whom had already shown their mettle at Pelusium and Jews Camp, plus further Jewish reinforcements from Egypt. He had his tried and trusted eight hundred German and Gallic cavalry, their horses having survived the conflict in Alexandria due to his determination to feed and preserve them. And he had several thousand allied light infantrymen and cavalry. His force now totaled some twenty thousand troops, almost exactly the same number he'd led to victory against Pompey at the Battle of Pharsalus.

An advance guard of cavalry and infantry always preceded a Roman army on the march, to ensure that the way ahead was free of enemy, and to build roads and bridges where necessary for the main force and its large baggage train to use without being delayed. When Caesar's advance guard reached the river chosen by the Egyptians as the location for their ambush, its legionaries set to work felling tall trees, which they then lay across the river. They next covered the logs with earth, to create a temporary bridge. The Roman troops labored in the hot sun for several hours to complete the bridge, just in time for the main force's arrival.

As the first troops began to cross the bridge, on the opposite bank hundreds of previously concealed Egyptian ambushers suddenly rose from behind rocks and undergrowth and pelted those crossing and the Roman units massed on the opposite bank with javelins and stones. The Roman advance came to a dead stop at this juncture as men hurriedly retreated across the temporary bridge.

According to Hirtius, the Roman troops who had been with Caesar in Alexandria were furious that they had been fighting these damnable Egyptians for so many months and still hadn't been able to get the better of them. But Caesar had a secret weapon, and now he employed it. Knowing the special skills of one contingent of his German cavalry bodyguard, Batavians from present-day Holland, Caesar quickly summoned their officers and ordered the Batavians to disperse up and down this river barrier and find fording places.

As ordered, the Batavian troopers scattered along the riverbank and were soon gone from sight. At one point the Batavians found a place where they could get their horses down the steep bank into the water. These troopers had a special talent: they could swim their horses across rivers while holding onto their saddles, in full equipment. Once on the far bank the soggy troopers were able to quickly remount and immediately go into action. This talent mastered by the Batavians would help Roman generals win numerous battles in times to come, and in the imperial era the Batavian Horse would become the Roman army's most elite cavalry regiment.

Out of nowhere, the Batavian cavalrymen came charging into the rear of the Egyptians occupying the riverbank facing Caesar's halted army. They took the Egyptian cavalry completely by surprise. The Egyptians would have dismounted to undertake the ambush; on foot, they were at a vital disadvantage. As the Batavians charged into the flat-footed Egyptians and set about them with flashing swords, Roman infantry was able to pour across the tree bridge in ever-increasing numbers and enter the fray from the front.

Sandwiched between the two attacking forces, Egyptians who stood and fought were cut to pieces. Most of those who ran were overtaken at the gallop and cut down. It was, says Hirtius, a rout, from which very few Egyptian cavalrymen were able to escape and return to their king with the news of their defeat.

With the blood lust of his men aroused, Caesar decided to drive home his advantage. As soon as his column had completed the river crossing, he marched directly toward the Egyptian camp seven miles away. Within two hours the Roman army appeared outside the Egyptian position. The Egyptians called their men to arms, and around all the walls of their defenses their troops ran to take up positions. There were about forty thousand of them, and they lined the walls of their camp and the adjacent fortified village almost shoulder to shoulder.

It was soon obvious that Ptolemy had no intention of sending his troops out to fight the Romans in the open, and Caesar's troops began calling on their commander to immediately send them against the enemy fortifications. While he appreciated his men's zeal, Caesar, seeing the extensive nature of the Egyptian forces and the excellent location of their camp, and knowing that his men were weary after marching, fighting, and then marching yet again for the better part of the day, decided against further hostilities and ordered a fortified camp built for the night not far from the Egyptian position.

While his men threw up the walls of their marching camp, and before the sun set, Caesar made a careful reconnoiter of the Egyptian position on horseback, analyzing its strengths and weaknesses. Beside him, his secretary Apollonius would have noted down his observations as he dictated; Caesar was famous for dictating to two and three secretaries at once when he was traveling—a different subject to each one.

That night, Caesar had orders circulated to his troops to prepare for an all-out assault on the Egyptian position the next day. While the troops were hard at work preparing ammunition and building scaling ladders and wooden hurdles to cross enemy trenches, Caesar, in his command tent, his *praetorium*, briefed his officers on what he intended doing the next day and what he required of each of them in the coming assault.

Shortly after dawn on the morning of March 27, having given his men a pep talk at morning assembly, Caesar marched his army out of camp, leaving a small guard behind, almost certainly made up of auxiliaries. But instead of attacking the main Egyptian camp, Caesar sent his entire force against the Egyptian village being held by the enemy. The objective was small, the defenders vastly outnumbered.

The overwhelming numbers of the attackers meant the village fell very quickly. As Caesar's legionaries came swarming up scaling ladders and swept over the front walls of the village's fortifications, knocking aside all opposition, hundreds of terrified Egyptian troops jumped from the rear walls of the village's fortifications and fled back to their main camp. The Roman attackers gave chase, as Caesar urged his men to maintain the initiative while the Egyptians were on the back foot. Leaving the village in ruins, the Roman army swept up the slope to the main Egyptian position. King Ptolemy's camp was soon under attack from the two most accessible sides.

When Caesar came riding up to join his men, he found that his troops had chased wide-eyed village stragglers all the way to the camp's front wall, which occupied the gently sloping side. The Egyptian refugees from the village begged their countrymen to let them into the camp, but the Egyptian troops inside dared not open the gate. Caesar's legionaries cut down every straggler there below the wall, in full view of their distraught comrades on the wall. The legionaries then began exchanging javelin fire with defenders on this wall. On the Nile side of the Egyptian camp there was a narrow approach between river and marsh, and some of the Roman troops were also going against the defenders there.

Ptolemy had assigned the defense of the camp's front wall to a large force of picked regular soldiers. Only a smaller number were defending the approach on the Nile side of the camp, but they were inflicting casualties on the Romans and their allies attacking from that quarter, because they were supported by a deadly barrage of arrows and slingshot coming from the Egyptians' many riverboats that had been drawn into the bank by their crews.

Even though his men weren't losing their enthusiasm for the assault, Caesar could see that he wasn't going to make progress the way things were going. The Roman general now noticed that the wall at the highest part of the Egyptian camp, that which rose above the cliff face to the rear, was all but deserted. Most of the defenders assigned to that sector, bored by inactivity and wanting to get into the fight, had deserted this wall and gone down to the two places on other walls that were under attack, some to help, some to watch.

Caesar sent for one of his most experienced centurions, Carfulenus, who was "outstanding both for dauntlessness and military skill," in the words of Hirtius. Pointing out the almost undefended but seemingly inaccessible wall, Caesar gave Centurion Carfulenus his instructions. The centurion and a handpicked group of Caesar's best men set off for the wall in question. It's almost certain that Carfulenus and his men were from the 6th Legion—recognized by Caesar as his best troops.

While Egyptian attention was focused on Roman attacks on the two walls elsewhere, Centurion Carfulenus and his men silently climbed the cliffs below the rear wall, apparently with the aid of scaling ladders, which they then used to mount the camp wall itself. The legionaries slid over the wall like demons, surprising and slaying the few sentries left on duty, who were all looking toward the hectic action on the lower walls. The other men meant to be guarding the rear wall, who had gone down to be closer to the action at the front wall, turned to see a tide of Roman legionaries washing over the rear wall, ran to engage the invaders, and called with alarm for support.

This yelling from the top of the camp caused confusion, consternation, and ultimately panic in Egyptian ranks elsewhere. Egyptian troops ran uncertainly to and from each of the three scenes of combat as their frantic officers tried to deal with the variety of threats. With attention now drawn to the rear wall, the Roman troops assaulting the front wall covered the outer trench with wicker hurdles and brought up scaling ladders.

Centurion Carfulenus and his men were now inside the enemy camp. They had cleared the rear ramparts of defenders, and now with bloodied

Egyptian corpses in their wake and with shields raised, they drove down the slope into enemy reinforcements sent to counter them. According to Hirtius, Carfulenus's unstoppable legionaries killed large numbers of Egyptians.

Now over the front wall came Jewish assault troops. Leading the Jewish forces as they fought their way onto the camp ramparts, showing neither fear nor hesitation, was Hyrcanus, the Jewish high priest. His fighting prowess, witnessed by Caesar's officers, was to impress Caesar. In a later citation to the people of Sidon quoted by Josephus, Caesar would say of Hyrcanus that during this battle he "showed himself superior in valor to all the rest" of the men in his Jewish force. Antipater, the Jewish commander, also was prominent during this assault, and he was wounded yet again.

Under attack from three directions now and in terror, Egyptian troops crushed toward the wall facing the Nile in their hundreds and then their thousands, intent on escaping the camp and reaching their river craft. Discipline did not break down entirely; at least one unit, possibly made up of the spearmen of the king's bodyguard, fought a resolute rearguard action to hold back the Romans attacking them from inside the camp.

This gave hundreds of other Egyptian soldiers the chance to jump from the riverside wall into the ditch running around its outside. These men were struggling to clamber from the ditch when the earth wall collapsed on top of them under the weight of thousands more men mounting it to escape. This collapse buried and suffocated those Egyptians in the ditch. It also created a large opening in the wall, making it easier for thousands more Egyptians to escape. Among the sea of men fleeing toward the Egyptian riverboats nudging the nearest Nile bank were King Ptolemy and members of his court.

At first, Egyptian archers and slingers on the boats provided covering fire to allow their retreating colleagues to reach the safety of the boats as Roman troops pressed after them. But as yelling, screaming men tried in wide-eyed desperation to board the craft, boatmen began to realize that all sense had deserted these fools, who in their desire to survive would only overload their vessels. Many boats began to put out from the shore, causing more panic among the desperate escapees. Here, a boat sank under the weight of too many passengers. There, men were killing fellow Egyptians to keep them from boarding. With piercing screams from its horrified occupants, another boat turned turtle. Then another, and another.

In the midst of this chaotic scene King Ptolemy was pulled aboard one vessel, which likewise tried to put out into midstream. But as the boat moved away from the riverbank to escape this "hell unleashed," as an Italian saying goes, men whose only thought was escape clung to its side. The king's boat began to heel over.

With swords and cudgels, crewmen and surviving members of the king's bodyguard tried to make the hundreds grasping onto the boat's rail let go. But too late. The boat containing the king rolled over, tipping all on board into the murky green-brown Nile, and went down. The young man was briefly seen struggling in the water, and then Ptolemy XIII, teenage king of Egypt, disappeared.

XVII

TO THE VICTOR, THE SPOILS

I n the last days of March 47 B.C., a large mounted force of several thousand men approached the city of Alexandria's Canopic Gate from the direction of the Nile River. Julius Caesar rode at the head of his personal cavalry and up to two thousand allied cavalry that had come south with Mithradates of Pergamum.

In addition to their own standards, the troopers would have carried the captured royal standard of King Ptolemy XIII. Several leading Egyptians would have ridden with them, too, their hands chained. These were men captured during and after the Battle of the Nile Delta, the battle that had destroyed the Egyptian army and brought about the demise of the Egyptian king. Ptolemy's body was never found. One of his advisers, Theodotus the rhetoric master, is known to have escaped from Egypt. Four years later he would be discovered in the province of Asia by Roman troops of the Liberators, and put to death there—on the orders of Marcus Brutus, according to Plutarch; on the orders of his colleague Cassius, according to Appian.

None of the Roman officers who had served in the Egyptian army, the Gabinians, survived the Battle of the Nile Delta. It seems that men such as Colonel Lucius Septimius and Centurion Salvius, Pompey the Great's assassins, either perished in the battle or were put to death immediately following it, as traitors to Rome. It was one thing to take up arms against Julius Caesar to serve under fellow Romans such as Pompey, but no Roman had sympathy for a fellow citizen who fought for a foreign foe.

Alexandria's Canopic Gate was opened to Caesar by the Egyptian troops left by Ptolemy to guard his capital, and the Roman general rode victoriously into the city. News of the battle and its outcome had preceded the conquering Romans, and all thought of resistance evaporated from the hearts

145

and minds of the people of Alexandria. Abandoning their fortifications, the troops of the city's guard and remaining militia came out and piled up their weapons. Civic leaders came to Caesar wearing mourning clothes, to throw themselves at his feet and beg his pardon. Heaping the sacred objects from their temples before him, they surrendered unconditionally.

After accepting the surrender of the leading Alexandrians and reassuring them that he would not carry out reprisals against them or their city, Caesar dismounted and passed through the former Egyptian lines to the sector of the city he and his men had occupied for six months in often grueling conditions. Here he reunited with the officers and men he had left behind to hold the Roman-occupied sector of the city. At the royal guesthouse that had been his quarters, he was greeted as victor by Cleopatra.

There, too, Cleopatra's ambitious and scheming sister Arsinoe was brought to Caesar. Cleopatra would have counseled Caesar to execute Arsinoe for leading the war against him for a time, but Caesar had boasted of his generosity to the defeated after his victories over Roman citizens during the civil war for the past two years, so he could hardly execute a woman. Instead of putting Arsinoe to death, he would magnanimously banish her to the Temple of Diana at Ephesus in Asia. But not before he took her back to Rome to display her as a trophy to the Roman people.

He would choose Arsinoe's place of exile for a quite deliberate reason. It was a reason full of irony, and the Romans loved irony. Years before, Arsinoe's father, Ptolemy XII, had sought sanctuary in the same temple, after Arsinoe's elder sister Berenice had overthrown him, and he had spent several humbled, frustrating years there. Whether Caesar intended Arsinoe to end her days at Ephesus we don't know. But that would be how it turned out—a decade later, Cleopatra, described by Josephus as a woman who hesitated at no wickedness, would convince Mark Antony to have Arsinoe executed at Ephesus, ridding her of a royal rival.

It also appears that at the same time that Arsinoe was handed over to Caesar, Ganymede, Arsinoe's former tutor and later the cunning commander of the Egyptian army, was presented to Caesar as a prisoner by the Egyptians.

Caesar now took charge of the entire royal palace of the Ptolemies, and in the throne room he formally installed Cleopatra as Queen of Egypt, in partnership now with her younger brother the twelve-year-old Ptolemy XIV. As part of the ceremony, Caesar had the will of Ptolemy XII read aloud, with emphasis on the article requiring that the late king's eldest daughter and eldest son occupy his throne after him, which, with Ptolemy

XIII drowned and out of the way and Ptolemy XIV the only surviving son, was now the case. In doing this, Caesar wanted the world to believe that he was not acting as a conqueror but as a liberator who was merely fulfilling the wishes of the late king of Egypt.

For the next two weeks, Caesar took a vacation. With Cleopatra lounging at his side, he sailed down the Nile in a fleet of riverboats and barges— four hundred of them, according to Appian. Caesar and the obviously pregnant Cleopatra traveled on a lavishly equipped royal barge, with many of his soldiers sailing in the other craft. It was party time for the victors. Suetonius says that Caesar and Cleopatra often dined till dawn. Suetonius also says that Caesar was so captivated by Cleopatra that he would have sailed all the way to Ethiopia with her on this leisurely concourse along the Nile. Certainly she would have wanted Caesar to stay for the birth of their child.

Yet, it wasn't all fun and games. Caesar also had a mind for matters of science, and the subject of the Roman calendar was playing on his mind. Wherever he had gone on his travels during his career he had studied and written about things that interested and intrigued him, always with the goal of scientific advancement. While briefly in Britain in 55 and 54 B.C., for example, he had conducted a study of the length of the days in that part of the world, having servants time the hours of daylight, using water clocks, while he was on the island, and noting down the results.

As Pontifex Maximus or Roman high priest since 61 B.C., Caesar had been in charge of the Roman calendar, which fixed the dates of the holy days each year when religious festivals were celebrated and Roman courts and businesses were closed. That calendar had been derived from the calendar of the Greeks—which, some scholars believe, went back as far as the eighth century B.C. It had been bothering Caesar for some time that the Roman calendar had become increasingly out of step with the seasons— and many Roman religious festivals, like later Christian successors, had a seasonal basis. The Roman calendar, which at that time was based on a year made up of 355 days, was woefully out of step with the phases of the moon, and was becoming even more so with each passing year. Yet, here in Egypt, the Egyptians, who had studied astronomy even before Rome existed, used a calendar that was closely aligned to the phases of the moon and was far more accurate than its Roman counterpart.

So, while he dallied in Egypt, Caesar conferred with local experts. One expert in particular, Sosigenes, an Alexandrian astronomer and scholar of Greek extraction, impressed him, and they talked at length about how the Roman calendar could be brought into sync with the phases of the moon. As Caesar would have told Sosigenes, the original Roman calendar was credited to Romulus, founder of Rome. Romulus's calendar had set March as the first month of the year, a year made up of ten months lasting a total of 304 days—six months of 30 days each, and four lasting 31 days. Just to complicate matters, there had been a brief uncounted winter gap between December and March.

A century after its introduction, this Romulan calendar had been corrected by Numa Pompilius, second king of Rome, who had added the months of January and February and extended the year to 355 days. Because the highly superstitious Romans had developed a dread of even numbers, Pompilius reduced the existing 30-day months to 29 days each and gave February 28 days; an even number was considered appropriate in this case, because February was a month devoted to the infernal gods.

Sosigenes explained to Caesar how and why the Egyptians had a 365-day calendar based on twelve months. Impressed by Sosigenes's knowledge and thinking, Caesar gave the Egyptian astronomer the task of coming up with a new Roman calendar, one he would introduce to replace the inefficient existing calendar.

That a new calendar would totally change the Roman way of life and would be resisted by many who were set in the old way did not concern Caesar. He had introduced major change to Rome before. Back in 59 B.C., when consul for the first time, he had created the world's first daily newspaper, the *Acta Diurnia,* written by hand at Rome every day. Circulated throughout the empire, it contained official news, court cases, appointments, chariot race results, even news of house fires in the capital. In that same year, Caesar had introduced traffic regulations banning most wheeled traffic from Rome's narrow, heavily congested streets by day; wagons and carts rolling in and out of the city could only do so at night. Hence Rome's reputation as the city that never slept.

Similar traffic regulations were later adopted by other large cities around the empire. This had been a reform that would have generated much complaint from Romans who had to become accustomed to the night-long sounds of wheels rolling over stone-paved streets, the cries of muleteers and the crack of their whips, the hubbub of thousands of conversations in the streets as most of the city tried to sleep.

Caesar was enjoying the break in Egypt, his rare vacation. He was enjoying his time with Cleopatra, enjoying exploring the Nile, enjoying long discussions with learned men such as Sosigenes. But, says, Suetonius, Caesar's soldiers objected to this dalliance. Increasingly, the mutterings and sour faces of the troops, even among men of the 6th, who would have been anxious to fulfill their obligation to Caesar by bringing the civil war to a close and then go home, could not be avoided. Caesar's staff would have reminded him that there was news of an army of republican legions gathering in Africa not so far away to the west that he must yet deal with his surviving Roman political opponents and their army before he could truly say the Roman Empire was his. There was also the matter of Pharnaces' occupation of Pontus.

In April, after two weeks on the Nile, Caesar gave in to the demands of his men and his colleagues and returned to Alexandria to put Egyptian affairs in order before departing from the country. Although Egypt would remain a kingdom in name, with Cleopatra and her youngest, powerless brother its joint sovereigns, in reality Egypt was now a protectorate of Rome. The country was firmly under Caesar's control, as were the funds in the Egyptian royal treasury, from which he would have taken the millions he claimed he was owed by Ptolemy XII, and a little more besides.

The Egyptian army was abolished on Caesar's orders. Never again as long as the Roman Empire existed would there be a separate Egyptian army. Instead, for now three of the four legions with Caesar would remain in Egypt—the 27th, 28th, and 37th. The most dilapidated relics of the Egyptian navy were burned; the more seaworthy would be taken to Rome for a public spectacle planned by Caesar.

Hirtius doesn't hide the fact that the subjugated Egyptians were not happy that their country was now occupied Roman territory. He says the three legions were left in Egypt because Cleopatra and her brother had neither the affection of their subjects—because they had sided with Caesar in the recent war—nor the power of authority over them. Besides, Caesar later told Hirtius, as long as the rulers of Egypt remained loyal to him and to Rome, the legions would protect them and their throne, while if they proved ungrateful, the legions would keep them in line.

Within a few years this garrison would increase to four legions. They would have two bases, one at Alexandria, the other at a site beside the Nile close to where the Battle of the Nile Delta was fought. Called Babylon Fossatum, because it would be surrounded on three sides by a moat, as Babylon was, this legion base would eventually become the location of the city of Cairo. In addition to housing a legionary garrison, Egypt would also in the future be required to provide auxiliaries to serve in the Roman army, under Roman officers. Within a century, Egypt was sufficiently acquiescent for the number of legions stationed there to be reduced to two.

According to Suetonius, Caesar would send one of his favorites out from Rome, the son of a freedman, to take charge of the legions now permanently stationed in Egypt, in the capacity of a prefect. This appointment was intended as a courtesy to Cleopatra. To appoint a Roman senator as Rome's man in Alexandria would have been a slap in the face to proud Cleopatra. Once Augustus became emperor and Egypt became a province, Augustus would continue the policy of appointing prefects to govern there. But Augustus did this for a different reason: the man who controlled Egypt, which produced a fourth to a third of Rome's grain needs, would have the power to control that grain supply. To eliminate the possibility of rivals gaining that power, Augustus decreed that no Roman of senatorial rank could even enter Egypt without his express permission.

In the autumn of 47 B.C., promising to send for Cleopatra once he was settled back in Rome, Caesar set off overland for Syria, via Pelusium, together with the Jewish leaders Hyrcanus and Antipater and their Jewish troops, as well as the allied forces supplied by the other leaders of the East. Mithradates of Pergamum also marched with Caesar. As his escorts Caesar took along his eight hundred cavalry and the men of the 6th Legion.

The tough veterans of the 6th, as Caesar had expected when he signed them up, had proven themselves by far his most effective and most reliable troops through the many difficult months in Egypt. The 6th had come out of this campaign virtually unscathed, unlike the other legions involved. It was a point that was not lost on Caesar or the less than one thousand men of the 6th. Legionary Publius Sertorius and his comrades would have begun to boast that it was as if the gods were now smiling on them and protecting them— after taking them to the brink of extermination at Farsala.

Leaving behind Alexandria, the Delta, and Pelusium, the column quickly marched up to the coastal plain of Idumaea. All the minor potentates of the region came flocking to Caesar once he arrived in Syria. He reaffirmed his friendship with them and Rome's determination to keep their lands safe from external enemies, with their help and while they maintained order within their realms, and he sent home most of the regional forces that had marched with him and fought for him in Egypt.

While he was in Syria he was joined by his cousin Sextus Caesar, who had come out from Rome with a fleet of ships. From Sextus and from letters he received from various leading people at Rome he learned that Mark Antony was doing an appalling job of running things at the capital in his absence. Caesar's bigheaded young relative Lucius Dolabella had been appointed a Tribune of the Plebs—the tribunes were at this time the only regular magistrates at Rome. Dolabella, to win public popularity, had been promising to abolish debts and eliminate rents. Aulus Trebellius, another of the tribunes, took exception to this, and the population had taken sides, until there were riots in the streets. Yet Antony, who was supposed to be in charge, had done nothing to prevent or terminate any of this.

Meanwhile, three of the four Spanish legions camped on the Field of Mars as they waited for Caesar's return to Rome had run out of patience. Encouraged by some of their senior officers to grab what was owed to them, the men of the 8th, 9th, and 10th Legions had gone on a looting spree in the city. The 7th Legion had kept out of this, and only when Antony brought the 7th into Rome to stand guard duty did the looting stop in the city. But then the three recalcitrant legions had gone on a rampage in Campania, south of Rome, looting the country estates of the rich. Leaving Sextus Caesar temporarily in charge at Rome, Antony had gone to Campania to convince the rampaging troops to go back to camp on the Field of Mars, where they now were once more. But the situation was still on a knife edge, and Caesar's friends in Rome were begging him to hurry home to fix things.

Despite the volatility in Rome, Caesar was determined to settle affairs in the East to his satisfaction. By this time he had become fully aware of Pharnaces' victory over General Domitius at Nicopolis and his subsequent brutal occupation of Pontus. Caesar had hoped that news of his victory in Egypt and subsequent arrival in Syria would be enough to scare Pharnaces into withdrawing from Pontus. But reports coming to Caesar while he was in Syria told him that Pharnaces was not budging. Those reports said that Pharnaces was puffed up with self-confidence in the wake of his defeat of General Domitius and his Roman army. Caesar began planning a military operation designed to terminate Pharnaces' occupation of Roman territory. But while he was prepared to use force, he was in no rush—perhaps the Bosporan king would lose his nerve if Caesar merely hovered just over the horizon, and save him the trouble of a military campaign.

So, through May and June, Caesar focused on administrative duties in Syria. He standardized the laws and judicial procedures of each district he passed through, and made various official appointments, firmly putting his personal imprint on the region. The most important of these appointments was that of Sextus Caesar as governor of the province of Syria, the post that had previously been held by Pompey's father-in-law, Scipio, who was now in Africa with the other surviving republican leaders. Sextus would take up residence at the governor's palace in Antioch, the Syrian capital. Caesar further decreed that from Antioch, Sextus also would have overall command of the legions based in Egypt and could, if circumstances required, summon them up from Egypt for military operations in the East.

Caesar also heard and passed judgment on local disputes, and distributed awards to individuals and Syrian communities. Among the many people who came to see him and place matters before him for judgment was Antigonus, son of Aristobulus, a former ruler of Judea who had been an opponent of Antipater and Hyrcanus before being poisoned and almost killed. In front of Caesar, Antigonus accused Antipater and Hyrcanus of having acted unjustly and extravagantly in Judea in the past. As for the help they'd just given Caesar in Egypt, he said they hadn't done it through goodwill to Caesar but rather to cover up the fact that they had previously been friends and supporters of Pompey the Great.

Given the chance to respond, Antipater dramatically disrobed in front of Caesar, to reveal a body scarred from numerous wounds, which, he said, he'd gained in the service of Rome and of Caesar. He would let his body do the talking, he said, although he suggested that if Antigonus were to gain power in Judea he would stir the Jews into revolt against Rome.

Caesar agreed wholeheartedly with Antipater. Sending his accuser Antigonus away, Caesar told Antipater that as his reward for his service in Egypt he could have whatever authority he wanted in his own country, and Antipater chose the post of Roman procurator of Judea. Caesar agreed to the appointment, also making Antipater a Roman citizen and freeing him from taxes for the rest of his life. Antipater subsequently made his eldest son, Phasaelus, governor of Jerusalem and his fifteen-year-old son Herod governor of Galilee. Antipater also received permission to rebuild the walls around Jerusalem, which Pompey and his legions had knocked down when they successfully besieged the city two decades earlier. High Priest Hyrcanus also was rewarded for his meritorious military service in Egypt—his high priesthood was confirmed on him for life by Caesar, who also decreed that Hyrcanus's children would succeed him as high priest after his death.

Hyrcanus and Antipater accompanied Caesar all the way through Syria until he left the province. Before he parted from the pair he vowed that the rewards he had bestowed on them would later be confirmed by decrees of the Senate at Rome, which they were, and would be inscribed in brass at Rome.

The Jewish people as a whole also received Caesar's thanks for the part their fighting men played in his victory in Egypt. The Jewish residents of Alexandria were made citizens of that city, with all the rights this entailed. And, over the next few years, the cities of the East would receive decrees from Caesar that pronounced that because devout Jews were required by their faith to observe one day in seven as a day of rest, and this was incompatible with military service, any Jew then serving in the Roman army was to be immediately discharged. No Jew was thereafter enrolled in the Roman army.

In late June of that year, 47 B.C., at the Syrian port of Laodicea, Caesar, the men of the 6th, and Caesar's eight hundred cavalry boarded his own fleet and the ships that Sextus Caesar had brought out from Italy. Always with an ear cocked for news of what Pharnaces was doing in Pontus, Caesar sailed to Tarsus, the principal city of Cilicia, and summoned all the leaders of the communities of Cilicia and neighboring states to a council.

On June 23, back in Egypt, Cleopatra gave birth to a son. She named him Ptolemy Philopater Philometor Caesar. He would soon become known simply as Caesarion. Later, for political reasons, Caesar's former friend and staff officer Gaius Oppius would write a document disclaiming Caesar's paternity of Cleopatra's son, but Caesar himself would claim Caesarion as his own flesh and blood, and Mark Antony would confirm it in the Senate.

At Tarsus in late June, unaware that his son had entered the world, Caesar was conducting his Cilician council, settling the affairs of the region. As he received submissions and settled disputes, couriers hurried dispatches from him to the Roman units that had fought in the Battle of Nicopolis and had been withdrawn to Asia by General Domitius. Those dispatches contained marching orders for the substantially intact 36th Legion and what remained of the Pontic Legion. They were both to march at once for Pontus, where Caesar would rendezvous with them. He himself would bring the 6th Legion and his cavalry.

Caesar had forgiven General Domitius for the disaster at Nicopolis. Before long Domitius would serve as a senior commander in Caesar's army when he took on the republican forces in Africa. But for now Caesar left Domitius in charge in Asia; he would appoint the former consul of 48 B.C., Publius Servilius Isauricus, to govern Asia in Domitius's stead in the new year. Now Caesar gave command of Domitius's two legions to General Caelius Vinicianus for the Pontus operation; apparently he had come out from Italy with Sextus Caesar.

After spending just a few days attending to matters of state in Tarsus, Caesar, impatient now to deal with the threat posed by the intransigent Pharnaces, set off overland with the 6th and his cavalry. In the first half of July, Caesar and his by now regular escort of two thousand infantry and cavalry arrived unexpectedly in the mountainous kingdom of Cappadocia after a series of forced marches from Cilicia.

Pontus, Pharnaces, and the Bosporan army were now just several days' march to the north.

XVIII

GOING AFTER
PHARNACES

After arriving in Cappadocia in mid-July 47 B.C., the Roman column spent two days at the city of Mazaca, today's Kayseri. This was the royal seat of the kings of Cappadocia, and, during his stay at the palace at Mazaca, Caesar pardoned Ariobazarnes, king of Cappadocia for the past five years, for having sided with Pompey and providing the republican side with cavalry at the Battle of Pharsalus.

Ariobazarnes had an ambitious younger brother, Ariarathes. To lessen the possibility of Ariarathes scheming to overthrow the king and causing instability in the region, Caesar gave the king's brother control of part of Armenia Minor. But Ariarathes would only be able to take control of the lands now assigned to him by Caesar once Pharnaces had been dealt with. This was a tangible incentive for Ariobazarnes and Ariarathes to provide their best cavalry to Caesar for the Roman leader's planned campaign against Pharnaces. With Pharnaces out of the way, Ariarathes would take charge in Armenia Minor and King Ariobazarnes would have his troublesome brother out of his hair. And Caesar would have two more grateful allies in the East.

Adding several hundred of the best Cappadocian cavalry to his column, Caesar moved on, continuing northwest along the principal Cappadocian highway to the city of Comana—not the city of the same name in Pontus. This Cappadocian Comana, the modern Sahr, also known as Chryse in Roman times to distinguish it from the Pontic Comana, was the site of a massive temple that was ancient even in Caesar's time. This was the shrine of the Hittite goddess Ma, who had been adopted by the Romans as the war goddess Bellona.

The shrine of Bellona at Comana was cared for by thousands of servants, and the goddess was so revered by Cappadocians that they ranked the senior priest of Comana second only to their king. The priesthood of Comana being vacant, Caesar stamped his authority on Cappadocian affairs by appointing a new priest, a Bythinian whose family had in the past traditionally provided the priests of this shrine.

As Caesar marched on through Cappadocia in the latter part of July, moving closer to Pontus with each passing day, he reached the borders of Cappadocia and Gallograecia, in what today is central-eastern Turkey. King Deiotarus had been ruling most of Gallograecia for a number of years with Pompey's blessing, although the Senate at Rome had actually styled him King of Armenia Minor. Old Deiotarus now came to Caesar.

Laying aside his fine clothes and royal insignia, King Deiotarus pros- trated himself before Caesar wearing simple unwashed clothes, and begged his forgiveness for having previously supported Pompey. The shrewd old king claimed that he had joined Pompey's army with six hundred cavalry for the Battle of Pharsalus because Pompey had commanded him to do so, and he had been afraid of disobeying the command because of Pompey's military might. He added that at the time there had been no forces of Caesar in the region to whom he could turn for help.

Caesar could read Deiotarus like a book. The king had thrown in his lot with Pompey because he had expected him to beat Caesar. From other reports, Caesar knew that Deiotarus and members of his family had enthu- siastically joined Pompey's war effort—Deiotarus's grandson Tarcondarius Castor also had been present at Pharsalus, leading three hundred Gallo- graecian cavalry for Pompey. And even after Pompey's defeat at Pharsalus, Deiotarus had met up with him in Thessaly when both were fleeing from Caesar's forces, where Deiotarus had asked Pompey what he should do. Pompey had told him to look after himself. This he had done, tracking down General Domitius when he arrived in the region and seeking help to oust Pharnaces from Armenia Minor.

Other regional nobles came in crowds to Caesar at Comana to speak up for Deiotarus, although the tetrarchs of the region asserted that the king had no hereditary claim to the Gallograecian territory he currently con- trolled and suggested that his lands be distributed among them instead.

Caesar was a pragmatic man who frequently overlooked the past crimes and misdemeanors of those who came over to his side. He was proud of the fact that he pardoned his enemies, and Deiotarus would be another who would benefit from his magnanimity. But before he pardoned the king he made him sweat a little. He reminded Deiotarus that when he was consul twelve years before he had conferred numerous benefits on him. He told him that a man of Deiotarus's intelligence should have known better than to support Pompey against Caesar, especially after Caesar had taken control at Rome in the spring of 49 B.C. and it was apparent who was the man in charge of Rome's destiny.

But in light of their old bonds of friendship, of Deiotarus's age and standing and the entreaties of his friends, Caesar said, he would pardon him for his folly. As to the matter of who controlled Gallograecia, he now advised the king and the other rulers of the region that he would settle that later, once he had dealt with more pressing affairs. Caesar had in fact already decided who would rule Gallograecia, and it was neither Deiotarus nor one of the other tetrarchs who had petitioned him for it. Leaving the king up in the air about his future, he then commanded Deiotarus to bring his infantry and all his cavalry to Pontus to join him in the campaign against Pharnaces.

According to Suetonius it was on July 28 that Caesar arrived in Pontus with his escort, including the 6th Legion men. There he was soon joined by the 36th Legion, the Pontic Legion, and Deiotarus and his infantry and cavalry. The survivors from the two legions of Deiotarus that had been much depleted by the defeat at Nicopolis had by now been formed into a single legion of close to full strength, and it took the name, then and long afterward, of the Deiotariana, or Deiotarus's Legion. Within sixteen years it would be given the vacant number of the 22nd Legion to become the 22nd Deiotariana, one of the legions of Rome's new standing army. Caesar had brought several thousand slaves with him from Cappadocia. The reason for this is not spelled out, but his intent was probably to make Pharnaces think he had more fighting men with him than he in fact possessed.

Unbeknownst to Caesar, Pharnaces was now also faced with problems back home in his Bosporan realm. Pharnaces had left his good friend and deputy Asander in charge at Kerch. But in his king's absence Asander had revolted and taken control of the kingdom in his own name. The ambitious Asander planned, says Cassius Dio, to ally himself to Rome and so receive Caesar's support against Pharnaces. Having only recently learned of Asander's betrayal, Pharnaces had mobilized his army and was marching for the northern coast of Pontus to join his fleet to return to Kerch and throw Asander off his throne, when he'd been informed that Caesar was approaching Pontus, marching an army in the direction of the Yesil River. Deciding to deal with the most immediate threat first, Pharnaces had then wheeled around and marched his army to the Yesil River valley, to stand in Caesar's way, setting up his headquarters at the town of Zela, modern-day Zile, in central Turkey.

Pharnaces' intent seems to have been to settle with Caesar, preferably through bluff or negotiation, and preserve his army for a confrontation with Asander. Yet, having already defeated one Roman army, and learning that much of the small army that Caesar was bringing against him was made up of the remnants of Domitius's defeated force, he was not averse to doing battle with him either. After all, a military victory over Caesar would end Asander's hopes of an alliance with the Roman leader, and in that case Asander probably would vacate the Bosporan throne of his own accord and flee for his life. Just the same, the cheapest and surest course for Pharnaces was to avoid battle with Caesar. If he could bluff Caesar into returning to Rome to sort out his own problems in his own capital, leaving Pharnaces still in control of Pontus, Pharnaces could then handle Asander with his army intact and with the reputation of having stared down Caesar and won. Either way, Asander's support back in the Bosporan Kingdom could be expected to melt away. With his course set, Pharnaces prepared for war but continued sending deputations to Caesar.

Envoys from Pharnaces now reached the Roman camp on the Yesil. Offering Caesar a golden crown as a gift from Pharnaces in recognition of his victory in Egypt, the ambassadors asked that Caesar not enter their country of Pontus as an enemy but as a friend. Pharnaces, they said, was prepared to obey all Caesar's commands. And they went to great pains to emphasize to Caesar that Pharnaces had never acceded to Pompey's requests for Bosporan troops prior to the Battle of Pharsalus. Yet they had heard that King Deiotarus, who had provided Pompey with troops, had lately been pardoned by Caesar. And they wondered where the fairness was in that.

"I will be absolutely fair to Pharnaces," Caesar replied mildly, so Hirtius writes, "if he does in fact fulfil his promises." But, Caesar warned the Bosporan envoys, they shouldn't be citing the case of Deiotarus or be too smug about not sending troops to Pompey. "I myself am never happier than when pardoning petitioners. But I can't overlook public outrages against the provinces by those who may have done me service."

He then reminded the envoys that Pharnaces's "good deed"—that of avoiding giving support to Pompey—had been more profitable for Pharnaces than it had been for Caesar. Now, he said, while he could not put right the terrible things that Pharnaces had done, Pharnaces could make some amends. He could speedily withdraw from Pontus, and he could free the men he'd enslaved and restore the property of Roman citizens and allies he'd confiscated. "When he's done this, then he can send me the gifts that generals are accustomed to receive from their friends after victory."

The envoys were sent back to Pharnaces with their golden crown. Yet Pharnaces was not unhappy at the reply the envoys conveyed to him; it was what he would have expected of Caesar. The envoys also brought him their assessment of the army that Caesar had with him. He had left most of his troops in Egypt, they would have said, and they confirmed that, as they had been hearing, many of those soldiers marching with him were the same men that Pharnaces had whipped at Nicopolis.

Pharnaces doubted that Caesar would commit to battle. He felt sure he was bluffing. Pharnaces, aware of the continuing disturbances in Rome, decided that if he could string Caesar along long enough the Roman leader would be forced to up stakes and hurry back to Rome.

So, from Zela, Pharnaces sent back word pledging to do everything that Caesar required of him. But for him and his court to overnight leave Pontus, his hereditary kingdom, was simply not possible, he said. He proposed a departure date some months in the future, and sent terms for a formal agreement that he desired Caesar and he would enter into. By the last week of July, Caesar could see that Pharnaces was stalling, and decided to act without further delay. Trumpets sounded "Prepare to march" throughout the Roman camp.

The men of the 6th Legion would have smiled among themselves. They were marching on Zela, to teach Pharnaces and his ragtag army of foreign mercenaries a lesson and to show Domitius's chastened amateurs how to fight and win. There was an old Roman saying about a javelin that never failed its owner, "Wherever you throw it, it will stand." The 6th Legion was just like that javelin—sharp, lethal, and ever dependable.

XIX

THE CHARIOTS
OF ZELA

T he valley of the Yesil Irmak, the Yesil River, was and is green and fertile. Today, watered by the murky Yesil and its tributaries, the valley is dominated by sugar beet and tobacco plantations. When, on the first day of August 47 B.C., the men of the 6th Legion and their comrades of Caesar's task force came up the valley from the direction of Cappadocian Comana with their backpacks over their shoulders, sugar and tobacco were unknown in the Roman world. Vineyards and orchards then lined the valley's steep surrounding foothills.

The Roman column had been marching since dawn, with a strong advance party of cavalry and infantry out front and a long baggage train of packmules and supply carts toward the rear. In the early morning, when it was twenty-five miles from the town of Zela, Caesar's column was met by another delegation from Pharnaces.

Caesar didn't halt the column. Instead, he dismounted and walked and talked with the Bosporan ambassadors as the army continued to march up the valley road. According to Appian, the envoys again sought to come to an arrangement for Pharnaces' withdrawal from Pontus, offering Caesar a golden crown yet again, then increasing their offer to include the hand in marriage of Pharnaces' daughter.

From Dio we know that the daughter's name was Dynamis, but her age at that time is not given. Dynamis would have been in her early teens or younger and must have been quite a beauty to be the subject of an offer of this nature. Apparently the girl was back at Kerch. The offer from Pharnaces, who probably, like his father, had several wives, was sponsored by Caesar's reputation as a purveyor of attractive women enhanced by his recent liaison with Cleopatra of Egypt. The fact that Dynamis was no doubt a virgin also would have added to her potential appeal.

Caesar rejected both crown and virgin out of hand. He had already decided his course as far as Pharnaces was concerned. According to Appian, Caesar said to the envoys in response to their offers, "Is a man who had killed his father to escape justice?" This referred to Mithradates the Great, who, while he hadn't been killed by Pharnaces personally, had met his end through his son's actions.

The envoys became incensed at this slight of their king. They reminded Caesar that the last time their army had met a Roman army it had easily come out the victor. And they boasted that their army was made up of vastly experienced veteran soldiers. That army, they declared, had fought forty-two battles and had won every one. Unimpressed, Caesar sent the envoys on their way. As they went galloping back to their master with Caesar's negative response, the Roman column continued its progress toward Zela.

The classical town of Zela sat on a low hill on the flat valley floor, its high, enclosing stone walls running around the base of the hill. The scenic valley backdrop was made up of a number of tall hills sliced by valleys. The highest of these surrounding hills was a little over three miles from the town, to which it was connected by tracks running over high ground. This hill was famous in this part of the world as the site of a 67 B.C. victory by an army led by Mithradates the Great over a Roman army commanded by Gaius Valerius Triarius, a general subordinate to the famous Lucius Lucullus. As a result of this defeat and other blunders, the Senate had replaced Lucullus as Rome's commander in chief in the East, installing Pompey the Great in his place.

On a rise next to this hill, Pharnaces had installed his army. He'd restored the fortress erected there on the rise twenty years before by his father, and this he developed as his base of operations against this latest Roman threat.

At about the middle of the day on August 1, Caesar pitched a marching camp on high ground five miles from the enemy position. While the legionaries set to work digging the entrenchments and throwing up the walls of their camp, the thousands of slaves in the party were sent to cut and collect timber from the nearby hill slopes for the camp gates, guard towers, corrals, and ramparts, and for the army's cooking fires.

The slaves played no part in the construction work itself. Legionaries built their own camps. Not even auxiliaries were permitted to lift a hand when it came to building Roman fortifications and siege works; they would be allocated the task of gathering water, firewood, and fodder. For centuries to come, this policy was to be employed by the Roman military.

Even, in A.D. 71, when General Lucillus Bassus was mopping up the last resistance of the Jewish Revolt in the Middle East and had access to many thousands of Jewish prisoners, he used his single depleted legion, the 10th, to build the siege works around the holdout town of Machaerus, merely employing the prisoners to carry his water.

Only legionaries were considered suitable for construction work by Rome's generals. Legionaries, Roman citizens, could be trusted to do the work with precision and efficiency, without fears of shoddy workmanship or sabotage, for they knew that their own lives would depend on their labor. Besides, the Romans adhered to the philosophy that hard work makes hard men. So it was the men of the 6th and their legionary colleagues who built Caesar's latest camp in the valley of the Yesil Irmak on August 1.

Pharnaces had been watching this construction work from the distance. When he went to his bed that night it was with a clear picture of where Caesar lay and confident that he knew what to expect to find the next morning. Yet, Julius Caesar had become famous for doing the most unexpected thing at the least expected time. Just as he had pulled off the surprise kidnapping of all four members of the Egyptian royal family at Alexandria, once again, here outside Zela, he caught his opponents by surprise. And once again he achieved it via a nocturnal operation.

In the early hours of the following morning, while it was still dark, Caesar quietly roused his legions and led them out of their new camp and across the valley floor toward the enemy position. Having left their baggage behind at the camp, the legionaries carried only their shields and weapons and were able to travel swiftly. Silently, they covered four miles in quick time.

As the sun rose on August 2, Pharnaces was astonished and infuriated to see Caesar's army now on the hill where his father had celebrated his great victory over the Romans—less than a mile from his own camp. It was as if Caesar and his troops had materialized from nowhere.

As soon as it was light, Caesar set the legions to work digging a new camp on the barren hillside they now occupied. On the hill above them there was a weathered stone monument, built by Mithradates the Great to celebrate his victory over Lucullus's Roman army. Caesar had no intention of emulating that result. While his troops worked, he sent orders for the slaves to take the building materials from the old camp and bring these and the army's baggage up to the new camp. A constant line of slaves was soon extending between the old camp and the new one under construction, as the legionaries concentrated on the building work.

Now it was Pharnaces' turn to deliver a surprise. Up to this point he had been under the impression that the slaves in the Roman column had been armed soldiers, as Caesar had wanted him to believe. But now as they toiled back and forth across the valley floor below with packmules and baggage carts he recognized them for what they were, and realized that the opposing military force was not as numerous as he had at first thought. In fact, Caesar had only about fifteen thousand fighting men here at Zela, and of those, no more than eight thousand were Roman legionaries. Pharnaces' army, probably by now thirty thousand strong, would have outnumbered Caesar's force by at least two to one.

With that knowledge, and once he had conducted a sacrifice and received favorable omens, and apparently driven by the belief that the hill on which Caesar had installed himself was unlucky for Romans but lucky for him because of his father's victory there, Pharnaces decided to act. Leaving just a few cohorts to guard the walls of his camp, he ordered the rest of his army to form up in battle order on the slope outside, facing the Romans on the hill across the valley a mile away.

On his two wings, in addition to cavalry, Pharnaces also placed a number of war chariots equipped with sharp scythes on their wheels. This is the first time we hear about Pharnaces possessing chariots. No mention is made of them participating in the Battle of Nicopolis. Hirtius describes these vehicles at Zela as royal chariots, suggesting they formed a special bodyguard unit for the Bosporan king. Indications are that Pharnaces received reinforcements from Kerch once he occupied Pontus, leaving behind only a small garrison that Asander was able to easily overcome or turn, so it is likely the chariots joined him after Nicopolis.

These vehicles would have been similar to Egyptian chariots of earlier ages, drawn by two horses each, light and fast, with leather bodywork stretched over wooden frames, and with the small compartment forward of the axle built to accommodate a standing driver and an archer or spearman.

Hirtius says that Caesar assumed the Bosporan troops were being drawn up outside their camp merely to intimidate him. Perhaps, Hirtius says Caesar reasoned, Pharnaces was trying to force him to also line up some of his own troops in battle order to counter the implied threat, which would take Romans out of the construction work and slow down progress on the building of his latest camp. Or maybe he thought, so Hirtius says, that Pharnaces was hoping Caesar would abandon his camp construction altogether to form all his men into battle lines.

Yet Caesar was not one to be intimidated by anyone. Just the same, he couldn't be reckless, so he issued orders for two-thirds of his men to continue working on the new camp. The troops who would normally form the first of his three battle lines were to take their positions on the slope below the camp, facing the Bosporans across the valley in their ranks and files.

In this lone battle line, Caesar assigned the honored right wing to the 6th Legion. Just two cohorts strong, they would all have formed up on the right of the line eight men deep. Almost certainly Caesar allotted the left wing to the 36th Legion, which had shown itself the best of the other legions at Nicopolis. The much reduced cohorts of the Pontic Legion and the single Deiotariana Legion would have occupied the center. Despite the fact that the Deiotarans were equipped and trained as heavy infantry, Caesar only rated them as auxiliaries, and not very reliable auxiliaries at that, after their poor performance at Nicopolis. While the majority of Caesar's men continued to dig, lift, and carry with a wary eye on the silent host of enemy soldiers in battle formation on the hill opposite, these selected battle line troops stood in battle formation on the hillside.

Now Pharnaces delivered his second surprise of the morning. Bosporan trumpets sounded, standards inclined, and Pharnaces and his entire army began to descend the steep side of the hill opposite. Hirtius says that Caesar was amused at first at the sight of this mass of men scuttling down the slope to the valley that separated the two armies, considering it a "vainglorious display." In his opinion, no sane enemy would attempt an attack in this fashion, and he ordered his men to keep digging.

Reaching the valley floor, the Bosporans bunched up as they caught their breath, but then, with Pharnaces leading, they began to charge up the hill toward the Roman position in good formation. Hirtius says that Caesar was caught completely off guard by the incredible rashness, or self-confidence, of Pharnaces' charge. Now Caesar was issuing a stream of orders: "Down tools! To arms! Battle order! Form second and third battle lines!"

At the unfinished Roman camp site, there was alarm and confusion as legionaries dropped their entrenching tools and dashed to where their helmets, shields, and javelins were stacked, then looked around to try to find their cohort's standard or to pick out their centurion's commands in the melee of yelling men running this way and that. Roman legionaries were trained to form up behind the nearest standard in emergencies, rather than waste time trying to find the standard of their own maniple or cohort. Whether this is what now took place as Caesar's officers strove to form second and third battle lines is unclear.

At Alexandria, Caesar had been in some tight situations, yet suddenly, now, seeing the enemy swarming up the hill and seeing much of his own army in disarray, Hirtius indicates that Caesar felt more in peril than ever before.

From the Bosporan flanks the chariots came speeding, bumping into the lead, coming up the slope with their horses straining and sweating under the whips of their drivers. They raced up the slope and were on the single Roman battle line before Caesar could form his second and third lines.

The normal battle tactic for chariots to employ in a situation such as this was to charge toward one wing of the enemy line, then swing and run all the way along the front of the line, giving their archers or spearmen ample opportunity to let loose their full arsenal of missiles on this attack run. At the end of the line the driver would turn his steeds away, and the chariot retreated, having softened up the opposition, to make way for the charging infantry. It seems that on the hill at Zela the Bosporan chariots chose to charge the Roman right wing—the 6th Legion's wing.

The men of the 6th Legion steadfastly held their positions as the chariots bore up on them. Then, on the command of their centurions, every man let fly with a javelin. Close to a thousand of these missiles sliced down the hill into the charging chariots. The legionaries immediately took up a second javelin, and again, on command, let fly.

The closely packed chariot formation was devastated by the barrages. Horses, pincushioned by javelins, tumbled through the air, or reared up, mortally wounded, then crashed to the ground, overturning their chariots and spilling out the occupants. Unarmed drivers of other chariots fell from their perches, impaled by javelins. Chariots coming up behind barreled into vehicles ahead that were driverless and out of control. Not a single chariot survived the charge.

On the command "Close ranks!" the men of the 6th shuffled into tight formation with their shields locked together, ready to meet the Bosporan infantry when they arrived, and armed with a grim satisfaction at having destroyed the chariots so effectively and with a steely resolve to now deliver death and destruction to the enemy infantry.

Letting out their battle cry, the Bosporan troops came rushing up to the thin, stationary Roman line of four thousand to five thousand men. Then, with a thunderous clash of shields, they came to grips. The men of the 6th received the enemy and stood their ground. The charge of the wild-eyed Bosporan mercenaries came to a shuddering halt at the Roman shield line.

For a long time it was a noisy, drawn-out stalemate as both sides fought shield to shield, toe to toe without any advantage. But being on the down-

slope, and having run down one hill and then up another in full equipment before engaging, the Bosporans had sapped their strength and were
at a disadvantage. On their wing, the 6th Legion began to exploit that
disadvantage.

Little by little at first, the Spaniards of the 6th commenced to push
the Bosporans in front of them back down the gradient, using their shields
like battering rams, jabbing over the top of the shields and into the faces
of the enemy with the point of their Spanish swords. One step at a time
at first; then slipping, sliding yards.

Soon the backpedaling became a rout on the right. Bosporans began to
turn, disengage from the fight, and run for their lives back down the hill.
Many tripped and fell on the uneven ground and over the wreckage of
chariots and the corpses of horses and chariot crews, and were trampled to
death by those who came fleeing after them and then by the steady, in-
exorable advance of the 6th.

On the Roman left wing and in the center, the Bosporans had held
their ground. But now they saw what was happening to their comrades on
their left, and were demoralized to see men of this army that had never
lost a battle now throwing away their weapons and fleeing back down the
hill in terror, then across the valley and all the way back to the fort on
the far hill. The Bosporans on the Roman left and in the center now also
gave way.

The men of the 6th, their adrenaline pulsing, chased the enemy all the
way across the valley and up the hill to the Bosporan camp. The cohorts
that Pharnaces had left on guard put up a spirited defense, but men who
have tasted blood become part animal, part machine, and nothing nor no
one was going to stand in their way now. Once joined by men from the
other legions, the troops of the 6th overwhelmed the guard units and
fought their way into the enemy camp and quickly, bloodily captured it.
Pharnaces' proud, boastful army ceased to exist that second day of August.
Virtually every member of it was either killed or captured in the Battle
of Zela.

Pharnaces himself managed to escape, fleeing on horseback with part
of his cavalry. Hirtius indicates that he was able to make his escape while
the Roman troops were busy looting his camp.

According to Appian, Pharnaces fled all the way back to the Bosporan
Kingdom, no doubt using the same ships that had brought his army to
Armenia Minor and Pontus. He was not to survive long. Dio says that
Pharnaces fought Asander, but came off second best, and was made a
prisoner. With no sympathy for his former ruler and friend, Asander soon
executed Pharnaces. To add insult to injury, Asander took as his wife

Pharnaces' beautiful young daughter Dynamis, the same girl who had been offered to Caesar by Pharnaces' ambassadors.

According to Hirtius, Caesar was overjoyed by the defeat of the Bosporans at Zela. It was "an easy victory [that] had befallen him in extraordinary circumstances," Hirtius remarked. He added that Caesar won many battles, but no victory made him happier than this one because the peril he had felt he was in at the commencement of the battle was etched permanently in his memory. Standing surveying the Bosporan corpses littering the battlefield and the thousands of humbled prisoners from Pharnaces' army, Caesar disdainfully remarked, according to both Appian and Suetonius, "Lucky Pompey! So these were the sort of enemies you met in your war against this man's father, Mithradates, when you were considered great and called Great."

The brief nature of Caesar's campaign to retake Pontus was immortalized in the equally brief message Caesar soon sent to Rome to announce his victory. Fond of word puns and alliteration, he simply said, "*Veni, vidi, vici*" (I came, I saw, I conquered).

At an assembly of his troops on the day following the Battle of Zela, Caesar honored individual soldiers for their bravery during the battle and doled out decorations and rewards. Pharnaces' royal treasure had been taken, and the proceeds from this were promised by Caesar to his troops. Money earned from the sale into slavery of the thousands of prisoners also would be distributed among the legionaries who had brought Caesar victory at Zela.

Caesar then announced the future postings of the units involved. Deiotarus's men were being sent back to home territory. This was not to be the end of their unit, however. Before long, the Deiotariana Legion would be stationed in Macedonia, and soon would be a permanent part of the Roman army, with its men granted Roman citizenship. The 36th Legion and the Pontic Legion were to be stationed in Pontus for the time being, under the command of General Caelius Vinicianus, whom Caesar appointed the new governor of the regained province.

But Caesar fully recognized that for his survival and ultimate victory in Egypt and now his rapid and decisive victory here at Zela he had one small group of soldiers to thank: the men of the 6th Legion, little more than nine hundred of them. And he would not forget the contribution made by the 6th, described by Hirtius as "a veteran legion that had undergone many toils and dangers" to this point.

"The Sixth Legion," Caesar announced from the tribunal, "is ordered to return to Italy to receive rewards and honors."

A cheer would have gone up from the men of the 6th. So as Caesar prepared to set off that same day with his omnipresent cavalry escort to continue to travel light and fast overland through Gallograecia and Bithynia to Asia, the men of the 6th prepared to march across Turkey and Greece to the Albanian coast, there to make a short sea journey from Durrës across the Strait of Otranto to Brindisi in Italy prior to the final leg up the Appian Way to Rome. They would head for the city at the heart of their empire, yet a city they had only heard about but never visited.

The men of the 6th would be marching chained Bosporan prisoners all the way to Rome with them—hundreds or even thousands of surrendered survivors from Pharnaces' army. Caesar had plans for these prisoners in Rome; already he was planning to celebrate a Triumph for his victory in Pontus, and these captives would be marched through the streets of Rome, displayed to the leering, jeering Roman people as trophies of war, prior to their being sold into slavery in the capital's slave market.

As the soldiers of the 6th packed up their personal belongings and their accumulated loot acquired from almost exactly a year's service under their agreement with Caesar, and wondered what manner of rewards and honors Caesar would bestow on them once he himself arrived back in Italy, they would have allowed themselves the luxury of thinking about their long overdue retirement. In their mind's eye they could see themselves hanging sword and shield on the wall of a comfortable farmhouse and settling down on a fine piece of land somewhere in the sun with an equally comfortable wife.

And the soldiers of the 6th would have marveled that since they had marched for Caesar they had led something of a charmed life. Their casualties, in Egypt and in Pontus, had been minimal, yet all around them other units had suffered greatly—the 37th Legion at the Hepstadion causeway in Alexandria, the 27th Legion at Jews Camp, the 36th and Pontic Legions at Nicopolis. It was almost, someone would have suggested, as if nothing could harm them, as if the 6th Legion were ironclad.

As the 6th marched away from Zela herding its chained column of humbled Bosporan prisoners with it, the men of the 36th Legion and the Pontic Legion were hard at work building a monument on the site of Caesar's victory, close to the twenty-year-old monument erected by Mithradates the Great to celebrate his victory over General Triarius. Dio says that Caesar did not dare tear down Mithradates' monument because it had been dedicated to the gods, essentially the same gods the Romans worshiped, but he had his own grander edifice thrown up within sight of it, to overshadow it.

As the 6th Legion proceeded west in his wake, Caesar arrived in Gallograecia. He'd given thought to King Deiotarus's contested claim to the region, and had decided that as Deiotarus had originally taken Gallograecia by force, that claim was not legitimate. But he would not give Gallograecia to one of the other claimants. Mithradates of Pergamum was riding with him, and now Caesar granted the tetrarchy of Gallograecia to him. And for good measure, Caesar also anointed Mithradates ruler of the Bosporan Kingdom, in Pharnaces' stead. There in Gallograecia the two firm friends parted, as Caesar continued west toward the province of Asia.

Mithradates of Pergamum would soon attempt to claim the Bosporan Kingdom as his own, but Asander had no intention of giving it up. To Caesar's great regret, Mithradates would be killed in the attempt. Asander was to reign over the Bosporan Kingdom for three decades, becoming a friend and client of Rome. Meanwhile, Dynamis's little brother Darius, son of Pharnaces and grandson of Mithradates, would be made ruler of Pontus by Mark Antony. On Asander's death in 13 B.C., the new ruler of Pontus, King Polemon, would invade the Bosporan Kingdom in an attempt to bring it under his rule. Asander's widow, Dynamis, the daughter of Pharnaces, would lead a spirited fight against the invaders until Rome brokered a peace.

Dynamis then married her opponent Polemon, but after a year they separated and resumed their war, which dragged on for years. In 8 B.C. the Bosporans would capture King Polemon and execute him. While Pontus became a Roman province once again, Dynamis was to rule the Bosporan Kingdom for the next fifteen years as its queen, with the approval of Rome, until her death in A.D. 8. In the imperial era, Rome would base forty warships of its Pontic Fleet in the Bosporan Kingdom, at the capital and naval city of Kerch, as part of its ongoing alliance with the Bosporan sovereigns.

Caesar could not have imagined, as he departed from Asia and set off back to Rome in the late summer of 47 B.C., that the virgin he had declined to take as a bride would one day rule her father's and her grandfather's kingdom.

Crossing the Hellespont, Caesar rode quickly along the Egnatian Way to Durrës, crossed to Brindisi, and then rode up the Appian Way, arriving at Rome far sooner than expected, just as the news of the swift and total victory at Zela was being digested at the capital.

He had been away a year and a half, but he came back as victor over Pompey, as conqueror of Egypt, and as liberator of the Roman East. The fact that he came back at all had much to do with the courage and fighting skills of the nine hundred men of the 6th Legion, and Caesar knew it.

XX

THE ROMAN TRIUMPHS
OF THE 6TH

T he 6th Legion had to wait for its promised rewards and honors.
Caesar still had a civil war to wrap up. And, as he learned when
he returned to Rome, his republican opponents had gathered a
massive army in the province of Africa—fourteen legions under the command of Pompey's father-in-law, Quintus Caecilius Metellus Pius Scipio
Nasica.

Scipio, as he was known, had pulled together ten Roman legions plus
the four native legions of King Juba of Numidia that had wiped out Caesar's ill-fated general Curio and his two legions in Africa two years back,
plus thousands of cavalry under Caesar's former loyal deputy, the ubiqui-
tous General Labienus, and 120 war elephants supplied by King Juba. In
all, the republican army under Scipio numbered more than eighty thousand men.

Of the ten Roman legions in this army that was now preparing to face
Caesar, two had comprised the original Roman garrison of the province of
Africa, units that had fought without distinction against Curio in 49 B.C.
when he'd invaded Africa from Sicily. Five were newly created legions
filled with hastily drafted local recruits, and three were units that had
been evacuated from Greece following the Battle of Pharsalus. The latter
three were the substantially intact 1st Legion, and the three cohorts of the
4th Legion and the two cohorts of the 6th Legion that had escaped with
their eagles across the Enipeus River at Farsala when the two remaining
cohorts of the 6th had been trapped and forced to surrender to Mark
Antony.

There would have been a temptation to combine these cohorts of the
4th and 6th Legions that reached Africa to create a single legion of five
cohorts, but the proud Spanish legionaries of the two units would not

169

have it. They had not saved their sacred eagles at the Battle of Pharsalus only to abandon one of them. So Scipio conscripted thousands of local African youths into the two units in an attempt to bring the 4th Legion and the 6th Legion back up to strength. Some of these recruits were Roman citizens, but with most available draftees of the right age and in good health enrolled in the five new legions created by Scipio's recruiting officers, the vast majority of the new men conscripted into the 4th and the 6th were slaves.

This was an unheard-of thing, slaves serving in a legion beside Roman citizens. Even the Egyptians had relegated the slaves they enlisted to the militia units that had fought Caesar at Alexandria and on the Nile, and had not tried to have them fight in the regular army. But Scipio was not a commander who was sensitive to the feelings of the men he led, and he ignored complaints from the experienced Spanish legionaries in the ranks of his 6th and the 4th Legions.

So a then unique situation arose that there were two Roman 6th Legions in this civil war, each born of Pompey's original 6th: one on Caesar's side, the other marching for the senatorial side under Scipio. The men of the 6th who had gone over to Caesar after Pharsalus had no desire to fight their former comrades of the 6th, men now serving Scipio who were their friends, relatives, and fellow townsmen, and they'd apparently stipulated this when they signed up for Caesar. So Caesar was not to include his now celebrated 6th in the task force he assembled for an invasion of Africa.

As soon as he returned to Rome in the late summer of 47 B.C., fresh from his successes in the East, Caesar acted decisively to end the administrative problems that had plagued Rome in his absence. Disappointed with the job that Mark Antony had done at Rome while he was away, he began by dismissing Antony from his post as his Master of Horse and chief deputy. To maintain order he brought the 7th Legion into Rome from the Field of Mars, where they had been camped for well over a year, and stationed the unit in the city and around his own house on the Sacred Way— the *domus publicus* of the Pontifex Maximus, the high priest of Rome, that he had been occupying since receiving the high priest's appointment for life in 63 B.C.

Antony was not happy at his removal from power, and even less happy when Caesar put up for auction all Pompey's property in and around the capital—his house in the Keels district that Antony had taken over as his own, another mansion on the Field of Mars, a magnificent estate on the Alban Mount south of Rome—all would eventually become property of the imperial family once the empire came under the rule of Augustus. Antony felt that Caesar should have given him Pompey's house for nothing. Sulking, Antony didn't volunteer to join Caesar for the planned African operation.

To succeed with that operation, Caesar felt he needed his best Spanish legions. The 7th was obeying his orders, but he wanted them to be joined by the 8th, 9th, and 10th to form the core of his African task force, a force of sufficient size and quality to take on the fourteen senatorial legions now assembled in North Africa. Even though they were back in camp on the Field of Mars, the men of these three rebellious legions were still refusing to obey orders and still demanding their promised bonuses and discharges.

To begin with, Caesar sent his staff officer Gaius Sallustius Crispus—who would become known to history as the writer Sallust—to the Field of Mars to address an assembly of the mutinous legions. When Caesar had parted with these legions at the Pharsalus battlefield back in August 48 B.C., he had declared that he could win this civil war without them, and his pride would not permit him to stand before them and admit that he did need them after all. It was Sallust's job to convince the Spanish legionaries to now march for Caesar in one last campaign. He did his best, but he was no Caesar. Even when he offered these men a substantial additional bonus, Sallust received an angry reaction from the troops. They rioted, and Sallust barely escaped with his life.

Caesar was forced to swallow his pride. He went himself to address the three legions on the Field of Mars. They assembled when summoned, but they were in no mood for fine speeches. They began to call for their discharge. In response, Caesar blithely said that, fine, they were now discharged, and he would continue the civil war with other legions. But only after he had won the war, he said, and when those other loyal legions had received their rewards, would he give these men their promised rewards. He was bluffing, of course, but stung by this, and by the fact that Caesar was now addressing them as "citizens" rather than "soldiers," the men begged him to reinstate them and to take them on his next campaign.

Leaving Mark Antony and other troublemakers at Rome, Caesar set off for Sicily, his jumping-off point for the planned African invasion. The 7th, 8th, 9th, and 10th Legions formed the vanguard of the army of eleven legions he created for the African operation. The other units included a new enlistment of the 5th, a legion that had previously marched for Pompey in Spain, plus the 13th and the 14th; these three units marched all the way from Spain to Sicily to take part in the invasion, joining the

25th, the 26th, and the 29th. Finally, because they had recent combat experience, the five cohorts of the 28th were summoned from their station in Egypt for this operation, and apparently came from Alexandria to Sicily by sea to join the landing force.

In the late fall, the men of Caesar's 6th Legion would have arrived at Rome, as they had been ordered, escorting their column of fearful Bosporan prisoners. Their arrival at the capital, probably at night to avoid the congested daytime streets, would have been an event to strike awe into the hearts of both the soldiers of the 6th and their prisoners. Its very size, spreading over some eight square miles around the famous seven hills of Rome, would have astonished them. This was a city that, within a hundred years, would boast a free population of 1.2 to 1.8 million people, according to one authoritative estimate based on the number of residences recorded in a census of A.D. 73. The number of slaves that further boosted the population can only be guessed at.

The new arrivals would have been dazzled by "the smoke, the show, and the noise of Rome," as one Roman author was to write. Even in the half light of torches and wall lamps the city, with its unending nightlife, would have intoxicated the virgin visitor. Wide-eyed with wonder, the otherwise tough men of the 6th would have herded the Bosporans into the Lautimiarum, the city prison of Rome, on the Street of the Banker below the Capitoline Mount and just outside the old city walls, then set up their tents on the open space on the Field of Mars where the 7th, 8th, 9th, and 10th Legions had previously been encamped.

For the legionaries, this was their first sight of the place from where their world was ruled—their careers prior to this had seen them born and raised in Spain, then serving in Spain and Gaul, Greece, Egypt, and the Roman East, but never setting foot in Italy. Here were the massive temples, the vast public buildings, the monuments, the symbols of power of which they had heard so much. Just as this would have daunted their prisoners, who would have dreaded what might lay in store for them, the experience would have made the soldiers of the 6th proud to be Romans.

They arrived at Rome to find that Caesar and his four veteran Spanish legions had weeks before marched for the south of Italy to be ferried to Sicily and from there to launch the invasion of North Africa. The 6th would have to wait for Caesar's return before they received their promised rewards. For the time being, they settled down to serve as the capital's guard unit until their commander in chief returned from what would be a five-month war in North Africa.

In late December, Caesar sailed from Sicily with the first of what would be a series of convoys, landing unopposed in Tunisia. Over the next

few months he engaged in skirmishes as he built up his forces via a number of troop convoys from Sicily. Twice during the early months of 46 B.C.
groups of Spanish veterans in Scipio's 6th Legion defected to Caesar—
they had become disgusted at the way Scipio had polluted their legion by
drafting slaves into the unit, and they had refused to march with such
inferiors any longer.

On April 4, Caesar's eleven legions did battle with Scipio's ten legions
and three of King Juba's legions and sixty war elephants, at Thapsus in
Tunisia. With the recent Spanish recruits of the 5th Legion dealing with
the elephants on the republican army's wings and the 10th Legion leading
a breakthrough on the enemy's left, the day-long battle was won by Caesar's army. Again the 1st Legion retained its discipline and escaped; it was
evacuated from the port of Utique to Spain's Balearic Isles to join Pompey
the Great's two sons, Gnaeus—the former lover of Cleopatra—and the
younger Sextus.

Scipio also escaped Africa by sea, but committed suicide after his ship
was forced into a bay by a storm and he was surrounded by hostile warships. General Afranius, the 6th Legion's commander in chief in Spain,
was caught trying to escape and executed. Afranius's deputy in Spain, General Petreius, fled inland with King Juba. They later had a dinner followed
by a duel to the death, the survivor of which then committed suicide.

Following the Battle of Thapsus, as Caesar advanced up the coast
toward Utica, the capital of the province of Africa, today's Utique, the
senatorial commander there, Cato the Younger, calmly organized the
evacuation by sea of as many republicans as he could. That night, Cato,
father-in-law of Marcus Brutus, and long a vehement critic of both Caesar
and Pompey before he chose to support the Senate in the civil war, committed suicide rather than surrender to Caesar.

When Caesar returned to Rome at the end of July 46 B.C., it seemed
that the civil war was over, that Caesar was undisputed ruler of the Roman
world. In a long speech delivered to the Senate, he told the senators,
according to Dio, that he would not be their master. Instead, he would be
their champion. "Not your tyrant, but your leader," he said. They should,
he urged them, "conduct yourselves toward me as a father." In return,
"I will take thought for you as for my children." Soon Caesar was being
referred to as the father of his country.

To celebrate his victories, Caesar now ordered that an unrivaled
extravaganza be laid on for the Roman people—four Triumphs during
September. For hundreds of years, the Triumph had been the ultimate
reward for a Roman general. Voted by the Senate and preceded by a number of days of public thanksgiving, the Triumph had several components.

There was a large cash prize, and a statue of the triumphant general, the *triumphator*, was set up in the Forum. But the major feature of any Triumph was a ceremonial procession through the streets of Rome, which were lined by the cheering population. For this street parade, the triumphator rode in a golden chariot, a *quadriga*, drawn by four white horses. He wore a special crimson cloak, and a crown of bay leaves. And he carried a laurel branch, the symbol of victory. Traditionally, too, a slave stood behind the general as he was driven past the adoring crowds; the slave whispered in his ear, over and over again, "You are not a god." Caesar, who would before long be worshiped as a god, dispensed with that humbling touch for his Triumphs.

Pompey had been awarded several Triumphs in his lifetime. Caesar had not celebrated a Triumph prior to this. He'd qualified for one with his 61 B.C. campaign in Spain, and the official thanksgiving at Rome, the prelude to a Triumph, had been decreed by the Senate and had taken place, but when given the choice of either accepting a Triumph or running for election as a consul in 60 B.C., he'd opted for the consulship—a case of power before glory. Now that Caesar had ultimate power, he was ready for an overdose of glory. For a man who seems to have been obsessed by the need to eclipse Pompey's record in all things, this was another way that Caesar could outshine his late rival.

The attraction of a Triumph was such that Cicero, a great critic of the vanities of other Romans, was most disappointed at the news that the civil war had broken out in 49 B.C., not because of what this meant for Rome, but because he would not be able to celebrate the Triumph he had been promised for his 51 B.C. campaign in Cilicia—the thanksgiving days had already been celebrated as a prelude to his Triumph. Plutarch was to consider Cicero guilty of "an uncontrollable appetite for distinction."

A Triumph could not be celebrated for the defeat of Romans. The victory had to be over foreigners. A Triumph for Caesar's conquest of Gaul was to be the first of the four he celebrated in 46 B.C. It would be followed by a Triumph for the defeat of the Egyptian army, then another for the victory in Pontus over Pharnaces and his Bosporans, and last of all a Triumph for his victory in Africa. To achieve this fourth Triumph, Caesar classed Thapsus as a victory over the Numidian legions of King Juba, ignoring the ten Roman legions he'd also defeated on that occasion.

In all Triumphal processions, the conquering general was borne along in his golden *quadriga* preceded by his lictors bearing his fasces entwined with laurel, the symbol of victory to which a general hailed as *imperator*, as Caesar had been, was entitled. Behind the general came prisoners taken in his campaign, all in chains, with their leaders prominent. Then came the spoils of war displayed on a succession of wagons, followed by more wagons bearing stage sets and large paintings depicting the battle in question, like floats in a modern-day parade, all with inscriptions in large letters so the public knew what they were looking at. Last of all came soldiers representing the general's army that had won the victory. These soldiers were permitted to march along the processional route singing bawdy ditties about their general, receiving the adulation of the cheering, applauding crowd as they passed.

The men of the 6th Legion camped at Rome now found themselves the stars of three out of four of Caesar's Triumphs. They had marched for him for two years during the Gallic War, they had won both the Egyptian campaign and Zela for him. And so they would march in the relevant Triumphs. The other Spanish legions, the 7th, 8th, 9th, and 10th, had returned from Africa, and it is likely they, too, marched in the Gallic Triumph with the 6th.

Caesar's Gallic War had been one of the bloodiest military episodes in Rome's history; according to Plutarch the Gallic War had resulted in the death of a million Gauls and had seen another million sold into slavery. It had certainly been the longest and ultimately most rewarding of Caesar's career. This was reflected in Caesar's Gallic Triumph, which was the first and by far the largest and most lavish of all his Triumphs.

At dawn on the September morning of the Gallic Triumph, the men of Caesar's 6th Legion formed up behind their standards on the Villa Publica, the public open space on the northern outskirts of the city, part of the Field of Mars and official assembly point for all Triumphs, where they were joined by the other troops who were taking part in the procession. All wore their red tunics and red cloaks, their heavy armor, their plumed helmets, their belted swords and daggers, their decorations for bravery. The laws of Rome prevented them from going "fully armed" into the city proper, so they would leave behind their shields and javelins. Those same laws gave them the right, as soldiers of a Triumphing general, to wear swords in the city. This glorious day, the men of the 6th would have told themselves, was worth all the pain over their years in military service.

Here, too, at the Villa Publica were assembled the many wagons of the procession, the small army of freedmen and slaves who were responsible for running the show, and the host of chained prisoners who would unhappily vie with the soldiers and Caesar himself as the main attractions.

At the appointed hour, Caesar himself arrived, carried in a litter. Alighting, he mounted the waiting golden *quadriga*. In addition to the bay leaf crown and the rich scarlet Triumphal cloak, he wore the *tunica palmata*, the tunic of the triumphator, which was embroidered with a palm frond design. The palm was the Roman symbol of a victor; winners in gladiatorial contests received small golden palms. Apart from a driver, Caesar rode in the chariot alone. Little more than sixty years later, when Germanicus Caesar rode through Rome's streets in celebration of a Triumph for his campaigns against the Germans, Germanicus would take his young children in the chariot with him. One of those children would be his son Caligula.

Behind Caesar this September day, toward the Tiber River, rose a huge, half-moon-shaped drama theater, Rome's largest, whose construction was close to completion. This was the Theater of Pompey, financed by Pompey personally when he was in power and given by him as a gift to the Roman people. Caesar had taken care not to portray Pompey on any of the giant paintings that would be shown in his Triumphs. He knew, as Appian was to say, that Pompey "was still much missed by all." Pompey's memory would not be easily erased.

And then the time had come to begin the parade. Caesar was possibly heralded by legion trumpeters—for all their love of pomp and splendor, the Romans had no marching bands, not even drummers. Then came Caesar himself, preceded by a small army of lictors, his official attendants, bearing his fasces. As Dictator, Caesar was legally entitled to twenty-four lictors, as opposed to the mere twelve of a consul. But, says Dio, in addition to his current lictors, Caesar had himself escorted by all the men who had served him as lictor over the years—the term of a lictor being just one year.

This throng of scores of lictors, says Dio, did not go down well with the status-conscious Roman elite, there being a set number of lictors permissible for magistrates under Roman law, from one for a quaestor up to the Dictator's twenty-four. To ignore that rule and give himself such a horde of attendants, while Caesar may have thought it an honor for his former lictors, was considered, at the very least, ostentatious.

The streets along the procession's route were lined with many hundreds of thousands of people, come to watch the parade—some to sit down to the free banquet for leading citizens that was to follow, and all to enjoy the free entertainments that were planned for the coming days. Word of the upcoming celebrations had been sent throughout Italy, and Suetonius says that people flocked to the capital from all directions, and that many of the spectators had to sleep in tents pitched along streets and roads, or on rooftops in the city. More than once during these Triumphs the crowds were so immense that people were crushed to death. According to Suetonius, two of the victims of these accidents were senators.

The roar of the crowd rose and became a constant crescendo as Caesar appeared. Then cheers turned to deafening boos and crude insults as Gallic soldiers taken prisoner six years before, in the failed Gallic Revolt, were led by. But by far the greatest reaction was reserved for the number one prisoner. His name was Vercingetorix. A noble of the Arverni tribe in south-central France, Vercingetorix had only been in his twenties when he led a revolt by many of the tribes of Gaul against the recently imposed rule of Rome. At first the Gallic rebels had posed great problems for the Romans, with Caesar being forced to abandon the siege of one rebel city, after taking heavy casualties, and retreat. But in the end Caesar had defeated Vercingetorix and destroyed a massive Gallic army at the 52 B.C. siege of Alesia. There, Vercingetorix had surrendered to Caesar, and he had been a prisoner in Rome ever since. Now the long-haired young man was dragged in chains past the booing, hooting, cursing, spitting mob.

Behind Vercingetorix came many of the spoils of Caesar's conquest in Gaul, followed by the wagons bearing stage sets and twenty massive paintings of the war, painted on vast canvases the size of ships' sails, showing key scenes of the Gallic conflict such as Vercingetorix's surrender to Caesar.

Agog at the sight of the humbled enemy, of the bloody war illustrated so dramatically before their eyes, and then the captured enemy weapons and glittering spoils that were also trailed past them—Appian was to write that a total of 2,822 captured golden crowns were displayed in the four Triumphs—the members of the crowd then turned their heads at the sound of rough voices singing even rougher songs. And they cheered with all their might at the sight of the legionaries of the 6th and their comrades of the other victorious legions striding along behind their silver eagles and other standards with beaming smiles on their faces and slanderous lyrics on their lips.

The songs they sang during this and the later Triumphs, according to Dio, ranged from ditties that poked fun at former fellow soldiers from the ranks, centurions such as Gaius Fuficius Fango, who had been appointed to the Senate by Caesar, to witty lines about Caesar's romance with Cleopatra. They also repeated a rumor that had been circulating for years, that in his youth Caesar had enjoyed a brief homosexual relationship with King Nicomedes of Bithynia while serving in the East. The anonymous lyricist responsible for this song implied that while Caesar had enslaved

the Gauls, Caesar had been enslaved by Nicomedes. According to Suetonius, the verse went like this:

> Gaul was brought to shame by Caesar,
> By King Nicomedes was he.
> There goes Caesar, wreathed in Triumph,
> For his Gallic victory.
> Nicomedes wears no laurels,
> Though he's the greatest of the three.

Caesar was not impressed by this particular ditty, and soon after went
to the trouble of declaring on oath that there had been no such intimate
relationship between King Nicomedes and himself. This, says Dio, only
made some people believe that where there was smoke, there was fire.

In another ribald verse recorded by Suetonius, the legionaries sang
about Caesar's sexual proclivities:

> Home we bring our bald whoremonger,
> Romans lock your wives away.
> All the bags of gold you loaned him,
> Went his Gallic whores to pay.

Dio noted that in the chorus of the last of their irreverent songs—
more of a chant than a song in this case, apparently—the soldiers in the
Triumph bellowed these almost seditious lines:

> If you do right, you will be punished,
> But if you do wrong, you will be king.

The time-honored processional route followed by the soldiers of the
6th and their commander in chief took them from the Field of Mars along
the Vicus Triumphalis, or Triumph Street, and through a gateway in Rome's
old Servian Walls called the Porta Triumphalis, whose thick wooden gate
was only raised into the open position during Triumphs and even then
merely for the exclusive use of the official procession. From there the Triumph proceeded to a low-lying, half-moon-shaped street within the old
city walls called the Velabrum.

There in the Velabrum, says Suetonius, right opposite the Temple of
Fortune, according to Dio, the axle of Caesar's golden chariot suddenly
broke, and Caesar almost tumbled out before he grabbed the side to steady
himself. Some among the very superstitious Romans witnessing this hic-

cup would have interpreted this as a sign that Caesar's fortunes were soon to take a tumble of a different kind. Attendants dashed to Caesar's aid, slaves hurried to pull the damaged chariot aside, the *quadriga* was quickly replaced by another chariot, and then the parade resumed as if nothing had happened.

The Triumphal procession moved into the Forum Boarium, home to Rome's meat market, then past the Temple of Janus and into and around the Circus Maximus. The banked wooden tiers of this massive stadium, home to Rome's chariot races, could seat hundreds of thousands (the Circus Maximus's capacity was said to then be at least 200,000, growing to 365,000 within another 200 years), and on Triumph day the circus was packed with excited, cheering, waving spectators.

After leaving the Circus Maximus, the procession progressed down the Via Triumphalis to the Via Sacra, the Sacred Way, swinging back toward the Capitol. Passing Caesar's mansion and the adjacent residence of the Vestal Virgins and their circular temple with its eternal flame, it continued toward the Capitoline Mount. In Rome's first days, the hill of the Capitol had been occupied by Romulus's walled citadel. Here, too, had stood his circular, mud-walled hut, and in reverence to and remembrance of Romulus, a round mud hut was still maintained on the Capitoline Mount at the very spot where tradition held that Romulus had lived.

Caesar's chariot passed through the Capitol's gateway and climbed an inclined street, the Clivus Capitolinus, to the hill's southern peak. There it came to a halt at the foot of the steps that led up to the huge, 450-year-old temple of Jupiter Optimus Maximus (Jupiter Best and Greatest). It was the largest temple in Rome, as befitted the principal god of the Romans, and rectangular in the classic Greek style, built of volcanic rock covered with stucco, its wooden roof supported by massive pillars. Every year, the first session of the Senate was traditionally held inside the temple, so that the senators—the "conscript fathers" as they were known—might gain divine guidance for their deliberations and decisions over the coming year.

Suetonius says that here, on this Triumph day, forty elephants were lined up, twenty on either side of the temple steps, each with a burning torch held in its trunk. In actuality they would have been lined up along the Clivus Capitolinus. Pompey also had displayed elephants in one of his Triumphs, and it seems that, as he did in other respects, Caesar was trying to outdo Pompey with his elephantine lineup.

These particular pachyderms had been captured from King Juba's troops by Caesar's 5th Legion at the Battle of Thapsus, and were subsequently shipped to Rome. They would be permanently based at Laurentum just outside Rome, for use in spectacles. Some ninety years later the descendants of these beasts would be put on standby for the emperor Claudius's invasion of Britain, but would never be used in it.

At the foot of the temple steps Caesar alighted from his ceremonial chariot. He and his lictors then ascended the broad stairway. Whether Caesar slowly, reverentially went up the long flight of steps on his knees, as tradition required of a Triumphing general, we are not told.

Meanwhile, part of the Triumphal procession had peeled off from its rear. The prisoner Vercingetorix was led away from the procession in chains to a small building called the Tullianum, situated beside the Gemonian Stairs, below the Capitoline Mount, next door to the city prison. There was a windowless chamber in a former cistern beneath the Tullianum that traditionally served as the state dungeon of Rome, and the long-haired Vercingetorix was led down the steps into the chamber, where, in the light of oil lamps, the executioner awaited him.

Inside the Temple of Jupiter, Caesar offered all-powerful Jove his laurel branch, and his lictors offered the laurels that had been wound around their fasces, in thanks for the general's victory. Caesar then emerged from the temple to host a giant feast for thousands of invited guests at hundreds of tables set up in the open. Much of the food for the banquet had been provided by leading members of society as they vied with each other to impress Caesar and seek his favor.

The banquet did not commence until a message had been received from the Tullianum to say that the leader of the Gallic Revolt, Vercingetorix, was dead. In the Tullianum basement, an executioner tightly bound the Gaul's neck with rope, then placed a hood over his head—this is how Tacitus describes the preliminaries of this form of execution. Then, standing behind the condemned man, the executioner tightened the garrote until Vercingetorix asphyxiated. Such executions were the traditional climax to Triumphs, but occasionally rebel leaders were permitted to live after being paraded. Caesar, despite the reputation for clemency of which he was proud, did not choose to pardon Vercingetorix.

In further celebration of his Gallic conquest, over the next five days Caesar presented a series of public entertainments that grew grander with each passing day. Plays were performed, in several languages, in all the then twelve districts of the city. Athletic contests were staged for three consecutive days in a temporary wooden stadium erected on the Field of Mars. But most of the entertainments involved the letting of blood, and death. There was a gladiatorial contest in the Forum, in which contestants included the son of a praetor who fought an ex-senator to the death.

An artificial lake had been dug on the Field of Mars, and here a naval battle took place between several of the old Egyptian warships that had fought against Caesar at Alexandria and had been sailed or towed up from Egypt since, along with their captive crews, and ships from Tyre in Syria. In preparation for this novel show, the organizers of the Triumphal spectacles would have had the ships manhandled overland from the Tiber River to the lake by thousands of slaves. Why the Tyrians were involved in this battle we are not told; it's possible the city of Tyre had declined to support Mithradates of Pergamum when he was gathering the force that he took to Caesar's aid in Egypt, and this was the city's punishment—to have their finest young men fight to the death aboard ships on the Field of Mars in front of Caesar and a vast, bloodthirsty Roman crowd.

Appian says that a total of four thousand rowers were involved, plus two thousand marines. The objective of the two contesting navies was to sink or capture the ships of the other side, for the amusement of the thousands of spectators sitting on tiers of temporary wooden seating that lined the banks of the lake. If this were an even contest, there would have been about two thousand men manning the oars belowdecks and a thousand fighting men above in each of two little flotillas of five or six cruisers per side. *Naumachiae*, or sea battle spectacles of this nature that were staged in the following century, ended only when the sun set or when all the ships of one side had been sunk or captured. It would seem that the same rules applied for Caesar's waterborne show.

At the Circus Maximus there were wild-beast hunts every morning for five days. One afternoon there were chariot races between young noblemen driving two-horse chariots and the more demanding four-horse chariots, and horse races where the riders rode two horses at once. On another day the Troy Games were staged, a sham battle between two troops of boys, sons of Roman knights. Once they came of age at fifteen, these sons of the nobility joined a society, the Collega Juvena, a kind of military cadet corps that trained them to ride and fight prior to their doing service in the army as officers, and these Troy Games offered them an opportunity to display their skills, albeit with blunt wooden weapons.

On the final day, a battle took place in the Circus Maximus between two armies, each consisting, says Suetonius, of five hundred infantry, thirty cavalry, and twenty elephants. The men involved were a mixture of POWs—captives from Caesar's Gallic campaign who had been paraded in his Triumph—and condemned criminals taken from the city's prison and armed for the show. As the audience watched, each force hurriedly built a fortified camp on the floor of the circus, from which the central spine had previously been removed just for this occasion. The object of the battle was to take the other side's camp. And it was to be no mock battle—this was a real life-and-death struggle for the men involved. The combatants were given a simple incentive to fight, and fight well: only the victors could expect to see another sunrise.

This battle in the circus was, according to Dio, a particularly bloody one, for which Caesar was to be criticized by some among the Roman aristocracy—they were to say that Rome had seen enough killing in the civil war, in which many sons of great families had given their lives, without Caesar so graphically reminding them of the nation's sacrifices in the name of entertainment.

A week later, with the population still reeling from the excesses of the Gallic Triumph, it was the turn of the Alexandrian Triumph, and this time, as the conquerors of the Egyptians, the men of the 6th really took center stage. The Alexandrian procession was much like that of the Gallic Triumph, but this time it wasn't followed by an extravagant series of public shows. Among the paintings displayed in this Triumph were scenes depicting the executions of Achillas and Pothinus, and Appian says the Roman crowd was exultant at the sight.

Leading the Egyptian prisoners being dragged through the streets on this occasion was Arsinoe, Cleopatra's younger sister and briefly queen of Egypt during the war with Caesar. Unlike Vercingetorix, she was not to be executed—following the Triumph she would be sent to Asia to begin her exile at Ephesus.

Just the same, a woman had never before been seen being led in a Roman Triumph, and this sight of a former queen being dragged at the end of a chain like a common criminal shocked many spectators. For her part, young Arsinoe was visibly distressed by the soul-destroying parade through the streets of Rome, and she won the sympathy of the crowd, arousing very great pity, according to Dio.

By this time Cleopatra was in Rome as Caesar's guest, staying at his suburban villa high on the Janiculum Hill, today's Gianicolo, across the Tiber River from the city. She was not alone, having been accompanied to Rome by her brother and "coruler," Ptolemy XIV, and the son she had borne Caesar, Caesarion, plus a bevy of servants. The three of them would remain at the capital for close to two years. Officially, the party had come to Rome at the invitation of the Senate. Cleopatra's presence in the capital was no secret; she was a foreign queen and Roman ally, and, officially at least, her visit was like that of many foreign dignitaries who had come to Rome before and would do so in the future.

Officially, Cleopatra was treated as a guest of the state, and no doubt many a senator, curious to see this by now famous Egyptian temptress, the Queen of the Nile, for themselves, made appointments to call on the visitor and in due course made the journey across the river using the bridges of Tiber Island, then climbed the slopes of the Gianicolo in litters carried by perspiring slaves to reach the villa crowning the summit of the hill. And there they would have presented their compliments to a bedecked Queen Cleopatra, and she would have charmed and beguiled them.

What Caesar's third wife, Calpurnia, daughter of former consul Lucius Piso, thought of Cleopatra's presence, even if the young queen was based outside the city during her stay, we can only imagine. It was almost expected of Roman nobles to have mistresses. Many a Roman marriage among the nobility was an arranged one, for the political benefit of the father of the bride, and a loving relationship between husband and wife was not always expected, just as long as each respected the other and did nothing to humiliate them in public. While decorum and decency were seen to prevail, a marriage lasted. Caesar had himself divorced his second wife, Pompeia, after a male admirer of hers had been scandalously caught in Caesar's house, the house of the high priest, when only women were supposed to be present during the celebration of the rites of a female deity, Bona Dea.

Cleopatra was wise enough to maintain a low profile while living on Rome's doorstep. There is no record of her actually entering the city. In fact, she probably infrequently ventured from her residence. As it was, Roman women of the upper class rarely ventured out; it was not considered seemly. When they did, they wore a head covering and veil, as Muslim women do today, and were conveyed about in a closed litter. Only freedwomen and female slaves were to be seen on the streets of Rome, while their mistresses led a restricted life, bound to the home, made bearable only by the fact that the wealthy owned many homes—typically, the house in Rome and several more at estates within a day or two of the city, as well as a seaside villa—on Italy's western coast in particular—and farming properties throughout the empire. Wives and daughters could travel among these at their leisure.

Caesar would have gone to visit Cleopatra, as he was entitled to do— she was a state visitor, and she was staying at his villa, after all. So, while it was common knowledge that Caesar and Cleopatra were intimately involved, and while Cleopatra was younger than she, and famous now as a temptress, Caesar's wife would have felt reassured that under old Roman law Caesar could not marry a foreigner. And while Caesar changed many a law once he came to power, to change that marriage law would have caused uproar among the Roman elite.

So, while she said nothing about the affair, Calpurnia was safe from divorce—on Cleopatra's account, at any rate. Besides, despite his affairs, Caesar seems to have retained great affection and respect for Calpurnia.

Just the same, it is likely that Cleopatra badgered Caesar to be able to witness his Alexandrian Triumph, especially as several of her greatest foes were to be paraded in chains during that Triumph. Later events suggest it is probable that Caesar arranged a discreet viewing place for Cleopatra in a building overlooking the Triumph's route, a place with a good view but where she could watch Caesar and her enemies pass by without being seen by the crowd or by the participants in the parade.

From that place she would have seen her sister Arsinoe's anguish. Perhaps Cleopatra initially smiled at what she saw, perhaps she enjoyed the fact that her treacherous sibling was suffering for her ambition. But from later events it would become clear that the event made an indelible impression, that Cleopatra never forgot the sight of her sister in chains, the subject of public derision and ridicule in Caesar's Triumph.

According to the first-century poet Lucan, the other principal prisoner displayed during this Triumph was Ganymede, Arsinoe's former tutor and commander of the Egyptian army during the latter stages of the war with Caesar in Egypt. As mentioned earlier, the author of *The Alexandrian War,* almost certainly Aulus Hirtius, was to quote several speeches in his book from Egyptian leaders, including Ganymede, and it is quite likely that Hirtius interviewed Ganymede once he was incarcerated behind the walls of Rome's prison. Either that, or another of Caesar's staff officers, such as Colonel Pollio, interviewed Ganymede following his capture, in Egypt or at Rome, and passed on the resulting information to Hirtius. If Ganymede was questioned while awaiting his appearance in the Alexandrian Triumph, it is easy to imagine the Egyptian willingly detailing his side of the story, reliving his few months of glory when he was commander of the Egyptian army and had Julius Caesar against the ropes in Alexandria.

We can assume that Ganymede's days ended in the Tullianum at the conclusion of the Alexandrian Triumph, meeting the executioner and his rope garrote just as the Gallic leader Vercingetorix had done. Both tradition and the clamoring crowd demanded a high-ranked victim as the climax to a Triumph, and Caesar would not have hesitated to do away with the likes of Ganymede.

A week later, the Pontic Triumph was celebrated, and again, as heroes of the Battle of Zela, the men of the 6th Legion would have led the military contingent in the parade. They may, in fact, have been the only unit fully represented in this Triumph, with the other legions that had taken part being still in the East. The Bosporan prisoners ushered to Rome by the men of the 6th were displayed in this Triumph, before being consigned to either slavery or gladiatorial schools. Such was the nature of the paintings displayed on wagons in this procession, with Pharnaces' men depicted running for their lives down the hill at Zela, that Appian says the Roman crowd lining the Pontic Triumph's route roared with laughter at the sight.

Years before, Pompey's Triumph for his conquest of the East had, after a string of painted wagons depicting the various nations he had subdued, finished with a wagon bearing a huge sign that read, "The Rest of the Known World." Caesar's Pontic Triumph was to mirror this graphic touch—Suetonius notes that one of the wagons in this procession simply carried a large banner that bore the words "I came, I saw, I conquered," Caesar's own description of his Pontic campaign in his original dispatch to Rome following his victory at Zela.

It is unlikely that the men of the 6th Legion took part in the fourth Triumph, the African. Apart from the fact that they had not been involved in the African campaign, the Triumph celebrated the defeat of their comrades of the 6th, and they would not have wanted any part of such an event.

Among the prisoners paraded in the African Triumph was a five-year-old boy, Juba, the son of the late King Juba of Numidia, the defeated cocommander of the senatorial forces at the Battle of Thapsus in Africa and the man responsible for the defeat of Curio and his two legions in Africa several years before. Far from being tarred with the same brush as his father, Juba Jr. would be raised and educated in Italy, growing up to display a talent with the pen and becoming a writer, in Greek, who was to gain some note among the Romans. Befriended by Caesar's great-nephew Octavian as he grew up among the leading members of Roman society, Juba would be granted the kingdoms of Numidia and Mauretania by Octavian once he become the emperor Augustus, and as King Juba II he would rule his father's former dominion, marrying Cleopatra Selene (Selene meaning the Moon), the only daughter of Cleopatra and Mark Antony. But that was yet some way in the future.

Perhaps becoming overconfident as a result of the laudatory public reception to his first three Triumphs, Caesar miscalculated with the African Triumph. While he refrained from depicting Pompey in this parade, he had no compunction about showing members of Pompey's party, Roman senators and former consuls, even though this Triumph was supposed to be celebrating the defeat of King Juba and his Numidians. In this parade the

Roman people were shown a picture of the Roman senatorial commander Scipio committing suicide by stabbing himself in the chest, then throwing himself into the Mediterranean. Another painting depicted General Petreius at his last, fatal meal with King Juba. Yet another showed the highly respected Cato the Younger bloodily taking his own life in the African capital, Utique, following the Thapsus defeat. Appian says that when they saw these pictures the Roman people lining the Triumph's route groaned out loud. These sights only served to remind Romans of the tragedies their country had only so recently gone through, Appian was to write.

The paintings in the African Triumph seemed to suggest that Caesar was gloating over the demise of his chief political adversaries, rather than celebrating the defeat of Rome's foreign enemies. Overall, the previous Triumphs had been successes. But as propaganda, the paintings in the African Triumph failed miserably. This miscalculation, this insensitivity, combined with the other excesses of the Triumphs, would not be forgotten by an increasing number of Caesar's critics in the years to come.

These critics reminded each other how Pompey the Great had celebrated his last Triumph seventeen years before. Voted a number of Triumphs by the Senate for his many victories in the East, Pompey had combined them into a single Triumph, and had rejected the vast majority of honors showered on him by a grateful Senate. As Cassius Dio was to remark, Pompey had declined honors and appointments that were liable to bring him envy and hate. Now Caesar, in his determination to outshine Pompey, showed no such modesty or restraint.

Perhaps it was during Caesar's African Triumph that a small demonstration of dissent from a member of Caesar's own handpicked Senate took place. During one of his Triumphs, says Suetonius, Caesar, riding in his quadriga, was passing the benches reserved for the ten Tribunes of the Plebs, almost certainly in the Circus Maximus, when all but one of them respectfully rose to their feet. The exception, who stayed stubbornly sitting in his place, was a tribune named Pontius Aquila.

"Hey there, Aquila the tribune!," Caesar called out to him. "Do you want me to restore the republic?" For a number of days after this incident, according to Suetonius, Caesar would sarcastically add to every undertaking he gave, "With the kind permission of Pontius Aquila."

Finally, following celebration of the Triumphs, Caesar distributed the promised rewards to his veteran troops. According to Suetonius, each legionary received 24,000 sesterces, and the men of the 6th Legion would have been awarded this and more. According to Appian, centurions received twice as much as the rank and file in this payout, and military tribunes and cavalry prefects twice as much as centurions. The Roman public also received a payment at Caesar's instigation—400 sesterces to every citizen, plus a large ration of grain and of olive oil.

Where did the hundreds of millions of sesterces come from for these payouts and for the extravagant Triumphs that preceded them, when just two years before, Caesar's purse had been so dramatically empty? Certainly Caesar now raised taxes throughout the empire, and he imposed big fines on cities, towns, and individuals who had supported Pompey and the republican Senate during the civil war. But the primary source of his vast and overnight expenditure was Egypt, the prize for which Caesar and the 6th Legion had fought so long and so stubbornly; for when he had won the war there, his spoils of victory had included the keys to the treasury of Alexandria.

Cassius Dio has Mark Antony say, in a 44 B.C. speech to the Roman people, while reciting a long list of instances of how Caesar had made Rome great, "How after this he brought Egypt to terms and how much money he brought to you from there, it would be superfluous to relate."

The legionaries also had been promised land grants, and the men of the 6th were assured that a colony was to be founded in Gaul just for them. But still Caesar would not discharge these troops for whom, officially, that discharge was now more than three years overdue. He knew that there was still soldiering to do; the civil war was not yet at an end after all. In western Spain, the Pompey brothers had landed from the Balearic Isles and gathered thousands of eager local recruits around their standard. They also had been joined by the 1st Legion after its evacuation from Africa, together with several of Scipio's best officers, including Generals Labienus and Varus.

What really made Caesar sit up and take notice of Pompey's sons was the news that two of his own legions, the 2nd and the Indigena, both former Pompeian units, had defected to Gnaeus and Sextus Pompey shortly after the pair set foot in Spain. Realizing that the civil war would not truly be over until he had dealt with Pompey's sons in Spain, Caesar issued orders for a task force of infantry and cavalry to be readied to march to Spain to deal with the Pompeys. The men of the 6th Legion at Rome were informed that they would be in that task force, and ordered to prepare for one last campaign for Caesar in the new year.

This Spanish campaign, Caesar would have assured the 6th and the other legions assigned to the campaign, would truly bring Rome's civil war to an end. And then they finally could receive their discharges, hang up their swords, and start their new lives as civilians and honored citizens.

XXI

ONE LAST BATTLE

efore he left Rome for Spain to take care of the Pompey brothers, Caesar attended to a great deal of public business. One item was unfinished business: the Roman calendar. It seems that Sosigenes, the Egyptian astronomer consulted by Caesar, had by this time come to Rome, possibly as a member of Cleopatra's party, with orders to advise Caesar and the College of Priests on the solution to the problem with the Roman calendar that Sosigenes and Caesar had discussed in Egypt.

Sosigenes told Caesar that the Roman republican calendar involving a year made up of 355 days divided into twelve months, with an extra month sandwiched in every four years to make up the lost days, had to go, and the attempt to match the calendar with the lunar cycles that had been behind the original Roman calendar just didn't work and must be abandoned. The system that Sosigenes recommended required the months to be arranged seasonally, based on the solar year, just like the Egyptian calendar. Sosigenes' precise year, with 365.25 days, meant that now the equinoxes would fall on the same date each year, and the seasons would always begin at the same time, year in, year out.

Caesar endorsed the astronomer's recommendations and instructed the College of Priests to implement his new Roman calendar at once. To account for the quarter day, the new calendar would involve one complete extra day every four years—creating what we know as a leap year, with 366 days, although the term "leap year" would not come into use until Anglo-Saxon times. Caesar ordered that the extra day, which he called the "point of time," be inserted into February, between the twenty-third and twenty-fourth of that month, to give February twenty-nine days every four years. Anyone born on this extra "point of time" day had his birthday recorded as and celebrated on February 23. This system of calculating the passage of time became known as the Julian calendar, which is the basis of our Western calendar today.

To bring the new Julian calendar into line with the seasons, with January falling in winter every year, that year, 46 B.C., was extended by Caesar by the addition of sixty-seven extra days, spread over two extra months inserted between November and December. This meant that 46 B.C. lasted fourteen months, and when January 1, 45 B.C. came around, it would fall on what had previously been March 1. It also meant that January 1, the first day of the year, fell in the first part of winter. Caesar even published an almanac for farmers, to guide them with their seasonal planting and harvesting according to his new calendar.

This was all very well, grumbled men of the 6th Legion as they waited in their camp on the Field of Mars through the two extra months. Caesar's almanac might be of some use to them down the road once they finally received their discharge from military service and took up the promised grants of government land and became farmers. But in the meantime, they would have complained, who was paying them for the extra two months' service? Legionaries were paid just once a year, before they went into winter camp. And there is no indication that Caesar paid his troops extra wages for the additional two months' service occasioned in 46 B.C. by his creation of 67 extra days, or that the time was credited toward the legionaries' eventual discharge date.

Caesar would have considered his troops well reimbursed after the huge payouts he'd made following the recent Triumphs. But as a Roman saying so aptly puts it, the love of money increases as wealth grows. Still, even though there would have been some among the ranks of the 6th who would not have been satisfied, it was not an issue the majority would have considered worth agitating over, not with their discharge seeming to be tantalizingly near. Soon the nine hundred men of the 6th were on the march again, heading for what they hoped and expected would be their last campaign before they finally received that discharge.

By December, more than twenty weeks after the month of four Triumphs, Caesar had himself set off for Spain. His best legions, including the 6th, had already gone on ahead. Initially, he rode up through Italy and crossed the Alps with a large cavalry escort; but, impatient to come to grips with his last adversaries, he made the journey from the south of France to Tarragona in eastern Spain by sea, leaving his cavalry behind to make their way over the Pyrenees Mountains and join him in eastern Spain.

When he came ashore in Spain, Caesar was stunned to learn that three of his veteran legions—the 8th, 9th, and 13th—also had deserted to the Pompey brothers, just as the 2nd and Indigena Legions had done months before. The 2nd and Indigena were both former Pompeian legions, so their defection was explainable—they were asserting their old loyalty to the Pompey family. But these three latest turncoat units were all veteran legions that had served Caesar for years, legions that had helped make him great.

The loss to the other side of these three legions would have stung Caesar. No explanation is given for this defection of some of Caesar's best and longest-serving units, but they apparently deserted him through a disintegration in their faith in Caesar and frustration with his endless promises of discharge—promises that were, as the Romans said, no more than cabbage warmed up a second time. But Caesar still had seven legions in Spain, including the heroes of his 6th and the famous 10th, demonstrably his two best units in his greatest battles. Once his cavalry joined him, he was also backed by four thousand troopers, the largest mounted force he had ever put into the field.

Back in Italy, there was much speculation and concern about the outcome of the war in Spain, which, despite Caesar's reputation and his veteran legions, was by no means certain now that five legions had gone over to the Pompey brothers and the locals in western Spain were giving them their heartfelt support. Young Gnaeus Pompey, who was in overall command of the rebel forces, had a reputation for a short temper and a vicious streak. He was not well liked in Italy, even by leading men who had once been faithful supporters of his father. Following the Battle of Pharsalus, when senatorial leaders had gathered on the western coast of Greece, Marcus Cicero had announced he was going back to Italy to become a neutral; Gnaeus Pompey had wanted to kill him, and had to be restrained by Cato the Younger.

Now, in January 45 B.C., Marcus Brutus's brother-in-law Gaius Cassius sent a letter to Cicero to say that he was deeply worried about the situation in Spain and about Caesar's prospects. "I'd rather have the easygoing old master than a cruel new one," he wrote. "You know what a fool Gnaeus is, how he takes cruelty for courage, how he thinks we always made fun of him. I'm afraid he may answer our frivolous banter with his sword."

After combining his legions and cavalry, Caesar pushed into western Spain, and in a series of skirmishing actions slowly drove Gnaeus's field army back along the Salsum River valley toward Córdoba, capital of Baetica, or Farther Spain, which was held by his younger brother Sextus.

The attitude of the men of the 6th to this Spanish campaign can only be guessed at. They were natives of eastern Spain, so they didn't feel the same way as the legionaries of the 8th and 9th Legions—natives of western Spain, they had objected to fighting their own people, and this had influenced the 8th and 9th's decision to defect to the Pompeys. But just the same, the soldiers of the 6th could not have been thrilled at the idea of fighting Spaniards on Spanish soil.

As it turned out, they were not to be at the forefront of the initial fighting. Only once did the 6th become involved in a serious engagement during the bloody weeks of skirmish and counterskirmish in the Salsum River valley, as Caesar advanced and Pompey fought a fighting withdrawal. And when they did go into action, the men of Caesar's smallest legion reminded everyone on both sides that they were the formidable 6th.

One morning in late winter, the men of the 6th were building en-trenchments near the river outside the town of Ategua, which was held by the opposition, when just after dawn they were attacked by a large Pompe-ian force with the objective of dislodging them from their position. Despite outnumbering the 6th Legion men, the attackers were driven back, all the way to the town, by the tough veterans of the 6th. There were heavy cas-ualties in the engagement on the Pompeian side, but there was hardly a scratch among the legionaries of the 6th.

This was the 6th Legion's sole fight of note prior to the major battle of the campaign, the Battle of Munda, which was to be the only set-piece battle of this last principal act of the civil war. The battle was fought near the hill town of Munda on March 17, 45 B.C.

With his support faltering in the face of his continual withdrawals, young Pompey brought on the battle to settle the issue once and for all, and Caesar was happy to oblige. Against Caesar's seven legions, the Pom-peians fielded thirteen, but most of these were made up of raw recruits. The 10th Legion was given Caesar's right; the 5th, famous now for neutralizing Juba's elephants at Thapsus, his left. The men of the 6th were in Caesar's center with four other virtually full-strength legions.

The battle didn't begin well for Caesar. He unwisely marched his men five miles to confront Pompey, then sent them charging up a slope at the eighty thousand troops of the other side, who stood waiting for them. This was reminiscent of Pharnaces' foolish tactics at Zela. Out of breath, being cut down by volleys of javelins coming down the slope at them, Caesar's thirty thousand men halted on the hillside. At that moment, says Appian, Caesar thought briefly of taking his own life. Instead, he dashed out in front of his front line, defied enemy javelins, and goaded his men into restarting their charge. In the end, Caesar won the Battle of Munda, his last battle, but, as he was to confess to his staff, he had never come closer to defeat.

Gnaeus Pompey escaped, but was tracked down and killed within days. Generals Labienus and Varus died in the fighting, and the famous 1st Legion could not slip from Caesar's grasp this time; badly mauled, it surrendered. Sextus Pompey slipped out of Córdoba while Caesar was besieging the city, and disappeared. He would survive for another decade, later retaking the stage to challenge Caesar's successors. Córdoba had to be stormed by Caesar's troops, and several other towns that held out against Caesar had to be besieged before resistance in Spain finally caved in, but essentially with the Battle of Munda the civil war came to a close.

As for the men of the 6th Legion, they had come through this Spanish campaign virtually untouched. Now they were increasingly referring to themselves as the *Ferrata*, the ironclad legion. Nothing could harm them. And finally, the men of Caesar's 6th, now four years past their due discharge, were allowed by Caesar to retire. He had promised them land, and now he delivered. They would be allowed to form a Roman colony, with all the privileges that colony status entailed, in the south of France. Caesar had assigned one of his most trusted generals, Major General Lucius Munatius Plancus, the task of settling the veterans of his best legions in Gaul. In many cases veterans from more than one legion would be settled in the new colonies, but the men of the 6th Legion were to have a colony all to themselves, despite their lack of numbers—colonies usually involved three thousand or more veterans.

General Plancus—a praetor, whom Caesar would the following year select to become a consul for 42 B.C. in a long list of appointments he planned five years in advance—obviously had orders to find the best colony site possible for the men of the 6th Legion, in recognition of the debt that Caesar owed them. The chosen location was the town of Arelate, today's Arles, in the Provence region of southern France. Situated northwest of Marseilles on the Camargue plain where the Rhône River divides for its run to the sea on the Côte D'Azur, Arles had been a noted town of Ligurian tribes in times past and now served as a Roman port for goods going up and down the Rhône. The town was situated in some of the most beautiful, fertile, and productive land in the Roman Empire. Caesar was truly keeping his word to the men of the 6th.

Earlier, when Caesar's four Spanish legions had demanded their discharge and land grants, they had made it clear they didn't want to be given land taken from private individuals who could later reclaim their land, via the courts or via appeals to influential Roman nobles. Yet over the next two decades this was to be a common and recurring fact of life, with many a landowner dispossessed and his farmland divided among discharged legionaries. As Arles was surrounded by prime agricultural land, it is probable that the land given to the men of the 6th was indeed confiscated from Gallic farmers, some of them descendants of settlers from Italy.

Four years after the 45 B.C. retirement of the veterans of the 6th, when large numbers of legionaries were discharged following the Battle of Philippi, tens of thousands of them, and they, too, were given their fifty-acre lots in various parts of the empire, much of that land had previously been confiscated by the authorities. One family affected by those confiscations of 41 B.C. was that of Publius Vergilius Maro, whom we know as the poet Virgil. Even though Virgil's father was a Roman citizen, his land and farmhouse at Andes beside the Mincio River, just north of the Po in Cisalpine Gaul, were swallowed up in these mass confiscations. Vergilius Sr. had built the farm up, taking his holdings from barely improved land and a humble cottage with a sod roof to a respectable villa surrounded by fields supporting a large goat herd and acres of flourishing wheat, plus pear orchards and vineyards on the distant valley slopes.

Virgil objected bitterly to the confiscation of his father's land, where he had been born and grew up. "These fallows, trimmed so fair," he was to write, "some brutal soldier will possess." It was all the fault of the civil wars, he lamented: "To what a pass has civil discord brought our hapless kinfolk?" He may have actually been present when the new owner, the veteran soldier, arrived to take possession of the Vergilius farm and eject its residents. "We have lived to see, what never yet we feared, an interloper own our little farm, and say, 'Be off, you former husbandmen! These fields are mine.' "

Virgil is known to have appealed to powerful friends for the restitution of his father's land, although it is uncertain whether his appeals were successful.

The father of Virgil's fellow poet and contemporary Horace (Quintus Horatius Flaccus) also lost his farm to soldier settlers in the confiscations of 41 B.C.—at Venusia in the hills of central Italy. In his case it was as a reprisal because Horace had served as a young tribune in command of one of Brutus's and Cassius's legions at Philippi. But within two years Horace had been pardoned by Octavian, so it is possible that he, too, attempted to have his father's property returned to him. Such were the clouds that could hang over the legality and certainty of many land grants to discharged legion veterans during this period.

Official Roman colony status would be bestowed by the Senate on the Arles settlement, which was named Colonia Julia Paterna Arelatensum Sextanorum. Among the long list of honors granted Caesar, a fawning

Senate bulging with his appointees had recently bestowed on him the title *Pater Patria,* or Father of His Country, and this influenced the colony's title, which means the Paternal Julian Colony of Arelate of the Soldiers of the Sixth. As with most Roman colonies, Arles would be a town without walls. In its forum would stand a statue of Marsyas, a naked male figure with his arms raised above his head as he stands chained to a column in the whipping position. This statue of Marsyas was a common sight in all Roman colonies, being the symbol of a colony's autonomy.

To administer its own affairs Arles was to have its own Senate, to which retirees from the 6th could be elected. Within a few years the city of Arles would fund and build a fine amphitheater for public shows, large enough to seat twenty thousand people and that is still in use today, as well as a hippodrome, a drama theater, and all the other grand public buildings that became part of the fabric of a Roman colony. And in the regular religious processions on the annual calendar, the men of the 6th would lead the way, dressed in white robes, with their former centurions and men who had received the highest bravery decorations during their years in military service at their head.

But the men of the 6th were not to take up their land grants at Arles overnight. Colony sites were very carefully surveyed and laid out, because the Roman bureaucracy was pedantically thorough and under instructions to ensure that there would not be any later title disputes between new owners, so this selection and surveying process took months.

In the meantime, Caesar took the men of several legions, including the veterans of the 6th, back to Rome with him once Spain had finally been subdued. When, in the fall of 45 B.C., news reached the capital that Caesar's column was marching south down the Aurelian Way from Genoa, thousands of people flooded out of Rome to line the road to welcome Caesar home. Those who went farthest were the magistrates and senators, and Caesar's relatives. Notable among the latter was his favorite, the youngest of the three grandsons of his late sister Julia, Gaius Octavius, who turned eighteen on September 23 and who had been living at Caesar's official residence on the Sacred Way since he turned fifteen.

But it was Mark Antony, for so long in Caesar's disfavor, and who had grown fat now after several years of idle, luxurious living, who went many miles out in advance of anyone else to greet Caesar on the road to Rome. Caesar forgave him for his poor performance during his long absence in the East, and allowed him to travel back to Rome with him in his litter. From this point on, Antony was to share power with Caesar, who appointed him his coconsul for 44 B.C., effective January 1.

Once back in the capital, Caesar celebrated one last Triumph, this time for his victory in Spain. Again he had to split hairs to justify this Triumph, which he said was a victory over the Spanish, not all of whom were Roman citizens at that time—universal Roman citizenship would not be granted to all the people of Spain until the reign of the emperor Vespasian 120 years later. There also had been a detachment of native troops from Mauretania in North Africa in the Pompey brothers' army, and this was an added justification for Caesar's latest extravagant street parade. And so, officially, this was another Triumph to celebrate a great victory in a foreign war.

Apparently Caesar had learned a lesson from the reaction to the excesses of his African Triumph. The sons of Pompey were neither mentioned nor depicted in this procession's wheeled dioramas. Neither were Titus Labienus nor Attius Varus, nor the many hundreds of other Roman noblemen who fought and died in Spain in the last contest of the civil war, or the thousands of Roman legionaries who perished with them, a number of them men who had previously marched for Caesar for almost two decades.

Once again the men of the 6th shared the procession with their general, and once again the streets were lined with cheering Romans. Yet there was a tense undertone about the whole affair, a feeling of threat and intimidation. Just as, in the Senate, senators were now vying with each other to vote various honors for Caesar to prove their loyalty to him, so some members of the ruling class felt they had to win his favor—especially those who had supported Pompey and the republican Senate previously—by providing items for his latest Triumph. In this way Gaius Lucilius Hirrus, a cousin of Pompey and a former Tribune of the Plebs who had been against Caesar prior to the defeat of Pompey at Pharsalus, donated six thousand fish for Caesar's public banquet on the occasion of the Spanish Triumph.

Following the Triumphal banquet, Caesar walked to his home on the Sacred Way, dressed in a white toga, wearing slippers and with his oak-leaf crown on his head, passing through the Julian Forum, the new forum he had just built in Rome as a place for public debate and given his name to. A vast, good-natured crowd of well-wishers followed him all the way to the mansion on the Via Sacra.

Soon the men of the 6th also went home—to their new properties in Arles. But Fate was not to permit them to enjoy retirement in the south of France for long.

XXII

PORCIA'S SECRET

T he day had come. A fine, late winter's day in mid-March of 44 B.C., almost exactly a year since the Battle of Munda had heralded the end of the civil war and of armed opposition to Julius Caesar. Before this day had ended, the history of Rome would be altered, dramatically and irrevocably.

At Rome this March morning, Gaius Cassius, former chief of staff to the triumvir Crassus at the Battle of Carrhae, an admiral under Pompey at the outset of the civil war, now a praetor, a senior judge, and trusted associate of Caesar, rose well before dawn. Cassius was a notoriously pale man, a worrier, with little patience, a short temper, and a sense of humor that had a sarcastic edge. His first duty, as it was every morning, was to say a prayer in his city house's small private chapel—of a kind that was in all Roman homes, often no more than a niche in the wall.

Having asked for divine aid in the day's venture, Cassius then readied himself and his household for guests, sending his servants bustling about in preparation. The Roman business day always commenced at sunup, and as the first rays of the new day streaked the eastern sky, Cassius's guests began to knock at his front door—friends, relatives, clients—and were admitted by his chief steward.

Roman society at the upper level was based on a client-patron system. Every man of substance had a gaggle of "clients" who owed their allegiance to him. Invariably some were relatives; others were business associates; others, former staff members. Every morning at dawn, clients would call on their patron and ask what service they could render, what favors they could do for him. The patron in turn would look after their interests, would recommend them and their sons for sought-after government posts, would support their applications to buy property at a reasonable price, act as their referees or advocates in legal cases, and so on. It was an open, aboveboard, "you scratch my back and I'll scratch yours" system that worked. Up until five years back, Gaius Cassius's patron had been Pompey the Great. Now it was Julius Caesar, the one man in Rome who didn't have a patron and who didn't need one.

It's from Plutarch that we know what took place at the house of Judge Cassius this particular morning. Once upward of a hundred male guests had assembled with Cassius in one of his reception rooms, his teenage son was ushered in by staff. We don't know the boy's name, only that he had turned fifteen and that this was his coming-of-age party. No women were present, not even Junia, the boy's mother. This "party" was a solemn, men-only affair, a religious ceremony, the *depositio barbae*.

There are numerous accounts of what took place at the *depositio*, from Petronius, Martial, and Juvenal, among others. The boy was seated on a stool in the middle of the room and was surrounded by a band of servants. A wrap of cambric or muslin was tied around his neck like a large napkin, and a servant dabbed his face with water from a silver bowl. Cassius's personal barber, his *tonsor*, then stepped up and produced an iron razor, which he sharpened with great show on a whetstone, lubricating it by spitting on it. He then proceeded to ceremoniously shave the young man as the beaming audience watched. This was the youngster's first ever encounter with a razor; until he came of age, a Roman boy of this era was not permitted to shave. Now, whether he'd managed a full growth or just a few wispy hairs jutting from his chin, the facial hair of the young man was removed.

As the barber worked, another servant stood close by with a bowl containing a poltus of spider webs soaked in oil and vinegar, commonly used to stop the bleeding caused by nicks of the tonsor's razor. But Cassius would have employed a skilled barber, and the shave required on this occasion is unlikely to have been particularly vigorous, so Cassius Jr. probably had no need of spider webs.

Every hair that was cut was deposited in a small golden casket, and once the boy's face was hair-free the tonsor closed the casket and presented it to his father. Cassius then left the room with the casket, going alone to the house's chapel. There he deposited the casket as an offering to Capitoline Jove. In the *Satyricon*, Petronius has his hero place his casket between the silver statuettes of his two *lares*, or household gods, and a statuette of Venus.

By the time Cassius had returned to the gathering, the boy's face would have been washed and freshened with water and pampered with soft, sweet-smelling oil. Now his father called on him to stand. Once the teenager was on his feet, Cassius, bursting with pride and accompanied by loud cheers and applause from those watching, took a toga from his valet and draped it around his son.

As the young man was about to learn, the application of a toga required some skill and practice. In wrapping it around his body, his father covered the boy's left arm but left his right arm free in the customary fashion. This was no regular toga, the formal garment and equivalent of our tuxedo adopted by the Romans from the Greeks for special occasions. This was the *toga virilis*, a white garment with a narrow purple border that marked the youth as a man and a member of the Equestrian Order.

As the boy was led away in his new toga by the proud, excited servants, Cassius conducted his friends out to his portico, looking over the enclosed garden at the center of the house. While they took refreshment, he moved among them, thanking them for coming, receiving their congratulations.

His brother-in-law Marcus Brutus was there. Brutus's half sister Junia Tertia was Cassius's wife. Even though Brutus had saved Cassius's life by gaining a pardon for him from Caesar when Brutus and Caesar had walked and talked about the pursuit of Pompey at Larisa back in August 48 B.C., the brothers-in-law had never been close. In fact, in recent months they had been quite at odds, but their relationship had been patched up a few weeks back by the need to unite in the interests of a common cause. When Cassius now asked Brutus if all was well with him, Brutus would have replied in the affirmative and gently patted his waist. Brutus had left home that morning wearing a belt beneath his tunic, and on the belt there hung a sheathed dagger.

Brutus was not in the habit of going about the city armed. For one thing, it was against the law. Earlier in the year he'd taken up the latest appointment granted to him by Caesar, the post of the most senior judge of Rome, the Urban Praetor, making him chiefly responsible for punishing lawbreakers within the city. Since reconciling with his "father" Caesar at Larisa following the Battle of Pharsalus, Brutus had been among the Dictator's most trusted subordinates, serving as governor of Cisalpine Gaul in 46 B.C. prior to his current highly prized appointment. But today Brutus was planning not only to break the law on an arms count; he also intended to commit murder.

Judge Cassius continued to circulate. He asked Senator Lucius Tillius Cimber if he was ready for all the day would bring, and Cimber acknowledged that he was. Cimber also carried a concealed weapon beneath his clothes. He had volunteered to be the one to make the first move in the assassination of Julius Caesar that was planned to take place this day, March 15, or the Ides of March, as it was known on the Roman calendar.

A meeting of the Senate was due to take place later that morning, the final sitting before Caesar set off for Syria in four days' time to lead a new military offensive he'd been contemplating for years and planning in detail for close to twelve months. This meticulously organized operation was aimed initially against the Parthians, involving sixteen legions and ten thousand cavalry, to punish Rome's old enemy for the humiliation of Carrhae. To create that army, and to leave additional legions stationed in Spain, Gaul, Illyricum, Africa, and the East, Caesar had ordered new enlistments to be raised for those of his legions that had discharged their veterans into retirement at the conclusion of the civil war—including the 6th.

Several colonels and generals assigned to the Parthian operation had already headed to the East, and the task force itself was currently being deployed. Six legions waited in Macedonia for Caesar to arrive from Italy. Eight more legions in the East, four of the units then stationed in Egypt, were due to march to join the 28th Legion at the operation's final assembly point, the city of Apamea, on the Orontes River to the east of Antioch in central Syria.

Apamea had been the traditional military headquarters of the Seleucid kings, rulers of the Middle East in centuries past, the place where they kept their cavalry, their war elephants, their armory. Caesar intended emulating the greatest military deeds of the Seleucids and more, with the largest army he had ever led and a campaign he expected could last as long as three years, first conquering Parthia and then invading Germany via the back door by going around the Caspian Sea, then returning through Gaul.

It was to be more than a campaign, it was to be a war of conquest, designed to destroy the power of Rome's enemies and create the greatest empire the world had ever known. Camped outside the city on Tiber Island, the men of the new enlistment of the 7th Legion, last of the sixteen legions assigned to the offensive, waited to escort their commander in chief on his march to the East commencing on March 19.

The upcoming Ides of March meeting of the Senate was seen by the assassination conspirators as the ideal opportunity, if not the last for as long as the three years that Caesar planned to be away, for their plot to be carried out. More than sixty senators were party to the conspiracy. The original murder plan had called for Caesar to be killed in the Forum during elections, but that location had been dropped in favor of the Senate's meeting place, for there the conspiratorial senators could get close to Caesar without raising suspicion.

The deadly deed had been planned with care, so that each man knew the part he was to play. Once Caesar was seated in his golden chair in the Senate chamber, Senator Cimber would approach him with a petition to have his brother returned from exile. As he did so, other conspirators would crowd around the Dictator's chair, vocally supporting Cimber's petition. Cimber would then grab Caesar's robe and pull it down over his arms so he couldn't defend himself. This would be the signal for the others to act, to draw their weapons, to plunge the blades into the body of Julius Caesar.

Now, in the chattering throng in the shade of his portico roof, Cassius came on Senator Publius Servilius Casca, the man who had volunteered to strike the first blow, to be the first to put the knife into Caesar. Casca's brother and fellow senator Gaius Casca also was in on the plot, but it was Publius who had the fire in the belly, who wanted the honor of striking first. Again, without speaking openly of the deed they were planning, Publius Casca confirmed to Cassius that he was ready, willing, and primed to act.

All the plotters were here now under Cassius's portico, mingling with other senators and knights who were oblivious to the real significance of the day. The coming-of-age ceremony for Cassius's son had been the perfect cover for the final gathering of the conspirators before they put the plot into effect, an opportunity to strengthen the resolve of any faint hearts. Seeing all these well-known and respected faces served as a graphic and reassuring reminder to the plotters that they were in solid company.

Their number not only included former supporters of Pompey. Some of Caesar's ablest and longest-serving generals were with them, men including Gaius Trebonius, who'd made his name as one of Caesar's most dependable subordinates during the conquest of Gaul, and Decimus Brutus Albinus, Caesar's best admiral. Even members of Caesar's inner circle such as Lucius Cornelius Cinna, son of the Cinna who'd been the consul Marius's great general and deputy, were conspirators. Cinna, another of Caesar's sixteen current praetors, was even related to him by marriage—his late sister Cornelia had been Caesar's first wife, and he was still considered family. Yet he, too, felt there was only one drastic course to be followed if Rome and democracy were to be saved.

This was the first time that all the conspirators had assembled under one roof. For security reasons they'd only met in small groups before now. Nothing had been put on paper, no one made a special sacrificial offering at a temple for the success of the venture that might have tipped off a priest or temple attendant that something suspicious was in the works. Not even the plotters' wives had been allowed to know what they were planning.

The core conspirators had sounded out potential recruits to the plot with extreme caution. One obvious candidate had been Brutus's good friend and Pompey's former dedicated aide Major General Marcus Favonius, who'd been pardoned by Caesar. But, Plutarch says, when Brutus had casually asked Favonius whether he preferred civil war to the worst and most illegal form of monarchy—as there was a feeling among some conspirators that Caesar's friends might go to war with the assassins to avenge his death—Favonius, who'd seen Pompey murdered at Pelusium, had said there could be no excuse for civil war. This was probably meant as a condemnation of Caesar's initiation of the civil war just passed, suggesting that Favonius could have joined the plotters, but to be on the safe side Brutus said no more to his friend on the subject.

It would have taken only one person to run to Caesar with information about what was in the offing for the plotters to be dead men. One hundred years later, a plot to kill the emperor Nero that also would involve some of the leading men of Rome would be discovered when one of the plotters ordered his steward to sharpen a rusty ceremonial dagger that normally was never taken from its sheath. The steward knew his master would soon be meeting with the emperor, and, suspicious, he would tip off a contact at the palace. That would be all it took for that particular plot to unravel—under torture one plotter after another would confess and spill the names of their colleagues.

Classical authorities agree that the plot to kill Caesar started with Cassius. Even though most acknowledge Cassius's reputation as a righteous man who could be counted on to stand up for a just cause, some still felt that his motives were ultimately personal. On the other hand, all authorities credit Brutus with the purest of patriotic motives for his involvement in the murder plot. Both Plutarch and Appian say that Cassius was unhappy with Caesar for giving Brutus the more important job of Urban Praetor while assigning him the less senior judgeship of Peregrine Praetor, who was responsible for judging legal cases involving issues beyond Rome's walls. According to both historians, Caesar had told friends that Cassius had the better claim to the Urban Praetor's job, but he chose Brutus anyway, out of favoritism. Plutarch says that following their appointment, Cassius had refused to talk to Brutus for weeks, or months.

Plutarch also says there was a story put about later by Cassius's detractors that his main reason for hating Caesar was that he'd confiscated a collection of African lions Cassius had put together at Megara in southern Greece in 48 B.C. when Cassius was still sailing for Pompey. This seemingly petty and out-of-date provocation to murder was, according to Plutarch, hogwash. He says that as far back as his school days Cassius had displayed a passionate hatred for tyranny in any form. And it was the tyranny of Julius Caesar that drove Gaius Cassius to plan his death.

Cassius's dissatisfaction with Caesar's rule had been simmering for many months. And that dissatisfaction had begun to show. In all the rush to vote Caesar a torrent of honors in the Senate over the past year or so, only one or two senators had dared to sometimes vote against this proposal or that, and Cassius had been among them, although Caesar had seemed not to notice. Some of the honors were so outrageous that even Caesar had turned them down. As it was, he now had special privileges in the Senate, in the theater, and at the circus. He had a special chair, a fabulous throne of gold and ivory, for his public appearances. The name of the seventh month of the year had been changed from Quintilis to July in his honor. It was also voted that Caesar was sacred and inviolate, as if he were a living god, and a new religious college was established to celebrate his divinity, with its own priesthood devoted to him. Temples were built to him, and one to him and Clemency with statues depicting Caesar and Clemency hand in hand, in commemoration of the clemency he had shown many of his civil war enemies.

Just the month before, in February 44 B.C., no one in the Senate had dared vote down a motion from Caesar's keenest supporters—a motion they knew had originated with Caesar himself—that he be appointed Dictator for life. There was no precedent in Roman history for this. Even Sulla had resigned the dictatorship and gone into reclusive retirement. As Dictator, Caesar was the sole ruler of Rome. As Dictator for life he could not be voted out of office. No man could remove him; only death could. In the eyes of some, this made him a king in everything but name. And Romans had an abhorrence of kings after a history prior to the republic of despotic rule by a succession of monarchs.

Under Caesar the Dictator, democracy died. Key offices of state were no longer filled via elections. The aediles, commissioners for public works and spectacles, still could be elected, because their roles involved prominence but little real power, but even then, Caesar wrote to the voters urging them to support the candidates he favored. Caesar selected and appointed the quaestors, or junior magistrates, the praetors, the consuls, the army commanders, the provincial governors, and for whatever length of term he saw fit.

He also ignored the constitution of the republic, which required men running for consul to be a minimum of forty-two years of age. To take over his consulship once he left Rome on March 19, Caesar appointed his relative Publius Dolabella, Cicero's son-in-law, who was just twenty-five, ignoring Dolabella's lack of years, his lack of restraint while a tribune at Rome during Caesar's enforced absence in the East, and his reputation as a flabby young fool.

The Senate had no say in any of this. Its sittings became less frequent, and when they did sit, the senators were left to debate, then to rubber-stamp one measure or another of Caesar's that was merely put up for decorum's sake. Caesar had become so contemptuous of the Senate that, without even troubling the House with any debate on the matter, let alone allowing the senators to put his nominees to the vote, he had recently published a list of appointments he'd decided on, extending over the next five years, as he planned to be absent from Rome for at least the next three years on his Parthian campaign. Rome was now ruled by the decree of Julius Caesar.

Plutarch says that during this period, Cicero, who had by now returned to public life after keeping a low profile over the past five years, and who had become increasingly unhappy with Caesar's management style, was told by an astrologer friend that a particular star would be rising the next night. "What? By decree?" Cicero is said to have sourly responded.

The chief conspirators had actually considered bringing the influential Cicero into the murder plot. They knew how much he had come to dislike Caesar's autocratic rule—even Caesar felt sure that Cicero detested him, so a member of Caesar's staff had recently told Cicero. The conspirators also knew how much Romans at large respected the former consul and great orator. But they decided against telling Cicero anything about the plot, for the simple reason, says Plutarch, that they feared Cicero would want to analyze every detail of the scheme, as was his habit. At best, wise but cautious Cicero could delay them and cause them to miss their opportunity to strike, and once Caesar was surrounded by his army in the East, he would be impregnable to attempts on his life from within. There was also the distinct possibility that Cicero might come up with too many reasons why they shouldn't risk carrying the plot forward. After all, when the passions are involved, some causes just don't stand up to rational analysis.

The passion among the most idealistic of the conspirators such as Brutus was for a return to the Republic as men such as Brutus's ancestor Junius Brutus had conceived it—a true democracy. The reality of the Republic over the past sixty years had not matched the ideal, with strongmen with strong armies, men such as Marius, Sulla, Pompey, and Caesar, dictating Rome's future with the point of a sword.

The pragmatic Caesar considered the Republic an illusion. Titus Ampius Balbus, who had been banished by Caesar after attempting to rob the Temple of Diana at Ephesus in 48 B.C., had been pardoned by him in 46 B.C., and he came to record Caesar's thoughts on a number of subjects. Suetonius quotes Ampius quoting Caesar on the Republic: "The Republic was nothing," said Caesar disdainfully, "a mere name without form or substance."

Caesar had come to ignore the fact that there were many leading Romans who hankered for the republican ideal, an ideal made all the more attractive by the fact that now that he was Dictator for life, Caesar's autocratic rule would last until the day he died, which may be another thirty years if nature were allowed to take her course. There was even the concern at the back of many of his critics' minds that Caesar intended to establish a ruling dynasty that continued after him. Already he'd caused a motion to be passed by the Senate decreeing that his son would be appointed Pontifex Maximus after his death, even though he did not yet have a legal son. Caesarion, his son by Cleopatra, was considered illegitimate under Roman law at that time, but that could easily be changed by yet another Senate decree. And after that there was nothing stopping Caesar from declaring his son heir not just to some of his titles and positions, but also to his throne. To the minds of the conspirators, there was only one way to stop Caesar, to liberate Romans from his autocracy, and to bring back the Republic for which they yearned.

Both Plutarch and Appian indicate that the plot was only four or five weeks old by the time the Ides of March came around. They say that a rumor reached Cassius in February that Caesar planned to call a meeting of the Senate for March 1, at which it would be proposed that his title be changed to "king." The rumor was given credence by what took place at the Lupercalia Festival at Rome on February 15, when Mark Antony had several times offered Caesar a crown, seeming to making a joke of it, and Caesar had turned it down each time, telling him to instead have the crown taken to the Temple of Capitoline Jove and placed on the statue of the god that stood there.

Cassius Dio would speculate that this rejection of a kingly crown was a deliberate act, a little scheme cooked up between Caesar and Antony to dispel the growing rumors that Caesar wanted to become the king of Rome. But the scheme had the reverse effect, and only stoked the rumors. After all, it was said, hadn't Caesar given his approval for a statue of him to be set up on the Capitol beside those of the seven ancient kings of Rome? As if he ranked himself as their equal.

Suetonius also reports a popular belief that the naming of Caesar as king of Rome was imminent in the late winter of 44 B.C., amid a flurry of rumors flying at the time. One rumor suggested that with Caesar about to embark on his Parthian offensive, the priestly keepers of the prophetic Sybaline Books would announce that as the books predicted that only a king could conquer the Parthians, then Caesar must be proclaimed king of Rome before he departed on March 19.

According to Suetonius, another rumor then current had Caesar planning to move the seat of government from Rome to Troy, or to Alexandria, where he could be closer to his mistress Cleopatra. Caesar couldn't
marry Cleopatra—Roman law prevented Roman citizens from marrying
foreigners. But Suetonius also says that Tribune of the Plebs Gaius Helvius
Cinna would later claim that Caesar had instructed him to draw up a bill
for approval by the Senate that would permit him to marry any woman
he chose, Roman or foreign, opening the way for him to make Cleopatra
his wife.

At this very moment, on March 15, the Egyptian queen was still in
residence with her younger brother Ptolemy XIV and her son Caesarion
just across the Tiber from Rome, where she had been living for many
months at Caesar's expense. No one seemed to mind that Caesar was so
blatantly keeping her there at his estate outside the city. No one had even
complained when Caesar set up a golden life-size statue of Cleopatra in
the new Temple of Venus Genetrix (Venus the Mother) that he erected at
Rome, setting Cleopatra's statue beside the statue of Venus herself—Venus
was Caesar's patron deity, with the family of the Caesars claiming descent
from the goddess. According to Appian, that statue of Cleopatra was still
there in the temple of Venus in his day, two hundred years later, despite
her ultimate role as an enemy of Rome—because it had been installed by
the deified Caesar. But for Caesar to marry the Egyptian queen, and, worse,
to move his capital to Alexandria—few at Rome would stomach such a
prospect.

In February, Cassius had been sufficiently concerned by these swirling
rumors, and the urgent need to do something about them before March 19
if anything was to be done at all, that he decided to make up with his
brother-in-law, and had hurried to discuss the matter with him. Brutus,
one of nature's gentlemen, greeted Cassius warmly, as if nothing had happened between them. But a frown must have clouded Brutus's face when
Cassius told him of the royal rumors.

Appian and Plutarch both record Cassius putting this question to Brutus: "What are we going to do if Caesar's friends do propose at the next
meeting of the Senate that he should become king?"

"I hadn't planned to attend the next sitting," Brutus replied.

"What if they send for us as praetors?" Cassius continued. "We'll have
to go."

"Then," Brutus said, according to Plutarch, "it will be my duty to not
hold my tongue but to boldly stand up and, if necessary, to die for my
country's liberty."

The plot to rid Rome of Julius Caesar was born that day. Both men began to canvass colleagues to find support for a drastic step that would eliminate the threat to democracy once and for all. Cassius's friend Antistius Labeo, another former admiral in Pompey's service who'd been pardoned by Caesar, quickly joined the scheme. Cassius and Labeo had then jointly approached Caesar's general Decimus Brutus Albinus, who was shortly to take up the post of governor of Cisalpine Gaul. As would soon be learned, Albinus was so much in Caesar's favor that he was included in the Dictator's will as his secondary heir; in the event of the death of Caesar's principal heir, Caesar's great-nephew Octavius, Albinus would inherit much of Caesar's by now massive estate.

After Cassius asked him to join the conspirators, Albinus had reserved his answer and had gone to see Brutus, who was a distant relative, to sound him out. When he received confirmation from the horse's mouth that Brutus was not only for the plot but also was one of the party's leaders, Albinus committed as well. He wouldn't be the last to join the conspiracy on learning of Brutus's involvement.

Like all the other conspirators, Albinus was at Cassius's house on the morning of March 15 for the coming-of-age celebration. When Cassius joined him in the garden, Albinus, trying to make it sound of no real importance for the sake of other listeners, told his host that the previous evening Caesar had taken him to dinner with Marcus Lepidus, at Lepidus's house. Lepidus now held the post of Master of Horse, making him the Dictator's official deputy.

According to Appian, as Caesar, Lepidus, and Albinus were drinking after their meal, Caesar had posed this question: "What do you think is the best sort of death for a man?" After Albinus and Lepidus had given their views, Caesar had said, "Personally, I think a sudden death is the best of all."

Cassius and Albinus would now have exchanged knowing glances, both with the same thought in mind—they and their colleagues in crime would soon oblige Caesar with his wish for a sudden death.

Before long the congregation at Judge Cassius's house broke up, as men hurried off to conduct their business of the morning before most of them answered Caesar's summons to attend the Senate sitting. The meeting was to take place at the Theater of Pompey, the massive complex erected at the western end of the Field of Mars by Pompey the Great. Construction had begun in 55 B.C. and had yet to be fully completed, but the majority of the building, the first drama theater to be built entirely of stone at Rome, was already in use.

The Senate House had been destroyed by fire during riots several years before and had yet to be repaired. In the interim, Senate meetings took place at convenient locations such as Pompey's Theater. Attached to the theater, now Rome's finest, were covered colonnades of one hundred massive columns under whose cover public business could be conducted. The theater also had a massive portico that was frequently used as a meeting hall, and it was here that the Senate sitting was due to take place.

The choice of the theater complex as the venue had everything to do with Brutus Albinus. He had been putting together a large band of gladiators for a major public show, and knowing that Caesar was a big fan of gladiators, even maintaining his own gladiatorial school, Albinus had suggested a demonstration by men from his collection in the huge, half-moon-shaped theater next door to the meeting hall once the Senate had finished its business, and Caesar had agreed.

With increased pulse rates, Cassius and Brutus left Cassius's house and made their way in litters to the theater complex dressed in their senatorial togas—white with a thick purple stripe to denote their status—and preceded by their lictors, the five official attendants bearing the fasces to which each was entitled as a praetor. As they arrived, somewhere around 8.30 A.M., they would have heard the distant sounds of metal on metal and wood as the gladiators rehearsed their show—the professional fighters had been at the theater for just that purpose since before dawn.

Rome's judges were required to make themselves available to the public on days like this to hear civil cases, so the praetors seated themselves on benches under the colonnades and called to order sittings of their individual courts, which would continue until just before the Senate convened.

Brutus had the most business before him that morning, and he tried to deal with each case with his usual unruffled manner and scrupulous fairness, listening to the advocates for the plaintiff and the defendant while trying to keep an open mind. But Brutus had other things on his mind. Not only could he feel the dagger at his waist, but his thoughts would have wandered from time to time to his new wife, Porcia. She was the daughter of Cato the Younger, Brutus's uncle. Although Brutus and she were first cousins, marriage between cousins was then legal. It would be outlawed before long, only to be legalized again for personal motives by the emperor Claudius in the following century.

Brutus was Porcia's second husband. She had married very young—perhaps close to the legal marrying age of twelve. Her first husband, Marcus Bibulus, had died not long after, leaving her a widow with a baby son,

Bibulus. Only the previous year, in the summer of 45 B.C., Brutus had divorced his previous wife to marry Porcia. It seems that Brutus and his stepson Bibulus, approaching or in his teens by 44 B.C., had an excellent relationship, for Bibulus would later write a favorable memoir of Brutus.

Brutus's new wife was to become the only wife of a conspirator to know what was planned for the Ides of March. Porcia was highly strung. And it's no wonder, having tragically lost a husband and a famous father, the latter in notoriously heroic circumstances when he'd taken his own life two years back at Utique in Africa rather than surrender to Caesar. Porcia's sensitivity made her alert to Brutus's mood, and as the month of March arrived, she began to sense that the husband she loved was keeping a secret from her. Was it another woman? Did Brutus have a health problem he was keeping from her? What was his secret? It drove her crazy not to know.

Plutarch says that one day, after sending her servants away and closing herself up in her bedroom, Porcia took a *cultellus*, a small iron knife about the size of a modern nail file normally used for cutting the fingernails, then stabbed herself in the thigh with it, causing a deep and painful gash. Bandaging the wound herself, Porcia kept it from her husband and her servants, but it became infected. When Porcia broke out in a fever, Brutus became concerned, but never once did she let on that she was in pain or reveal how her "illness" had originated, until, just days before the Ides, she revealed her act of self-mutilation to Brutus.

Appalled, he asked her why she would do such a thing. According to Plutarch, Porcia answered that if she had the strength to defy pain and prove she was no weak woman, and at the same time keep such a nasty wound secret, she could keep Brutus's secrets, too. After all, she said, she'd married him to share his fortunes, good or bad. So Brutus had shared his secret with his wife, despite the agreement he'd made with his coconspirators that no wives would be let in on the plot. When Brutus had prepared to go off to Cassius's house before dawn on March 15, the devoted Porcia had helped him strap on his concealed dagger.

At the court sitting at the theater colonnade, Brutus made a ruling in what was to be the last case brought before him that morning. When Brutus decided against the plaintiff, the man in question was far from happy. According to Plutarch, the plaintiff jumped up and angrily, noisily protested. "You can't do this to me! I'll appeal to Caesar. He'll see me right!"

Plutarch says that, in response, Brutus cast his eyes around those present and then said, calmly and deliberately to the unhappy plaintiff, "Caesar doesn't prevent me, nor will he, from doing my duty according to the laws of Rome."

Once he'd terminated the court session, and his lictors had joined with those of the other praetors to clear the public from the colonnade, Brutus strolled to join Cassius and a growing number of senators who were milling at the top of the steps to the meeting hall and looking east along the street that ran beside the Villa Publicus, which Caesar was expected to use to reach the theater. It was moments before the fifth hour in the Roman way of keeping time, or, close to 10.00 A.M., as the modern clock would say.

According to the praetors' water clock, which had been carefully set by attendants using a portable sundial, the hour nominated by Caesar for the start of the Senate sitting had arrived. Even allowing for the vagaries of Rome's water clocks—Seneca was to say that it was easier to get the philosophers of Rome to agree among themselves than the clocks—Caesar could be expected to be already on his way from his home on the Via Sacra in downtown Rome. Carried in a litter, the trip would take him perhaps fifteen minutes.

At the top of the long, broad flight of steps, Cassius and Brutus would have nodded to each other as they came together in the crowd of toga-clad senators and their attendants, but very little would have passed between them. Just for a moment, the pensive Cassius may have turned his gaze southwest across the Tiber River, to the slopes of the Gianicolo, rising above the far bank. Then, as now, lush gardens sprawled along the slope. Then, the gardens were owned by Julius Caesar. And, set among the greenery was a mansion, a guesthouse, also the property of Caesar. Cassius would have been aware that the mansion contained a guest of Caesar that day—Cleopatra, Queen of Egypt.

It's probable that Caesar had plans for Cleopatra to accompany him when he set off for the East on March 19—parting in Syria, they would go their separate ways for the time being, he leading his army into Parthia, she going home to Alexandria. That being the case, Cleopatra's servants would have been busy preparing a massive baggage train for her departure even as Cassius looked up to the house on the hill through the haze of smoke that typically hung over the city from the cooking and work-shop fires of Rome. Did Gaius Cassius and his friends have a surprise for Cleopatra!

The tension was rising among the men clustered at the top of the theater steps; Caesar was late. Was he still coming? As the waiting senators chatted in low voices and wondered where Caesar might be, one of their number went up to Senator Publius Casca, the man who was primed to be the first to strike Caesar. Appian and Plutarch say the senator took Casca's free right hand, and, with a wink and a smile, said, "You kept the secret from us, my friend, but Brutus has told me everything."

Casca's heart missed a beat. He was convinced the assassination plot had been exposed. In an instant, the blood would have drained from his face. He opened his mouth, and was about to beg the man to keep the secret of the murder conspiracy to himself when, Plutarch says, the anonymous senator burst out laughing at the obvious surprise he'd caused.

"How come, Casca," the senator went on, "you're so rich all of a sudden you can afford to put your name up to become an aedile?"

This wasn't to be the only scare the plotters had that morning. While Brutus had been conducting his court session, he'd noticed runners from his domestic staff appear in the public gallery and try to attract his attention, and each time he'd waved them away. Now, as Brutus stood at the top of the steps outside the meeting hall, one of those runners tugged at his sleeve.

"Master, my mistress Porcia, your wife, is dying!" Plutarch says the breathless messenger advised. "You must come quickly."

Horror-struck, Brutus demanded to know what was going on. It turned out that ever since he'd left home that morning, Porcia, well aware of the dangerous mission he'd embarked on, had become increasingly anxious for his safety and had repeatedly sent messengers to determine his welfare and report back. Porcia was still weak from her stab wound, and as the hours passed and her anxiety grew while she waited for the deed to be done at the Senate sitting, she'd become dizzy, then passed out while seated with her female servants. Although Porcia had soon come around, Brutus's chief steward had panicked and sent the latest message to say that Porcia was dying.

Brutus, confident that he knew the cause of Porcia's fainting spell, sent the runner back to his wife with the message that he had public business to attend to but would hurry home to her as soon as he had accomplished all that had to be accomplished. Naturally, Brutus's worried colleagues wanted to know what the urgent message was all about. He was just assuring Cassius that his wife, Cassius's sister, was unwell but not so unwell that he needed to depart from his public purpose, when Senator Popilius Laenas came up to the pair. Laenus, descendant of a censor of Rome who had given the city its first civic water clock, greeted Cassius and Brutus more boisterously than usual.

Then Laenus leaned in close to the pair and whispered, "My hopes are with you, my friends, that you can accomplish what you have in mind. And I urge you to do it without delay, as the thing is no longer a secret."

As Laenus hurried away, Cassius and Brutus looked at each other in shock. There could be no mistake this time—there was definitely a leak in the conspiratorial ring. And Brutus would have guiltily wondered whether his wife, Porcia, had been the source of that leak. But two questions were uppermost in the minds of Brutus and Cassius now: Was Laenus genuinely with them? And, had he kept the secret to himself? As the ringleaders contemplated awful failure, and their agreement that if things went wrong on the day they would all take their own lives, there was a sudden buzz of excitement from the crowd: Caesar was coming. Someone was going to die on this day. Cassius and Brutus would soon know whether it was them, or Caesar.

Two enclosed litters came into view, each being carried by burly slaves along the street beside the Villa Publicus toward Pompey's Theater. The first litter was preceded by junior magistrates of the city and the twenty-four lictors of the Dictator, each lictor carrying a fasces. The second litter followed the twelve lictors of a consul, conveying Mark Antony. A vast crowd of servants and curious citizens came along behind the official procession.

No military guard accompanied the litters. As recently as the previous December, Caesar had been traveling outside Rome on a visit to the western coast of Italy with a mounted bodyguard of two thousand men. But in the city he went without armed guards. The German and Gallic cavalry-men who'd ridden with him throughout the war in Gaul and then from the beginning to the end of the civil war seem to have been given their discharges and sent home. These long-serving troopers had shared the fighting in Alexandria, then beside the Nile, and at Zela with the men of the 6th. Like all Caesar's troops who had remained loyal to the last, they would have received the long-promised victory bonus. Caesar probably also granted Roman citizenship to the troopers of the bodyguard. Now, within Rome, Caesar merely used his lictors as an escort; their only weapon was their staff of office.

Not that military muscle was far away if the Dictator needed it. The 7th Legion was, after all, camped on Tiber Island, in the middle of the Tiber River just west of the old city walls, its ten cohorts of Spanish legionaries at full strength after a recent reenlistment. But Caesar had resisted calls from his inner circle to use the men from the 7th as his personal bodyguard inside the city, as he had back in 46 B.C. To surround himself with bodyguards, he had recently said, was only to say to the world that he had something to fear, and to invite trouble.

Up on a balcony at the Gianicolo that morning, Cleopatra may well have been looking out over the sprawling gardens of Caesar's villa, beyond the dirty brown Tiber and across the red-tiled rooftops of the city toward the Theater of Pompey. Caesar would have told her that he planned to attend a meeting of the Senate at the fifth hour, the last such meeting before he began his journey to the East with his Egyptian mistress on March 19.

Cleopatra would have been looking forward to setting off, to going home. For close to two years she had been a virtual prisoner up here on the hill overlooking smoky, noisy Rome, with the man she loved so near, yet so far away. She would have missed the wide, regulated streets and grand architecture of her capital, missed the sweet air of Alexandria, the mild nights with their soft, caressing breezes, and the warm waters of the Mediterranean lapping at her door.

There on the Gianicolo balcony she may have been holding her son and Caesar's son, Caesarion, pointing to the buildings on the Field of Mars, and telling the child that "Daddy" was down there. Little Caesarion also would have been looking forward to going "home." Almost three years old now, he would have been talking, in halting Greek, about the crocodiles and palm trees and pyramids that his mother and servants would have told him about. Too young to remember the place of his birth, he could only know "home" from their stories. There, in exotic Egypt, Caesarion's mother would have promised him, he would one day reign as king of Egypt.

It is unlikely that Cleopatra would have been able to make out Caesar's litter as it and Mark Antony's conveyance were carried along the Street of the Banker and then by the Villa Publicus to Pompey's Theater. The massive theater itself would have been visible from up on the hilltop, but Caesar was much too far away for his mistress to actually see him when he stepped from his litter. Nor would she have had any inkling of what was about to take place there.

Had she been on the spot, Cleopatra would have seen Decimus Brutus Albinus and Gaius Trebonius, two of the assassination conspirators, trot down the steps to meet the pair of litters as they halted at the bottom of the theater steps. Albinus and Trebonius had been delegated to greet the arrivals. Albinus, as the sponsor of the gladiatorial display later in the morning, would officially welcome Caesar. Trebonius, as a friend of Mark Antony's, was to detain Antony in conversation and prevent his intervention in the assassination, for, as copresident of the House, the physically powerful Antony would take his seat right next to Caesar, where he was in a position to intervene against assassins.

Antony would later put it about that Caesar had seriously considered sending him to cancel the Senate sitting, following two unfavorable sacrifices before Caesar in his capacity of high priest of Rome. But Brutus Albinus had convinced Caesar to attend. Not a superstitious man himself, and impatient to have the meeting out of the way so he could return to his final preparations for the journey to Syria and the massive military operation that would follow, Caesar had needed little persuasion to go to Pompey's Theater despite the poor omens.

Julius Caesar climbed out of the first litter, taking Albinus's hand as he came to his feet, and exchanging brief pleasantries. Caesar was wearing his senatorial toga. He had a crown of oak leaves on his head, and was wearing a richly embroidered crimson cloak, both the trappings of a general who had celebrated a Triumph, which Caesar was required to wear when he took the auspices as high priest.

As Caesar began to move up the steps, an eager crowd swamped around him, and his lictors had to struggle to clear a path. From all directions hands thrust petitions at Caesar. He took every roll of parchment, but without opening any passed them on to his personal secretary Quintus Faberius and the undersecretaries trailing him, for later consideration. One of these documents, it was later learned, was a letter from a Greek teacher, warning Caesar of a plot against his life.

From the top of the steps, with Caesar slowly making his way up through the throng, Cassius and Brutus could see that Trebonius was performing his allotted task, detaining solid, muscular Antony in animated conversation at the bottom of the steps. Senators were flooding into the meeting hall, to be in their places ahead of Caesar. As Cassius, Brutus, and several other conspirators were about to do the same, Plutarch says they saw Senator Laenas emerge from the crowd, take Caesar's arm, and begin to speak animatedly close to his ear. This was the same Laenas who'd revealed he knew all about the conspiracy. In the general hubbub there was no way Cassius or Brutus could hear what was being said, and for a moment they were certain that the game was up, that Laenas was blowing the whistle on them.

Hands were reaching under robes to draw weapons, for murder or for suicide, when Brutus realized from Laenas's hand gestures that he was asking rather than telling, that he was beseeching Caesar for a favor, and Brutus stayed his colleagues' hands. Then Caesar nodded, and Laenas briefly kissed his hand in thanks before Caesar moved on and continued to ascend the steps through a narrow avenue of lictors holding back the crowd.

Now Cassius and Brutus and the last of those by the portico doorway turned and hurried indoors. Inside, the meeting hall had been sealed off from the rest of the theater complex by temporary screens. A giant statue of Pompey the Great, benefactor of the theater complex, stood larger than life at one end of the vast room. Wooden benches had been arrayed in a semicircle in front of the curile chair of a consul. Beside it, attendants were hurriedly placing the chair of the Dictator, Caesar's gold and ivory throne.

Cassius Dio says that when Caesar's arrival was delayed, the attendants responsible for the chair had carried it out of the meeting hall, believing that the Dictator would not be attending the sitting after all. When news of his approach reached the theater, there had been a flurry of activity as the attendants rushed to return the chair to its place of honor.

The voices of hundreds of senators all talking at once echoed around the portico stones—Caesar had appointed nine hundred men to the Senate, but not all were in Rome at this time. Conspirators were filling the front benches. With the current praetors and former consuls traditionally occupying the first row as a right, Cassius and Brutus took their seats at the front, side by side.

Nearby they saw Cimber, tense and drawn, his rolled petition in hand, and Cinna, and Servius Galba, Sextius Naso, Quintus Ligarius, Marcus Spurius, Munucius Basilus, Rubrius Ruga, and Pontius Aquila, the tribune who had been humiliated in public by Caesar, and scores of other senators whose hands were edging close to weapons concealed beneath their garments.

According to Plutarch, Cassius now turned and looked up at the marble statue of Pompey. Several times life size, the standing figure was dressed in a toga; its right hand was outstretched, as if Pompey had been frozen in the middle of a speech, a typical pose for statues of this kind. Pompey had placed the statue there himself. Later it would be removed from the meeting hall and placed on top of a Triumphal arch erected opposite the theater complex, for the whole world to see.

As he looked up at Pompey's face, Plutarch says, Cassius addressed a silent prayer to the marble figure, in the hope that the dead general might somehow help them succeed in what they were about to do. And then a hush fell over the meeting hall. Cassius looked around. Holding his fasces, Caesar's chief lictor was standing in the doorway. "Make way for the Dictator," the lictor called in a formal, self-important tone.

All conversation ceased, a hush came over the hall, and every man present came to his feet. Then, his footsteps echoing around the cavernous interior, Gaius Julius Caesar made his entrance.

XXIII

AFTER THE MURDER

At Arles in France, the retirees of the 6th Legion were still coming to terms with civilian life after twenty years in the military when, late in March, the stunning news reached the town that on the Ides of March Julius Caesar had been murdered in the Theater of Pompey at Rome. The veterans of the 6th heard how Caesar had received twenty-three stab wounds. How Brutus had been wounded in the hand in the frantic flurry of strikes at the seated dictator. How, in the panic that swept the city, Antony had disappeared, only to be located later inside his barricaded house. How the conspirators had marched to the Capitoline Mount escorted by Albinus's gladiators, and there from the temple steps Brutus had made a speech in support of the assassination, a speech that had been elegant but that lacked passion or power. How Marcus Lepidus had led the 7th Legion from Tiber Island to the Theater of Pompey, before the legion decided that with Caesar dead, Lepidus no longer had the authority to command them, and they'd returned to the island.

A story would have soon reached Arles, a story later related by Suetonius, about an event in Campania that involved legion veterans and that would have intrigued the highly superstitious retired legionaries of the 6th. Back in January, a group of veterans who had been settled near Capua, the Roman Casilinum, in Campania, south of Rome, had been out looking for stone with which to build houses on their newly allotted farmland. These were men from either or both the 7th and 10th Legions, Spaniards like the veterans of the 6th, men who had fought against the 6th at Pharsalus and with them at Munda.

With the bonuses and booty they'd gathered over their years in military service, these veterans could have won many a maiden's heart by buying all the expensive perfumes on prosperous Capua's Via Seplasia, a street renowned for its perfume shops—and still had plenty of change. But, having come by their money through years of blood, sweat, and toil, they

215

were not about to pay for anything they didn't have to. So when they set about building their farmhouses, avoiding the local quarry operators, they'd gone looking for ancient stone tombs they'd heard were in the area, in search of free stone.

Finding the tombs in question, irreverently and enthusiastically they'd attacked them with sledgehammers and crowbars as if they were enemy fortifications, breaking them up and carting away the stones for their farmhouses. Breaking into one tomb, their eyes had lit up when they'd discovered a large hoard of ancient vases, which they'd also taken away, to sell. The story went that one of these looted tombs proved to be that of Capys, the Greek who had founded the town of Capua centuries before, and in it the scavenging veterans found a bronze tablet with an inscription in Greek: "Disturb the bones of Capys, and a man of Trojan stock will be murdered by his kindred and later avenged at great cost to Italy."

In the wake of Caesar's assassination, this was taken to be an omen for the death of Caesar, who, like many noble Romans, was considered to have descended from Trojan soldiers who had fled to Italy after the fall of Troy. According to Suetonius, this tale was recorded by Lucius Cornelius Balbus, Caesar's former staff officer who published Caesar's memoirs. At the time of Caesar's murder, Balbus was serving in western Spain as quaestor to Asinius Pollio, who Caesar had made a major general and governor of Baetica after the Battle of Munda. While in Spain, Balbus may well have heard this story of the inscription in the tomb, from Spanish relatives of the Spanish colonists of Capua, who in turn had heard it via letters from their kin the veterans.

Through the last days of March and into April news of rapidly changing events at Rome would have reached Arles daily. The agitated men of the 6th heard how Antony and Lepidus had made a deal with Brutus and Cassius, after which the Senate had voted to pardon all conspirators. How Antony had convinced Brutus, as City Praetor, to permit Caesar's funeral to take place inside the city—cremations and burials were normally only permitted outside the city walls—and how Antony had used his funeral oration for Caesar to turn the population against the conspirators. The ex-soldiers also would have been interested to learn that Antony also had recalled six thousand retired veterans who were living near Rome, putting them in the reformed Praetorian Guard, an ancient corps that had fallen into disuse over recent decades, and was using the Praetorians as his private protection force.

All this would have generated considerable unrest among the veterans at Arles. Their legion had been Caesar's elite unit through the last key phases of the civil war, and he had recognized them and honored them accordingly. They would have wanted to wreak vengeance against Brutus and Cassius and their leader's other assassins, ridiculing the conspirators' claim that they were the Liberators of Rome. Veterans of the 6th such as Publius Sertorius and Lucius Acilius would have taken swords and shields down from the walls of their homes, and brought out the whetstone to sharpen blades. The terms of their military discharge required them to be available to serve a total of another four years in emergencies, and this, to them, was definitely an emergency. The 6th Legion veterans would have met to dictate messages to Consul Antony and sent pledges to him that they were ready to re-form behind their standards and march against Caesar's murderers as soon as they received the order.

Word would have come back from Antony that he wanted the veterans of the 6th to be ready for active service by conducting regular arms drills, and their military equipment was to be inspected monthly by their colony's senior officials—instructions that Antony delivered personally to veterans settled closer to Rome during visits to their colonies during this period.

In the June twilight, with tears running down her cheeks and with her son Bibulus at her side holding her hand, Porcia watched the cargo vessel slowly draw level with Cape Palinuro, heading south into the Tyrrhenian Sea off Italy's western coast, until its stern light was all that was visible. And then that, too, was gone, as the ship slipped beyond the point and disappeared into the growing darkness.

On board the vessel were Porcia's husband, Brutus, and her brother Cassius, together with their most loyal friends and servants. It had been a wretched farewell. Porcia had wanted to go with Brutus, to share his fortunes as she had ever since they'd left Rome within days of the Ides of March. But Brutus feared that what lay ahead for Cassius and himself was not something he could subject his wife and stepson to, and once they'd reached the seaside village of Velia, near modern Elea, south of Salerno, he'd instructed her to travel back to their house at Rome and wait for him to return as the savior of the Republic.

This flight from Italy by the two principal Liberators, as history would come to know them, had been sparked by Mark Antony's funeral oration for Julius Caesar. Whipped up into a rage against Caesar's murderers by Antony, the crowd in the Forum had stripped wooden furniture from nearby buildings and from the front of curbside stores lining the Forum, piled it high, and cremated Caesar's body right there, in the Forum, ignoring Rome's laws and conventions.

Then, with burning brands in their hands, members of the throng had run to the houses of Cassius and Brutus and tried to set them alight. The houses' servants had been able to keep the mob out, but Cassius and Brutus had realized that their lives and those of their families were now at risk. They'd quickly gathered up family and staff and left the capital, going to a seaside villa on the West Coast at Anzio, the Roman town of Antium.

This was an outcome that Mark Antony would have been hoping for. It would have been preferable if Brutus and Cassius had been killed by the mob, but to have them driven out of the capital suited his purposes well enough. Now he could do as he pleased in Rome. Antony subsequently made his move on power through April and May, issuing decrees that used the heading "Memorandum of Caesar," implying they had been made by Caesar before he died.

These memoranda appointed friends and relatives of Antony to senior posts, freed men from prison, and recalled exiles. And as the veterans of the 6th had heard, Antony also re-formed the defunct Praetorian Guard as his personal bodyguard. It was the only military unit at the capital now, in the wake of the transfer by the Senate of the 7th Legion from Rome to Albe in central Italy. From Anzio, Cassius and Brutus had tried to counter Antony politically, through their supporters in the Senate.

On June 5, while Cassius and Brutus waited nervously at Anzio, those supporters had pushed a motion through the Senate appointing the pair to the newly created posts of Special Commissioners for the Grain Supply, with a roving commission to travel to any part of Italy or the empire to inquire into the provision of Rome's vital grain imports. This gave Cassius and Brutus a valid reason to stay outside the capital and not meet their obligations as praetors in the city. But Brutus had been in favor of returning to Rome and confronting their opponents, most particularly Mark Antony. For the moment, he had been talked out of it by his friends.

On June 7, Brutus and Cassius were joined at Anzio by Marcus Cicero. Brutus had sent for Cicero, as he wanted his advice on what he and Cassius should do. Arriving before midday, Cicero was warmly welcomed by Brutus and ushered into a room crowded with the family and friends of Brutus and Cassius, including Brutus's wife, Porcia; Cassius's wife; Brutus's sister Junia; and Brutus's mother, fifty-four-year-old Servilia, onetime lover of Caesar. Servilia and Caesar had continued to remain close over the years, although not intimate—he'd reputedly given her a fabulous pearl worth a fortune when he was consul for the first time in 59 B.C., had given her other gifts during the Civil War, and had conveyed several properties to her for a song when auctioning off the confiscated assets of Pompey and his closest supporters.

Also present at the Anzio gathering was General Marcus Favonius, Pompey's former aide and Brutus's good friend. Contrary to the earlier fears of the plotters, Favonius had unhesitatingly supported the assassination of Caesar once the deed was done, and had quickly thrown his support behind the assassination conspirators and against Antony.

In his own words, Cicero didn't trust Antony a yard. He was not alone. He had heard that Aulus Hirtius, Caesar's former staff officer and now a consul elect, considered Antony's present disposition "as bad and as treacherous as can be." As Cicero would later record in detail in a letter to a friend, he began to give Brutus the advice he had been formulating on the way to Anzio—that Brutus and Cassius should accept the appointments as grain commissioners and get out of Italy before Antony mobilized Caesar's retired army veterans against them. As far as Cicero was concerned, Brutus was the bulwark of the Republic, and his safety was paramount.

As Cicero was giving this advice, Cassius walked into the room, so Cicero repeated his advice in full for Cassius's benefit. Cassius agreed with Cicero's assessment that the Liberators should leave Italy. He said that he himself would go to Greece.

Cicero would record the exact words that followed, for posterity. "What about you, Brutus?" he asked, turning to the other chief Liberator.

"To Rome, if you agree," the forty-one-year-old Brutus replied.

"But I don't agree at all," Cicero responded. "You wouldn't be safe there."

"Supposing I could be safe? Would you approve?"

"Of course. And what's more, I would be against your leaving for a province either now or following your praetorship. But I can't ask you to risk your life at Rome."

Cicero knew that Antony, in his capacity as consul, had already sent subordinates to the retired legion veterans in Italy, telling them to have their arms ready and to be prepared to defend the decrees of Caesar. And it was clear that the veterans of Caesar's legions, men such as the retirees of the 6th, incensed by Caesar's murder and ready to revenge his death, were looking to Antony for direction. Soon nowhere in Italy would be safe for any opponent of Mark Antony.

The conversation then lapsed into recriminations about what should have and shouldn't have been done by the conspirators on the Ides of

March, with Decimus Brutus Albinus in particular coming in for criticism for failing to use the muscle of his gladiators to enforce the will of the conspirators. In essence, the Liberators had underestimated Antony, and they were paying the price for it. As it turned out, Cicero, had he known the assassination was planned, would have urged that Antony also be killed. But, as he now told Brutus and Cassius, it was no use crying over spilled milk. At the very least, he said, Brutus and Cassius should have summoned the Senate and the pair of them taken over leadership of the empire before Antony had a chance to act.

To this, Brutus's mother, Caesar's former lover, exclaimed: "Upon my word! I never heard the like!"

Cicero held his tongue after that, for he could see that Brutus and his family had no ambitions for personal power. Brutus had merely wanted to see the Republic of old restored, but, naively, he had thought that with the dictator out of the way, that idealistic Republic would somehow reemerge of its own accord. In killing Caesar, all he had done was allow another despot, Antony, to rise in the place of the first.

"I found the ship going to pieces," Cicero was to despondently write to his friend Atticus that night, following this meeting with Brutus and Cassius. "No plan, no thought, no method." Cicero could see that the disorganized republican movement was doomed. And he could see that he himself might not be able to look forward to a long future if his bitter enemy Antony had his way. "I have the feeling the sands are running out," Cicero wrote to Atticus that night in June.

But at least Cicero did manage to convince Brutus that returning to Rome was not an option. Brutus and Cassius began to plan their departure from Italy, but in the greatest secrecy; if Antony realized what they were up to, he would certainly try to stop them.

As Urban Praetor, Brutus was responsible for organizing the annual Ludi Apollinares, the Festival of Apollo, due to take place in Rome from July 7 to July 13. In late June, under the pretext of checking out a troupe of actors in Naples for the festival, Brutus traveled there from Anzio. After booking the Naples troupe for the festival, Brutus, his family, and his friends hadn't returned to Anzio. Instead, they'd quickly proceeded down the coast road toward Salerno. Continuing through old Paestum, they'd rendezvoused with Cassius and his party at a villa at the seaside town of Velia.

The next day, Brutus and Cassius boarded a cargo ship with their aides and servants and sailed with the evening tide, leaving their wives and young children behind. Their planned route would take them down through the

Strait of Messina, around the boot of Italy, and across the Ionian Sea to Piraeus, the port of Athens. There, Brutus and his party would leave the ship to base themselves in Athens, from where he would commence to build support in Greece, while Cassius continued on to Syria.

Officially, Cassius and Brutus would be carrying out their jobs as grain commissioners in the East. But once Antony and his supporters came to hear of their destinations, they would realize the pair was up to something, and would guess they were raising money and men for a military tilt at Antony.

At Velia, once the ship carrying their menfolk had disappeared from view, and as the night closed around the relatives of the two men, sobbing women escorted by helpless servants made their way down from the promontory from which they'd watched the craft depart. As Brutus' wife, Porcia, and her son Bibulus climbed into a litter, Porcia was inconsolable. At dawn next day they would begin the journey back to Rome and back to uncertainty, but for now they would return to the house at Velia, where they'd spent the previous night with Brutus.

Plutarch says Porcia's son Bibulus later wrote that on a wall of that villa at Velia there was a painting of Hector, chief warrior of Troy, parting for the last time from his wife, Andromache, as he set off for war. Porcia, he says, had been in tears ever since she'd arrived at the villa and first laid eyes on the picture. Porcia's dread, says Plutarch, was that, like Andromache, she would never see her husband again. And so it would turn out to be.

XXIV

THE WOLF'S TWINS

ow there were two 6th Legions. In 45 B.C., to give himself sixteen full-strength legions for the invasion of Parthia plus enough legions to garrison Spain, Gaul, Italy, Illyricum, Africa, and the East while he was campaigning in Parthia, Caesar had ordered new enlistments enrolled for the units he'd allowed to discharge their veterans into honorable retirement. The 7th, 8th, 9th, and 10th Legions had all received new intakes in this process, with some of their veterans voluntarily returning to march in their senior cohorts, and others taking up appointments as centurions to train and lead the new recruits. Many of those recruits were former Pompeian soldiers who had surrendered in Spain after the defeat of the forces led by the Pompey brothers.

Caesar's 6th Legion also had received a new intake, following the discharge of their now famous veterans in the wake of their participation in the Spanish Triumph at Rome. Meanwhile, in Africa a year before, the other half of Pompey's original republican 6th Legion had surrendered at the 46 B.C. Battle of Thapsus, and Caesar had ordered it, and the 4th Legion, remnants of which also surrendered at Thapsus, to likewise be brought up to full strength with a new enlistment. In this case the new enlistment would have been made up mostly of men who had fought on the republican side in Africa and been made POWs.

By 44 B.C., then, the Roman army included these two separate 6th Legions, both approaching full strength, and both linked by a common birth, as if they were twins. As someone in authority at Rome must have pointed out, they were just like Romulus and Remus, the legendary founders of Rome. That legend had it that the mother of Romulus and Remus was Rhea Silvia, daughter of Numitor, the deposed king of the central Italian city of Alba Longa, while their father was Mars, the god of war. Rhea had been forced by her uncle Amulius, who had overthrown Numitor, to become a vestal virgin and make a vow of chastity so she could not breed sons who might claim his throne. Then Mars had his way with Rhea, after which Amulius ordered Rhea to drown her baby twins in the Tiber. But the container in which Rhea placed them floated down the flooded river and came to rest at the future site of Rome, close to a fig tree on the river-bank that would be considered sacred in later times.

Here, so the legend went, baby Romulus and Remus were found by a she-wolf and a woodpecker, both of which were to become sacred to the god Mars. Wolf and woodpecker suckled and protected the boys until they were found by the shepherd Faustulus, who took them home to his wife, Acca Larentia. The boys were raised by Faustulus and his wife, and in their youth joined a band of adventurous young men who killed King Amulius and restored Numitor to the throne of Alba Longa. The boys established the settlement of Rome on the Palatine Hill, but before long they quar-reled, and Romulus killed Remus, after which the city took Romulus's name.

As Romulus increased his power he welcomed exiles and fugitives, including Trojans fleeing the Trojan War. To provide his men with wives he invited the Sabine tribe from the nearby Quirinal Hill to a festival at Rome, then abducted the Sabines' wives. This was the famous rape of the Sabine women that was later reenacted in the Roman wedding ceremony, and, like many Roman wedding practices such as the wedding ring, bridal veil, and wedding cake, found its way into modern Western culture, in this case as the act of the groom carrying his bride over the threshold. The Romans and the Sabines soon combined. Romulus eventually disappeared mysteriously in a storm, apparently on the Quirinal Hill. He was there-after worshiped by the Roman people as the god Quirinus, ranking close to Jupiter and Mars in the Roman pantheon.

By the first century B.C., the image of the she-wolf suckling the twins Romulus and Remus was common throughout the Roman Empire, and the two 6th Legions now took this symbol as their own. From now on, in addition to the bull emblem that continued to adorn the shields and stan-dards of both 6th Legions, in recognition of their joint origin both 6th Legions would also proudly carry the symbol of the she-wolf and the twins on their standards. It's also likely that both units also adopted Quirinus as their patron deity.

By early 43 B.C., Rome was again locked in a civil war, and both 6th Legions were engaged in the conflict. It wasn't Cassius and Brutus who were now the subjects of dissension—the two leading Liberators remained in the East, building their power base and enjoying strong support from many senators back at home. A new player had emerged on the scene.

Caesar's eighteen-year-old great-nephew Octavius, the son of his niece Attia, who was in turn daughter of Caesar's late sister Julia, had been studying at the famous learning center at Apollonia in Greece when the Dictator was assassinated. Caesar had taken Octavius into his household when the boy was fifteen and treated him like a son, making him his principal heir.

Caesar had intended taking the young man along on the Parthian operation as a member of his staff, and Octavius had been in Apollonia preparing to join Caesar in Macedonia during the spring for the march to Syria. In the months leading up to 44 B.C.'s Ides of March, senior officers from the legions in Macedonia had gone down to Apollonia to pay their respects to Octavius and to participate in his military training for the upcoming operation in Parthia.

Shortly after the assassination, the young man arrived at Rome accompanied by his best friend, nineteen-year-old Marcus Agrippa, and claimed his inheritance. Antony, who was executor of Caesar's estate, was now enforcing his will at Rome with his six thousand Praetorian guardsmen but facing unrelenting criticism from the likes of Cicero and other leading senators. Antony fobbed off the youth, who under the terms of Caesar's will was now his adopted son and so took Caesar's name, becoming Gaius Julius Caesar Octavianus. While the boy was now called Caesar by his contemporaries, history would refer to him—for the next seventeen years, anyhow—as Octavian. But young Octavian was not to be fobbed off for long.

Antony had wanted the governorship of Cisalpine Gaul then held by Brutus Albinus, one of Caesar's assassins. When the Senate refused to give it to him, Antony summoned five of the six legions sitting uselessly in Macedonia waiting for the Parthian operation, which would not now go ahead, and four legions landed at Brindisi late in the year, to be soon joined by the fifth. There they went into camp, to await Antony's orders; meanwhile, he was hoping to use the legions' presence in Italy to intimidate his opponents and get his own way.

Early in the new year of 43 B.C., while matters were coming to a head in Italy, an event took place that would give the retirees of the 6th Legion great satisfaction and considerable amusement. Flabby young Publius Dolabella, who had divorced Cicero's daughter Tullia in 46 B.C. and had become Antony's supporter following Caesar's assassination, was appointed governor of Syria by the Senate. Dolabella quickly set off overland to Macedonia, on his way to Syria.

In Macedonia early in the new year, Dolabella picked up the only legion that Antony had left there of the six that Caesar had originally assembled in Macedonia for his Parthian operation. This happened to be the Deiotariana Legion, the unit that had served beside the 6th at the Battle of Zela, recalled by Caesar for the Parthian invasion and given Roman citizenship and Roman officers. Dolabella continued eastward, leading the Deiotariana to Asia. Since the previous year this province had been governed by Lieutenant General Gaius Trebonius. One of Caesar's senior commanders during the last four years of the Gallic War, Trebonius had governed Farther Spain in 47–46 B.C. and been a consul in 45 B.C., but despite his favored status with Caesar he had joined Brutus and Cassius and the other conspirators and had taken part in Caesar's assassination.

Forty-seven-year-old General Trebonius became aware that Dolabella was in his province with a legion and was trying to buy provisions for his march to Syria. Trebonius had no time for either Antony or Dolabella. He gave orders that Dolabella was not to be granted admittance to any city in his province. Turned away from Pergamum, Dolabella arrived outside Trebonius's provincial capital, the port city of Smyrna (present-day Izmir), on Turkey's Aegean coast, with his hungry troops. Trebonius disdainfully told him he would have to go another fifty miles south, to Ephesus, for supplies, and Dolabella's column wearily continued its march.

Trebonius sent a detachment from the legion under his command in Asia—thought to be the 36th—to shadow Dolabella. But Dolabella's rear guard lured this shadowing force into a trap; then, when these men surrendered without a fight, executed every one of them. The Deiotariana Legion then quickly and quietly marched back to Izmir, and in the early morning hours silently scaled the city walls. The first that General Trebonius knew that his capital was in the hands of Dolabella's troops was when he was roughly shaken awake and found a sword at his throat.

"Get up!" snarled a centurion of the Deiotariana Legion.

Two legionaries grabbed Trebonius and dragged him from his bed. Appian describes what followed.

"There's no need for that," Trebonius protested. "Take me to Publius Cornelius Dolabella. I'm quite willing to go with you without resisting."

The centurion looked at the haughty general, one of Caesar's assassins, with a mixture of amusement and disgust. "You can go where you like," he sarcastically responded. "But leave your head behind. Our orders are only to bring your head."

With the troops crowding into his bedchamber laughing at their centurion's darkly dry humor, the suddenly pale General Trebonius was pressed to his knees. And there at Izmir, Gaius Trebonius had his head sliced from his shoulders. As the retired veterans of the 6th Legion would have happily remarked when the story reached them, Trebonius was the first of Caesar's murderers to die. Even though the assassination conspirators in the Senate soon pushed through a vote that decreed Dolabella a public enemy for this execution, if the men of the 6th had their way Trebonius would not be the last to be meted out the ultimate punishment.

Back in Italy, two of Antony's five legions deserted him after he decimated them for insubordination, going over to young Octavian. Undeterred, Antony pressed on to Cisalpine Gaul with the other three and a number of new local recruits and lay siege to Albinus at Mutina, today's Modena, in north-central Italy. The Senate declared Antony an enemy of the state and sent several armies marching north to relieve Albinus at Modena. Two of these forces were commanded by the consuls that Caesar had previously designated for 43 b.c., his former aide and biographer Aulus Hirtius and General Gaius Vibius Pansa. The third force was commanded by Octavian.

In two battles at Modena in April, Antony was badly mauled, losing half his men, and was forced to withdraw across the Alps into Transalpine Gaul, the south of France. But both consuls, Hirtius and Pansa, were killed in the fighting. This left the door open for young Octavian to assimilate their legions into his army. In the south of France, Marcus Lepidus, ordered by the Senate to take on Antony's depleted force, was in command of seven legions, including new enlistments of both the 6th and the 10th Legions.

By the summer of 44 b.c., too, the renowned retired veterans of the 6th at Arles—Cleopatra's kidnappers—had rejoined their legion, which was part of Marcus Lepidus's army then in camp at the Var River, not far from Arles. The veterans had been called up to honor the terms of their discharge and serve for up to four more years in emergencies, but it is likely they would have voluntarily taken the field anyway, to avenge the murder of Caesar. In the same way, veterans of the 10th had rejoined their legion from retirement at their colony at Narbonne as Lepidus marched through the town.

Despite their thirst for revenge, the 6th's veterans would have hoped that this would involve just a short period of service, until Caesar's murderers were dealt with and this current period of frustrating political instability had been brought to an end. It would have frustrated the veterans, too, to have to serve one of Caesar's loyal deputies and confront Antony, another of his deputies, when their principal objective was the punishment of Caesar's chief assassins, Cassius and Brutus.

Lepidus was an insipid and uninspiring military commander. There was a Roman saying, "He is great in trifles," and so it was in the case of Marcus Lepidus. Led by the famous 10th, which, like the 6th, was considered to have had a special relationship with Caesar, all seven of Lepidus's units, including the 6th, turned their backs on him and defected to Antony when he set up camp on the far side of the Var. With no other choice, Lepidus then also allied himself with Antony. Soon the two legions stationed in Farther Spain crossed the Pyrenees on Senate orders to tackle Antony. But they, too, led by General Gaius Pollio, Caesar's former staff officer, also joined Antony. Then another three legions—led by Major General Marcus Plancus, the general who had settled the men of the 6th in Gaul—sent by the Senate to shadow Antony, refused to go against him. And Major General Publius Ventidius, with three legions he had raised on his own authority as a current praetor, threw his support behind Antony.

Only weeks before, Antony had led a disheveled and beaten force over the Alps, drinking dirty water from alpine puddles at the roadside to survive. Now he could call on upward of twenty legions, some of them the most famous in the Roman army, including Caesar's 6th and his favorite 10th, together with several of Rome's leading generals.

Instead of going head to head with Antony, the astute young Octavian, who himself had ten legions at his disposal, subsequently sat down with Antony and Lepidus in north-central Italy and worked out a deal. Now that they controlled all Rome's legions in the West between them, the three men agreed to share power, in what became known as the Second Triumvirate, and to sideline the now powerless Senate. One of the first acts of the "triumvirs" was to draw up a list of 300 senators and 1,000 knights they wanted to eliminate. Each man submitted his own list of 100 senators and some 330 knights to create the grand execution list. A price of 100,000 sesterces was offered for the head of each proscribed man. If a slave delivered up a wanted man, he would not only be paid, he also would receive his freedom and Roman citizenship. At the top of Antony's list of the men he wanted dead was his bitter enemy Marcus Cicero. Octavian initially argued against Cicero's execution but eventually gave in to the determined, vengeful Antony.

In November 43 B.C., the three triumvirs arrived in Rome, leading a single legion each and the Praetorian cohorts, bent on spilling the blood of their foes and seizing their property. Controlling more than thirty legions among them, they could ignore the law and discard all sense of propriety as they eliminated adversaries and critics. "Laws are silent in the midst of arms," as a Roman saying goes, and such was the case during these bloody months of the 43–42 B.C. pogrom of the triumvirs.

Most of the men on the extermination list were subsequently hunted down by Praetorian death squads sent by Antony and Octavian and executed wherever they were found. Some of the wanted men managed to escape, a number to Sicily, a few to Brutus and Cassius in the East, several by dressing as centurions, but Cicero was not among the lucky ones who kept their heads. Antony had ordered that not only should Cicero's severed head be delivered to him, he wanted to see his right hand as well—the hand that had written the speeches, the *Philippics*, that were highly critical of him.

Cicero fled, but guided by an informant, his hunters found him near the port town of Caieta, modern Gaeta, a little north of Naples, on the western coast of Italy. His execution squad was led by Tribune Popillius, a man whom Cicero had successfully defended in court when he'd been charged with murder. On December 7, 43 B.C., sixty-three-year-old Cicero, lawyer, author, general, statesman, considered the greatest orator of his day, was beheaded by a blow from the sword of Popillius's deputy, Centurion Herennius. The head and both hands of Cicero were duly brought to Antony, and were later displayed on the rostra at Rome for all the world to see. Antony was so delighted to have Cicero's head that he paid Tribune Popillius ten times the reward that had been offered for it; the tribune walked away an instant millionaire.

Hundreds more suffered Cicero's fate. As Seneca wrote a century later, Antony had "the heads of his country's leading men brought to him at the dinner table, identifying the hands and liquidated features during banquets marked by sumptuous magnificence and regal pomp, still thirsting for blood when filled with wine." With the vast majority of their opponents and critics out of the way, the Board of Three for the Ordering of State—as Antony, Octavian, and Lepidus now called themselves—turned their attention to dealing with Brutus and Cassius, who had been beyond their reach.

The two Liberators had by this time taken full control of the Roman East. Cassius had won the loyalty of twelve legions, including those Caesar had left in Egypt with Cleopatra, and assembled a powerful navy provided by Eastern maritime cities. He led his army against Dolabella, trapping him and his two legions—the Deiotariana and the late General Trebonius's 36th—inside Laodicea in Syria. Uninspiring Dolabella was subsequently betrayed by one of his own centurions, who opened one of Laodicea's smaller gates to Cassius. As Cassius's troops flooded into the city, Dolabella showed courage enough to have one of his bodyguards behead him rather than fall into the hands of the vindictive Cassius. Adding Dolabella's legions to his growing army, Cassius set about occupying Syria. When four predominantly Jewish cities of the Middle East—Gophna,

Emmaus, Lod, and Thamna—closed their gates to him, Cassius took them by storm, and sold their inhabitants into slavery.

Cassius then successfully invaded the island of Rhodes, where he had been brought up, the island that had provided Julius Caesar with the flotilla of warships that had performed so well for him during his Egyptian campaign. Rhodes had refused to support Cassius, and paid a savage price for its defiance after Cassius's fleet defeated its ships in two sea battles and then his legionaries stormed the famous island. Cassius subsequently marched his army through the provinces of the East, crossed the Dardanelles, and arrived in Macedonia, where he linked up with Brutus, who had taken control of eight legions in the region and levied several new units. Between them, the pair now commanded twenty-two legions, many auxiliaries, and thousands of cavalry.

The Liberators marched most of their troops to the Macedonian town of Philippi, today's Filippoi. There they blocked the Egnatian Way, the military highway linking East and West, by building extensive fortifications for a mile across the valley traversed by the highway, linking their two fortified camps, each on a hill on either side of the highway. Entrenchments dug by their troops ran all the way to the coast, eight miles away.

Mark Antony, in a letter to Hyrcanus, Jewish high priest at Jerusalem, which would be quoted by Josephus, said of Brutus and Cassius's tactic of digging in at Philippi, "They seized on the places that were proper for their purpose and as it were walled them around with mountains to the very sea, and where the passage was possible only through a single gate."

In the summer of 42 B.C., Antony and Octavian shipped an advance party of eight legions from Italy to Greece, and these units skirted around Philippi and blocked access to the Liberators' army from the East. Leaving Lepidus in charge at Rome, Antony and Octavian then took a convoy to Greece loaded with another twenty legions, these units being split evenly between the two commanders. The 4th Legion, filled out by a new enlistment since its surrender at Thapsus, was in Antony's army. He also had a 6th Legion in his force, and from its subsequent posting this is likely to have been Caesar's by now famous 6th—the Ferrata, as many of its men had come to call it, bolstered by its veterans who had been recalled from retirement at Arles.

As for the second 6th Legion, the unit that was re-formed by Caesar from the men of the original 6th who had survived the Battle of Thapsus, Octavian and Antony had left three legions sitting outside Rome, with Lepidus, and the second 6th may have been among those units now guarding the capital.

Despite the fact that the Liberators had a powerful naval force at their disposal, the vast convoy of Antony and Octavian managed to reach Greece without being intercepted. With Octavian falling ill, Antony left one of his legions at Amphipolis to guard the baggage and pressed on to Philippi with the remaining nineteen. Octavian had only just rejoined him when, in early October 42 B.C., the first of two Battles of Philippi was launched by an unheralded charge by Antony's nine legions, while Octavian's surprised troops stood by and watched. Brutus's legions counter-charged without waiting for orders from their generals. The legion on Brutus's extreme right almost wiped out Antony's 4th Legion, the old marching companion of the 6th, which became overextended on Antony's left wing. The 4th fought bravely, if in vain, to halt Brutus's advance, taking heavy casualties, and following the battle the survivors of the 4th would call their legion the 4th Macedonica in remembrance of this bloody day on the Macedonian plain. In time, the title would become official.

The drive by Brutus's troops overran the triumvirs' camp, and Octavian narrowly escaped with his life. But, at the same time, Antony took Cassius's camp, and Cassius and his staff hurriedly withdrew up the hill behind it. In all the confusion and clouds of dust kicked up by the tens of thousands of infantry and cavalry, on seeing Antony's troops in his headquarters below him Cassius thought the battle lost. Toward the end of the day Cassius, survivor of Carrhae, admiral under Pompey, senior judge under Caesar, and subsequently chief architect of his assassination, committed suicide on the hilltop.

In reality, the Liberators' army had come off better from the day's fierce fighting in terms of number of casualties. Brutus withdrew a distance and regrouped, and a week later was convinced by his subordinates to do battle again in an attempt to win total victory. But this time Brutus's army fared much worse. Forced to retreat, he was surrounded. His remaining fourteen thousand men from four legions refused to continue the fight, and sought peace terms. On a lonely Macedonian hill, Marcus Brutus, "son" of Julius Caesar, also took his own life—by having an associate run him through. While Brutus's head would be displayed at Rome, Octavian had the rest of Brutus's remains cremated, and sent the ashes to Brutus's mother, Servilia.

After Brutus's devoted though neurotic wife, Porcia, who'd waited anxiously back in Italy for news of him, learned of her husband's death, her servants put her on a suicide watch. But she outwitted them, swallowing hot embers from the fire in her room and dying a horrible, self-inflicted death. Cassius's wife, Brutus's sister Junia, would live to ripe old age, at least into her eighties and perhaps older, dying, of natural causes, an extremely wealthy woman in A.D. 22, during the reign of the emperor Tiberius. Roman historian Tacitus would note that Junia would mention many leading Romans in her will, but contrary to custom the emperor Tiberius, stepson of Octavian, was not one of them. In Junia's funeral cortege, says Tacitus, the busts of many of her family members would be carried, as was the custom at Roman funerals. But the busts of Brutus and Cassius were notably absent—on orders from the emperor, it would seem.

Many other leading men of Rome apart from Brutus and Cassius also perished as a result of the defeat at Philippi. Some fell on the battlefield, some committed suicide, others were executed after the battle by the victors. Among them were Brutus's cousin and Porcia's brother Marcus Cato Jr., and Brutus's best friend, the fiery young general Marcus Favonius. Before long, not one of the senators who had participated in the murder of Julius Caesar would still be alive.

Mark Antony wrote to Hyrcanus at Jerusalem after the Philippi victory: "We have overcome that confused rout of men, half mad with spite against us." The revenge the men of the 6th Legion and other Caesarian veterans had sought had been obtained. "We have taken vengeance on those who had been the authors of great injustice toward men, and of great wickedness toward the gods," Antony told Hyrcanus. He added that Brutus "became a partaker of the same destruction as Cassius. And now that these men have received their punishment, we suppose we may enjoy peace for the time to come."

With that sentiment in mind, and with Antony, Octavian, and Lepidus now indisputable rulers of the Roman world, many of the legions of the Liberators were disbanded, as were some of the triumvirs' legions. The remaining units were now divided among Antony, Octavian, and Lepidus. Octavian would control the West, Antony the East, with Lepidus left the crumbs—the province of Africa, and the post of Pontifex Maximus for life. Of these legions, the 6th Ferrata went with Antony to the East, to be based in Syria, and the second 6th came under Octavian's control—by 40 B.C. it was stationed in Spain.

The veterans who had come out of retirement to serve during the short war were now discharged, and the triumvirs' veterans given land grants. According to Appian, Antony only wanted to give land to men of the twenty-eight legions that had served the triumvirs in Macedonia against the Liberators, but Octavian, who took charge of the land allocations in Italy, also included six legions that had been left in the West. Even so, other Second Triumvirate legions, such as the 14th, which was back at its Africa station following Philippi, were not included in the discharge and settlement of veterans, which some estimates suggest involved up to thirty-two thousand retirees.

When the veterans had been recalled the previous year, they had been promised land in the eighteen rich Italian cities nominated publicly for confiscation by the Triumvirs in 43 B.C. A number of retirees from the 6th did not go back to Arles, but instead were now allocated farms outside one of those eighteen Italian cities, Beneventum, fifty miles east of Capua in Campania. Prosperous Beneventum, modern Benevento, sat astride the Appian Way on a ridge between the Sabato and Calore Rivers, northeast of Naples. The 6th's new settlement program was again supervised by General Plancus. The size of each land grant at Benevento was some fifty acres per retiree, with most allotments valued at 50,000 to 60,000 sesterces.

So it was that men who had gone over to Caesar at Farsala and saved his skin in Egypt and at Zela took up new land grants in the Benevento region in the spring of 41 B.C. Until land surveying was completed, the veterans camped on the Field of Mars outside Rome. Then, when each city was ready to receive them, the retirees were marched to the places in question. Octavian himself led at least one of these marches, ignoring the thousands of dispossessed farmers who flocked to Rome to protest the loss of their land.

There at Benevento the men of the 6th Ferrata occupied their farm holdings and spent the rest of their days, having more than served out the four extra years they were expected to put in once they had served their full enlistments. Many of the men of the 6th would have played leading roles in the civic affairs of Benevento, especially during the year's many religious festivals. The more ambitious among them would be elected to the town senate, to become big fish in a small rural pond.

Among the numerous tombstones of men of the 6th Legion found in the area in recently modern times none were of centurions, or even of standard-bearers. This is not to say that no NCOs lived and died among the retired 6th Legion veterans of Benevento, but that is a possibility. Perhaps the veteran NCOs continued to serve in the army—one in five veterans did choose to continue in service with the legions after Philippi—or perhaps they were given more substantial land elsewhere; we don't know. We do know that former centurions were regularly appointed to serve as lictors, or official attendants, of magistrates at Rome, and it is highly likely that the NCOs of the 6th Ferrata who survived the civil wars took up such official posts at Rome and other large cities once they received their military discharges.

From their farms around Benevento, the retired veterans of the 6th would have followed unfolding events and the adventures of their former unit with acute interest, for both 6th Legions were to play roles in the tumultuous affairs of the next ten years.

The veterans would have learned, with immense satisfaction, that the last conspirators involved in the murder of Julius Caesar were dead by the time they were taking up their land grants in 41 B.C. That same year they also heard an intriguing story about Cleopatra, the Egyptian queen they had kept under lock and key in Alexandria.

They would have come to know that immediately following Caesar's death Cleopatra had hurried back to Alexandria with her brother Ptolemy XIV and son Caesarion. Under the terms of Caesar's will, his estate on the Gianicolo where the Egyptian party had been staying became the property of the Roman people on his death, and the hillside Gardens of Caesar were to become a feature of the city. With all the political infighting at Rome following Caesar's death, there would have been no way that the shocked and distraught Cleopatra would have wanted to remain there.

In July, shortly after the return to the Egyptian capital of Cleopatra and her entourage, her younger brother Ptolemy died, poisoned. The men of the 6th would have had no doubts that Cleopatra had been behind his murder, particularly as she now named Caesarion, her infant son by Caesar, her new coruler, giving him the title of Ptolemy XV. Cleopatra was now in effect sole ruler of Egypt, and although Roman legions were then still stationed at Alexandria, she was pretty much free to do what she pleased. Her independence increased even more when Cassius took the legions based in Egypt into his army and led them to Macedonia to join Brutus's force.

Cleopatra remained there at Alexandria, sitting on the fence, holding back the rejuvenated Egyptian navy, and not supporting any one party while she waited to see who would emerge from the turmoil as Rome's new strongman. Now, in 41 B.C., she received a summons from Mark Antony. He wanted her to explain to him, to his face, why she hadn't been more supportive of the triumvir's war efforts against Caesar's murderers Cassius and Brutus and their "madness of arms"—as he described their Eastern campaign in a letter to the people of Tyre in Syria quoted by Josephus.

After stalling for a time, Cleopatra arrived at Tarsus in Cilicia, where Antony was then staying. She made her arrival in a golden barge and promptly seduced Antony. Totally smitten with her, he'd gone back to Alexandria with Cleopatra, where the pair lived a life of total hedonism, calling themselves the "inimitable livers" as they dined and drank for days on end. Meanwhile, back in Rome, Antony's wife, Fulvia, was blithely promoting his interests and fermenting revolt against Octavian. When she died in 40 B.C., Antony returned to Rome, where, to cement his relationship with Octavian, he married his colleague's sister Octavia, with whom he was to have several children. Although this was a political marriage, Antony was, according to Appian, very much in love with Octavia to begin with.

In 39 B.C., Antony's deputy in the East, Lieutenant General Publius Ventidius, went to war against the Parthians, who had successfully invaded Syria in partnership with Quintus Labienus, the son of General Titus Labienus, Caesar's onetime deputy who'd defected to Pompey and perished at the Battle of Munda. Labienus Jr. had sided with the Liberators in 43–42 B.C., and prior to the Battle of Philippi had been sent by Cassius to meet with the king of Parthia, Orodes II, with hopes of convincing him to provide the Liberators with aid for their war against Octavian and Antony. Quintus Labienus had been in the middle of discussions with the Parthians when news of the defeat of Brutus and Cassius at Philippi reached the Parthian capital, Ctesiphon.

Only death as a proscribed person awaited Labienus in Roman territory, so he remained at the Parthian court and made a deal with King Orodes under which Labienus invaded Syria with a Parthian army, serving as cocommander with Pacorus, son of the king, and the Parthian generals Barzapharnes and Pharnapates. Initially, the Parthian invasion was virtually bloodless, with the Roman troops then stationed in Syria going over to Labienus in remembrance of his father and of the Liberators. While Pacorus and his Parthian troops advanced south into Palestine, Labienus and his mixed Roman/Parthian force moved north, planning to roll up Rome's allied states and provinces of the East.

As Labienus occupied Cilicia and southern Anatolia, Antony gave the colorful but very capable General Ventidius the job of ejecting him. A man in his fifties, Publius Ventidius had risen from being a prisoner as a boy during the civil war between Sulla and Marius and then a mule contractor as a young man to become a consul of Rome, a career path made possible by sheer ability. His current appointment was also a product of his steadfast loyalty to Antony. Among the numerous legions assigned to Ventidius for this job in the East were the 6th Ferrata and the 3rd—the 6th's former Pompeian marching partners in Spain prior to and in the early stages of the civil war.

While General Ventidius's Eastern campaign was launched under Antony's direction from afar, the triumvirs had other problems to deal with closer to Rome, problems all to do with a Pompey; for between 39 and 36 B.C., Pompey the Great's surviving son, Sextus, threatened to break the Second Triumvirate's grip on power.

Sextus Pompey had emerged from the dust of the conclusion of the civil war in Spain in 45 B.C. to conduct a troublesome guerrilla war in western Spain, so Marcus Lepidus, then governor of Nearer Spain, had negotiated a deal with him that Antony pushed through the Senate: in exchange for 50 million sesterces in compensation for property owned by his father, Pompey the Great, that had been seized by Caesar during the civil war, plus command of a Roman fleet in the western Mediterranean, Sextus agreed to leave Spain. These measures had been designed to keep Pompey quiet and prevent him from becoming a rallying point for men who still harbored affection for the old republican ideals. And for a time these objectives were achieved.

Sextus had spent several years building a power base, using his fleet to dominate the western Mediterranean and convincing three legions stationed on Corsica and Sardinia to swear allegiance to him, taking control of the two islands. By 39 B.C., Sextus was securely installed in Sicily, the governorship of which had been promised to him by the triumvirs but never given. A number of legions came over to the last son of Pompey, who had been joined by many republicans who had fled the proscriptions of 43–42 B.C. and family members including his sister Pompeia and her children; when Pompeia's husband, Lucius Cornelius Sulla Faustus, son of the late Roman dictator Sulla, had been killed after the Battle of Thapsus in Africa, Caesar had allowed Pompeia to sail to Spain to join her brothers.

To Sicily, too, came Tiberius Claudius Nero, Caesar's former quaestor and naval commander when the 6th Legion had been fighting in Egypt. Nero had fallen out with Antony and Octavian, and, fearing for his life, sought refuge with the Pompey family. But while Pompeia was kind to Tiberius Nero, her brother Sextus would not even talk to him, and Tiberius Nero had to continue his flight. Eventually he would receive Octavian's pardon.

After a series of naval battles through 38–37 B.C. in which Octavian had fared badly and nearly lost his life, the triumvirs had decided to take the battle onto land, where they would have a marked superiority in troop numbers. In 36 B.C. Octavian and Lepidus landed on Sicily with twenty-four legions to dislodge Sextus. The second 6th Legion was one of Octavian's units during these operations.

On land the triumvirs gained the upper hand, but in 36 B.C. the deciding battles were fought on the water, with twenty-six-year-old Octavian's

best friend, Marcus Agrippa, in command of his fleet and decisively defeating the thirty-year-old Pompey that same year. Sextus fled to the East
with his few remaining warships and threw himself on Mark Antony's
mercy, to no avail; in 35 B.C. one of Antony's deputies, General Marcus
Titius, executed him. With Sextus's death, so, too, died the Pompey
dynasty.

In Sicily, Lepidus, suddenly finding himself with dozens of legions—his
own plus Sextus's surrendered units—made a grab for power, convincing
all the troops to vow allegiance to him, and him alone. Young Octavian
had then come to Lepidus's huge camp and won over the troops. After
that, Lepidus retired into semi-exile in southern Italy, and his fellow triumvirs again carved up the empire between them, with Octavian to control the West, including Africa, and Antony the East.

Meanwhile, in the East, General Ventidius had repulsed Quintus Labienus's army in the Battle of the Cilician Gates in 39 B.C., a bloody encounter in a mountain pass leading into Cilicia in which Labienus Jr. himself
was killed. The next year, 38 B.C., Ventidius lured the army of the Parthian
prince Pacorus into battle, and his legions, including the 6th Ferrata, had
killed Pacorus and won another resounding victory over the Parthians,
this time at Mount Gindarus.

With Labienus dead and the surviving Roman troops who had followed him going over to General Ventidius, the Parthians were driven
from all Roman territory, with Ventidius reclaiming Cilicia and Syria for
Rome. Ventidius returned home to Rome that same year and celebrated
a Triumph, the first since Caesar's 45 B.C. Spanish Triumph. This Triumph, like the last, celebrated a victory in which the 6th had played a
leading role. Ventidius died shortly after. His loss would impact severely
on Antony's future fortunes.

Antony returned to Alexandria following Ventidius's successes in the
East and resumed his relationship with Cleopatra, who was to bear him
three children. In 36 B.C., Antony, determined to prove that he was a better general than Ventidius, invaded Parthian territory with sixteen
legions, having recruited a number of additional units in the East—he is
known to have had at least twenty-three legions operating in various parts
of the East. Again, among the units taking part in operations against the
Parthians were the 6th Ferrata and 3rd Legions.

Later historians would assess Antony as a brave soldier but inept general who was served by often exceptional underlings such as Ventidius.
Antony's Parthian campaign, conceived and led by him, turned into an
unmitigated disaster. All went well at first, as Antony's army of a hundred
thousand men advanced through Armenia into Media, a country allied to

Parthia. A Parthian counteroffensive was led by the new king of Parthia, Phraates IV, who had killed his father, Orodes, to take the throne. Antony reached the Median city of Phraata and lay siege to it. But in his impatience to reach Phraata he had allowed his massive baggage train, which included all his artillery and a battering ram eighty feet long, to fall behind him on the march. The Parthians circled behind Antony, cut off the baggage train, and slaughtered all ten thousand soldiers and noncombatants traveling with it. Without supplies or the right equipment, the long siege of Phraata fizzled, and as the weather deteriorated, Antony finally conceded that he would have to withdraw to Roman territory.

When Antony finally managed to extricate himself from Media, after a bloody retreat that had lasted weeks, he had lost twenty-four thousand men to starvation, to appalling winter weather, and to King Phraates, who pursued him relentlessly with his heavy cavalry and famous mounted archers. Good men of the 6th numbered among those whose bodies were left where they fell on that horrendous retreat. Antony in fact owed his life to the 3rd Legion, whose rearguard action saved the entire force from another disaster of the magnitude of Carrhae seventeen years before.

Having divorced Octavia by this time, Antony returned to Cleopatra, and, despite his bloody Median reverse, in 34 B.C. celebrated a fantastic pseudo-Triumph in Alexandria, as if he had won a great victory against the Parthians. In this Triumph Cleopatra and Antony were carried through the streets seated on golden thrones, accompanied by their three young children and Caesar's son, Caesarion. To Caesarion, Cleopatra gave the title king of kings, and to herself, queen of kings. Antony had by this time given her a variety of Roman territories throughout the East, which incensed many in Rome, not the least of whom was Octavian, who was also deeply offended at the way Antony had treated his sister Octavia.

There was little that Antony would not give Cleopatra. By some accounts they even married, although under Roman law such a marriage was illegal. Only once did he deny her. In 40 B.C., while Antony was back in Rome, Cleopatra had entertained Herod, son of the late Jewish leader Antipater, at Alexandria. Herod had paid Antony to have the Roman Senate make him king of Judea, but Cleopatra had her covetous eyes on Judea as well. She even tried to seduce Herod, but he rejected her advances, which infuriated her. So she tried to convince Antony to give her Herod's territory. But Antony was Herod's firm friend. Despite all Cleopatra's persuasive powers, while she did convince Antony to give her Arabia and a small part of Judea, Cleopatra never got her hands on the richest parts of Herod's kingdom, for which Herod was for the rest of his days grateful to Antony.

Octavian had put up with Antony and Cleopatra long enough, and he decided to act to eliminate them. First, he failed to renew the Second Triumvirate when the latest five-year agreement expired. Before long, in 31 B.C., he declared war—not on Antony, a Roman, but on the foreigner Cleopatra and her Egyptians.

Antony moved most of his land forces to Macedonia, then to southern Greece, where he linked up with Cleopatra and their combined naval forces. When Octavian and his deputy Agrippa arrived with land and sea forces, Antony and Cleopatra chose to break out at Actium and flee back to Egypt. To achieve that breakout, their fleet had to fight the Battle of Actium, a naval battle, on September 2, 31 B.C. The breakout cost them the majority of their ships and troops. Antony's abandoned legions on shore surrendered a week later.

Octavian now disbanded many of his legions and legions that had marched for Antony, sending his own veterans into retirement in colonies throughout the Roman world. The legionaries he retained were non-Italians, men from the provinces, for it was Octavian's policy that Italians from south of the Po River should not have to serve in the Roman army— that would fall to provincials from now on, he decreed. The only exception was to be the Praetorian Guard, which, under Octavian/Augustus and many of his successors, would be recruited exclusively in Italy south of the Po.

When Octavian, now thirty-two, marched into Egypt in the summer of 30 B.C., the garrison at Pelusium surrendered to him—on Cleopatra's orders according to Octavian himself, unbeknownst to Antony. Antony's remaining troops put up only mild resistance outside Alexandria, and he, realizing that it was all over, fell on his sword, dying slowly and painfully. At first Cleopatra negotiated with Octavian, but, dreading the prospect of being dragged through the streets of Rome in Octavian's inevitable Egyptian Triumph, remembering how her sister Arsinoe had suffered that fate in 46 B.C. in Caesar's Egyptian Triumph, she, too, took her own life. The reputed suicide method was the bite of an asp, but most historians think she also took poison, as both her female attendants did.

Through years of uncertainty and threat during her childhood, years that had made her and her siblings mature fast, Cleopatra had developed a finely tuned instinct for survival. As she realized her talent for manipulation, she had gone from a clever but vulnerable teenager to a scheming and covetous vixen who didn't know where to stop. Even in her last days she tried to seduce Octavian, and only when that failed did she realize that her career and her life had reached their inevitable ends.

As Octavian had advanced into Egypt, Cleopatra had sent the son she had by Caesar, Caesarion, a.k.a. Ptolemy XV, who was now seventeen—and closely resembling his father in appearance and gait, according to Suetonius—fleeing south. Caesarion went into hiding at the port of Berenice on Upper Egypt's Red Sea coast. Soon betrayed by his tutor, Caesarion fell into Octavian's clutches. Once Caesarion was in his control, Octavian promptly had him strangled. In doing so, Octavian eliminated a potential rival who may have had, in the eyes of some, stronger claims to Caesar's inheritance than his own. The three children of Antony and Cleopatra—the only girl, Cleopatra Selene, and the boys Alaexander Helios (meaning the Sun) and the youngest, another Ptolemy, were sent to Rome by Octavian, where they were taken into the home of Octavian's sister Octavia, Antony's deserted second wife, who raised them with her own children.

Octavian was now sole ruler of the Roman Empire, and, like Caesar, he now had the keys to the fabulously rich Egyptian treasury. Unlike Caesar, he turned Egypt into a Roman province and emptied the treasury—the contents went to Rome, to be used to pay his retired troops' overdue pay and retirement bonuses. Funds left over were enough to finance Rome's standing army for years to come. Among the twenty-eight legions that now made up that standing army were the two 6th Legions: the 6th Ferrata and the second 6th.

In 30 B.C. the 6th Ferrata was stationed at the Syrian port city of Laodicea. Shortly it would move southeast to build a new permanent camp for itself at Raphaneae, near the Euphrates River. From there it could maintain a permanent watch on the Parthians as one of the complement of four legions now permanently assigned to the Syria station under the command of the governor of Syria, who had his headquarters at the provincial capital, Antioch. The second 6th went back to Farther Spain, which was now its permanent station.

By 30 B.C., a decade after the 6th Ferrata veterans had taken up their land grants around Benevento, veterans of the 30th Legion also were settled in the Benevento region, in overdue mass discharges in the wake of Octavian's defeat of Antony and Cleopatra at Actium. These men of the 30th, originally recruited in Italy, had fought against the 6th in Spain in 49 B.C., with them at Munda in 45 B.C., and with them again under Antony's command following Caesar's death, before the 30th Legion ended up in Octavian's army. The parents of some of the 30th Legion's Italian veterans moved onto their farms with them, suggesting that the original family homes had not been too far from Benevento. This had not been the case with the 6th Legion veterans, whose parents were far away in Spain.

Nine tombstones of the tough veterans of the original 6th Legion—nine of the famous nine hundred—survived in the Benevento area to modern times; and names are only visible on seven. Legionary Publius Sertorius was buried there by his brother Marcus, Legionary Quintus Tetarfenus by his brother Marcus. Legionary Gaius Figilius married once he was discharged, and he was buried here by his wife. Legionary Gaius Numisius was buried by his freedmen, his former slaves, several of whom were later interred around him. We don't know who buried Legionary Lucius Caienus. Legionary Lucius Acilius married local girl Marcia Tertia once he retired, and it was she who buried him.

On the Via Appia east of Benevento, Legionary Lucius Labicius's tombstone was raised. His was the only one of all the 6th Legion tombstones to include the title Ferrata in its inscription. Labicius had obviously been immensely proud to be an Ironclad, one of the nine hundred Roman soldiers who had become Cleopatra's kidnappers and who changed Roman history.

XXV

THE IMPERIAL 6THS

I n 27 B.C. Octavian took the name Augustus, a title meaning "revered," which was bestowed on him by the Senate. It was as Caesar Augustus that he would reign for the next forty years; history came to know him as the first emperor of Rome.

Early in that reign, Augustus reformed the Roman army so that each of his twenty-eight permanent legions spread around the empire now had a command structure that began with a commander of brigadier general rank. One military tribune, now called a tribune of the broad stripe, served as each legion's second in command, and a newly created position, that of camp prefect, a former centurion, was third in command. Five officer cadets—tribunes of the thin stripe and all members of the Equestrian Order—served postings of six months with a legion, from March to October, before moving on to the next step up the promotional ladder, appointment as a prefect in charge of auxiliaries. During those six months the junior tribune served on the legion commander's staff for three months (later two), and was free to spend the remaining three months at leisure. Some became tourists in the provinces where their legion was stationed, while the more conscientious did voluntary administrative work at the legion headquarters.

After several appointments as a prefect of both light infantry and cavalry over as many as seven or eight years, the young Roman noble qualified for promotion to senior tribune, and then entry into the Senate at age thirty, and a legion command.

The legion was now a self-contained fighting force, with its own small cavalry unit of 124 officers and men plus artillery—ten heavy ballistas and fifty scorpion dart throwers per legion. The imperial legion created by Augustus was made up of ten cohorts, nine of 480 men each and a "double strength" first cohort of 800. The latter was responsible for guarding the legion's golden eagle standard and always accompanied the legion commander. Under Augustus, a maximum of two legions could be stationed at any one base over winter, and no legion was based in the area where its men were recruited.

Those recruitments took place in mass intakes of young men of seventeen and above, mostly conscripts, with the average recruit being age twenty. Until 6 B.C., recruits signed up for sixteen years of legion service plus another four years of service in the Evocati militia during emergencies once they retired. Between 6 B.C. and A.D. 11, as discharge and reenlistment dates came up for the legions, the service period for legionaries was extended by Augustus from sixteen to twenty years, the service period for members of the Praetorian Guard from twelve to sixteen years, and the obligatory Evocati period postdischarge extended to a total of five years' service from four.

To fund his standing army of twenty-eight legions, Augustus set up a military treasury that was separate from the Treasury of Saturn, the general treasury. The military treasury was administered by a staff headed by three former praetors, each appointed for three years. Initially, Augustus deposited a large sum into the military treasury from his own funds—most of his fortune was based on the treasure of the Ptolemies that he had "liberated" from Egypt following Cleopatra's death. For ongoing military funding he depended on contributions from foreign kings and communities and a 5 percent death tax, which he introduced specifically for this purpose. The military treasury bore the cost of paying, feeding, and equipping the legions, and of paying the bonuses that the emperors gave the troops from time to time—on the emperor's birthday each year, for example.

The 6th Ferrata Legion continued to be stationed in the East through the last part of the first century B.C. and throughout the first century A.D., always based at Raphaneae in Syria, sharing that base with the 12th Legion for several decades. The 6th's title of Ferrata would be in official use by the third century, but it is unknown at what point Ferrata went from an honorific used only by the men of the legion to a title recognized by the Palatium, the emperor's headquarters at Rome. It is possible that the legion was among the first to replace its jackets of iron mail with segmented metal armor, the *segmentia lorica*, in about A.D. 25, from which its proud old Ironclad name of Caesar's day may have found more general usage, although no Roman writer officially ascribes the title to the legion in the first century A.D.

In A.D. 19–20, the 6th Ferrata conducted an operation to arrest the governor of Syria, Gnaeus Calpurnius Piso, who was accused of the poisoning murder of Germanicus Caesar, a famous, hero-worshiped young Roman general and heir to the emperor Tiberius. Germanicus was the eldest son of Tiberius' brother Drusus Caesar—both were the sons of Tiberius Claudius Nero. Drusus had married Octavia, daughter of Mark Antony, making Germanicus Antony's grandson. On Drusus's death on campaign in Germany, Tiberius had adopted his eldest boy, Germanicus, at the insistence of Augustus.

The blame for Germanicus's murder, which took place at Daphne near Antioch in Syria, had fallen on Governor Piso, although it was generally believed that the emperor Tiberius had been behind the murder, for he was jealous and fearful of his nephew and adopted son's fame and popularity. Piso barricaded himself in the fortress of Celenderis in Cilicia, which the 6th laid siege to, led by their commander, Brigadier General Pacuvius, who had refused to support Piso even though some of his own 6th Ferrata centurions had accepted bribes from Piso in return for their loyalty.

With no alternative, Piso surrendered and went back to Rome to face trial in the Senate, only to take his own life in mysterious circumstances just when it seemed likely he would be acquitted. The historian Tacitus and many other Romans felt sure that the insecure Tiberius had been behind the death of his heir, Germanicus, and had forced Piso to suicide.

In A.D. 54, Lieutenant General Gnaeus Domitius Corbulo arrived in the Middle East with secret orders from the young emperor Nero, grandson of Germanicus. A Parthian prince now ruled Armenia, a kingdom that Germanicus had brought into the Roman sphere of influence in A.D. 18. General Corbulo's orders were to reclaim Armenia for Rome. To achieve this task he took charge of two of the four legions of the Syrian station, the 6th Ferrata and the 10th. Finding both units lamentably run down after years of inactivity, he discharged their most unfit and elderly men; then, using special authority invested in him by the emperor, he instituted a draft among young Roman citizens in Cappadocia and Galatia to fill the empty places in the 6th and the 10th.

This was highly unusual—as a rule the legions did not have their ranks replenished until their twenty-year discharge and reenlistment came around, and by the end of their enlistments legion numbers were usually well below the nominal imperial figure of 5,247 officers and men. Only in the most dire circumstances were legion numbers made up during the course of the normal twenty-year enlistment span. For example, six years later, in A.D. 60, Nero would authorize the transfer of 2,000 new recruits from the 21st Rapax Legion on the Rhine to fill the ranks of the 9th Hispana Legion after it was savaged by Queen Boudicca's rebels in the British

Revolt. In that case the revolt still had to be put down and the reinforcements were urgently needed. The men involved remained with the 9th for the remainder of their enlistment, and the 21st continued understrength for the remainder of its enlistment period.

In A.D. 54 General Corbulo considered the personnel situation of the 6th Ferrata and 10th Legions dire enough to warrant the recruitment of new men to fill their much-depleted ranks. He had been given a task by the emperor, and, methodical and cautious by nature, Corbulo was determined to have his legions at maximum strength before he took on the Parthians. This meant that in the future the 6th Ferrata would have two discharge and reenlistment dates during each twenty-year span—part of the legion would have been discharged, and the empty places filled with a partial new enlistment every ten years thereafter.

Once the 6th and the 10th had their ranks filled out with the new recruits from Galatia and Cappadocia, General Corbulo marched the two legions and half the Syrian station's auxiliary light infantry and cavalry up into the mountains of Cappadocia, where he trained them relentlessly for four years. In 58 B.C., Corbulo and his legions swept unexpectedly into Armenia, drove out the Parthians, and installed a new king chosen by Rome on the Armenian throne. Four years later, after the Parthians invaded Armenia and then threatened Syria, Corbulo, reinforced by the 15th Apollinaris Legion from Pannonia, took the 6th Ferrata back into Armenia and drove the Parthians out a second time.

During this second campaign, Corbulo's inept deputy Lieutenant General Caessenius Paetus, leading the ill-prepared 4th Scythica and 12th Legions, surrendered his camp to the Parthians, after which he returned to Rome in disgrace. Fortunately for Rome, his failures were made up for by the efforts of Corbulo and his legions.

In A.D. 66, the 6th Ferrata was intimately involved in the campaigns to put down the Jewish Revolt, losing its commander, Brigadier General Tyrennius Priscus, and a number of men in the initial bungled counteroffensive in Judea led by the governor of Syria, Lieutenant General Cestius Gallus. The new Roman commander appointed by the emperor Nero to put down the revolt, Lieutenant General Titus Vespasianus, who would become the Roman emperor Vespasian, recovered Galilee and most of Judea between A.D. 67 and 69. His son Titus finally took Jerusalem in A.D. 70 after a bloody siege that ended with the destruction of the Jewish Temple.

The 6th Legion played no part in these later Judean operations, sitting out the last three years of the Jewish Revolt at their base at Raphaneae, anxiously watching the Euphrates in case the Parthians decided to invade Roman territory while the Romans were focused on defeating the Jewish rebels. The 6th was in fact the only legion guarding against a Parthian attack, but the Parthians, knowing that another half dozen legions and elements of several others were close by in Judea and Egypt, and that the very capable Vespasian was in command, made no move to threaten Roman territory.

In the summer of A.D. 69, when the legions in the East and several on the Danube and in the Balkans swore allegiance to Vespasian, the war of succession that had erupted the previous year with Nero's demise moved into a new phase. Now Vespasian challenged the new emperor, Vitellius, who in April had taken the throne from the short-lived emperor Otho, and the 6th Ferrata found itself suddenly in the forefront of the action.

With all the legions of the region but the 6th engaged in the siege of Jerusalem, when the governor of Syria, Lieutenant General Licinius Mucianus, agreed to lead a force from Syria to Rome to make Vespasian emperor, the 6th Ferrata was the only legion available for the daunting task. To support the 6th, Mucianus called up thirteen thousand retired legion veterans living in Syria to march behind their Evocati militia standards, and assembled a number of auxiliaries, creating a force of some twenty-five thousand men.

Mucianus led the 6th and the remainder of his force overland from Syria, through the provinces of the East, across the straits from Asia to Macedonia, then up through the Balkans. While Mucianus was on the march, units in Moesia, today's Bulgaria, and elsewhere in the Balkans were advancing into Italy to take on the forces of the emperor Vitellius for Vespasian, led by the ambitious Brigadier General Primus Antonius, commander of the 7th Galbiana Legion. Mucianus sent orders ahead for Antonius to wait for him and the 6th Ferrata at Aquileia in northeastern Italy while he dealt with another problem—for, once the legions stationed in Moesia had moved toward Italy, hordes of mounted Sarmatian raiders had flooded across the Danube into Moesia behind their backs, killing the province's Roman governor and overrunning auxiliary outposts before pillaging and occupying Roman settlements.

Mucianus and the 6th Ferrata swung north, and marched for the Danube to take on the Sarmatian invaders. The details of this campaign are sketchy, but the action was so rapid and the fighting so decisive that the surprised Sarmatian cavalry suffered thousands of casualties. The bloodied Sarmatian survivors quickly fled back across the Danube, while the 6th Ferrata seems to have suffered only minimal losses.

Meanwhile, General Antonius hadn't waited for Mucianus as instructed. Marching down into Italy, his pro-Vespasian forces had defeated Vitellius's army at Cremona and then continued on to Rome itself, crossing the Apennines through heavy snow and then, led by the 3rd Gallica Legion, taking the capital in a day of bloody fighting. When Mucianus and the 6th Ferrata arrived a few days later, Vitellius had been killed, his army had surrendered, and the throne was Vespasian's.

Vespasian was declared emperor by the Senate on December 21, A.D. 69, having deposed Vitellius, who'd deposed Otho, who'd deposed Galba, who'd replaced Nero during two tumultuous years for Rome. In A.D. 70 the 6th Ferrata marched all the way back to its station in Syria, as its brother legion, the 6th Victrix, marched from Spain to help put down a Gallic uprising on the Rhine. Within a year, the empire was settling into a period of peace and prosperity after the harrowing war of succession.

General Mucianus, now acting as Vespasian's tough right-hand man, was voted a Triumph by the Senate for the 6th Ferrata's victory over the Sarmatians on the way to Italy, the first Triumph associated with the 6th Ferrata since General Ventidius's Parthian Triumph of 38 B.C.

The veterans of the original 6th had long since made old bones, at Benevento, Arles, and elsewhere, but the story of the gallant deeds in Egypt and at Zela of Cleopatra's kidnappers and Pharnaces' destroyers would have been told to each new enlistment of the 6th when they joined the unit, by their centurions. The strong esprit de corps of the legions was founded on such battle honors. Tacitus tells of how, in A.D. 69, the men of the 3rd Gallica Legion, fighting at the Battle of Cremona for Vespasian, were reminded by General Primus Antonius of how their legion had saved Mark Antony's skin from the Parthians in Media back in 36 B.C.

There can be no doubt that the soldiers of this enlistment of the 6th Ferrata would have been fully aware of the 6th's shining record, of its Gallic, Egyptian, Pontic, and Spanish Triumphs of 46–45 B.C., and of its Parthian Triumph of 38 B.C. Their officers would have told the new men how proud their predecessors would have been of them for emulating one of their feats and for maintaining their record by earning a Triumph.

But this time the men of the 6th would not be parading through the streets of Rome. Instead of a street parade, Vespasian awarded Mucianus all the honors associated with a Triumph, including the cash prize, Forum statue, and so-called Triumphal Decorations—the cloak, bay leaf crown, and laurel branch. Vespasian and Titus also celebrated a Triumph, a joint one, for crushing the Jewish Revolt, but they went all the way, with the full street procession. Vespasian and Titus each rode in a golden *quadriga* in the procession, while Vespasian's youngest son, Domitian, rode a horse. As tradition required, the parade ended with the execution of a senior prisoner in the Tullianum basement. In this case it was one of the leaders of the Jewish partisans who died by the garrote.

In A.D. 71 Paetus, the Roman general who had disgraced himself in Armenia a decade and a half earlier, came back to Syria, this time as the province's governor. Two years later, seeking glory at home to rank him with the likes of General Mucianus, he invaded the friendly allied state of Commagene with the 6th Ferrata, on the pretext that the king, Antiochus IV, was planning to change allegiance to the Parthians. Paetus had written to Vespasian to say that he had intelligence to this effect, and sought Vespasian's permission for the operation. Although Vespasian was surprised, for Antiochus had been a model client and ally until then, he told Paetus to do what he thought best. That was all the invitation needed by Paetus, who was looking for a Triumph.

The Commagenian king's sons attempted to resist with their small local army, but they were no match for the 6th Ferrata, and the little war was quickly over. The whole affair proved an embarrassment to Vespasian, but he could not lose face and reverse matters. The best he could do was allow the ousted King Antiochus and his family to live in exile at Rome, while Commagene became a Roman province. For his pains, General Paetus earned himself no Triumph.

In the second century the 6th Ferrata participated in the emperor Trajan's conquests in the East. Between A.D. 113 and 116, those campaigns saw Trajan's legions reclaim Armenia from yet another Parthian invasion, annex Mesopotamia and the Nabataean part of Arabia, and briefly occupy the Parthian capital, Ctesiphon. In A.D. 114–115, Trajan had two triumphal arches built in Italy to celebrate his military victories. One was erected at the Adriatic port city of Ancona, one of his favorite places. The other arch was built at Benevento, where it still stands today. Why Benevento was honored with the arch we can only speculate. Perhaps the 6th Ferrata performed so creditably for Trajan in his battles against the Parthians that he chose to honor the town that was the traditional settling place of veterans of the 6th.

By A.D. 119 the 6th Ferrata had left its longtime base at Raphaneae, taking up a new permanent station in Arabia. Between A.D. 132 and 135 the legion was brought in to help put down the Second Jewish Revolt in Judea. This was a grueling campaign in which thousands died on both sides before the revolt was finally crushed and Jews were permanently banned from all of Judea.

Immediately following the revolt, the 6th Ferrata was transferred to Legio in northern Spain, a town that grew around a legion base—from which the town took its name. Under Trajan's successor, Hadrian, men of the legion adopted the new fashion, established by Hadrian, of wearing neat beards. By this time, too, legionaries had increasingly taken to wearing short, tight-fitting breeches under their tunics, following the habit of auxiliaries, who had worn breeches for some time prior to this.

During the reign of Septimius Severus (A.D. 193–211) the 6th Ferrata again served briefly in the Middle East—in A.D. 194, Severus first defeated the rebellious governor of Syria, Gaius Pescennius Niger, and in 197–198 he defeated the Parthians after they invaded Mesopotamia. Under Severus, the single men of the legions were for the first time permitted to marry while still serving in the army. And Severus was the first emperor to permanently station a legion in Italy south of the Po River, installing the new 2nd Parthicae Legion at Albano, the ancient town of Alba Longa, just south of Rome. "What were once vices," the Romans were wont to say, "are now customs." Severus also increased the basic rate of pay for legionaries, their first pay raise in more than a century.

By early in the third century, the 6th's Ferrata title had become official, and this may have been because of the legion's loyal service to Severus. By A.D. 300, the 6th Ferrata was firmly entrenched at its regular base at Legio in northwestern Spain, its last known station.

The 6th Ferrata's twin, the second 6th, remained in the West throughout its career. It was based in Nearer Spain from 40 B.C., serving in the Cantabrian War of 29–19 B.C. in northern Spain, which resulted in the final conquest of all of Spain for Rome. The legion continued to be based in Nearer Spain once the war was brought to a close in 19 B.C. It marched to the Balkans to serve in the Pannonian War of A.D. 6–9, which put down the revolt of Pannonian and Dalmatian partisans. As a result of its service in one or other of these campaigns the legion was officially granted the title Victrix, meaning "Conqueror," by the emperor Augustus. It was officially known as the 6th Victrix thereafter.

The 6th Victrix Legion was based in Nearer Spain for six decades following the Pannonian War. In A.D. 68–69 the 6th Victrix threw its loyalty behind Sulpicius Galba, governor of Nearer Spain, who took Nero's throne and became the first Roman emperor without any family connection with Caesar. When Galba marched on Rome with a new legion he'd raised in Spain, the 7th Galbiana, or Galba's 7th, he left the loyal 6th Victrix behind to control Spain in his name.

In A.D. 70, once Vespasian became emperor, a new enlistment of the 6th Victrix Legion was ordered to march to the Rhine to participate in a combined operation to put down a massive Gallic uprising led by a Batavian auxiliary commander, Julius Civilis, who had served with Vespasian in Britain. The Civilis Revolt had resulted in the loss of all Roman bases on the Rhine from the North Sea to Switzerland.

Led by its latest commander, Brigadier General Sextus Caelius Tuscus, the 6th Victrix marched up from Spain to join the deputy commander of the operation, Major General Petilius Cerialis, at Mainz, on the Rhine. General Cerialis not only added the 6th Victrix to his army for his continued push along the Rhine, he also took the 6th's tribune, its second in command, Colonel Gaius Minicius, and made him commander of one wing of the Singularian Horse, the regiment of German cavalry created the previous year to serve as the emperor's household cavalry, the mounted arm of the Praetorian Guard.

On the face of it this was a demotion for Minicius, but Cerialis wanted someone he could trust in a senior position with the Singularians, whose Batavian commander, Briganticus, was related to the rebel leader, Civilis. As it turned out, Briganticus was killed in the fighting and Colonel Minicius, a native of Aquileia, led the Singularians in an action that resulted in a spectacular victory for General Cerialis's army against the rebels beside the Rhine in the Battle of Old Camp. The recently recruited troops of this enlistment of the 6th Victrix performed creditably in the battle, although they advanced too eagerly at one point and it took the 14th Gemina Legion, then the most famous legion in the Roman army, to come up on their flank and drive the enemy back.

Following the termination of the revolt with the surrender of Civilis, the 6th Victrix stayed on the Rhine, based at Neuss in Germany. During Trajan's reign it moved to Vetera, today's Xanten in Holland. In A.D. 122 the legion was hurriedly transferred across the North Sea to York, Roman Eburacum, in north-central England, to replace the 9th Hispana Legion, which had mysteriously disappeared, apparently wiped out by Celtic invaders from Scotland. There in Britain the 6th remained until A.D. 406.

The other two legions stationed on the island, the 2nd Adiutrix and the 20th Valeria Victrix, were withdrawn in the year 395 to help defend Gaul and Italy from the barbarian invasions, and eleven years later the 6th Victrix became the last legion to be pulled out of Britain. Despite repeated requests from the Britons for Rome to return legions to British soil to help the islanders fight off raiders from Scotland, Germany, and

Scandinavia, no legion ever returned to Britain, and the locals had to raise their own troops and organize their own defense.

Many Britons today are descended from Roman settlers who made England, Wales, and southern Scotland their home between the landings of A.D. 43 and the withdrawal of the legions some 350 years later. A number would be descended from retired legionaries of the 6th Victrix Legion, whose retirees would have increasingly been settled in Britain. There is no way of knowing how many retired legionaries made their homes in Britain, but based on the settlement of veterans from three legions every twenty years in and around the colonies of Britain, at least 170,000 legion retirees would have made their homes on the island and died there, with many raising British families.

As for the 6th Victrix itself, after 406, from the time it landed in Gaul, the legion disappeared from the pages of history, swallowed up in the bloody disintegration of the Western Roman Empire. All this was a long way from the heroics of the little more than nine hundred Spaniards of the 6th Legion who had been plucked from the edge of death at Farsala to kidnap Cleopatra, and to come, to see, and to conquer with Caesar at Zela. We know so much about this legion and its activities during the first centuries B.C. and A.D. because this was the most documented period of Roman history. Later records are less numerous, less detailed, and less reliable.

Other legions would occasionally rise to prominence in later centuries—the 12th Fulminata Legion, winning a battle against Germanic invaders in a thunderstorm for Marcus Aurelius in A.D. 174, for example, after which the emperor formalized the legion's old republican title of Fulminata (Thunderer). But overall, in later times individual legions seem not to have played such dramatic roles in history as did the 3rd Gallica in saving Mark Antony in Media or in making Vespasian emperor, the 10th in Caesar's first century B.C. conquest of Gaul and at the Battles of Pharsalus and Munda, the 14th in defeating Boudicca's rampaging British hordes in A.D. 60, and the sensational 6th's performance in Egypt and Pontus.

Were the legionaries of that period tougher, more resolute than those who followed them in later centuries? It was not as if they were invincible, were superior fighters to every opponent they faced—whole legions were wiped out during these two centuries. Were their generals better? Certainly, in Caesar and Pompey, Ventidius, Drusus, Germanicus, Corbulo, and Paulinus, Rome had exceptional generals, men who combined courage with charisma, tactics with tenacity.

The men of Caesar's sensational 6th would have told you that they were a different breed from those who succeeded them. They had not been permitted to marry while in service. Their legion had not been recruited in the areas where they were stationed, as the legions were from the second century. All their men were recruited in the same location, creating a solid camaraderie, but as early as the reign of Nero, in the second half of the first century, different cohorts of the same legion were increasingly recruited in different parts of the world.

Of course, the men of the sensational 6th would tell you that they were different from every soldier who ever served Rome. Publius Sertorius and his comrades in arms would tell you that after years of reverses the Roman gods had looked favorably on them and made them ironclad for the last two years of their service. With the gods looking after them they would have gone wherever they had been sent, kidnap whomever they were told to kidnap, and resolutely fought whoever stood in their way, confident of their ironclad status.

As the old proverb said, wherever they were thrown, there the heroes of the 6th Legion would stand.

APPENDIX A

REPUBLICAN ROMAN MILITARY RANKS, FIRST CENTURY B.C., AND THEIR MODERN-DAY EQUIVALENTS

Rank	Description	Equivalent
Miles gregarius	Literally, a "common soldier" of the legion.	Private
Signifer	Standard-bearer for legion cohort and maniple. No real authority.	Corporal
Aquilifer	Eagle-bearer of the legion. Most prestigious post for a standard-bearer.	Corporal
Tesserarius	Orderly sergeant; sergeant of the guard.	Sergeant
Optio	Second in command of a century and of a cavalry squadron. Unit training, administration, and records officer.	Sergeant major
Decurio	Decurion. Officer of Roman cavalry.	Second lieutenant
Centurio	Centurion. Officer commanding a century, maniple, and cohort. Sixty to a legion, including six primi ordines. Eleven grades, including primi ordines and primus pilus. Seniority usually determined by length of service.	First lieutenant
Primi ordines	Most senior "first rank" centurions of a legion, serving in the first cohort.	Captain
Primus pilus	Literally the "first spear," chief centurion, a legion's most senior centurion, one of the primi ordines.	Major

Rank	Description	Equivalent
Praefectus fabricus	Originally prefect of engineers, he became the adjutant of an army commander.	Lieutenant colonel
Tribunus militaris	Military tribune, one of six officers of Equestrian Order rank who commanded a legion among them for two months each, on rotation, with the other five each commanding two cohorts of the legion.	Colonel
Quaestor	A provincial governor's chief of staff and quartermaster. On military campaigns often given his own command. By imperial times, while he still had responsibility for military recruiting, his role became a civil one, mostly involving financial and legal affairs. Election as a quaestor also brought a Senate seat for life.	Brigadier general
Legatus	A commander of one or more legions or military detachment, of senatorial rank, a deputy of a general of consular rank.	Brigadier general
Praetor	A senior magistrate at Rome, second only to the consuls. Praetors and former praetors could command a legion and armies in the field.	Major general
Consul	A consul was the highest official at Rome. The two consuls for the year shared the presidency of the Senate and gave their names to the year. Consuls or former consuls normally commanded Roman field armies. Seniority was determined by the number of consulships held and when. For example, Pompey had held two consulships and was therefore senior to all other generals. To eclipse him, Caesar had himself voted four consulships once he was in power, to give him a total of five.	Lieutenant general
Proconsul	Governor of a Roman province. A former consul. (See the glossary for details.)	Lieutenant general

APPENDIX B

IMPERIAL POSTINGS OF THE TWO 6TH LEGIONS

6th Ferrata Legion

30 B.C.–A.D. 113: Raphaneae, Syria

A.D. 113–116: Mesopotamian and Parthian Campaigns of Trajan

A.D. 116–119: Raphaneae, Syria

A.D. 119–132: Arabia

A.D. 132–135: Judea (Second Jewish Revolt)

A.D. 135–194: Legio, Spain

A.D. 194–198: Middle East (campaigns of Severus)

A.D. 198–300: Legio, Spain

6th Victrix Legion

30 B.C.–A.D. 6: Nearer Spain (including Cantabrian War, 29–19 B.C.)

A.D. 6–9: Pannonia (Pannonian War)

A.D. 9–70: Nearer Spain

A.D. 70–103: Neuss (Novaesium), Lower Germany

A.D. 103–122: Xanten (Vetera), Lower Germany

A.D. 122–406: York (Eburacum), Lower Britain

APPENDIX C

SOURCES

Primary Sources

The books in this series are based primarily on classical texts; inscriptions; and, to a lesser extent, coins. Some epigraphic material is on stone monuments small and large. Some source material is in the form of documents inscribed on metal, velum, and papyrus, such as the discharge notices of legionaries and citizenship certificates of retired auxiliaries, and the pleas of soldiers to the gods associated with temple offerings. The letters of officers' wives on the British frontier even exist, exchanging gossip and dinner invitations, and the letter from an Egyptian cavalry officer to his mother at home in Egypt asking her to send him more money.

Inscriptions and written records can generally be taken at face value, even if some inscriptions raise more questions than they answer. In the late first century B.C., for example, a number of former legionaries had honorific titles inscribed on their tombstones relating to the legions in which they had served, but frequently those honorifics were neither official nor in widespread use.

Classical coins can be an invaluable guide to the stations and movements of Roman legions. The men of the legions were paid once a year, the gold coins of their pay generally being minted with the name of the legion in question as well as sufficient information for the era of the minting to be determined as well as the place where the issue took place.

Classical texts, however, have to be approached with the eye of an historical detective, for some classical authors hovered between the worlds of novelist and historian, tending to spice up their narratives with exaggeration and anecdote. Many speeches in classical texts were invented by their authors—even if basing them on firsthand sources—and few writers could escape coloring their writings with personal prejudices and preferences. So in trawling classical sources for the facts, comparison, analysis, and objectivity are essential tools.

In the thirty-four years of research and writing that went into this book, the many classical and contemporary written sources listed below were consulted. Primarily, this work was made possible by the following classical sources, listed alphabetically.

Acts of the Apostles from the **Holy Bible.** These provide a contemporary insight and an on-the-spot account, albeit from a layman's point of view, regarding several aspects of legion activity during the first century.

Appian. Born in about A.D. 95 at Alexandria, of Greek stock, Appian worked as an advocate in the courts at Rome and later served as a financial administrator in the provinces. In the middle of the second century he wrote a number of books on Roman history, of which his *Civil Wars* is the most helpful to writers interested in the legions. He is the least well regarded of the Greek historians of the Roman Empire, but for the historical events in the Roman Empire between 133 B.C. and 70 B.C. he is considered the only continuous source of any reliability.

His work is at times disjointed; at others, error-strewn. He sometimes also lapsed into what have been described as rhetorical flourishes, or just plain fiction. Despite this, Appian used many well-placed sources and his work provides a useful basis of comparison, particularly when considered alongside Plutarch, Suetonius, and Cassius Dio.

Recommended English translations: *Appian: Roman History*, trans. H. White (1889), rev. for Loeb series by I. Robinson (London: Loeb, 1913); and *Appian: The Civil Wars*, trans. J. Carter (London: Penguin, 1996).

Julius Caesar. *The Gallic War* and *The Civil War*, together with *The Alexandrian War*, *The African War*, and *The Spanish War* by other hands. Caesar wrote his *Commentaries*, his memoirs, with the first volumes, dealing with his conquest of Gaul and covering the period 58–51 B.C., being published in his lifetime. He was still working on his account of the civil war, which leaves off after the Battle of Pharsalus, when he was murdered in 44 B.C. At the urging of Caesar's former chief of staff Lucius Cornelius Balbus, these published and unpublished works were collated by Caesar's loyal staff officer Aulus Hirtius shortly after the dictator's death. Hirtius, promoted to general, would himself be dead within another year. Hirtius combined them with additional material, some of which he wrote himself, the rest apparently penned by officers who had been on the scene for the last battles of the civil war, before they were published by Balbus.

Caesar's own writings are in the third person, as if produced by an independent observer, and strive to paint Caesar in the best light possible while denigrating his opponents. Despite the propagandist overtones, they still provide a fascinating insight into one of history's most brilliant generals and engineers, and of his campaigns. Most importantly to an historian seeking data on the legions of Rome, Caesar regularly identifies the legions involved in his various campaigns and battles.

In the associated material, Hirtius strove to both emulate and praise his master, sometimes distorting the facts to paint Caesar's adversary Pompey the Great in a bad light. Other authors, such as Plutarch, occasionally give us a truer picture, such as the time Pompey loaned Caesar a legion, the 6th, in 52 B.C., when Caesar was in trouble in Gaul, without the approval of the Senate. Plutarch tells us Pompey was greatly criticized by the likes of Cato the Younger for helping Caesar in this way, but you wouldn't know it from Hirtius's narrative.

Often, where there were passages in Caesar's original text that told of an error of judgment or setback on Caesar's account, Hirtius—or possibly Balbus—cut it out. We know this because there are several instances where Caesar says "as mentioned before" or the like, and the before-mentioned material is missing. Fortunately, sufficient references were overlooked by the editors in their hasty editing for the truth to emerge. In their haste, too, the editors missed passages in the additional material that don't exactly flatter Caesar, with a picture of an impatient and sometimes petty man emerging.

Another of Caesar's loyal staff officers, Gaius Asinius Pollio, who features in this particular book, is quoted by Suetonius as writing that he felt Caesar's memoirs showed signs of carelessness and inaccuracy. Pollio, who became a consul and gained renown in his own time as an author—although none of his works has come down to us—said that in his experience Caesar didn't always check the truth of reports that came in, and he had been either disingenuous or forgetful in describing his own actions. But Cicero, also quoted by Suetonius, said that Caesar wrote admirably, composing his memoirs cleanly, directly, and gracefully. Cicero added that Caesar's sole intention had been to supply historians with factual material, and that subsequently "several fools have been pleased to primp up his narrative for their own glorification." The fools in question were Hirtius and Balbus.

Despite the distortions of the "fools," and the fact that Caesar himself wasn't entirely honest in his writings, with himself or with his readers, Caesar's memoirs are still a rare, lively, and informative resource.

Recommended English translations: Among the best are *The Commentaries of Caesar*, trans. W. Duncan (London: Dodsley, 1779); *Caesar: Commentaries on the Gallic and Civil Wars*, trans. W. A. M'Devitte and W. S. Bohm (London: Bell, 1890); *Caesar: The Gallic War and the Civil War*, trans. T. Rice Holmes, Loeb series (London: 1914–1955); *Caesar: The Conquest of Gaul*, trans. S. A. Handford (1951), rev. J. F. Gardner (1967) (London: Penguin, 1967); and *Caesar: The Civil War*, trans. J. F. Gardner (London: Penguin, 1967).

Cicero. Marcus Tullius Cicero (106–43 B.C.) was one of the most noted orators of his day. A leading senator and famous defense counsel, he was a prodigious author. Cicero's younger brother Quintus served on Caesar's staff in Gaul in 54–52 B.C., commanding the 14th Legion during one disastrous period, and he no doubt kept Cicero informed of Caesar's activities. Having served as a military tribune under Pompey's father, and owing his life to Pompey's intervention, Cicero allied himself to Pompey through much of his career, deserting him when he felt that Caesar would win the civil war. Cicero despised Mark Antony and badly misjudged the ability of young Octavian, which resulted in them ordering his death. Many of his works have come down to us, but it is his collected letters that are of most interest when it comes to the legions. Cicero's letters provide insight into the tumultuous events surrounding Caesar's invasion of Italy and Mark Antony's quest for power on the death of Caesar.

Recommended English translations of his correspondence include: *Cicero: Letters to Atticus*, trans. O. E. Winstedt, Loeb series (Cambridge, Mass.: Harvard University Press, 1912–1958); *Cicero: Letters to His Friends*, trans. W. Glynn Williams, M. Cary, and M. Henderson, Loeb series (Cambridge, Mass.: Harvard University Press, 1912–1958); *Letters of Cicero*, trans. L. P. Wilkinson (London: Hutchinson, 1949); and *Cicero: Selected Letters*, trans. D. R. Shackleton Bailey (London: Penguin, 1986).

Cassius Dio. Also referred to as Dio Cassius and Dion Cassius (his father also was a Cassius, his grandfather a Dio), his full name was Cassius Dio Cocceianus. This Greek historian was born in the Roman province of Bithynia in about A.D. 150. Son of a proconsul, he joined the Senate under the emperor Commodus. Twice a consul, and governor of Africa, Dalmatia, and Upper Pannonia during his long career, he had military experience and was well versed in the ways of the legions. He wrote a history of the Roman Empire in eighty books in the years leading up to his death in 235; the history took the form of a year-by-year synopsis of major events, with occasional diversion into anecdote.

Dio worked from existing sources and obviously based much of his first-century narrative on Tacitus. With the A.D. 37–47 chapters of Tacitus's *Annals* lost to us, it is from Dio that we glean much of what we know about Claudius's invasion of Britain. We also can see where Dio borrowed from Suetonius in his books on the first centuries B.C. and A.D., although some of his errors and exaggerations are glaringly original—for instance, he has Titus save his father, Vespasian, on a Welsh battlefield in A.D. 47, when the boy was only seven. Dio also assumed, incorrectly, that some customs of his day had been current in earlier times.

Unlike Tacitus, Dio rarely makes reference to individual legions, but he provides an invaluable list of all the legions in existence in his day, with brief background information on each, which serves as a proverbial bookend to any history of the legions of the early imperial era. Despite his failings, Dio is still a valuable source.

Recommended English translations: *Dio's Roman History*, trans. E. Cary, Loeb series (London: 1914–1927); and *Cassius Dio, the Roman History: The Reign of Augustus*, trans. I. Scott-Kilvert (London: Penguin, 1987).

Josephus. Born in about A.D. 37, Joseph ben Matthias was a young Jewish general who commanded Galilee for the partisans during the first year of the Jewish Revolt of A.D. 66–70, and who later took the Roman name Flavius Josephus after being captured at Jefat in A.D. 67 and becoming a Roman collaborator. He claims he won his freedom and the favor of Vespasian and Titus by predicting that both would become emperor of Rome. He wrote extensively over twenty-five years, under the patronage of all three Flavian emperors. Josephus's coverage of the A.D. 66–70 Jewish Revolt, his *Jewish War*, is very useful to those interested in the legions. Several glaring errors in that work—he puts legionaries' swords on their left hips, for example—may be those of later copyists. Josephus's *Life* (of Josephus) provides more on the Jewish Revolt. *Jewish Antiquities*, published after the death of Titus in A.D. 81, provides rare information about the participation of Jewish troops in the relief force that helped Julius Caesar conquer Egypt in 47 B.C., about the favors Caesar subsequently granted Jews because of this support, and also rare verbatim quotations from letters of Mark Antony.

Vespasian gave Josephus an estate in Judea, a pension, and use of an apartment in his own family house on Pomegranate Street in the 6th Precinct at Rome. The year of his death is uncertain. Some scholars make it in A.D. 100; others place it in A.D. 92 or 93.

Recommended English translations: *The Jewish War*, trans. H. St. John Thackery, R. Marcus, and L. H. Feldman (London: Loeb, 1926); also, the trans. of G. A. Williamson (London: Penguin, 1959, rev. 1970); *The Complete Works of Josephus*, which includes *Jewish Antiquities*, trans. W. Whiston (1737; repub. as *The New Complete Works of Josephus* [Grand Rapids, Mich.: Kregel, 1999]).

Pliny the Younger. Gaius Plinius Caecilius Secundus, nephew and heir of Pliny the Elder, was a consul in A.D. 100 and governor of Bithynia-Pontus between A.D. 111 and 113. His correspondence, in particular with the emperor Trajan at Rome on matters that came before Pliny for judgment, give a fascinating insight into Roman provincial government. His legion-specific usefulness is limited—he only had auxiliary troops under his control, and sought the emperor's approval for even minor troop movements.

Recommended English translations: *The Letters of Pliny the Consul*, trans. W. Melmoth (1746; rev. W. M. Hutchinson [London, Loeb, 1915]); *Pliny's Letters*, trans. A. J. Church and W. A. Brodribb (Edinburgh: Blackwood, 1872); and *The Letters of the Younger Pliny*, trans. B. Radice (London: Penguin, 1963).

Plutarch. Plutarchos (A.D. 46–c. 120), was a Greek scholar who wrote in the reigns of the Roman emperors Nerva, Trajan, and Hadrian. Shakespeare used Plutarch's *Parallel Lives* as the basis for his plays *Julius Caesar* and *Antony and Cleopatra*. This, Plutarch's great work, gives short biographies of numerous historical figures and provides background material on key players in the history of the legions: Sulla, Marius, Lucullus, Sertorius, Cato the Younger, Crassus, Pompey the Great, Julius Caesar, Mark Antony, Brutus, Cassius, Cicero, and the emperors Galba and Otho.

Plutarch, who considered himself more biographer than historian, occasionally makes reference to his sources, most of which have not come down to us, such as Emphylus, a rhetorician and colleague of Caesar's assassin Brutus and who, in Plutarch's words, produced "a short but well-written history of the death of Caesar" titled *Brutus*.

The author of hundreds of books and essays, Plutarch was well respected in his own day. Occasionally biased, often colorful, but only once in a while making a demonstrable error, he remains a valuable resource on people and events related to the legions.

Recommended English translations: Sir Thomas North's 1579 translation— the one used by Shakespeare—can be heavy going with its Tudor English, but sometimes presents a different picture than later versions. Easier reads are John Dryden's *The Lives of the Noble Grecians and Romans* (1683–1686; reprint, Chicago: Encyclopaedia Britannica, 1952); *Plutarch's Lives of Illustrious Men*, trans. J. and W. Lanhome (London: Chatto & Windus, 1875); and *Plutarch's Lives*, trans. B. Perrin, Loeb series (London: Loeb, 1914–1926).

Polybius. This Greek statesman and historian lived between 200 and 118 B.C. At Rome, initially as a hostage, he became a friend of and adviser to Scipio Aemilianus, the Roman consul and general who conquered Carthage. Traveling widely, Polybius wrote his *History of Rome* after returning to Greece in 150 B.C. With broad experience of Roman political and military matters he wrote with intelligence and authority about the Roman army of the mid-second century B.C. Some chapters are so detailed they read like a legion owner's manual. It's from Polybius that we know so much about legion practices and procedures, many of which remained essentially unchanged for centuries after, from camp layout to bravery decorations, sentry details to punishments.

Recommended English translations: *The Histories of Polybius*, trans. E. Shuckburgh (London: Macmillan, 1889); *Polybius: Histories*, trans. W. R. Paton (London: Loeb, 1922–1927); and *Polybius: The Rise of the Roman Empire*, trans. I. Scott-Kilvert (London: Penguin, 1979).

Suetonius. Biographer Gaius Suetonius Tranquillus was born in A.D. 69, in the middle of the war of succession that followed Nero's demise. At the time, Suetonius's father was serving as a tribune and second in command with the 13th Gemina Legion. Young Suetonius apparently had no taste for army life. When his friend Pliny the Younger obtained an appointment for him as a tribune of the broad stripe, which would have made him second in command of a legion, he asked that it be given instead to a relative, Caesennius Silvanus.

Suetonius pursued a career in the service of the Palatium, rising to be briefly in charge of the imperial archives at Rome, which were closed to the public. Married but childless at age forty-three, through Pliny the Younger he obtained from the emperor Trajan the financial privileges of a father of three. After Pliny died in about A.D. 113, Suetonius found a new patron, the powerful Septicius Clarus, a Prefect of the Praetorian Guard early in Hadrian's reign before falling from grace. Suetonius dedicated his post-A.D. 117 book on the Caesars to Clarus. Through the prefect's influence he won the position of senior correspondence secretary to the emperor Hadrian, but in about A.D. 123 was fired for disrespect to the empress Sabina while Hadrian was away touring the empire.

After this, out of favor, Suetonius was denied access to the official records, but it is clear from his collection of pocket biographies, *Lives of the Caesars*, that he had begun researching a book on Roman leaders while running the archives. His biographies of Julius Caesar, Augustus, and Tiberius are filled with detail that could only come from official sources—excerpts from emperors' private letters, for example—while his later biographies rely on gossip, hearsay, myth, exaggeration, and sensational anecdote in place of hard fact, suggesting that his researches had only reached Tiberius at the time of his dismissal. Even in territory where he had good source material to work with he managed glaring errors; mostly, it seems, from sloppiness.

Suetonius wrote a number of books, including those aimed at capturing a broad market, such as *The Lives of Famous Whores*, *The Physical Defects of Mankind*, and *Greek Terms of Abuse*. But his *Lives of the Caesars* captured most interest down through the ages. Despite his errors and imperfections, his access to official records makes him a source that cannot be ignored, even if a critical eye must be employed.

Recommended English translations: *Lives of the Twelve Caesars*, transl. P. Holland (1606; reprint, New York: New York Limited Editions Club) (1963; rev. trans., London: F. Etchells and H. Macdonald, 1931). A 1796 translation by A. Thompson, reprint, Williamstown, Mass.: Corner House, 1978; Loeb series, trans. J. C. Rolfe (London, 1914); and *The Twelve Caesars*, trans. R. Graves (1957; rev. M. Grant [London: Penguin, 1979]).

Tacitus. Publius Cornelius Tacitus was the king of Roman historians. His *Annals* and *Histories* and, to a lesser extent, his *Agricola* and *Germania* are treasure troves of information about Rome and her empire in the first century A.D. Living between A.D. 55 and 117, Tacitus, an intimate friend of the writer Pliny the Younger, was a consul in A.D. 97 and governor of the province of Asia in A.D. 112. With apparently unlimited access to the official archives, his hugely detailed books abound with facts and figures taken directly from the records of the proceedings of the Senate and other sources as varied as back issues of the *Acta Diurnia*. He acknowledges liberal use of the work of numerous other writers, much since lost—men such as Pliny the Elder, whose twenty-volume *German Wars*, commenced while serving with the legions on the Rhine, helped shape Tacitus's attitude to Germany, Germanicus, and Arminius. Tacitus also acknowledges the works of serving soldiers such as Vipstanus Messalla, second in command of the 7th Claudia Legion during the crucial war of succession battles of A.D. 69, who went on to write his memoirs.

While his *Agricola* was rushed—it is sometimes inaccurate, contradictory, or just plain vague—his *Annals* and *Histories,* completed two decades later, are products of detailed research and careful construction. For the period A.D. 14–70, Tacitus can be read as the unrivaled authority on the legions of the first century. He identifies the legions taking part in wars, campaigns, and battles, inclusive of their names, commanders, and frequently the names of individual officers and enlisted men. Usually resisting gossipy anecdote in favor of documented fact, Tacitus renders any imperial legion history possible.

Recommended English translations: *Annals & Histories,* trans. A. J. Church and W. J. Brodribb, London (1869–1872); reprint, Chicago: Encyclopaedia Britannica, 1952; also trans. W. Peterson, Loeb series (1914–1937); reprint, Franklin, Pa.: Franklin Library, 1982; *Annals,* trans. M. Grant (London: Penguin, 1966); *Annals,* trans. D. R. Dudley (New York: Mentor, 1966); *History,* trans. A. Murphy (London: Dent, 1900); *The Agricola and the Germania,* trans. A. J. Church and W. J. Brodribb (London: Macmillan, 1869–1872); *Tacitus,* trans. H. Mattingly and S. A. Handford (London: Penguin, 1948); *Tacitus,* a combination of all his works, trans. C. H. Moore and J. Jackson (London: Heinemann/Putnam, 1931).

Virgil. Publius Vergilius Maro was Rome's most revered poet. His *Aeneid* was said to have been read by every Roman schoolboy subsequent to its publication. He was born in 70 B.C. on a farm on the banks of the Mincio River, near Mantua in Cisalpine Gaul. His father, a farmer and pottery works owner, sent him to the school of Epidius at Rome, whose pupils also included Mark Antony and Octavian. Virgil's references to the 41 B.C. land confiscations for discharged legion veterans in the *Ecologues,* and his contemporary references to Egypt in the *Aeneid* have been used in this work.

Among the many English translations available: *The Poems of Virgil,* trans. James Rhoades (Chicago: Encyclopaedia Britannica, 1952); and H. R. Fairclough's translation for the Loeb series (Cambridge, Mass.: Harvard University Press, 1935).

Additional Sources: A Selected Bibliography

Abbott, F. F., and Johnson, A. C. *Municipal Administration in the Roman Empire.* Princeton, N.J.: Princeton University Press, 1926.

Arrian. *History of Alexander, and Indica.* Translated by P. Brunt. Loeb series. Cambridge, Mass.: Harvard University Press, 1976.

Aurelius, M. *Meditations.* Translated by G. Long. Chicago: Encyclopaedia Britannica, 1952.

Azzaroli, A. *An Early History of Horsemanship.* London: E. J. Brill, 1985.

Birley, A. *Marcus Aurelius.* London: Eyre & Spottiswoode, 1966.

Birley, E. *Roman Britain and the Roman Army*. Kendal, U.K.: Titus Wilson, 1953.

Boardman, J., J. Griffin, and O. Murray. *The Oxford History of the Classical World*. Oxford, U.K.: Oxford University Press, 1986.

Bouchier, E. S. *Spain under the Roman Empire*. Oxford, U.K.: B. H. Blackwell, 1914.

Boyne, W., with H. Stuart Jones. *A Manual of Roman Coins*. Chicago: Ammon, 1968.

Brogen, O. *Roman Gaul*. London: Bell, 1953.

Broughton, T. R. S. *The Romanization of Africa Proconsularis*. New York: Greenwood, 1968.

Bryant, A. *The Age of Elegance*. London: Collins, 1954.

Buchan, J. *Augustus*. London: Hodder & Stoughton, 1937.

Caracalla. *Historia Augusta*. Loeb series. Cambridge, Mass.: Harvard University Press, 1923.

Carcopino, J. *Daily Life in Ancient Rome*. London: Pelican, 1956.

Casson, L. *Ancient Egypt*. Alexandria, Va.: Time-Life, 1965.

Cave, W. *Lives, Acts, and Martyrdoms of the Holy Apostles*. London: Hatchard, 1836.

Chevalier, R. *Roman Roads*. Translated by N. H. Field. London: Batsford, 1976.

Church, A. J. *Roman Life in the Days of Cicero*. London: Seeley, 1923.

Clausewitz, C. P. G. von. *On War*. Translated by J. J. Graham. New York: Penguin, 1968.

Colledge, M. A. R. *The Parthians*. Leiden: E. J. Brill, 1986.

Collingwood, R. C. *Roman Britain*. Oxford, U.K.: Oxford University Press, 1932.

Cottrell, L. *Enemy of Rome*. London: Pan, 1962.

———. *The Great Invasion*. London: Evans, 1958.

Cowell, F. R. *Cicero and the Roman Republic*. Harmondsworth, U.K.: Penguin, 1956.

Croft, P. *Roman Mythology*. London: Octopus, 1974.

Cunliffe, B. *The Celtic World*. London: Bodley Head, 1979.

———. *Rome and Her Empire*. Maidenhead, U.K.: McGraw-Hill, 1978.

———. *The Roman Baths at Bath*. Bath, U.K.: Bath Archeological Trust, 1993.

De La Billiere, Gen. Sir P. *Looking for Trouble*. London: HarperCollins, 1994.

Delbruck, H. *History of the Art of War*. Translated by J. Walter Renfroe Jr. Lincoln: University of Nebraska Press, Bison Books, 1990.

Divine, A. *Secrets and Stories of the War: Miracle at Dunkirk*. London: Reader's Digest Association, 1963.

Duff, J. D. *Lucan*. Cambridge, Mass.: Harvard University Press, 1977.

Dupuy, R. E. and T. N. Dupuy. *The Encyclopedia of Military History: From 3500 B.C. to the Present*. London: Military Book Society, 1970.

Emile, T. *Roman Life under the Caesars*. New York: Putnam, 1908.

Forestier, A. *The Roman Soldier*. London: A. & C. Black, 1928.

Frank, T., ed. *An Economic Survey of Ancient Rome*. Peterson, N.J.: Pageant, 1959.

Frere, S. S. *Britannia, a History of Roman Britain*. London: Routledge & Kegan Paul, 1987.

Frontinus, S. J. *Stratagems and Aqueducts*. Translated by C. E. Bennet and M. B. McElwain. London: Loeb, 1969.

Fuller, J. *Julius Caesar: Man, Soldier, and Tyrant*. London: Eyre & Spottiswoode, 1965.

Furneaux, R. *The Roman Siege of Jerusalem*. London: Rupert Hart-Davis, 1973.

Gardner, J. F. *Family and Familia in Roman Law and Life*. Oxford, U.K.: Oxford University Press, 1998.

Gibbon, E. *The Decline and Fall of the Roman Empire*. Chicago: Encyclopaedia Britannica, 1932.

Grant, M. *The Army of the Caesars*. Harmondsworth, U.K.: Penguin, 1974.

——— . *Cleopatra*. Harmondsworth, U.K.: Penguin, 1972.

——— . *Gladiators*. Harmondsworth, U.K.: Penguin, 1967.

——— . *History of Rome*. Harmondsworth, U.K.: Penguin, 1978.

——— . *The Jews of the Roman World*. Harmondsworth, U.K.: Penguin, 1973.

——— . *Julius Caesar*. Harmondsworth, U.K.: Penguin, 1969.

——— . *The Roman Emperors*. Harmondsworth, U.K.: Penguin, 1985.

——— . *Roman History from Coins*. New York: Barnes & Noble, 1995.

Graves, R. *I, Claudius*. London: Arthur Barker, 1934.

Haywood, R. M. *Ancient Greece and the Near East*. London: Vision, 1964.

——— . *Ancient Rome*. London: Vision, 1967.

Highet, G. *Juvenal the Satirist*. Oxford, U.K.: Clarendon, 1954.

Hill, W. T. *Buried London*. London: Phoenix House, 1955.

Home, G. C. *Roman London*. London: Eyre & Spottiswoode, 1948.

Jimenez, R. *Caesar against the Celts*. Conshohocken, Pa.: Sarpedon, 1996.

Jones, A. H. M. *Augustus*. New York: W. W. Norton, 1972.

Keppie, L. *Colonisation and Veteran Settlement in Italy, 47–14 B.C.* London: British School at Rome, 1983.

——— . *The Making of the Roman Army: From Republic to Empire*. Totowa, N.J.: Barnes & Noble, 1984.

——— . *Roman Inscribed and Sculpted Stones in the Huntorian Museum University of Glasgow*. London: Society for Promotion of Roman Studies, 1999.

Ker, W. C. A. *Martial*. London: Loeb, 1919–1920.

Laking, G. F. *A Record of European Armour and Arms through Seven Centuries*. New York: A.M.S., 1934.

Leach, J. *Pompey the Great*. New York: Croom Helm, 1978.

Livy. *The War with Hannibal*. Translated by E. de Selincourt. Harmondsworth, U.K.: Penguin, 1965.

MacArthur, B., ed. *The Penguin Book of Twentieth-Century Speeches*. London: Penguin, 1992.

MacMullen, R. *Soldier and Civilian in the Later Roman Empire*. Cambridge, Mass.: Harvard University Press, 1967.

Mannix, D. P. *Those about to Die*. London: Mayflower, 1960.

Margary, I. D. *Roman Roads in Britain*. London: Phoenix House, 1957.

Marsden, E. W. *Greek and Roman Artillery*. Oxford, U.K.: Oxford University Press, 1969.

Mattingly, H. *Roman Coins from the Earliest Times to the Fall of the Western Empire*. London: Methuen, 1927.

Merrifield, R. *London: City of the Romans*. London: Batsford, 1983.

Mommsen, T. *The Provinces of the Roman Empire*. Edited by T. R. S. Broughton. Chicago: University of Chicago Press, Phoenix Books, 1968.

Morton, H. V. *In the Steps of the Master*. London: Rich & Cowan, 1934.

Mothersole, J. *In Roman Scotland*. London: John Lane the Bodley Head, 1927.

Napthali, L. *Life in Egypt under Roman Rule*. Oxford, U.K.: Clarendon, 1983.

Parker, H. D. M. *The Roman Legions*. New York: Barnes & Noble, 1958.

Payne-Gallwey, Sir R. *The Crossbow: Mediaeval and Modern, with a Treatise on the Ballista and Catapults of the Ancients*. 1903. Reprint, London: Holland Press, 1995.

Peterson, D. *The Roman Legions Re-created in Color*. London: Windrow & Greene, 1992.

Petronius Arbiter, G. *The Satyricon*. Translated by M. Heseltine. London: Loeb, 1913.

Philo Judaeus. *The Works of Philo*. Translated by C. D. Yonge. Peabody, Mass.: Hendrickson, 1993.

Plato. *The Dialogues*. Translated by B. Jowlett. Reprint, Chicago: Encyclopaedia Britannica, 1952.

Pliny the Elder. *Natural History*. Edited and translated by H. Rackman. London: Loeb, 1938–1963.

Raven, S. *Rome in Africa*. London: Longman, 1969.

Robertson, D. S. *Greek and Roman Architecture*. Cambridge, U.K.: Cambridge University Press, 1943.

Robinson, H. R. *The Armour of Imperial Rome*. Oxford, U.K.: Oxford University Press, 1975.

Romer, J. *Testament: The Bible and History*. London: Michael O'Mara, 1988.

Rossi, L. *Trajan's Column and the Dacian Wars*. London: Thames & Hudson, 1974.

Rostovtzeff, M. I. *The Social and Economic History of the Roman Empire*. New York: Biblio & Tannen, 1957.

Salway, P. *Roman Britain*. Oxford, U.K.: Oxford University Press, 1981.

Schwarzkopf, General H. N. *It Doesn't Take a Hero*. New York: Bantam, 1992.

Seager, R. *Tiberius*. London: Eyre Methuen, 1972.

Seneca. *Letters from a Stoic*. Translated by R. Campbell. Harmondsworth, U.K.: Penguin, 1969.

Sherwin-White, A. N. *The Roman Citizenship*. Oxford, U.K.: Oxford University Press, 1939.

Simkins, M. *Warriors of Rome*. London: Blandford, 1988.

Smith, F. E. *Waterloo*. London: Pan, 1970.

Starr, C. G. *Roman Imperial Navy, 31* B.C.–A.D. *324*. Ithaca, N.Y.: Cornell University Press, 1941.

Statius. *Collected Works*. Translated by J. H. Mozley. Cambridge, Mass.: Loeb, 1928.

Strabo. *The Geography of Strabo*. Translated by H. L. Jones. Cambridge, Mass.: Loeb, 1924.

Sulimirski, T. *The Sarmatians*. New York: Praeger, 1970.

Syme, R. *Ammianus and the Historia Augusta*. Oxford, U.K.: Oxford University Press, 1968.

——————. *Historia Augusta Papers*. Oxford, U.K.: Clarendon, 1983.

——————. *History in Ovid*. Oxford, U.K.: Oxford University Press, 1979.

Times (London). *Concise Atlas of World History*. London: Times, 1982.

Todd, M. *The Early Germans*. Oxford, U.K.: Blackwell, 1992.

——————. *The Northern Barbarians, 1000* B.C.–A.D. *300*. New York: Blackwell, 1987.

Trench, C. C. *A History of Horsemanship*. Garden City, N.Y.: Doubleday, 1970.

[U.K.] War Office. *Field Service Regulations*. London: H.M. Stationery Office, 1914.

[U.S.] Department of the Army. *U.S. Army Survival Manual: FM 21-76*. New York: Dorset, 1991.

Utley, R. M. *The Lance and the Shield*. New York: Henry Holt, 1993.

Vernam, G. R. *Man on Horseback*. Garden City, N.Y.: Doubleday, 1964.

Waldeck, C. *Secrets and Stories of the War*. London: Reader's Digest Association, 1963.

Wallace, L. *Ben Hur*. London: Ward, Lock, 1880.

Ward, G. C., with R. and K. Burns. *The Civil War*. New York: Alfred A. Knopf, 1991.

Warmington, E. H. *Nero*. Harmondsworth, U.K.: Penguin, 1969.

Warry, J. *Warfare in the Classical World*. London: Salamander, 1989.

Watson, G. R. *The Roman Soldier*. Ithaca, N.Y.: Cornell University Press, 1969.

Webster, G. and Dudley, D. R. *The Rebellion of Boudicca*. New York: Barnes & Noble, 1962.

——————. *The Roman Conquest of Britain*. London: Pan, 1973.

Webster's New Twentieth-Century Dictionary of the English Language. Cleveland: World, 1953.

Weigall, A. *Nero, Emperor of Rome*. London: Butterworth, 1930.

Wheeler, R. M. *Rome beyond the Imperial Frontiers*. London: Bell, 1954.

White, K. D. *Greek & Roman Technology*. Ithaca, N.Y.: Cornell University Press, 1983.

Wightman, E. M. *Roman Trier and the Treveri*. New York: Praeger, 1970.

Wiseman, F. J. *Roman Spain*. New York: Bell, 1956.

GLOSSARY

ACTA DIURNIA   Rome's *Daily News*, world's first newspaper. Handwritten daily by the Palatium at Rome and sent around the empire. Founded by Julius Caesar in 59 B.C. when he was consul for the first time.

AQUILIFER   Standard-bearer who carried the *aquila*, the legion's eagle. Eagle-bearer.

AUXILIARY   Noncitizen serving in Roman army. Light infantry and cavalry. Recruited throughout empire. In imperial times served twenty-five years. Paid less than legionary. From the first century A.D., granted Roman citizenship on discharge. Commanded by prefects.

BATAVIAN HORSE   Elite auxiliary cavalry unit of Roman army. Recruited in present-day Holland. Its troopers were famous for being able to swim rivers with their horses in full equipment. Initially, Batavians formed the core of Julius Caesar's personal bodyguard of three hundred "Germans." By the third century A.D., the Batavian Horse regiment was the emperor's household cavalry unit.

BATTLESHIP   Roman warship of Deceres class; 572 oarsmen, 30 sailors, 250 marines.

BOLT   Large metal-tipped arrow fired by archers and *scorpio* catapults.

CAMP PREFECT   *Campus praefectus*. Imperial legion officer, third in command after commander and senior tribune. Promoted from centurion. Quartermaster, commander of major legion detachments. Took over the role filled by quaestors in republican armies.

CAMPAIGNING SEASON   Traditionally, early March to the Festival of the October Horse on October 19, when legions conducted military campaigns, after which they went into winter quarters. The terms "seasoned campaigner" and "seasoned soldier" derive from this.

CENTURION   Legion, Praetorian/City Guard, and Marines officer, sixty to a republican legion, in eleven grades. Equivalent to first lieutenant and captain. Enlisted man promoted from ranks, although there were some Equestrian Order centurions in the late republic/early empire.

CENTURY   Legion subunit made up of ten squads. In republican times, of a hundred men. In imperial times, of eighty men. Commanded by a centurion.

CHIEF CENTURION *Primus pilus* (first spear). Legion's most senior centurion.

CIVIC CROWN Crown of oak leaves, military bravery award for saving the life of a Roman citizen in battle. Rarely awarded, highly prized. Julius Caesar was a recipient.

COHORT Battalion. Ten to a legion. In Caesar's time, of 600 men. In imperial times, cohorts 10 through 2 had 480 men, the senior first cohort, 800.

COLONEL See TRIBUNE and PREFECT.

CONQUISITOR Roman army recruiting officer.

CONSUL Highest official at Rome; president of Senate. Two held office annually. Also commanded Roman armies, with equivalent rank of lieutenant general. The minimum age in the Republic was forty-two; in the imperial era the minimum age was thirty-seven, except for members of imperial family.

CONTUBERNIUM Legion subunit; the squad. In the Republic, of ten men; in the empire, of eight men.

CRUISER Midsize warship, including *bireme*, *trireme*, and *quinquereme*. The latter was 120 feet long, with a beam of 17 feet, a crew of 270 oarsmen at 3 banks of oars, 30 sailors, and 160 marines.

CURSUS PUBLICUS "The state's very fast runner." Imperial Rome's courier service. Founded by emperor Augustus with runners on foot; soon expanded to wheeled vehicles and mounted couriers. Horses changed at way stations, checked by inspectors every 6 to 10 miles. Covered up to 170 miles per day. It was a capital offense to interfere with *cursus publicus* couriers or their load.

DECIMATION Literally, to reduce by a tenth. Legions punished for mutiny or cowardice by one man in ten being clubbed to death by their comrades after drawing lots. Ordered to be carried out by both Caesar and Antony on units under their command. The 9th Legion, later the 9th Hispana, was the only legion on record to be decimated twice, the second time being in the first century during the reign of Tiberius.

DECUMAN GATE The main gate of legion camp, it faced away from the enemy.

DECURION Legion cavalry officer. Equivalent of a second lieutenant. Four to each legion cavalry squadron. Also, a senior elected civil official of a Roman town.

DICTATOR Supreme and sole chief of Rome. An ancient appointment, made by the Senate in emergencies, intended to last a maximum of six months. Sulla used the position to make himself ruler of the Roman Republic. Julius Caesar appropriated the title, with several temporary appointments, before becoming Dictator for life in February 44 B.C.

EAGLE The *aquila*, sacred standard of a legion; originally silver, later gold.

EQUESTRIAN   Member of Roman order of knighthood. Qualified for posts as tribune, prefect, procurator, and Senate membership. Required net worth of 400,000 sesterces. In the imperial era served a mandatory six-month legion cadetship as junior tribune at age eighteen or nineteen.

EVOCATI   In republican times, the general term for legion veterans. In the imperial era, a militia corps of retired legion veterans serving behind their old standards in emergencies and controlled by their provincial governor. Cassius Dio described them as "the recalled," because they were from time to time recalled to military duty.

FASCES   Symbol of Roman magistrate's power to punish and execute, an ax head protruding from a bundle of wooden rods. Carried by lictors. Denoted rank: quaestors had one, legates five, praetors six, consuls and most emperors twelve, dictator and some emperors twenty-four.

FIRST-RANK CENTURIONS   *Primi ordines*; a legion's six most senior centurions.

FORUM   Open space, usually rectangular, in all Roman cities and towns where law courts, meeting halls, temples, markets, and speakers' platforms were located.

FREEDMAN   Former slave, officially granted freedom.

FRIGATE   Liburnan; light, fast warship. Length, 108 feet; beam, 12 feet; crew, 144 rowers, ten to fifteen sailors, and forty marines.

FURLOUGH FEES   In camp, one legionary in four could take leave by paying a set fee to his centurion. The state took the responsibility for paying centurions these fees in A.D. 69.

GEMINA LEGION   "Twin" legion formed by merger of two existing legions.

GERMAN GUARD   Elite bodyguard unit of a Roman emperor, made up of hand-picked German auxiliaries. Instituted by Augustus.

GLADIATORS   Professional fighters used in public shows throughout the empire. Usually slaves. Gladiatorial contests originated as funeral rites. Sometimes used as soldiers in civil wars, but usually without success, as they lacked unit training or discipline.

GLADIUS   Roman legionary sword, twenty inches long, double edged, with a pointed end.

IMPERATOR   Title. Literally, chief or master. Highest honor for a general. Became reserved for emperors after their armies' victories. Title "emperor" grew from *imperator*.

IMPERIAL   Relating to the period of Roman history from 27 B.C. to the fall of the empire.

IMPERIAL PROVINCE   In the imperial era, an "armed" frontline province bordering unfriendly states, administered by the Palatium. Garrisoned by at least two legions plus auxiliaries. Governed by a propraetor (lieutenant general), a former consul whose appointment, by the emperor, was open-ended. A propraetor commanded all troops in his province, could wear a sword and uniform and levy recruits, and had capital punishment power.

JUVENA COLLEGA   Young Men's Association. Ancient guild for sons of Roman nobility in Italy. Fostered by Augustus. Boys joined at age seventeen. Learned horsemanship, weapons skills, manliness, etc., as a prelude to entering the army at eighteen as officer cadets.

LEGION   Regiment. Main operational unit of the Roman army. From *legio* (levy, or draft). In 10 cohorts. Republican legion nominal strength, 6,000 men; imperial, 5,246 officers and men, including own cavalry unit of 124 officers and men. At the beginning of the first century A.D. there were 28 legions; by A.D. 102, 30; and in A.D. 233, 33.

LEGIONARY   Soldier of a legion. Mostly a draftee. A Roman citizen (with very rare exceptions). Most recruited outside Italy in the imperial era. Republican military age, seventeen to forty-six, served sixteen years; imperial, average age twenty, served twenty years from late in Augustus's reign.

LICTORS   Unarmed attendants of Roman magistrates, carrying their fasces.

LUSTRATION   The Lustration Exercise, religious ceremony performed by legions in March. Standards were purified with perfumes and garlands prior to each new campaign.

MANIPLE   Company. Legion subunit, of 200 men in the republic, 160 in imperial times. Three to a cohort.

MANTLET   Wooden shed, on wheels, used in siege works.

MARCHING CAMP   Fortified camp built by legions at the end of every day's march.

MARINE   Soldier with the Roman navy. Freedman. Served twenty-six years, paid less than an auxiliary. Commanded by centurions. Organized by cohorts; unit titles unknown.

MURAL CROWN   Crown of gold awarded to the first Roman soldier over an enemy city wall.

NAVY   In republican times Rome relied on her allies to provide ships and men to act as Rome's navy. In imperial times Rome introduced her own navy, with two battle fleets: the Tyrrhenian Fleet, based at Micenum, with a squadron also at Fréjus in southern France; and the Adriatic Fleet, at Ravenna. Other, smaller fleets were the *Classis Britannica*, at Boulogne; the *Classis Germanica*, on the Rhine; the *Classis Moesica*, on the Lower Danube; the *Classis Pannonica*, on the

Upper Danube, and the *Classis Pontica,* with part based in Pontus and forty vessels based at Kersh to cover the Black and Azov Seas.

OPTIO Sergeant major. Deputy to centurion and decurion. Unit records and training officer. One to a century, four to legion cavalry units.

ORBIS The ring, the Roman legion's circular formation of last resort.

OVATION Lesser form of a Triumph. Celebrant rode in horseback through Rome.

PALATIUM Origin of the word "palace." Residence and military headquarters of emperors at Rome. First established by Augustus on Palatine Hill, from which its name derived. All emperors' headquarters were thereafter called the Palatium, even when new palaces were built by other emperors, including Tiberius, Caligula, Nero, and Domitian. Domitian's new palace, the Domus Augustana, served as the Palatium of many later emperors. Augustus's original, absorbed into Domitian's palace, had become known as the Old Palatium.

PALUDAMENTUM Roman general's cloak. Scarlet in republican times. In imperial times, legion commanders wore a scarlet cloak; commanders in chief, a purple cloak.

PILUM A Roman legionary's javelin. Metal-tipped, weighted end, six to seven feet long.

PRAETOR Senior magistrate and major general. Sixteen appointed annually once Caesar came to power. Could command legions and armies.

PRAETORIAN GATE Gate of a legion camp that faced the enemy.

PRAETORIAN GUARD Elite unit founded in Republic to guard Rome. Re-formed by Mark Antony immediately following the murder of Caesar in 44 B.C. with six thousand recently retired legion veterans. Elite imperial military police force under the emperors.

PRAETORIUM Headquarters in a legion camp.

PREFECT Commander of auxiliary units, Praetorian Guard, City Guard, Night Watch, and naval fleets. A citizen of Equestrian Order status. Prefects governed Egypt and, between A.D. 6 and 41, Judea.

PROCONSUL Literally, "as good as a consul." See SENATORIAL PROVINCE.

PROCURATOR Provincial official of Equestrian Order rank, deputy of governor, superior to prefect. Financial administrator and tax gatherer. Sometimes governed small provinces and subprovinces (e.g., Macedonia and Judea). Had capital punishment power. Annual salary, 60,000 to 100,000 sesterces.

PROPRAETOR Literally, "as good as a praetor." See IMPERIAL PROVINCE.

QUADRIGA A Roman chariot drawn by four horses. A golden quadriga was used in Triumphs.

QUAESTOR Literally, "investigator." Most junior Roman magistrate, entitled to one lictor. One assisted each consul at Rome on treasury matters; several others appointed to assist provincial governors on matters including finance, military recruiting, etc. Appointment as a quaestor meant immediate entry into the Senate once a man had served out his appointment. Caesar appointed twenty annually once he was in power. In his time, a provincial governor's quaestor also served as his chief of staff and quartermaster, with the equivalent modern-day rank of brigadier general, and in this capacity a quaestor could lead legions or armies. Among Caesar's quaestors in Gaul were young Crassus and Mark Antony.

RANK AND FILE Enlisted soldiers of a legion.

ROSTRA Speakers' place in the Forum at Rome.

SATURNALIA Festival of Saturn. Originally on December 17, extended to four days, then five, then seven. Slaves could dress like their masters, dice playing was legal, and patrons gave their clients gifts. Origin of Christian Christmas festival and of Christmas gift-giving.

SCORPION *Scorpio*, quick-firing artillery piece using metal-tipped bolts. Each legion was equipped with fifty of them, plus ten heavy stone-throwing catapults.

SEAL Every Roman of Equestrian Order or Senatorial rank wore a gold signet ring on his left hand. The ring bore his personal seal, which was affixed to all his documents and correspondence. Pompey the Great's seal was of a lion with a sword in one paw. Caesar's family seal was the elephant, but once he was Dictator his seal depicted the goddess Venus, from whom Caesar claimed to be descended, wearing helmet and armor. Augustus's seal, called the Sardonychis and introduced in 27 B.C., was used by most subsequent emperors. It bore an image of Augustus cut by the artisan Dioscurides. For three years prior, Augustus's seal carried the image of a sphinx, celebrating his victory in Egypt over Antony and Cleopatra. The sphinx was briefly replaced, according to Suetonius, by the head of Alexander the Great. The Sardonychis seal was possibly named for the superior quality wax used, resembling onyx. Also: the Palatium's outbound correspondence department, so called because the Sardonychis seal was the last thing added to outgoing letters.

SECOND ENLISTMENT MEN Legionaries who voluntarily served another sixteen- or twenty-year enlistment with their legion when their first enlistment expired.

SEGMENTIA LORICA Segmented metal armor adopted by the men of Rome's legions in the first century A.D. to replace iron mail armor.

SENATE Rome's most powerful elected body. Members, needing a net worth of 1 million sesterces, qualified for legion commands, praetorships, and consulships.

Minimum age 30 in imperial times. In Caesar's time, some 350 to 400 members, increased by him to 900. At the start of the reign of Augustus, 1,000 members; he subsequently limited it to 600 members.

SENATORIAL PROVINCE   In the imperial era, a province with a governor appointed by the Senate for a year, by lot, from its members. With the rank of proconsul (lieutenant general) the governor had capital punishment power but couldn't wear a uniform or sword or levy troops. Garrison of auxiliaries (except in Africa, where one legion was stationed). Asia and Africa were the most highly prized, best-paid appointments—up to 400,000 sesterces a year.

SIGNIFER   Literally, a signaler; the standard-bearer of legion subunits.

SPATHA   Roman cavalry sword. It had a round end, and was longer than the *gladius*.

TESSERA   A small wax sheet on which was inscribed the legion's watchword for the day.

TESSERARIUS   Legion guard/orderly sergeant. Distributed the *tessera* to his men.

TESTUDO   "Tortoise" formation. Legionaries locked shields over their heads and at their sides.

THIRD ENLISTMENT MEN   Legionaries voluntarily serving a third enlistment.

TORQUE   Neck chain of twisted gold. Among the Roman army's highest bravery awards.

TRIBUNAL   Reviewing stand in a legion camp; built in front of tribunes' quarters.

TRIBUNE (MILITARY)   Legion, Praetorian Guard, and City Guard officer. Six of equal rank in republican legions shared command. In imperial legion, a "thin stripe" junior tribune was an officer-cadet serving a mandatory six months; five to a legion. One "broad stripe" senior tribune (a so-called military tribune) per legion was a full colonel and legion second in command. Senior tribunes commanded Praetorian Guard and City Guard cohorts. From the reign of Claudius, for promotion purposes, twenty-five senior tribunes were appointed annually, but not all were given legion or Praetorian posts.

TRIBUNE OF THE PLEBEIANS   Ten Tribunes of the Plebeians were elected at Rome, sitting in the Senate. In the Republic they had the power of veto over Senate votes. This power was absorbed by the emperor in imperial times.

TRIUMPH   Parade through Rome in a gold quadriga by a victorious general, followed by his soldiers, prisoners, and spoils. He also received T.D.s and a large cash prize. Initially granted by the Senate, later by emperors, and usually only to generals of consular rank.

TRIUMPHAL DECORATIONS (T.D.s)   A crimson cloak, crown of bay leaves, laurel branch, and statue in the Forum for generals celebrating a Triumph.

TRIUMPHATOR   Roman general celebrating a Triumph.

TRIUMVIRS   Members of the 43–33 B.C. Board of Three for the Ordering of State—Octavian, Antony, and Lepidus. Prior to that, unofficially, Caesar, Pompey, and Crassus.

TUNICA PALMATA   The palm tunic. A tunic embroidered with a palm frond design worn by generals celebrating a Triumph.

VEXILLUM   Square cloth banner of auxiliary units and legion detachments.

WATCH   Time in Roman military camps was divided into watches of three hours, at the end of which sentries changed, on a trumpet call. The officer of the watch was a tribune.

WATCHWORD   Password in a Roman military camp. Daily, just prior to sunset, the tribune of the watch presented the most senior officer in camp with a register of the number of men fit for duty, and in return was given the watchword for the next twenty-four hours. This was distributed to the sentries by the guard cohort's *tesserarii*. In imperial times, the watch tribune of the Praetorian Guard obtained the guard's watchword from the emperor.

WINTER CAMP   A permanent base where a legion usually spent October to March.

INDEX